£9.99

# THE STUDENT WRITER'S GUIDE

An A to Z of Writing and Language

# THE STUDENT WRITER'S GUIDE

## An A to Z of Writing and Language

*Edited by Nigel Kent*

Stanley Thornes (Publishers) Ltd

Text © Jacaranda Wiley Ltd 1989
Additional material © Nigel Kent 1990

First published in 1989 by
The Jacaranda Press, Australia

This edition published in 1990 by:
Stanley Thornes (Publishers) Ltd
Old Station Drive
Leckhampton
CHELTENHAM GL53 0DN
UK

Illustrations by Allan Stomann.

The editors and publishers are grateful to the
following for permission to reproduce material:

*Fast Forward* magazine (BBC Enterprises Ltd),
page 30; Friends of the Earth, page 33 (bottom);
Greenpeace, page 33 (top); *The Gloucestershire Echo*,
29 August 1989, page 53; *The Independent*, 15
August 1989, page 58.

Every effort has been made to contact copyright
holders and we apologise if any have been
overlooked.

British Library Cataloguing in Publication Data

---

British Library Cataloguing in Publication Data
The student writer's guide: an A to Z of writing and
language
  1. English language. Composition. Techniques
  I. Kent, Nigel
  808.042

ISBN 0-7487-0499-X

---

Typeset in 11½/12½ and 10½/11 pt Plantin

Printed and bound in Great Britain at
The Bath Press, Avon

# Contents

# Editorial Staff

## Writers and Editors

Pam Peters — *General Editor*

David Blair — *Contributing Editor*

Richard Tardif — *Executive Editor*

Helen Bateman — *Senior Editor*

Susan Butler

Linsay Knight

Alison Moore

Nigel Kent — *Editor of UK edition*

## Computer Systems

William E. Smith

## Editorial Assistants

Kristine Burnet

Maureen Leslie

Anne Teong

## Consultants to the Project

### Victoria

Joan P. Stewart — *Coordinator (Education Programs) School Support Centre*

### New South Wales

Rhonda Jenkins — *Language Consultant*

Chris Carroll — *Inspector of Schools*

### Queensland

John Carr — *Senior Education Officer Curriculum Services Branch*

### South Australia

Pamela Ball — *Education Editor*

### Western Australia

Peter Forrestal — *Freelance writer and publisher with Chalkface Press*

Further assistance was provided by members of the Australian Education Council's Working Party on Spelling and Punctuation, chaired by Dr L. W. Louden.

## Acknowledgements

We would like to express our thanks to Mrs Heather Donoghue and the students of the Weston Creek High School, and to Mr Robert McGregor and other staff and students of Barker College, through whose cooperation and help we had a good range of student writing to draw upon. Particular thanks are due to Adam Cole, Kylie Ellis, John Gardiner, Adam Hale, Felicity Peters, Gregory Peters, and Rohan Smith, who allowed us to use their work in the "Writing Workshop" (Australian edition), and to Grace Crossley, Rachael Etheridge, Mandy Little, Ian Moir, Kerry Murphy, Kevin O'Leary (UK edition).

# To the student — making the most of this book

When you have something to write, there's much to be done. You have to think about *what* you're going to say and *how* you're going to say it. You have to decide what shape and structure it's to have, and what style of expression is best. You can't do all that at once!

## The writing process

This book shows you how to handle your writing step by step. The steps of the writing process are explained in the book's first section — the "Writing Workshop". The first part of the Writing Workshop shows you how to work from basic ideas and raw material through to a plan, and then on to a draft. Once the essay is drafted, you can think more about its overall shape, structure and style. The second part of the Writing Workshop — "From me to it" — suggests ways of modifying your style, if you want to for a particular audience. The third part — "Forms of writing" — is a showcase of different kinds of writing, with notes to show you what to aim for with them. The layout of letters is explained in Appendix E.

## Editing your writing

Whenever you revise and edit your work, there are thousands of questions about language to sort out:
    Why does this word look strange?
    Do I need an apostrophe here?
    How should I spell this word?
    What's wrong with this sentence?
Sometimes it's a matter of right or wrong. Sometimes a matter of choice. The second section of this book — the "A to Z Guide to Writing and Language" will answer many of these questions.

## Looking words up

The A to Z Guide is in alphabetical order, so you just look words up as you would in a dictionary. If the word doesn't seem to be there, you may be looking under the wrong spelling. Check with Appendix A, which sets out different ways of spelling the same sounds in English.

Once you've located the word, you may find it's presented as one of a pair which either look or sound alike. Both will be discussed in the entry. Some of the words you may be looking up follow a particular pattern of spelling. With them you may be directed to a larger group entry, which explains how a whole set of words behaves.

## Choices in spelling

With some words you have a choice of spelling. The book explains why you might choose one or the other, but both are correct and the choice is yours. In writing this book we too have made choices, and you'll find that we use the spellings that are more regular.

## Consistency

Whenever you have a choice − in spelling, punctuation or anything else − the most important thing is to make it and stick to it. If you decide to use *-ise* in *organise* and *realise*, make sure you use it in *civilise* and *recognise* too. If on the other hand you decide to use *-ize*, those words should be *organize, realize, recognize* and *civilize*.

Being consistent is important whether you're choosing spellings, or the right kind of expression for your writing. In general you keep to formal or informal language in a particular piece, unless you're aiming at some special effect.

## A polished piece of writing

By thinking of all those things at different stages of your writing, you'll take control of it. You'll have a technique for writing, whatever the task is. What's more, you'll be able to develop ideas into a polished piece which you can be proud to share with anyone. Good luck!

*Pam Peters*
*General Editor*

# Writing
# workshop

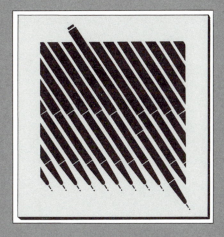

# Part 1: The writing process

## Step by step
## Computers and writing

# Step by step

What is writing?   Writing is so many different things . . .
> Writing is pushing a pen.
> Writing is your handwriting.
> Writing is making notes.
> Writing is sorting out what you want to say first.
> Writing is telling someone something on paper.
> Writing is explaining something to someone on paper.
> Writing is getting your spelling and grammar right.
> Writing is that essay you've just written.
> > and so on . . .

Why are there so many answers to that question? It's because writing is a *process*. You can answer the question at the beginning or end of the process, or somewhere in the middle.

Often people think of writing as just the end product – the finished essay. It looks great, of course. But it may seem a long way away when you're still scratching your head about what to write. You may need help with what to do in the early stages of the writing process:
- How do I get ideas together and develop them?
- How do I get something going on that sheet of paper?

In this first section of the "Writing Workshop", we show you step by step how to put a piece of writing together. It never happens all at once. Few people – even professional writers – can put a piece of writing together at one attempt. Most people develop their writing through the four broad stages shown below.

1. *Brainstorming and composing:* Don't worry about how you're going to get your ideas down on paper during this stage. Just jot down any ideas that occur to you which might be relevant to the piece of writing you're about to undertake.

   As soon as you feel you're running out of ideas, stop. Look to see if any of the ideas you've jotted down seem to go together. If they don't, you'll need to carry on brainstorming. Sometimes it is a good idea to leave brainstorming for a little while and have a break. When you return, you'll start fresh and may find new relevant ideas occur to you.

   Once you feel you've got a list of ideas which seem to connect with one another, you need to start thinking about finding the best order or structure for them.

2. *Drafting:* You should by now have a clear idea of what you want to include in your piece of writing and of what direction you want to go in. Now you need to find appropriate words and sentences to capture your ideas. In this stage you experiment: you write out your ideas in full to see how they look and sound. As you write you may find that new ideas occur to you, or that your ideas begin to grow. This is to be expected; often writers only discover what they really think or believe when they start writing.

3. *Revising and editing:* Once you have drafted out your ideas, you have to look at your work critically. Have you said what you wanted to say? Have you said it in a way that your reader can understand and respond to? The latter question is the harder to answer. Even some experienced writers find it difficult to put themselves in the place of the reader and recognise the problems they might have created for him. At this stage, therefore, it is useful to test out your draft on a partner. Ask him to read your work and tell you what he thought about it. Also ask him to feedback the difficulties he has had in following and understanding what you've written. Listen to his comments carefully and note down any adjustments to the content, structure and expression which you will need to make when you're revising your first draft.

   Having reached the stage when you're happy with the content, structure and expression of your piece, you are ready to polish the spelling, grammar and punctuation. Use any resources that are available to you at this stage to help you do this. A dictionary, a thesaurus, your teacher and *The Student Writer's Guide* are useful sources of the support you may need.

4. *Publishing:* The final stage of the writing process is when you go public – when you hand your writing over to your reader. Whether it goes to the teacher for marking, or to the editor of the school magazine or to someone outside the school, it is out of your hands as a finished piece of writing. This stage will involve you in a consideration of layout and presentation. Does the work merit illustrations? Where should diagrams be placed on the page? Where should page breaks occur? Should print style be consistent or can it be varied for effect? Does the piece need headings? All your answers to these questions will be determined by your need to support the meaning and effect of your piece by the presentation of the text on the page.

These are the four stages in the writing process. Of course the process isn't always so streamlined: the stages often overlap. For the moment, let's talk about the three stages that lead up to the publication, and show how they work for two different kinds of writing.

# Example A: a personal essay

When you write a personal essay, you often have a lot of scope to talk about your own ideas and experiences. You're free to tackle the topic in your own way, and you choose the subject matter.

The freedom is great, but there are difficulties – *you* must decide on the limits of the topic, and you have to lick it into shape. An essay isn't just a ramble through bits and pieces of thought. It has to develop a structure.

Here's how it's done.

## Stage 1    Brainstorming and composing

Say you were asked to write about *growing up*, as Mandy was. Growing up? 'What on earth do I write about?' you ask yourself.

Mandy asking herself the same question, jotted down the first things that came into her head when she thought about growing up:

dyeing my hair
my first date
GCSE exams
baby sitting
spots, greasy hair

going to secondary school
arguments with mum and dad
work experience
leaving home

These were mixed up thoughts. At this stage she wasn't worried about ideas that connected or linked in any way. She was brainstorming, exploring the possibilities of her essay on growing up.

When she felt that she had explored these possibilities as fully as she could, she looked back at her list. What could she do with the ideas? Leaving home wasn't something that she had experienced yet, whilst all the others she had. Dyeing her hair had been part of a preparation for her first date and had caused difficulties at school and with her parents. She felt that this incident typified growing up for her: it was typical of the sort of scrapes she seemed to be getting into nowadays and if she were to describe that incident it would bring out other aspects of growing up – the changing relationship with her parents and her developing interest in members of the opposite sex. It seemed to provide a useful link between some of the ideas she had.

As Mandy looked at the results of her brainstorming session, she was beginning to develop an idea that would form the basis of her essay. She began to jot down further ideas and develop a framework or structure for her writing.

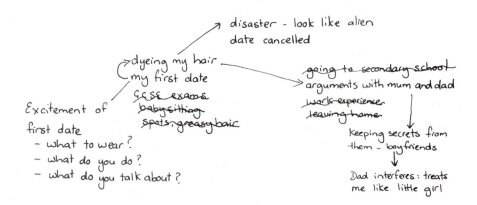

She now knew what she wanted to include and the direction she would take when she started writing.

## Stage 2 Drafting

Using her notes to guide her Mandy produced the first draft of her essay, shown on page 8.

It's very much a first draft. That's why it's full of corrections. She was sorting things out as she went along, sometimes finding a better way of saying something, sometimes thinking of extra things to say. She was creating and writing at the same time. She wasn't concerned too much about accuracy of spelling and punctuation at this stage, she could deal with those later. Getting the ideas down in the best way was her most important priority at this stage.

As you write you develop your main idea, adding to it and changing it as you consider appropriate. Notice that, though Mandy started with the simple idea of the hair-dyeing incident, it grew to cover key aspects of growing up, such as the changing relationships of adolescence and the teenager's desire for independence.

## Stage 3 Revising and editing

Mandy was fairly happy with her first draft. She felt that she had captured her feelings about growing up but wanted to test it out on a reader to see if the reader understood what she was trying to say. She realised that having only just finished writing the piece, she was still too close to it to see the weaknesses.

She asked her friend to read it aloud to see if the essay sounded like she wanted it to sound. Then she asked her friend to give her some practical advice about how she might improve it.

This is what her friend said:

> "I thought it was very realistic; it's just the sort of thing that does happen. I thought it ended a bit quickly. I wanted to know more about what your dad did and how you got out of the situation."

Mandy found this advice helpful. When she had finished she had felt the ending wasn't as good as the beginning but couldn't pin down what was wrong. Furthermore, when she listened to her friend reading the piece, it became clear to her that there were a few things that either weren't clear or which didn't read as smoothly as she would have liked. She decided to redraft her piece to try to improve the content, structure and style.

When she finished the second draft, she asked her friend and her teacher to look through it once more to help her pick up any punctuation, grammar, usage or spelling errors that might spoil the effect of the piece.

Mandy's revised draft is shown on pp 9–10, with the suggested corrections and the improvements Mandy made to the content. It's come a long way from the scatty thoughts about growing up during the brainstorming section (p 6).

If you'd like to see the finished product, all ready for publication, it's on pp 20–1.

## Draft 1

Your father ~~gives~~ hands you a letter and you don't know ~~who~~ recognise the handwriting and you wonder who it is. You open it and start reading — |" Dear Mandy, ~~Do you~~ Will you go out, Do you want to go with me to see Superman III on thursday? If you do, I will be outside the Odeon at 7.15, I will wait for you for ten minutes. If your not there, I'll know you ~~will~~ won't be coming. I hope you do. Luv Martyn." Wow! It's your first date and it's Martyn. Yes, Martyn, Captain of the football team and the only boy in your class who doesn't suffer from greasy hair and ~~pimples~~ acne. Do you want to go. Will you go? Yes, of course you'll go!

Your father is watching you across the breakfast table so you put the letter as carmly back into the envelope as you can. "Is it Something intresting?" "No," you lie, "It's from Julie – she wants me to go to the pictures with her on thursday" As soon as you've said it you know it's a mistake. "Why's Julie writing to you, she only lives round the corner." Get out of that one Mandy. You conveniently spot the time and say, "God, I'm going to be late" pick up your sandwich box, your bag, your coat and shout bye as you run out the door.

All the way to school your thinking about what your going to wear. The red dress or the brown skirt and wrap over blouse. ~~than flash~~ Then it occurs to you. Why not dye your hair. Boys like blondes much better than mousy browns. If you walk to school and back you can save your bus fare and you will have enough to buy the dye.

In the evening you can't do your homework because your thinking all the time of Martyn. Do you kiss on the first date who makes the first move? What are you going to talk about. You decide to have a bath and use the hair dye you've brought and you lock yourself in the bathroom and rub it into your hair.

30 minutes later you rinse it off and instead of a cool sophisticated blond in the mirror you see a green haired alien staring back at you. You scream in horror and dad comes rushing up the stairs to see ~~what is the matter~~ what the matter is. You let him in, "What do you think you've done?" he says, He makes you wash your hair thirty times that night and when it makes no difference. "You can't go to school tommorrow looking like that," he says. "I'm not having my little girl called a punk." "But tomorrows thursday," you say, "I can wear a hat!" "No, and that's final," he says, That's growing up, I suppose.

## Draft 2

Your father hands you a letter ~~and~~ you don't
recognise the handwriting and you wonder who it _so_
is. You open it and start reading it "Dear Mandy,
~~Will you go out.~~ Do you want to go with me to see
Superman III on Thursday? If you do, I will be
outside the Odeon at 7.15, I will wate for you
for ten minutes. If you're not there, I'll know you
~~will~~ won't be coming. I hope you do. Luv Martyn."
Wow! It's your first date and it's Martyn. Yes,
Martyn, Captain of the football team and the only
boy in your class who doesn't suffer from greasy
hair and acne. Will you go? Yes, of course you'll go!

_who might be writing to you_ (annotation near "is")

_— put as separate paragraph + then block it out as letter_ (annotation right margin)

_new line_ (left margin annotation)
_new paragraph_ (left margin annotation)

Your father is watching you across the breakfast
table so you put the letter as calmly back into
the envelope as you can. "Something interesting?"
Do you tell him "~~No~~, you lie "It's from Julie —
she wants me to go to the pictures with her on
Thursday" As soon as you've said it you know
it's a mistake. "Why's Julie writing to you? She
only lives round the corner." Get out of that one,
Mandy. You conveniently spot the time and
say, "God, I'm going to be late" pick up
your sandwich box, your bag, your coat and
shout bye as you run out the door. Phew

_new line he asks_ (right margin)
_set out on separate lines_ (left margin)
_the truth or do_ / _...You lie_ (annotations)
_new paragraph_ (right margin)
_You_ (insertion) _and_ (insertion) _Phew_ (insertion)

All the way to school your thinking about
what you're going to wear. Then it occurs to
you. Why not dye your hair. Boys like blondes
much better than mousy browns. If you walk
to school and back you can save your bus fare
and you ~~can~~ will have enough to buy the dye.

In the evening you can't do your homework
because your thinking all the time of Martyn Do
you kiss on the first date? Who makes the first
move? What are you going to talk about? You
decide ~~to~~ have a bath and use the hair dye
you've bought ~~and you lock yourself in the~~
~~bathroom and rub it into you hair.~~

_you're_ (insertion) _about your date with_ (insertion) _tomorrow_ (insertion)
_think about it. It's time to_ (insertion)

30 minutes later you rinse ~~it~~ the dye off and look at yourself in the mirror. Oh no!

Instead of a cool sofisticated blonde ~~in the mirror~~ there's ~~you see~~ a green haired alien staring back at you. You scream in horror and dad comes rushing up the stairs to see ~~"what is the matter"~~ what the matter is. You let him in.

*write out on separate lines*

"What do you think you've done?" he ~~says~~ shouts.

"~~You cannot answer,~~ "~~what do you want to~~ Have you been dyeing ~~go dyeing~~ your hair ~~for~~?" no answer. "What for?" You can see the horror in his face as he recognises that his little girl isn't a little girl any more. "I don't know, I just wanted to." You can't tell him the truth, it'll only make things worse. "Get in the bathroom and wash it out! You can't go to school like that. I don't want you walking down the street like some demented punk." what will people think?

In a flash it hits you. If he doesn't let you out, the date will be off. No pictures and no

*Separate lines*

Martyn. "But it's Thursday tomorrow," you say, unable to hold the words in. "What's so special about Thursday?" he asks. Do you tell him or don't you? It'll only make things worse. You keep your mouth shut and start running the water, to try and wash the dye out. This growing up is no fun you know.

## Example B: a factual essay

When you write an essay in history (or geography, economics or business studies) you begin with facts or a body of information. You could call these essays *factual* ones. But their purpose is to show that you *understand* the facts, and how they fit together to make a larger picture. Often you are interpreting them or examining the issues in them.

You can present factual material either in a personal way (as if you were there yourself), or in a straight informative way. Your teacher will normally tell you which approach is expected. (If you'd like to compare two types of presentation, see pp 48–9.) Either way there's less room to move than in our first essay (Example A) because you must work with set pieces of information. On the other hand, at least you know what to write about!

In Example B you'll see a straight informative essay. It's written in response to the instruction: "Describe the positive effects of the Second World War."

## Stage 1   Brainstorming and composing

Kerry's first reaction to the question was to write down all the effects she could think of:

destruction                             UNO

Cold War                         NATO

Welfare State                    peace

rebuilding with American money    rise of Socialism

independence for India etc        bankruptcy

new alliances between countries

When she had run out of ideas, she selected those which seemed to fit with the theme of "positive effects" and then drew a diagram to see how she might link them. At this stage she also thought it might be useful to note down any other material which might prove helpful in developing these ideas.

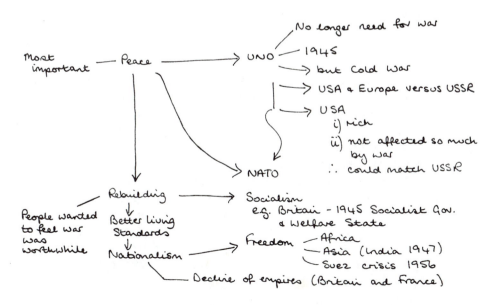

By now Kerry had a fairly clear idea of the material she wished to include in her essay. Before she started, however, she decided to work out a sequence or order of material for her essay. She produced this as three headings:

1. Peace
2. Socialism
3. Nationalism.

## Stage 2  Drafting

With the headings Kerry knew what the whole of her essay was going to be about, and so she could write a short introduction for it. Essay introductions are always easier to write when you have an overview of all the main points you're going to develop. The introduction gives your reader a few points to whet the appetite and shows how you're going to tackle the question.

After drafting the introduction, Kerry went on to talk about each of her main headings. The first draft (page 13) was rather messy, because she was getting things down and working them out at the same time. In the rush of drafting, she didn't try to write words with much care, and some of the details got repeated and tangled up. Furthermore, the essay didn't flow, for she hadn't used *topic sentences*. These are sentences that give the reader some indication of what will be discussed in the paragraph that follows and which help tie the whole essay together. But at this stage it didn't matter. This was only the first draft, it could be tidied up later. The most important thing for her was to work out and develop the ideas she had.

## Stage 3  Revising and editing

Kerry let her essay "cool" for a couple of days and then read it through again, trying to put herself in the place of the reader and noting down any weaknesses she found as she read. As she did so, she noticed where some of the words were not quite right, so she changed them before discussing her work with her teacher.

Her teacher read it to get the overall effect and immediately picked up the weakness in the organisation of the piece. She explained to Kerry the use of topic sentences and drew her attention to the ending of the essay, making the point that it was rather abrupt and that this could be avoided if she wrote a conclusion, which draws the main points together in a summary statement. Kerry's teacher also made suggestions about using different words when the flow of the essay was spoiled by the repetition of the same word or phrase, and she praised Kerry for the accuracy of her spelling and punctuation, particularly her use of capital letters. They are particularly important in writing of this sort because of all the proper names that the writer is likely to use. In Kerry's handwriting, however, the capital letter 'A' wasn't always clear, so her teacher suggested that she attend to this point in her final draft.

## Draft 1

The Second World War had a devastating effect on the lives of people in Europe. The warring countries were bankrupt and many of their people were left hungry, homeless or both. If good was to come out the war Europe's politicians faced a number of challenges rebuilding their economic prosperity; to ensure that such a war never happened again and deal with the new aspirations of their people.

In 1945 the Charter of the United Nations Organisation was signed by over fifty countries to produce a peace that would last. Whilst experience has proved that the UNO has affected in a good way the relationships between nations, it could not prevent the hostility that began to grow between the USSR and the USA called the cold war. The USSR had survived as the most powerful nation in Europe. The smaller nations felt threatened. Only the USA could match its power. The USA had the technology, the resources and the economic strength to develop an army to stop the USSR. The USA also formed the North Atlantic Treaty Organisation. This was an agreement between the non-Communist countries in Europe and Canada and the USA to develop military defence strategy against the USSR and its allies in East Europe. Even though the tension between the USSR and the USA has lessened recently NATO still exists for the Europe's and the USA's protection.

The people who had fought and who had suffered in the war in Europe had new expectations. They wanted rewards for the war they had fought such as better living standards. Though most political parties tried to develop policies to meet these demands, it was Socialists who proved most successful in improving living standards. For example, in 1945 Britain elected a Socialist Government who set about improving living standards through the Welfare State to fulfil the ordinary man's new aspirations.

Many countries also got independence. The countries, who had supported Europe in their fight against Nazi Germany began to seek a reward — independence. All over africa and asia European dependencies began to call for self-rule. Quickly the empires of countries like Britain and France began to fall apart. The process of granting independence was not always a simple one and frequently led to new hostilities, as Britian found out in 1947 in India and in the Suez Crisis in 1956. However, the process could not be resisted. The days of Colonial Empires were over.

Looking again at the essay, Kerry felt that there were other changes that she would like to make. She thought the second paragraph would benefit from being split into two separate paragraphs: the first would deal with the UNO and the second NATO. This might also improve the flow, particularly if she could find an effective topic sentence. She also felt that her comment on NATO still existing today didn't add much to the essay and she could strike out that sentence and replace it with something more *relevant*, such as how NATO has managed to keep the peace in Europe since 1945. If she did this, it would further justify her decision to split paragraph two in the way she proposed, for she would be developing the positive effects of NATO in sufficient detail to warrant a separate paragraph.

With the help of her teacher, and all the things she'd noticed herself, Kerry was set to produce the final version of her essay. The second draft is shown on pp 15–16, with all the suggested corrections and revisions. On pp 22–3 you'll find the published version, one she could proudly share with anyone.

## Checklist for redrafting and proof-reading

1. *What is revising?*
   Revising is making changes to your writing, to make sure you can be understood by your reader. It means checking the content of the writing, the way you have organised your ideas and the way you have expressed them. It is hard to think of all three at once, so it's best to do it in three stages. When you revise you can
   > add something
   > delete something
   > move something
   > change something.

2. *How do I know what to redraft?*
   - Try reading your work aloud to yourself (if you're on your own). Does it read smoothly and easily? Or are there gaps where something's missing? Or spots where things are vague or unclear? Are there spots where you've said the same thing twice? Or ones where you need to add more details to make your point properly? Or have you included any material that isn't strictly related to the main point of your writing?

## Draft 2

The Second World War had a devastating effect on the lives of people in Europe. The warring countries were bankrupt and many of their people were left hungry, homeless, or both. If good was to come out the war Europe's politicians faced a number of challenges to rebuilding their economic prosperity; to ensure that such a war never happened again and to deal with the new aspirations of their people.

*— Put in a topic sentence*

In 1945 the Charter of the United Nations Organisation *The aim of the UNO was to provide a means of solving disputes* was signed by over fifty countries. / to produce a *between countries without war and to create economic prosperity* peace that would last. Whilst experience has proved that the UNO has had *an effect* affected in a *on* good way the relationships between nations, it could not prevent the *growing tension* hostility that began to grow between both the USSR and the USA *during the years following the war*, called the cold war. / The USSR had survived as the most powerful nation in Europe. The smaller *European* nations felt threatened *and looked to the USA for protection for only* Only the USA could match *the USSR's* its power. *It* The USA had the technology, the resources *our* and the economic strength to *provide the necessary check on* develop an *military strength might* army to stop the USSR's *'s possible advance*. The USA also formed the North Atlantic Treaty Organisation. This was an agreement between the non-Communist countries in Europe and Canada and the USA to develop a military defence strategy against the USSR and its allies in East Europe. Even though the tension between the USSR and the USA has lessened recently, NATO still exists for the Europe's and the USA's protection.

*Split into new paragraph with a topic sentence*

*Explain how NATO works*

*Topic Sentence* The people who had fought and who had suffered in the war in Europe had new expectations. They wanted rewards for the war they had fought such as better living standards. Though most political parties tried to develop policies to meet these demands, it was Socialists who proved most successful in improving living standards. For example, in 1945 Britain elected a Socialist government who set about *establishing the Welfare State* improving living standards through the Welfare State to fulfil the ordinary man's new aspirations.

*(continued)*

> Topic / sentence
>
> / Many countries also got independence. The countries, who had supported Europe in their fight against Nazi Germany began to seek a reward / independence. All over Africa and Asia European dependencies began to call for self-rule. Quickly the /colonial/ empires of countries like Britain and France began to fall apart. The process of granting independence was not always a simple one and frequently led to new hostilities, as Britain found out in 1947 in India and in the Suez Crisis in 1956. However, the process could not be resisted. The days of Colonial Empires were over.

- Try turning sentences over in your mind (if you're in the classroom). Does the sentence work? Do the words go together? Is there one word which doesn't sound quite right? Could it be replaced by a word or a phrase which would make the sentence sound better?
- Remember to use the resources available to you. If you have help to hand, ask your partner to read your work to you. This can often help you identify parts of your writing that are not working. Furthermore, a partner can often suggest ideas which will help you improve weak spots.

3. *How do I redraft the structure of my writing?*
   - Check the beginning. Does it say clearly what is to come? What have you done to encourage the reader to read on?
   - Check individual paragraphs. Is there a topic sentence? Does the paragraph develop just one idea?
   - Check the order of paragraphs. Is there a good reason for them being in that order?
   - Check the closing paragraph. Does it work like a conclusion, rounding things off?

4. *How do I edit my expression?*
   - Check the sound of the piece. Is it the sort of language the reader will expect to meet in work of this sort? Does the language used match the reader and the purpose of the writing? Or is the reader likely to be confused, shocked, surprised or even offended by some of the language?
   - Check individual words. If you seem to be repeating a word, see if there are others you could use instead by using a thesaurus. If you're not quite sure of the meaning of a word, check it in a dictionary. Then write it down in your own special "Word Book".

- Check the spelling of words you're not sure of. Some words offer you a choice, as this book shows, and then you just have to make sure you use the same spelling each time. (Be consistent.)
- Check your sentences. Are they either too short or too long? If they're short they *may* be incomplete and lack a proper verb. (Read them aloud on their own, and you'll see if this is so.) If they're long, they may really contain enough ideas for two or three sentences and should be divided up. If you've repeated or half-repeated anything, it should be trimmed.
- Check your punctuation. Questions need question marks. Quotations need quotation marks at the beginning and end. (It's easy to forget them at the end.) Some sentences need a comma or two to help the meaning become clear.

# Computers and writing

Question: Do you think of computers as:
        hi-tech toys for scientists and executives?
        machines for electronic games and amusements?
        instruments to help in education?

If you answered "yes" to the last of those questions, your school probably has computers. You may even have been introduced to them in class. If you have used a computer in a *writing* class you are extra lucky, because it is a useful tool.

Computers are useful at all three stages of the writing process, as we shall see. You can just as well use pen or pencil to brainstorm, draft or edit, but when it comes to publishing your work, the computer is the ideal thing to have. With it you can make your work look like something out of a printed book, and show it to others at its best. Whether or not you use computers in the writing process, we hope your school has one for you to use at the publication stage.

### Computers at the beginning of the writing process — brainstorming and composing (stage 1)

When you begin to write, you're just tossing ideas around. It's often just a list which you add to at random. You cross things off and squeeze things in, with much chewing of the pen. Though it looks a mess, it's vital planning for the essay.

All this can be done perfectly well with a pen. But if you can get to a computer at this stage, you could do the same thing on the computer screen, and avoid the mess. With any *word-processing program* you can make a list of words and headings, and alter the list until things are in the right order for drafting.

Some computers will run *brainstorming programs* to help you sort your ideas out. (You type a heading in as a sentence, and the computer will ask you questions about it, to help develop the idea.) But they're not really necessary, and you could do the same for yourself without the computer.

## Computers and drafting (stage 2)

The computer can help you quite a lot with drafting your essay, though once again, they're not essential. You could do the same with just pen and paper, as Mandy and Kerry did. In fact many writers prefer to draft with pen and paper, because they find the mechanics of the computer and its screen get in the way of thinking and writing.

Yet your draft will certainly look tidier if it's done on computer, and you'll be able to remove all the false starts and obvious mistakes straight away. With a *word-processing program* you just zap them away. It's so easy to correct writing mistakes on the computer, and there's no temptation to ignore them or pretend that they don't matter!

To use a word-processor on the computer, you *don't* have to be a good typist. You don't have to be any kind of typist at all. Whatever mistakes come up, you get rid of them immediately, and the computer will print out your work cleanly and evenly. If you're a two-finger typist, it doesn't let on! Still, if your school offers courses in touch-typing, you should take advantage of them.

## Computers, revising and editing (stage 3)

With a word-processor you may actually begin revising your work as you draft it out. But still the most important revision will happen after you've shown your work to a friend or teacher, and heard their comments on it.

Once again, it's so easy to correct and change things with the *word-processing program* — not just change words and spellings, but move sentences and even paragraphs into a better place in the essay. No worries. The computer will remove all trace of where they were, and install them in the new place as if they'd always been there. A word-processor should help you to be bolder in your revision. You don't have to worry about how much effort it will take to make *big* changes. And the finished product will be all the better for them.

Some computers will run special *editing programs* as an additional help at this stage. There are *spelling checkers* which will check all your words against a computerised dictionary to see if they're correctly spelled. They have their limits, though. The dictionary is unlikely to have all the proper names you'll need in history or geography. And it may not have words in their plural form, or with tense endings. Another problem is that the spelling checker can't tell if you've used a good word in the wrong place. It won't pick up when you've used *their* instead of *there*, because each one is a correct spelling. However, the checker will pick up words which are wrongly spelled (or wrongly typed).

Other computer programs which are useful to you when editing are the *style checkers*. They can tell you how long your sentences are, and how often you use prepositions, or abstract words (those ending in *-ion*), or passive verbs (ones where the object has become the subject). Some programs will generate synonyms for you from an in-built thesaurus. They are useful aids, though they cannot automatically improve your style. They show you what your style is like, and may suggest some alternatives; but you have to decide what to do about it.

## Computers and publication

Computers and their word-processing programs are at their most useful when you want to publish your writing. They give you a clear, perfectly printed copy to share with others — one with the best points from revision built in, and all the mistakes taken out.

When you become experienced in the use of the word-processor you can begin to experiment with its facilities for varying the layout and presentation of your work. You can begin to design the appearance of your writing to match its audience and purpose. You can vary such features as the shape and position of the text on the page, the print style and the spacing.

On the next four pages you'll find the finished and published versions of the two essays we saw in production earlier in this section. Both now read well.

The published version of Mandy's essay "Growing Up" now looks very professional. Compare the earlier version on pp 9–10.

The published version of Kerry's essay "Describe the Positive Effects of the Second World War" is significantly different. Each point has been developed; she has now introduced topic sentences and the essay flows elegantly towards its conclusion.

Neither essay shows any signs of the changes that have been made during the production. They just look like good finished products.

### GROWING UP BY MANDY LITTLE

Your father hands you a letter.  You don't recognise the handwriting
so you wonder who it is who might be writing to you.  You open it and start
reading:

"Dear Mandy,

Do you want to go with me to see Superman III on Thursday?  If
you do, I will be outside the Odeon at 7.15.  I will wait for you
for ten minutes.  If you're not there, I'll know you won't be coming.

I hope you do,

Luv

Martyn"

Wow!  It's your first date and it's Martyn.  Yes, Martyn.  Captain of the
football team and the only boy in your class who doesn't suffer from greasy
hair and acne.  Will you go? Yes, of course you'll go!

Your father is watching you across the breakfast table so you put the
letter calmly back into the envelope.

"Something interesting?" he asks.

Do you tell the truth or do you lie?...You lie.

"It's from Julie — she wants me to go to the pictures with her on
Thursday."

As soon as you've said it you know it's a mistake.

"Why's Julie writing to you?  She only lives round the corner."

Get out of that one, Mandy.  You conveniently spot the time and say,
"God I'm going to be late." You pick up your sandwich box, your bag and
your coat and shout bye as you run out the door.  Phew!

All the way to school you think about what you're going to wear.  Then
it occurs to you.  Why not dye your hair?  Boys like blondes much better
than mousy browns.  If you walk to school and back you can save your bus
fare and you will have enough to buy the dye.

*(continued)*

In the evening you can't do your homework because you're thinking all the time about your date with Martyn tomorrow.  Do you kiss on the first date?  Who makes the first move?  What are you going to talk about?  Have a bath and think about it.  It's time to use the hair dye you've bought.

30 minutes later you rinse the dye off and look at yourself in the mirror.  Oh no!  Instead of a cool sophisticated blonde, there's a green haired alien staring back at you.  You scream in horror and dad comes rushing up the stairs to see what the matter is.  You have to let him in.

"What do you think you've done?" he shouts.

You cannot answer.

"Have you been dyeing your hair?"

No answer.

"What for?" You can see the horror in his face as he recognises that his little girl isn't a little girl any more.

"I don't know.  I just wanted to."  You can't tell him the truth, it'll only make things worse.

"Get in the bathroom and wash it out!  You can't go to school like that.  I don't want you walking down the street like some punk.  What will people think?"

In a flash it hits you.  If he doesn't let you out, the date will be off.  No pictures and no Martyn.  No!  It's not fair.

"But it's Thursday tomorrow," you say, unable to hold the words in.

"What's so special about Thursday?" he asks.

Do you tell him or don't you?  It'll only make things worse.  You keep your mouth shut and start running the water, to try and wash the dye out, resigning yourself to the fact that the date with Martyn will have to wait.

This growing up is no fun, you know.

DESCRIBE THE POSITIVE EFFECTS OF THE SECOND WORLD WAR

BY KERRY MURPHY

The Second World War had a devastating effect on the lives of people in Europe. The warring countries were bankrupt and many of their people were left hungry, homeless or both. If good was to come out of the war Europe's politicians faced a number of challenges: to rebuild their economic prosperity; to ensure that such a war never happened again and to deal with the new aspirations of their people.

Perhaps their most important priority was to build a peace that would last. In 1945 the Charter of the United Nations Organisation was signed by over fifty countries. The aims of the UNO were to provide a means of solving disputes between countries without the need for war and with the financial help of the USA to create the conditions for economic prosperity. Whilst experience has proved that the UNO has had an effect on the relationships between nations, it could not prevent the growing tension that began to arise between the USSR and the USA during the years following the war. Despite the ravages of World War II, the USSR had survived as the most powerful nation in Europe. The smaller European nations felt threatened and looked to the USA for protection for only the USA could match the USSR's potential power. It had the technology, the resources and the economic strength to develop a military might to provide the necessary check on the USSR's possible advance.

In order to strengthen the alliance between the USA and the non-Communist European countries, in 1949 the North Atlantic Treaty Organisation was established. This consisted of a formal agreement between the non-Communist countries in Europe and Canada and the USA to develop a military defence strategy to protect against the USSR and its allies in Eastern Europe. This strategy was based on the idea that if the Western World powers could match or even exceed the military power of the USSR, the USSR would realise they could not win a Third World War and therefore, would not try to take over the smaller countries in Europe.

The second challenge for politicians in Europe was to be sensitive to the new political climate in their own countries. The people in Europe had new expectations. They wanted rewards for the war they had fought, such as better living standards. Though most political parties tried to develop policies to meet these demands, it was Socialists who generally proved most successful. For example, in 1945 Britain elected a Socialist government who set about establishing the Welfare State to fulfil the ordinary man's new aspirations.

*(continued)*

The final important challenge was to respond to the growth of nationalism, which the war had stimulated. Many countries, who had supported the allies in their fight against Nazi Germany began to seek a reward – their independence. All over Africa and Asia European dependencies began to call for self-rule. Quickly the colonial empires of countries like Britain and France began to disintegrate. The process of granting independence was not always a simple one and frequently led to new tensions and hostilities, as Britain found out in 1947 in India and 1956 in the Suez Crisis. However, the process could not be resisted. The days of colonial empires were over.

With hindsight in 1989, we can with some certainty say that the lives of those who fought in 1939–45 have not been wasted. Out of the Second World War grew a better world – one of peace, economic prosperity and freedom.

# Part 2: From me to it

*Begin with yourself*
*Turning things over and*
*inside out*

# Begin with yourself

When we speak, we often start with ourselves. "I" is actually one of the commonest words people use. We use it in explaining what we've been doing, as in: "I went for a ride . . . " And it's there when we say what's on our minds: "I think", "I know", "I like" or "I can't stand it". What happens to us, and the way it affects us, is often what we want to share with others.

When writing, it's again easier to begin with yourself. Even if the topic seems remote, you can always get a grip on it by asking: "How does it affect *me*?" This is what Mandy did when she had to write about growing up (p 6). She thought about her experience of growing up as a teenage girl and used this as a basis for her essay. With English essays, in particular, you can often use your own experiences and feelings as the content.

## Put yourself in the picture

It's the same for writing in other subjects, such as history, geography, sociology or economics, though in a slightly different way. The facts for a history essay will come from books and magazines, or a lesson, and they may be completely new to you. Yet you will be able to get a grip on them by asking: "What do *I* find the most interesting fact in all that?" In her essay on the positive effects of the Second World War, Kerry began with the idea of peace in Europe since 1945 and in exploring that idea she was encouraged to look at the other changes that accompanied that peace. In exploring one fact you'll find yourself involved in other related facts, and that will get you inside the subject.

Once you've got yourself into the essay, you'll find things start to come easy, and you'll have plenty to say and present. Then it's just a matter of presenting it all in the most interesting way for the reader. The funny thing is that the harder you try to express the way things look to *you*, the better they will come across to the reader!

## A personal essay

On the next page you'll see how one student began by writing about herself, and soon found she was talking about things that would interest any reader.

Grace, like Mandy, was asked to consider the subject of *growing up*. Her approach is very different. She chooses to describe herself and how growing up is affecting her at the time she is writing. In doing so, she presents the ups and downs of teenage life and discusses the value of music and art to her. When we finish reading this essay, we not only know Grace better but we've also had to reflect on issues that affect us all.

## Growing up
## By Grace Crossley

Grace Crossley, born Huddersfield, 3rd August 1972, medium build, mid-length brown hair, blue eyes, oval face, sallow complexion. A Sixth Form student at Cheltenham Sixth Form Centre.

But who is the real me? A few years ago I could have answered the question easily. I felt happy and secure, and I could not imagine life being much different. But growing up has brought a whole new world of experiences, pressures, responsibilities, excitements and . . . confusion. I stand in a whirlwind of decisions, too far away from childhood to feel secure, but not near enough to adulthood to see a clear way ahead.

I sense that my role in the family is changing. I am trying to sever the ties and pull away. Sometimes I pull a little too hard and have to recoil to the safety of my home which still means so much to me. My friends find that hard to understand and it is difficult to explain to them that the love of my family means much more than the possessions that they seem to value so much. And yet such close love can be claustrophobic and heated arguments can result. I have a canny knack of knowing just how to irritate my mum and anger her. I do not think that part of me has grown up yet.

Yet something is happening to me. I am much moodier than I used to be. Dad insists that they did not have moods when he was young. Somehow I doubt whether that's right. Some days I feel like a ship lost in the fog, totally isolated and unable to find my way through it, the fog distorting the shape of everything in my world. These are the black days which vanish as quickly as they appear. On other days everything goes right. I want to sing and dance and savour everything around me. All my senses seem alert and life has a sharpness and a relevance.

If I need relief from the black moods, I can always turn to music, which has been an unchanging part of my life from the time when I could sing nursery rhymes. My mother often used to sing Latin nouns to me when I was a baby and now I relish playing a musical instrument – the flute. Music provides a refuge when I am feeling down; it can arouse strong emotions and awake dormant feelings, at times almost reducing me to tears. Yet I cannot imagine life without this pleasure and if I lived in a world without other people's music I would have to make my own.

Art too has played, and will always play, a significant part in my life. I cannot remember a time when I have not been interested in the subject. I have been brought up in an artistic world, where visits to exhibitions and galleries were as frequent as visits to relatives. As a family we have always enjoyed making things. Even though I can afford to buy gifts myself now, I still prefer to make them, as I feel that I am also giving a part of me. And giving seems so much more important than taking nowadays.

Music and art then have been constant threads through my life and they are links with my childhood that will stay with me in the future. Yet the future will bring more changes, new bridges to be crossed, new roads to travel down, new joys and new sorrows – but on this day, this is me.

# Turning things over and inside out

When you put yourself at the heart of what you write, you'll go a long way. Tell your readers what interests *you*, and you've a good chance of interesting them. What's more, you'll have plenty to say, and a sheet of blank paper won't faze you.

Once you feel confident about writing, you're ready to start experimenting . . . and whole new worlds of writing will open up!

## Turn things over

Experimenting is firstly playing with words for different effects. See what happens when you replace one word with another. You can start with an observation: "The headmaster was angry and so were the students", and then replace *angry* with *fuming*, or with the simile *as mad as a rabid dog*. What you are doing is finding synonyms for *angry*, and each one changes the effect a little. Both *fuming* and *mad as a rabid dog* make the sentence more dramatic and they give you alternatives, so that you don't have to repeat the same word: "The students were angry and the headmaster was as mad as a rabid dog." In the case of the simile you can not only say something about the emotional state of the headmaster, you can also get across to the reader your feelings towards him. *Mad as a rabid dog* suggests fear and dislike, whereas a different simile, such as *mad as a March hare* would have a completely different effect — one of sympathy and amusement.

## In other words . . .

By looking for other words and phrases you can begin to create different styles. If you say: "It's brill", you create a very different effect from when you say: "It's excellent". It's the same point, but the style is different. You could say that it's a matter of saying something to a different audience, for the chances are you'd say "It's brill" to a fellow student, and "It's excellent" to your teacher. What you're doing is adapting your language for the audience. You're using slang to create an informal style in the first case, and Standard English words for a more formal style in the second. If you fail to make an appropriate choice you can confuse or even offend your reader.

You might like to try "translating" other slang idioms into more formal language, just for fun. What about "It's wicked", "take a gander", "it fair blew our socks off"? Then try "translating" the other way too. Start with some formal idioms and turn them into slang.

Differences in expression like these help to make the very different styles of, say, a novel and a textbook. Or the difference between what you write in your personal journal (if you keep one) and the language of your history essay or science report.

# Turn it inside out

But there are other things than words that also make the difference
between a novel and a textbook. It's the way they look at their subject,
their perspective on it. The novel tries to get inside its subject, while the
textbook stands back and comments from outside. The novel uses "I" and
"me", or "she" or "he", whereas the textbook uses "it". You'll see the
difference if you start with a personal sentence (one with "I" in it), and
then turn it inside out, by using "the student" in the same place. For
example:

"After school I can go into town"    would become

"After school, the student is allowed to go into the city."

It is as if someone else was writing about you, and you have to think
about yourself in a more objective way. It's the difference between a
personal and an impersonal way of saying things.

When you translate "from me to it" like this, you'll find you have to
adapt other things as well. You often have to add extra details to fill out
the picture. We blur things and take them for granted when talking
informally, and they have to be made explicit in more formal writing.
These things are all part of the more objective style which you'll need,
sooner or later, for writing in history and geography, or economics and
science.

On the next two pages, you'll find two pairs of texts, each pair about
the same subject. However, within each pair you'll find contrasting styles
and effects – so different that they seem to belong to different worlds.

The first pair are about pop star and soap-opera actor, Jason Donovan.
But one piece is like the script of a live interview, with Jason Donovan
speaking for himself, while the other is like a feature article written by a
journalist for the newspaper.

The second is about a region in Australia called the Blue Mountains
where people go bushwalking. The style of the first piece will take you
there along with the bushwalkers, while the second is like something
written in a geography textbook.

# Check the details

When you look more closely, you'll see that the second text in each pair
is really only a "translation" or transformation of the first. See how many
points they have in common.

## Jason Donovan talks about his school life

**A**

*What did you want to be when you grew up?*
Like most boys that age at Malvern Central School I was really into flying and aircraft, and I wanted to be a jet pilot.

*Were you a bit of a goody at school or did you muck about?*
I suppose I was a bit of a tearaway when I was 14 or 15! I was really into underground music at the time and I'd sneak into night clubs with a friend and we'd be out 'till all hours raging!

*Were you a bright spark?*
I slogged my guts out to pass my Higher School Certificate putting about ten hours a day in the two weeks leading up to the exams!! I'm not that clever so I'm the sort of person who has to try that much harder at everything. I was pleased I did because soon after that I got the part of Scott in *Neighbours*.

*What were your fave subjects?*
My best subject by a long way was art. In fact I've still got a painting of a warrior I did at school on the wall at home. I was also OK at English but I was pretty hopeless at Maths.

**B**

Star of *Neighbours* and successful pop singer, Jason Donovan, admits he did not find school work easy. He attributes his limited academic success to sheer hard work, having to study for ten hours a day in the weeks leading up to his Higher School Certificate to ensure a pass. Yet he still found enough time to indulge his interest in underground music by stopping out late to frequent night clubs where such music was to be found. It is scarcely surprising, therefore, that Mr Donovan's dream of becoming a jet pilot was never fulfilled and that he became a soap-opera actor and singer instead.

# From speech to Standard English

What's the same in the two pieces? Information about Jason Donovan:
He aspired to being a jet pilot.
He liked underground music.
He stopped out late to go to night clubs.
He passed his Higher School Certificate through hard work.
What's different?
- A is a dialogue between two people. B is a statement by one person and so is a monologue.
- A has questions and answers. B is continuous reporting.

- A   has Jason Donovan speaking for himself as "I" (the view from the inside). B   presents him as "he" (the view from the outside).
- A   has more informal language such as "really into", "a bit of a tearaway", "sneak into", "raging", "slogged my guts out". B   has more formal language, such as "indulge", "frequent", "sheer hard work".
- A   takes things for granted, such as the audience knowing what *Neighbours* is. B   explains this basic point to the reader.

## The Kanangra Walls area

**A**

. . . The next day we set out from Dex Creek through a gently sloping area of short, dense scrub, with only our compasses to guide us. There were no tracks, only rabbit paths, so we had to make our way through a forest of waist-high bushes, which took an aggressive attitude towards our legs. Jenny's shins looked like the work of Jackson Pollock. Once through there, we discovered we were in the wrong place, and needed to do more bush-bashing to get to the western side of Moko Creek. We followed that ridge to the well-named Mount Strongleg.

To descend Strongleg Buttress we had to drop 600 metres in about one and a half kilometres. It's spurs like this which made us think longingly of chairlifts and hang-gliders. But we managed the descent in about 50 minutes, and were glad to wallow in the Kanangra Creek. After a very long lunch we moved on downstream. Unfortunately the grassy banks of the Cox's River had been ripped out by a flood the previous August, so there was a lot of slow rock-scrambling. We stopped for the night on Kooriekirra Creek, and feasted on hot muffins and Stefan's delicious, pure Australian honey (not an advertisement) . . .

**B**

Below Kanangra Walls, the Gangerang Plateau stretches northeast, and is drained by several creeks, including Dex Creek to the south, and Moko Creek to the north. The soil of the plateau is mostly sedimentary material. But it is exposed to all weather conditions, and only supports sclerophyll vegetation and acacia. The same vegetation extends along the ridges to Kooriekirra Top and, ultimately, Mt Strongleg.

The precipitous flanks of Mt Strongleg rise 600 metres above the Kanangra Creek. The peak forms one side of the northern end of the Kanangra Gorge, and it diverts the Kanangra Creek westwards before it can resume its northward course to the Cox's River. The steep descent of Kanangra Creek and others promotes a savage flow of water in the Cox's River. It can transport basalt boulders far downstream, which continually scour the banks of the river and modify its course . . .

## From informal report to scientific description

What's the same? Information on:

> landmarks such as Dex Creek, Moko Creek, Kanangra Creek,
>    Cox's River, Mt Strongleg
> the tough vegetation
> the steepness of Mt Strongleg
> large rocks in the bed of the Cox's River
> changes in the profile of Cox's River

What's different?

- A  is a personal account from one of the walkers, hence "we". B  is an impersonal description with no people in it at all.
- A  takes you stage by stage on the walk. B  presents things in relation to the two main geographical features of the area, Gangerang Plateau and Mt Strongleg.
- A  takes the details of the landscape for granted. B  adds in a lot of "hard" information about the landmarks and their orientation.
- A  tells you what the walkers experience along the way. B  gives you geological causes and effects.
- A  uses everyday words and images, such as "waist-high", "bush-bashing", "wallow", "ripped out", "feasted". B  contains technical words, such as "drained", "sedimentary", "sclerophyll", "vegetation", "basalt".
- A's purpose is to entertain the reader. B's purpose is to explain the geography of the area.

# Finding a purpose . . .

The final factor affecting the sort of language you use when writing is your purpose. Knowing why you're writing helps you find the right style. It should force you into choosing certain types of word in preference to others, into preferring certain types of sentences and into selecting certain ways of sequencing and setting out your ideas. Below you will find two very different types of language which serve two very different purposes.

## Emotive

There will be times when you want to persuade your readers by appealing to their emotions. The English language is full of words which when used in certain situations appeal straight to the reader's heart — words like *slavery, freedom, liberty, justice, equality*. When such words are used in conjunction with vivid imagery and other poetic techniques like *alliteration, repetition* and *assonance,* the effect can be awesome. Politicians know this, as do advertisers and other propagandists. They frequently resort to this type of language to manipulate us. This excerpt from a Greenpeace leaflet is typical. Look at the emotive vocabulary and imagery that has been highlighted in bold print:

---

### Planet Earth is 4 600 million years old

If we condense this inconceivable timespan into an understandable concept, we can liken Earth to a person 46 years of age . . .

Modern man has been around for 4 hours. During the last hour Man discovered agriculture. The industrial revolution began a minute ago.

During those sixty seconds of biological time, Modern Man has made a **rubbish tip** of **Paradise**.

He has multiplied his numbers to **plague** proportions, caused the **extinction** of 500 species of animals, **ransacked** the planet for fuels and now stands **like a brutish infant, gloating** over his meteoric rise to ascendancy, on the brink of **a war to end all wars** and of effectively destroying this **oasis** of life in the solar system.

# Explanatory

There will be other times when you will want to appeal to your reader's intellect. When you want to explain a process in writing, your desire for clarity will influence the language you use. It is likely that you will opt for short sentences with clear, simple vocabulary. If you need to use technical words, which the reader may not be familiar with, you will make their meaning clear through their context or with some form of explanation. Furthermore, your paragraphs will be as brief as possible, because you will want to avoid overloading your reader with too much information.

---

### The ozone story simply told

The ozone layer in the atmosphere allows life on Earth to flourish. It absorbs damaging ultraviolet radiation (UV-B) from the sun.

The damage to the ozone layer is being done by chemicals called chlorofluorocarbons (CFCs) which are used in a wide range of industrial processes.

Every year, a hole in the ozone layer appears over the Antarctic. It has gradually been getting bigger, and now covers an area the size of the United States.

The biggest single use of CFCs is as propellants in aerosol sprays. In the US, they were banned for this purpose back in 1978. Other major uses are in foam packaging (in hamburger cartons, for instance), air conditioning units and refrigerants.

# Part 3: Forms of writing

*Giving shape and structure to your material*

*Forms to help both writer and reader*

*A journal*

*Narratives*

*Descriptions*

*Essays*

*Science reports*

*News reports*

*Advertisements*

*Letters*

# Giving shape and structure to your material

Whenever you sit down to write, you should give some thought to the overall shape and structure of whatever you're writing. The best pieces of writing aren't just a string of paragraphs loaded with information. Rather, the paragraphs and sections help to structure the information into a total shape. And the shape or form shows the purpose of the information.

*Letters and their form:* One form which everyone knows is the letter form. It is an obvious one because its beginning and end are shown in a regular way. Letters always begin with "Dear So-and-so", and end with a greeting or courtesy, and the name of the writer. These are part of the standard letter form, whatever the letter's purpose. The message or business of the letter is always framed in this way, with the name of the intended reader at the beginning, and that of the writer at the end. Have a look at the letters on pp 56–7 for some examples.

*The form of science reports:* Another standard form which you may know is the one used in formal science reports. They usually have five sections: 1. Aim; 2. Apparatus; 3. Method; 4. Results; 5. Conclusion. Each of the sections is labelled, which makes them quite obvious. A particular kind of information goes into each section, as explained on p 50. As a set, the sections form a logical order for reporting experiments.

*Story form and narratives:* Some writing forms are not so obvious because there are no labels or fixed sets of words that go with each section or stage. But the form is there, just below the surface. It is in the structure and the order in which the writer presents things to you. Stories are usually told in the order of events, to show how things happened. Even so, story form is more than just one thing after another. The best stories take shape around a climax, and the build-up to the climax helps to frame it. A story cannot go straight to its climax, or it wouldn't be a story. First things first. You must meet the main characters, and the situation they're in, and then things can develop towards the climax. The standard parts of a story are explained.

*Descriptions:* There is no single way of structuring descriptions. The sequence of details and ideas will be dictated by the nature of the subject and the effect you're striving for. For example, you might wish to show what the day in the life of a village is like by describing the changing scene throughout the day, beginning with dawn, moving to midday and ending with dusk. Or you might wish to capture a scene from a hill-top by describing first what can be seen in the background and then gradually moving towards the foreground. Or you might want to capture your impressions of a particular experience by building your description around a contrast – the stadium during the football game, followed by the stadium after the game. Other possible methods of structuring a description are discussed on p 45.

*Getting the order right:* The order you write things down in is always important. It is already there in some forms of writing: story narratives have it in the order of events, and science reports in their logical order. But in other forms you have to decide for yourself. In essays you have to decide whether you can use the order of events, as you can when you're writing about a historical or natural process. But when there is no time-line (or cause and effect) underlying your material, you will have to think of a logical order — perhaps comparison, or from most to least important.

# Forms to help both writer and reader

The form which structures and frames your writing is important in two ways:

1. It helps you to plan and compose your writing (Stage 1 of the writing process, p 4). You'll know what kind of material to present when. Each piece will have its place and you'll have a clear idea of *why* it is there — what purpose it serves in your writing. Most people write better when they know what purpose each section of their writing is meant to serve.
2. It helps your readers to know where they are in your writing, and to anticipate the purpose behind what you say. They can meet you halfway in your writing.

In the following pages you'll find examples of eight well-known forms of writing, each of which has its own order or structure. Some of them you probably use already. (The others you'll know from reading the newspaper or whatever arrives in the letterbox.) Each one has some notes beside it to explain how it works, and there are diagrams to show the underlying structure. You'll find:

- journal writing
- story or narrative
- description
- essays — argumentative and factual
- science reports — formal and informal
- news report
- advertisements — "hard-sell" and "soft-sell"
- letters — private and public

As a change from essay writing, why not try your hand at one of the other forms in the list. You could take whatever topic you've been tackling in history or social studies, and try writing a news article about it. Pretend you're an eyewitness reporter. Or you could write advertisements ("hard-sell" and "soft-sell") for a bicycle or a computer. Or a letter about what your school needs, to the minister of education.

## A journal: Records of Scott's expedition to the South Pole

These are some of the final extracts from Robert Falcon Scott's disastrous attempt to lead the first team of men to the South Pole in 1912.

*Wednesday, January 18 1912*
. . . Great God! This is an awful place and terrible enough for us to have laboured to it without the reward of priority . . .

Now for the run home and a desperate struggle. I wonder if we can do it. . . .

*Friday, March 16 or Saturday 17*
Lost track of dates, but think the last correct. Tragedy all along the line. At lunch, the day before yesterday, poor Titus Oates said he couldn't go on; he proposed we should leave him in his sleeping bag. That we could not do, and we induced him to come on, on the afternoon march. In spite of its awful nature for him he struggled on and we made a few miles. At night he was worse and we knew the end had come . . .

. . . This was the end. He slept through the night before last, hoping not to wake; but he woke in the morning — yesterday. It was blowing a blizzard. He said, "I am just going outside and may be some time." He went out into the blizzard and we have not seen him since. . . .

*Monday, March 19*
Lunch. We camped with difficulty last night, and were dreadfully cold till after our supper of cold pemmican and biscuit and a half a pannikin of cocoa cooked over the spirit. Then, contrary to expectation, we got warm and all slept well. Today we started in the usual dragging manner. Sledge dreadfully heavy. We are 15½ miles from the depot and ought to get there in three days. What progress! We have two days' food but barely a day's fuel. All our feet are getting bad — Wilson's best, my right foot worst, left all right. There is no chance to nurse one's feet till we can get hot food into us. Amputation is the least I can hope for now, but will the trouble spread? That is the serious question. The weather doesn't give us a chance — the wind from N. to N.W. and — 40° temp. today.

*Wednesday, March 21*
Got within 11 miles of depot Monday night; had to lay up all yesterday in severe blizzard. Today forlorn hope, Wilson and Bowers going to depot for fuel.

*Thursday, March 22 and 23*
Blizzard bad as ever — Wilson and Bowers unable to start — tomorrow last chance — no fuel and only one or two of food left — must be near the end. Have decided it shall be natural — we shall march for the depot with or without our effects and die in our tracks.

*Thursday, March 29*
Since the 21st we have had a continuous gale from W.S.W. and S.W. We had fuel to make two cups of tea apiece and bare food for two days on the 20th. Every day we have been ready to start for our depot *11 miles* away, but outside the door of the tent it remains a scene of whirling drift. I do not think we can hope for any better things now. We shall stick it out to the end, but we are getting weaker, of course, and the end cannot be far.

It seems a pity, but I do not think I can write more.

Last entry.
For God's sake look after our people.

## Notes on journals

When you write a journal day by day, you may be doing it to keep regular records, or to have somewhere to keep notes on things which seem important and interesting. At the time of writing you cannot tell what will be important later, but this doesn't matter. Journals and diaries are always a mixture, with entries which in time will seem only trivial, and ones which become extremely important.

Journal entries are often uneven in length. On some days there will be a lot to report apart from the regular records; on others there is nothing remarkable to add. But the shape and size of the entries is no more important than the overall length of the journal. The form of the journal is simply that it puts things down in small, one-day-at-a-time sections. Unlike all the other forms shown on the next few pages, it is written in parts, and not as a whole.

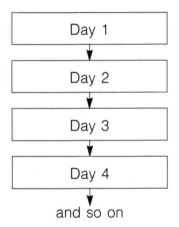

and so on          *Diagram of a journal*

## Uses of journals

Since journals are a way of keeping notes on things, you can use them to record your reactions to lessons in any subject, day by day. When you reread them at the end of term, they will give you an overview of what has been tackled, and help you in revising. You may be surprised to read how you first reacted to something, as "strange", "hard", "boring" . . . and how it seems later. Try keeping a journal in maths on the methods and problems you're being taught, or in English, on your reactions to the book you're currently reading.

# Narratives

Stories come in a variety of forms, shapes and sizes. They might be as brief as one of Aesop's fables or as long as Tolstoy's *War and Peace*. They might take the form of a diary or journal like Daniel Keyes' *Flowers for Algernon*, or a collection of letters like Samuel Richardson's *Pamela*, or a playscript like Shakespeare's tragedies, or an interior monologue like Alan Sillitoe's *The Loneliness of the Long Distance Runner*. Whatever their form, most stories share the same underlying shape or structure. Read this story written by Rachael and look at the way in which she's ordered the sequence of events she describes.

## The Mistake
## by Rachael Etheridge

9.00 a.m. and my rushed breakfast was turning dangerously in my stomach every time we sped round a corner. "If this is travelling first class on British Rail," I thought, "I hate to think what travelling second class must be like. Even harder seats and even harder ham sandwiches, I dare say."

Taking a train up North meant that at Birmingham I had to change trains. This procedure usually meant great inconvenience but at this time in the morning with my breakfast giving me terrible indigestion, the thought of stepping down from the train was bliss. I almost looked forward to sitting down and drinking a cup of tea — even British Rail tea — without jolting from side to side.

When the train finally came to a halt, I collected my handbag and briefcase and struggled to the door of the carriages. As I pushed down the handle, I half expected it to be stuck and imagined myself locked in a first class compartment on a British Rail train, surviving on their very own cardboard ham sandwiches for the rest of my life. But no, to my surprise, the door suddenly swung open and I was ejected out of the train and onto the platform, briefcase flying before me. Quickly I gathered up my briefcase and with as much dignity as possible I walked purposefully towards the British Rail cafe, eyes fixed on the entrance.

I had recaptured some of my composure and thanked God that I had passed through the cafe door safely. Looking around me I saw that all the tables were taken and there were only a few chairs left.

I stood in the queue, hoping and praying I hadn't scagged my new tights but not daring to look down in case.

Now with my feet firmly planted on terra firma I felt my unsettled stomach could handle a Kit-Kat with my tea. I replaced my purse and struggled to carry all my belongings as I sought out a vacant seat. I was keeping a sharp eye open for people's feet and stray chair legs but apart from dropping my briefcase twice, I arrived at a table safely. I found myself sitting uncomfortably next to a delightful young man with shoulder-length, greasy hair. He sat hunched over the table like an old man, looking decidedly unwell. "Oh, come on!" I thought. "British Rail isn't really that bad!"

I was firmly seated and was making a mental note never to travel this way again, when suddenly a long, thin hand reached out and picked up the Kit-Kat. I watched, amazed at what I saw, as the long, dirty fingers unwrapped it.

*(continued)*

I looked questioningly from the chocolate to the youth's face. He looked back at me with glazed eyes and shrugged. Did he realise he was eating my Kit-Kat or did he honestly believe he had a right to it?

My surprise was overtaken by anger. I was not about to sit there watching some long-haired lout eat my Kit-Kat. I reached out, grabbed the remaining half and stuffed it defiantly into my mouth. I glared at him, expecting embarrassment, but his facial expression barely changed. He merely stood up and shuffled to the counter. Maybe he was going to buy another Kit-Kat.

I felt pleased with myself. I had proved that I would not give in to the younger generation of today. I smiled and took a sip of tea. It wasn't particularly enjoyable but I felt proud of myself and the taste of the tea was irrelevant.

The lovely gentleman decided to honour me with his presence yet again. He slowly seated himself, hair dropping in front of his glazed eyes. There on the plate in front of him was a large doughnut, dripping in sugar. He slumped in his chair, stirring figures of eight in his tea.

I stared at his doughnut, a sly smile spreading across my face. My stomach didn't really feel like a cake but to prove a point it would just have to suffer. As quick as lightning my hand shot out, spilling tea as it did so. My slim fingers wrapped around the bulging cake before the young hooligan realised. Pausing to reconsider just momentarily, I shoved as much of the sticky cake as I could into my wide open mouth.

'Well, he won't steal another Kit-Kat in a hurry,' I said to myself, laughing inwardly. My eyes sparkled as my cheeks bulged with cake and jam rolled down my chin. I finished my huge mouthful and daintily wiped my lips with my napkin. My train was now being called. I gathered up my belongings carefully, my face showing no emotion. I stood up and gave the young man the benefit of one of my icy stares. He was slumped in his chair staring at the empty plate in front of him.

I made my way towards the platform, shoulders back, feeling a million dollars, even if my face was a little sticky. Climbing aboard the train, I was extremely careful not to trip. I contentedly sank down. I could now study my tights to see if they had scagged. They hadn't. I undid the zip to my crammed full shoulder bag, thinking I would read a magazine, when I saw it! The red wrapper. There, sitting alongside my purse was a Kit-Kat. It couldn't possibly be the Kit-Kat I had bought in the cafe . . . could it? Dropping my bag in dismay I sank down into my seat, turning to the window in embarrassment.

As we pulled slowly out of the station I saw the young man with long shoulder-length greasy hair and a fixed, glazed expression.

## Notes on narratives

Rachael's story, "The Mistake", demonstrates well how narratives are structured around a climax. The art of story-telling is in building up to the climax and taking time over the details in order to increase suspense. The details should trigger the reader's imagination and bring the story's characters and situation to life. You can speak and exchange words with each other to heighten the drama. Then having involved the reader in your situation, you deliver the climax and take your leave gracefully.

## Uses of narrative

You're most likely to be writing narratives in English classes, whether it's a story of what happened to you last Christmas, or your own imaginative creation or perhaps science fiction. But narratives are also a good way of presenting things from history and from art, as in a historical novel. You take the chief characters from a historical event, or from a painting, and write about what was going on around them as if you were following the drama with them.

| |
|---|
| INTRODUCTION TO CHARACTERS AND SETTING |
| SIGNIFICANT EVENT OR CHAIN OF EVENTS |
| CLIMAX |
| DENOUEMENT OR CONCLUSION |

*Diagram of a narrative*

# Descriptions

> ### The Station
> ### By Ian Moir
> Lower Galstone station is situated on the outskirts of the town, its dark corrugated rooves and ramshackle walls appearing as a cancerous growth between the gas works and the oppressive council flats, those dismal monoliths of poverty. Access to the station is via a narrow walled passage which from the main road runs parallel with the front of the gasworks for a hundred yards, then turns a right angle to enter the station car park. This frequently causes problems, what with gas tankers and cars manoeuvring in the same area and long vehicles continually becoming stuck in the bend. This happens so frequently that people often question the original motives of the planning commission.
>
> The car park itself is a cramped tarmac affair with a single lamp post in the centre, which, had it not been vandalised, might still supply the surrounding four parking spaces with enough light to appreciate the potholed surface. At this time in the morning, however, there was sufficient light to appreciate not only the potholes but the generous scattering of litter and broken glass.

*(continued)*

A vast estate car arrived, scrunching up the debris. It was an old model —
as were all the other cars in the car park — for only the most naive of American
tourists dared leave a new car here in the night's dark embrace. The car stopped
and almost immediately a hoard of small duffle coated children piled out of
the tailgate — three, four, no five youngsters — for whom the station was an
adventure playground. They scuttled like rats in front of the moving cars, then
headed towards the station entrance, a widish gap with rusted gates and or-
namental curls of plaster. The architect had unfortunately failed to predict the
phenomenon of acid rain, and as a result the stonework resembled wax that
had melted, flowed and reset again. The children passed through, running soft
pink fingers over the rusty railings.

The first thing to strike anyone passing through the station gate is the smell.
Although there is no physical barrier it suddenly appears on entering and disappears just as abruptly when leaving. A few steps inside brings upon some
frightening nasal experiences. The reek of diesel fumes blends with the stifling
smell of cigarette smoke and unsanitised lavatories to produce a pungent odour
surely unmatched by any station in England.

Today the major source of the unpleasant emissions appeared to be a
doorway to the left, leading into a dull, grey waiting room. Even though it was
still an hour to the half-nine rush, the room contained enough smokers to make
the air as dull and grey as the room. A tramp shuffled out the men's opposite,
retying his outsized trousers with electric flex. His eyes flitted round the room,
noting the drab walls, the sagging ceiling and the out-of-order coffee machine.
He started towards the vacant seat by the single radiator, a quart of liquor
clutched in one grimy claw like a baby's rattle.

A queue of haggard looking people sprawled across the centre of the room,
waiting for the privilege of shouting through three inches of glass to an even
more haggard looking ticket seller. One middle-aged woman turned to ask the
time of a black leather-clad youth behind her but was rewarded with a puff
of smoke. She tried to nudge her husband into some sort of action, but he only
murmured something dismissive behind his RAF moustache.

The queue did not part for the tramp so he was forced to go round the back
of it, a course which took his shoddy shoes through the edge of a pile of saw-
dust soaked with disinfectant. The only other exit from the waiting room led
out onto the platform and the promise of a slightly fresher atmosphere. A
station porter wheeled a squeaky trolley loaded with crates through the
opening.

The platform stretched towards the left, a long, thin slab of concrete. It was
new and gave the impression of a filling in the decay ridden surroundings. The
walls were covered with posters advertising out of date cheap day returns and
age old graffiti, the wall having been filled up with untidy scrawl a long time
ago. Against the wall was a row of cast iron seats. These were usually unoc-
cupied and today was no exception. A closer look provided the reason. Above
was a long gash in the corrugated roofing, which let in rain and pigeon drop-
pings. The family of duffle coated children, with the exception of the smallest
boy, sat on matching suitcases, swinging their legs. He had managed to drag
his coat through one of the thin trails of spilled coke which ran across the

*(continued)*

platform. His mother, flushed and breathless, caught up with him and began dabbing frantically with a tissue.

A thin man with a guitar case leaned against a pillar nearby, apparently observing the scene, but in fact his hazel eyes were focused somewhere distant and not on the children. He whistled through yellowed teeth while his coarse fingers drummed out a rhythm on the peeling paint of the pillar behind him. He stopped momentarily when a pack of Brownies noisily scuffled out onto the platform, giggling and skipping. Two overweight twins attempted to push a tiny bespectacled wretch onto the tracks below but were thwarted by a long stare down their Brown Owl's beaky nose. Another cheeky-faced girl argued with her friends whilst snatching glances at the man with the guitar. "It is him! Look, I'll go and ask him, shall I?" she said, then sauntered up to him, mouthing insistently back to her friends, "It is!"

"Excuse me, er . . . are you Eric Clapton?" she enquired sweetly.

The man smiled briefly at this then walked off down the platform leaving the girl to a volley of "I told you so" remarks from her friends. He settled again, leaning on the pillar down the platform. From here it was possible to see the ripped "Keep Britain Tidy" notice and the pile of litter on the floor beneath the empty litter bin. This transformed the pillar into a totem pole surrounded by offerings of banana skins and chewing gum to the guitarist — the garbage god.

A short walk further down the platform brought into view a lead lined window set into the wall on the left. Three of its many panes were smashed. A look through one of the holes — the remaining ones being too dingy to pass as transparent — revealed a small, dark room with an old walnut desk, one leg supported by a heavy volume with "REGULATIONS" embossed on the spine. An oil lamp sat on one end and under it in a drawer surprisingly obvious from the window was a half-filled bottle of whiskey. Pictures of famous steam engines cluttered the wall and had been used to cover cracks in the plaster.

Two sidesteps to the right was a green door. The single word, "Stationmaster", was painted across it.

I sighed and let myself into my office . . .

## Notes on description

There will be times when you will be asked to describe a person, an experience or a scene. You do it all the time when you're speaking — "It was a nightmare! You should've seen him . . . He went beserk, throwing the books down on the table, screaming at the top of his voice. His hair was all over the place, his shirt was hanging out . . . I thought he was going to explode, he was that red in the face." In order to recreate the scene for your listener, you rattle off a series of details, hoping that when the listener assembles them, he will not only recreate in his imagination what you have just described, but he will also share your feelings about it.

You have similar intentions when you're writing a description. If you are to be successful you need to have a clear sense of what you're trying to get across to your reader; you have to select those details that will create both the scene and your response, and you have to find the right words to capture them as exactly as possible. Of course, when you're writing you have the time to select those details and words more carefully. You also have the opportunity to put those details in the sequence which will best capture the scene and your response. Just as when you're writing narrative, you need to think about how you're going to begin your piece, how it will progress and how it will end. However, the answers to these questions are not always as obvious as when you're writing narrative. The way you structure a description will be dictated by the nature of your subject and the effect you're striving for. As you read Ian's description of Lower Galstone station, look at the way in which he has sequenced the piece. It has two distinct strands. He moves from the outside of the station to the interior, and he moves from a description of the general scene towards a focus on the specific details of the Stationmaster's office.

## Uses of description

You're most likely to be writing descriptions in English classes. Sometimes these descriptions will form part of narratives; sometimes they will form parts of personal letters; sometimes they will be set pieces. You might find, however, that you're asked to write a description in history, geography or religious education. Teachers in these subject areas like to use descriptions as a means of helping you bring to life cold, factual accounts of a period, event or time.

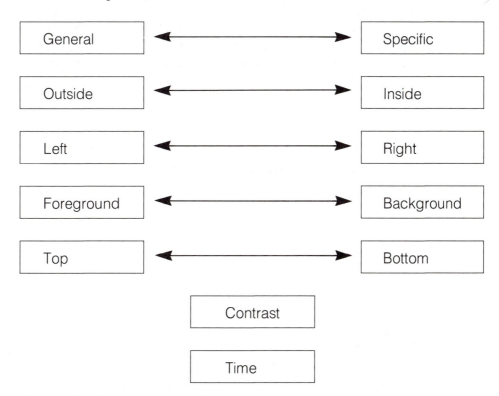

*Diagram of possible structures for description*

# Essays

At school you write a lot of longish pieces or prose which are loosely called "essays". What goes into them, and the purpose behind them is likely to differ slightly from subject to subject and from year to year.

During the GCSE years you are likely to be called upon to write more abstract essays that contain a series of thoughts or reflections or an argument. There is a reflective essay on p 27, Grace's "Growing Up" and an argumentative one, Kevin's "The Case against Homework" on p 47. With essays like these, the form and order must be decided by the logic of your material, because there's no order of events to follow. The structure of the argumentative essays is shown below.

In subjects like history, geography, sociology, economics, business studies and home economics, you will be asked to write some kind of factual essay. The purpose of such essays is to bring together a body of information, and to interpret it or give it some meaningful shape or theme. The meaning you are expected to find may be indicated by the set question, as with the first Viking essay (p 48): "What influence did the Vikings have on England?" Your task as essay writer is to select information that will answer the question, and to present the information in a logical way (perhaps moving from what's most important to what's least important). It is also possible to present information from a personal perspective, as shown in the other Viking essay: "Over to England" (p 49).

On other occasions in these subjects you will have to produce argumentative and critical essays. In such essays you will be using your information to support a point of view. Once again, the order in which you present things has to be a logical one for the material.

| INTRODUCTION: Statement of point of view |
| --- |
| Argument 1 |
| Argument 2 |
| Argument 3 |
| Argument 4 |
| CONCLUSION |

*Diagram of an argumentative essay*

# An argumentative essay

### The case against homework
### by Kevin O'Leary

You arrive home from school exhausted. The day's lessons have taken their toll. Your head is spinning with facts; your body is battered and bruised from an afternoon of Games and all you want to do is to collapse in front of the television or go round your friend's house and forget about school. But can you? Of course you cannot. School does not end at 3.25; it extends into the evening, and when GCSE coursework assignments are due, it does not stop there — you can be working until the early hours of the morning. Is this really fair?

The introduction of GCSE has resulted in an increase in homework for all fifteen- and sixteen-year-olds. A survey conducted by 4B has shown that pupils in the fourth year in this school spend on average between two and three hours per night on homework. Virtually every pupil interviewed said he felt he no longer had enough time to himself. Others said that in order to make room for their homework they were having to give up their hobbies. The time they used to spend on activities such as go-carting, playing sport and building models has to be used for completing Geography and CDT projects. How are we supposed to become individuals if we are not allowed to follow our own interests?

This burden of homework also destroys relationships and causes tensions in families. Many pupils reported that they do not have the time to see friends outside school hours. They feel that they are becoming prisoners in their own bedrooms. Homework even interferes with family events. One pupil described finishing his Design project on Christmas morning; others stated that they normally work all day on Sunday so that they do not fall behind. Sunday is supposed to be the day for the family, a day of rest! Even mums and dads are allowed Sundays off. When are families supposed to talk to each other and do things together?

The justification for such a massive load of homework is that it will help us succeed in our exams. Yet the result can be exactly the opposite. The survey showed that most pupils felt tired in the mornings because they had been working late the night before. Common sense should tell teachers and examiners that pupils will learn more effectively if they are fresh. You cannot think up clever and imaginative ideas for English essays, if all you want to do is close your eyes, put your head on the table and go to sleep. However teachers do not seem to recognise what they are putting their pupils through. We get blamed for carelessness, for mistakes that we make because we are too tired to think straight and if you try to pace yourselves in lessons so that you have got something left at the end of the day to do your homework, you are called lazy or are labelled "a daydreamer". You just cannot win!

Teenage years are precious. To use a cliché, we only have them once in a lifetime. Although success at school is important and our futures do depend upon it; our futures also depend upon us becoming individuals with our own personalities and with our own relationships. Homework is hindering this part of our development.

## Notes on essays

An essay should always have an underlying purpose, whether it's factual or argumentative. This is what you introduce in the introduction: say what kind of interpretation or point of view you are going to provide. It's important to tell your readers what to expect from the essay overall.

Each paragraph in the main body should present an individual point or unit of information. It should be stated in the topic (or first) sentence of the paragraph, before you go on to detail it. Notice how this is done in the Viking essay below.

In the last paragraph (conclusion) you should draw the main points together in a summary statement. It should recall the points but express them in a more general way. This helps to avoid sheer repetition, and widens the impact of your essay.

## A factual–informative essay                                   Essay I

---

### "What influence did the Vikings have on England?"
### by John Gardiner

From their first raid on English shores, the Vikings had a profound effect upon England's culture and history. They brought with them new skills, customs, language, religion and ideas. Far from being destructive heathens as they are so often portrayed, they contributed much to England. Many traces of the Vikings can still be found in today's society, especially in our language and legal system.

The first major influence the Vikings had upon England were their raids. To start with they travelled from their native lands only to plunder England's coastal towns and churches, but later began to colonise the area. These attacks had several effects upon the people already living in England. Families who had lived in the same region for generations were forced off their farms. Churches and monasteries were major targets for Viking attacks and many priceless objects were taken from them. Gradually, however, they began to settle down in England and the raids subsided.

As the Vikings settled in England they brought many new skills and customs with them. They loved brightly coloured clothes and often wore gold or silver ornaments. Men dressed in trousers, a long sleeved shirt and a tunic. Women wore a silk vest under a dress, and an overgarment fastened with a pair of brooches. Viking craftsmen often produced beautiful jewellery with animal designs. The Vikings also made magnificent weapons, and were renowned for their skill in wood-carving and boat-building.

Many of the words in today's English are derived from the tongue of the Vikings. Our days of the week — Tuesday, Wednesday, Thursday and Friday are named after the Viking gods Tyr, Woden or Odin, Thor and Frigg. Many places in England still bear Viking place names. The Vikings also left behind them many poems and tales which even today make good reading.

For their time, the Vikings had a very advanced system of parliament and laws. Both of these they brought with them to England. All Viking men considered each other to be equal, and women had many more rights than in other societies of the time. Even slaves were allowed to earn their freedom. Penalties for crimes or wrong-doings were usually paid in the form of a fine. However, if the offender could not pay, he faced the risk of banishment or hanging.

Taking everything into account, the Vikings contributed much to many aspects of English society. They were not savages who revelled in the destruction of beauty, but a just, artistic and peaceful race. Even today, we have much to thank them for.

## A factual–personal essay

Essay II

Over to England — The view of a Viking immigrant

I came to England with my parents when I was 16 years old. We moved after my uncle Bragar the Bold had been there on a "business trip". He was one of the real old Viking soldiers, always ready to talk tough and pick a fight. He used to disappear overseas with his sword all sharpened up, and return with gold cups and silver candlesticks. He never told us exactly how he got them, only that he did business on the edge of his sword, and that the sword made people very generous!

But he talked a lot about all the good land in England, and my parents were convinced it must be better than the swampy ground they had been trying to farm in Denmark. So we packed up a few things, and let Bragar fix up a long-ship for us to travel on. The longship (named *Surf Dragon*) was like an enormous canoe, open to wind and weather. However I soon realised how well it was built when we struck giant waves, and the ship simply flexed its way through them.

As we reached the English coast, I wondered what the locals were like. Yet there was no sign of them. The first few farms we came to were all either burnt or deserted. We stopped at one of them, and have stayed here ever since. It gave us a roof over our heads, and some land to work. Uncle Bragar disappeared again "on business", and returned with a few animals to stock the farm. After that he settled down with us. He works the forge and makes all kinds of metal products, tools for the farm, and even brooches and jewellery for my mother.

Bragar has become our local district leader. He helped to set up a system of law, with equal rights for most people. He'd never spent much time on things like that before, but now he's putting all his energy into making the new settlement work.

Gradually we have begun to make contact with English people around here. They're a quiet lot and we never have any trouble from them. Their language isn't so different from ours, and they've been quite interested in some of our old legends and stories. Actually we've been swapping stories. We tell a Viking one, and then they tell a Christian one.

## Notes on factual essays — personal and informative

When you have information to present you can choose to make a personal narrative out of it like Essay II above. It draws on the same raw material (facts and pictures) as Essay I, but it links things together imaginatively, and with a certain amount of common sense and general knowledge. The order of presentation is the order of events, just as in a story.

When you compare it with Essay I, you'll see how the writer there presents things impersonally, not as if they were part of himself. He groups facts together to make a topic for each paragraph — like words and literature for a paragraph on how the Vikings influenced the English language.

# Science reports
## A formal report on a school science experiment

Experiment 3

Aim: To compare amounts of carbon dioxide ($CO_2$) in exhaled air when
sitting and when active.

Apparatus: Stopwatch, three mixing beakers, limewater, straw.

Method: The subject's pulse rate was measured three times, once in
normal classroom circumstances, once after he had been for a
walk, and once after a brisk run. After having his pulse
taken, he was asked to bubble air through limewater in a
beaker. The limewater in each beaker was examined and
compared to see which contained the most precipitate.

Results: (Data table)

| TEST | CONDITIONS | HEARTRATE | LIMEWATER |
|---|---|---|---|
| 1 | normal classroom | 67 b/m | a watered down milky consistency |
| 2 | after walk | 82 b/m | same as before, possibly thicker |
| 3 | after run | 102 b/m | slightly thicker than both of above |

In tests 1 and 2, the differences in consistency were very slight, to the
point of being doubtful. Test 3 did show a thicker consistency,
though not by very much.

Conclusion: Physical activity increases the amount of carbon
dioxide breathed out.

## Notes on formal science reports

Scientists use this form of writing when writing up experiments because
it shows exactly what they did, the results that came out of it, and what
was concluded. Anyone who wanted to duplicate the experiment could do
so. All the necessary details are there. Science reports usually have five
sections:

| |
|---|
| Aim (what you were investigating in the experiment) |
| Apparatus (the equipment you used) |
| Method (what you did as part of experimental procedure) |
| Results (your measurements and observations, and any extra comments on what happened) |
| Conclusion (what the experiment showed) |

*Diagram of a science report*

**An informal science report**

> ## Breathing and exercise
>
> Our breathing changes in more than one way when we have some exercise. When we come home panting from a run, we're obviously breathing more quickly, and the volume of air we breathe in and out is larger. The lungs seem to be working harder than usual all round.
>
> Another interesting difference is that the chemistry of the air we breathe out changes a bit after exercise. We can prove this by making a kind of breathalyser, which shows how much carbon dioxide we are breathing out.
>
> The "breathalyser" is only a beaker with limewater in it, and you simply bubble air through a straw into the liquid. The limewater is a thin liquid, almost clear, but it gets thicker and whiter the more carbon dioxide is mixed with it.
>
> To see this effect at different levels of exercise, we decided to compare sitting, walking and running. We checked our pulse rate on each activity, to show that they really were different levels. First we blew air into the limewater while sitting at the bench, and found that it began to turn cloudy. After that we got up and walked up and down the corridor to get the pulse rate up. Then when we blew into the limewater it became whitish and a bit thicker in consistency. Finally, we did a brisk run around the school block, and this time the limewater became noticeably thicker and more intensely white. It shows that the air we breathe out contains more carbon dioxide, the harder we exercise.
>
> What happens chemically is that the limewater (calcium hydroxide) reacts with carbon dioxide to form calcium carbonate (a white precipitate) and water.
>
> The formula is $CO_2 + Ca(OH)_2 \rightarrow CaCO_3 + H_2O$.

## Notes on informal reports

Informal reports can present the same information as the formal kind, but they explain and interpret things along the way, instead of saving it up for the conclusion. The informal report draws less attention to the way the experiment was conducted, and talks more about the larger issues that make up the context. (In the informal report, it is clear that the experiment was part of a general study of breathing.)

The order of paragraphs in an informal report is decided by what has to be explained first (= logical order), or else the order of events.

## Uses of formal and informal reports

Formal reports are used in science to make the records of experiments as objective as possible. The individual sections help to keep the facts and results of the experiment separate from any conclusions.

An informal report does not have these sections, and observations are blended with interpretation. Just how and why the observations were made does not have to be so tightly defined. You simply have to explain what you observed or did, in a reasonable order (often the order of events).

The report of the bushwalk on p 31 is also an informal report. You may have good reason to use informal reports in field work in geography, agriculture and commerce, and also in home economics and technology, when explaining how you made something.

# News reports

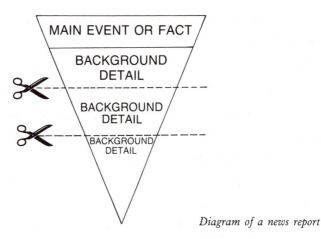

*Diagram of a news report*

## A news report from a local paper

# In the running for top race

FLEET-footed Lisa Clifford is hoping to give fellow athletes the run-around when the cross country season starts in a few weeks.

The 14-year-old Cheltenham schoolgirl is shaping up by entering fun runs and training three times a week.

She is the best for her age in Cheltenham and hopes to fight off other contenders with a rigorous training programme.

Cheltenham Harrier, Lisa was the first woman to cross the line in the recent one-mile Echo fun run round Pittville Park.

She won easily, but she knows not all her races will be so simple and she is aiming to compete in the national cross country championships later this year.

"I go running in the parks on Tuesday, track racing on Thursdays and do about four miles on a Sunday. I also do some hill training," she said.

"Training can be hard and lots of people give up." But she admits there is a pleasurable side to it. "It makes you feel as though you have achieved something and you also meet lots of friends. I think running keeps me fit and helps me stay really happy."

Cheltenham Harriers coach David Riggs said: "Lisa is good. She's a natural and extremely determined and the best for her age in Cheltenham."

He said he would recommend the sport to anyone. It helped keep youngsters off the streets.

Lisa Clifford, the best runner for her age in Cheltenham.

## Notes on newspaper reports

When journalists write an article for a newspaper, they don't know exactly how many words there will be room for on the printed page. The article could be cut off halfway through if there's only limited space. So the journalist puts the most important fact at the very beginning, in the first sentence or two, and then goes on to give what is really background information. As the article continues, the information is less and less connected with the fact reported at the start. You call this sort of writing a "pyramid structure", because it's like an upside-down pyramid (or triangle). The diagram on p 52 shows you how the most important information is kept, even if the article is cut short.

## Uses of news reports

News reports are an interesting form for you to recast historical information in. Pick out the most important point for a start (as the top of the pyramid), and then fill in the background, bit by bit. (Make sure you explain who, what, when, where, why and how.) You could also write news articles about some of the issues in social studies, economics or health education. Try to find a current event to highlight the issue as your starting point.

# Advertisements: "Hard sell" and "soft sell" for hamburgers

### Notes on advertisements

The purpose of an advertisement is to sell something. The way you advertise partly depends on whether it's a cereal or a luxury car you're selling. But it's also a matter of the audience you're trying to reach with the advertisement. For some audiences, you need a direct, "hard sell" approach; for others, the more subtle "soft sell" approach is the one. Whichever you choose, the pictures have to support the approach.

The "hard sell" approach tries to make you rush out and buy, and often commands you with a set of imperatives, e.g. "Buy", "Present". It tries to grab your attention with the practical virtues of the product – how easy and quick and comfortable it is, and especially, how cheap it is.

The "soft sell" advertisement tries instead to build up a context in which you and the product go together. It presents the product as something which will help you to achieve some goal in life.

In both advertisements, the approach is shown by the words in the largest print.

### Uses of advertisements

From your work in commerce or home economics, you could try writing advertisements for a particular product – first something ordinary and necessary, and then a luxury item. Then you might draft an advertisement for the school play or concert. Or an advertisement for whatever you've made in technology.

# McDonald's™ Family Bonus

## Buy a Big Mac™ get 2 Cheeseburgers
# FREE

Just present this voucher when you next purchase a Big Mac and it will be our pleasure to give you 2 Cheeseburgers absolutely FREE!

**Valid only at McDonald's**

**Vine Street, Evesbury**

Only one coupon per person per day.
Not to be used in conjunction with
any other McDonald's food offer.

**Balance.**

Meat, potatoes and orange juice.
Balance comes from eating a variety of foods.
Because nutritionists agree, no one food provides all the necessary nutrients.
At McDonald's, we offer 100% pure Australian beef. We offer fish and poultry. Lettuce and tomatoes. And more.
Variety in our menu means you can balance what you order.
And make sure your McDonald's meal balances with other meals you eat.
Because we want McDonald's food to fit comfortably into your own well-balanced diet.
Better for you. Better for us.

**IT'S A GOOD TIME FOR THE GREAT TASTE.**

McD5534/87

# Private letters
## A personal letter

> St Anne's Hotel
> Flapthorne
> Evesbury
> Worcs
> 20th July 1989
>
> Dear Julie,
>
> Here we are in gorgeous Evesbury! Actually we're just outside it in what is jokingly called a village. It seems to consist of the hotel we're stopping in, a gypsy caravan parked in a lay-by down the road, a broken down old cottage and a telephone box. In fact, Evesbury's not much better. Have you ever been there? If you haven't you'd never believe such a place existed! I reckon life stopped in Evesbury in the fifties. I saw a gang of boys about our age walking down the High Street in Evesbury dressed in Teddy Boy gear! Yes, Teddy Boy gear — velvet collared jackets, brothel creepers, drainpipe trousers — the lot! I would have killed myself laughing if I hadn't been so depressed with the thought of having to spend another twelve days here.
>
> I can't understand my mum and dad. They've been looking forward to this holiday for months. It's the highlight of their year. They seem to enjoy doing nothing all day. They don't think about what I'd like to do. I have to fit in with them. Take yesterday for instance, we got up at about eight, had breakfast, went for a drive, stopped at a local pub at about twelve, went for another drive, stopped at a tea shop at four for a cream tea, got back to the hotel at six, had dinner at 7.30, talked to the other guests in the hotel — two old-age pensioners — and went to bed at nine. Sounds fun, doesn't it? I told my dad that he ought to slow down or he'd give himself a heart attack. Too much excitement could be dangerous. He wasn't amused and gave me a lecture about "being grateful" and about all the other kids of my age who aren't lucky enough to have a holiday. Lucky? I'd change places with them any day. Why can't we go to Torremolinos or Corfu — somewhere exciting where there's a bit of night-life? Perhaps not. He really would have a heart attack if we went somewhere like that!
>
> I'll have to go now. I need to save my strength for tomorrow. See you when I get back. I'll spend all of five minutes describing the exciting things that have happened to me on holiday. Hope you're having a better time at home.
>
> Love
> Beth

## A business letter

---

### *Surety Insurance Company*
Registered address:
19 Farrier Street, Bristol BS7 0TR


29 April 1989


Mr S Keating
29 Church Street
Hillfield
Cheltenham
GL54 2FG


Dear Mr Keating

Re: Insurance theft of boy's bicycle

In answer to your letter of 25 April, the company regrets to
inform you that your present insurance policy does not cover
the theft of your son's bicycle.  Unfortunately your policy only
safeguards personal property of this nature when it is at home.
To provide insurance cover for personal property which is removed
from home, as was the case at the time of the theft of your son's
bicycle, you will need an additional policy made out against loss
and/or theft.  It would nominate each item for which such cover
is required and declare the circumstances under which each may
come to be removed.  Details are available on request.

Yours sincerely

B. Reece

B Reece
Manager

## Notes on personal and business letters

For people away from home, letters are a way of bridging the gap. If you're the person away, you want to tell your family and friends some of your experiences. And for those at home, the letters are an exciting way of sharing in someone's travels. Letters like these give you personal information, and often sound as if the travellers themselves were there talking to you.

Letters are of course also written for reasons of business. The letter may be written on behalf of a company, or some institution, such as a school or government office. The letter may have to give advice on a particular problem, or to explain an official action. Letters like these are not usually so friendly, because the letter writer represents an institution, not himself or herself as an individual.

## Uses of private letters

Just how personal a letter is will depend on who you're writing to. Try writing a letter applying for the kind of job you hope to get when you leave school, and you'll be writing in a rather formal way to a future employer. Then write a letter to a penpal overseas, in a country you've studied in geography or your foreign language class. It will probably be much more friendly.

Details of the different formats used in personal and business letters are explained in Appendix E.

# Public letters
## A letter to the editor

Dear Sir,

With the Government at last addressing itself to the problem of uncared-for dogs, should this not be the moment to tackle the wider question of freedom of movement across international frontiers for domestic animals.

Each year millions of Britons travel to rabid countries on holiday, business or, because of the nature of their work, to live (service families, diplomats), with no apparent worry.

With the imminent linkage of our island to the Continent, and armed with the latest technological and scientific facts, surely the moment has come to brush the dust off this issue and review calmly and unemotionally potential changes.

Should not the following be considered:

(1) Compulsory registration of all dogs and cats through a national computer system (this already works in other countries), with the animal tattooed in the ear or inner thigh, as collars can come off or fail to be put on.

(2) With this system operational all unmarked strays would be classified as abandoned and could be destroyed.

(3) Availability of the rabies vaccine administered by Ministry of Agriculture-approved veterinaries, enabling those who wish to travel abroad with their pets to do so. On re-entering this country, customs or immigration officials would check, through the national computer link, that the animal was correctly vaccinated.

This issue raises high emotions generally based on lack of information and outdated facts, but it would be interesting to know the answers to the following:

(a) How many of the thousands of vaccinated dogs and cats passing through quarantine develop rabies?

(b) How is it possible for horses to enter and leave this country freely when they also are potential rabies carriers?

Yours faithfully,
MARY FRETWELL
(Lady Fretwell)
London SW18
11 August

## Notes on public letters

People who want to contact the public at large sometimes do it through letters. They may have a viewpoint which they want to express publicly, so that many people will talk about it and perhaps do something about it. The difficulty is how to reach the public.

Most newspapers publish "letters to the editor", and anyone, young or old, can express their views this way. You just address the letter to the Editor of your local newspaper, and if it raises interesting issues you may see it in print!

Other people with something to say to the public at large are advertisers, and they too sometimes use letters for the purpose. The advertiser can mass-produce them for a letter-box drop, or pay to have the letter printed in a newspaper or magazine. The advertising letter often takes you by surprise. It may address you in person (with your name taken from a computerised mailing list), and it may try to give you information in a personal way. But the further you read, the clearer it is that the letter is only an advertisement in disguise. Its purpose is really to get your money into the advertiser's pocket!

## Uses of public letters

You could write a letter to the editor about any of the kinds of public issues you've talked about in social studies. Or the letter might be about public behaviour, or language that gets you down.

Then try writing an advertising letter to people, perhaps about a service available to them, or about what kind of training your school can offer to students.

## An advertising letter

### *Student Loan Inc.*

High Street
Milford Road
London

11 November 1989

Ms Holly Reece
3a Phoenix Hall
Evebury College of Education
Glos
GL50 9RA

Dear Ms Reece

Congratulations! You've passed your 'A' levels; you've got a place at College
and your dreams are about to come true! Nothing's going to stop you now but
are you sure?

When it comes to paying bills for textbooks, accommodation, travel, clothes,
the poll tax and the odd record or two, the difficulties begin. Your grant
disappears before you know it and debts begin to mount. You could try ringing
mum and dad but they've got bills of their own; you could try a high street bank
but you won't be able to afford their rates of interest; you could try a part-time
job, but that would interfere with your studies. You don't know where to turn
and the dream rapidly becomes a nightmare ...

But wait! It needn't be like that! Student Loan Inc. offers banking
services specifically for people like you. We know what it is like to be a
student so we offer a range of low interest, no security loans to help you meet
those bills and let you concentrate on your studies.

But what's the point of borrowing money, if I can't afford to pay it back, you
might ask. Don't worry! We don't want a single penny from you until you secure
full-time employment, when we will agree between us what you can afford to pay
and when.

Sounds too good to be true, doesn't it? Don't let your dream become a nightmare.
Complete the enclosed loan application form or pop in for a chat with our friendly
staff and let us invest in your future.

Yours sincerely

*A. Burrows*

A Burrows
Manager

# Part 4: Using reference books

*Reference books for research and drafting*

*Reference books for revising*

*Using your references*

# Reference books for researching and drafting

When writing essays you often want to check the facts you have, or to fill in a detail which you missed in the lesson. Where can you go?

The most useful general reference is the *encyclopedia*. It has entries and mini-essays on most subjects you can think of. The entries are arranged alphabetically so it's easy to find what you want. Ask the librarian for the encyclopedia which is right for your age level. Some encyclopedias are written for adults, others for students. The adult ones have more information but they're harder to read. Encyclopedias will give you the core of most subjects, though they're not necessarily up-to-date. If you want to know the latest on who is the minister for something, you'll need to consult a *Year Book*, or a *Who's Who* — again in your nearest library.

Another useful reference is the *atlas*. It always helps to know where places are, and this is true in history and social studies and economics, as well as geography. The larger the atlas, the more likely it is to show even small places, and to have extra maps and diagrams of things like land use, population density and so on. It all helps to give you the local context in which things happen.

# Reference books for revising

When it comes to revising your draft essay, you may need other reference books to help with checking your expression. A *style guide* like this book explains many details of language — spelling, punctuation and grammar. It will also help you to see the difference between words which are rather alike in meaning or sound or spelling. If you are looking for fresh words to vary your expression, a *thesaurus* will give you some choices. You should still check them in a *dictionary*, to be sure they have the right shade of meaning for your purpose. The dictionary is, of course, the complete reference on words. You need to have one which is right for your age level, and one which is more or less up-to-date.

# Using your references

When you take some words or a statement from another book, you must take care in presenting them in your essay. If you repeat the exact words of another writer, you should:
(a) put them into quotation marks
(b) say what book they come from.
This is a way of showing that they are really someone else's idea. But it also shows that you're making careful use of your reading.

# Plagiarism

If you use someone else's words without showing that it is a quotation, you're really committing *plagiarism*. It's like stealing someone's property and pretending it's yours. The higher you go in your education, the more you're expected to write and think independently of your sources.

Of course, it's always okay if you use your own words to express ideas you've gathered from your references. If you *paraphrase* ideas, you won't ever be guilty of plagiarism. What's more, it's good for developing your own expression.

# Quoting

When you do quote the exact words of another writer, there are three things to remember:

(a) *Put quotation marks around the words you've borrowed.* You can choose either single (' ') or double (" ") quotation marks. For more about this, and about using other punctuation marks when quoting, see *quotation marks* in the "A to Z Guide to Writing and Language".

(b) *Make sure the quotation blends in with the sentence that carries it.* The words of the quotation have to dovetail with the grammar of the sentence. So make sure you don't do this:

> The Chief Examiner in his report said that he: "I have noted an improvement in standards this year."

You will have noticed that this doesn't read very fluently; the sentence has a hiccup in the middle where the quotation comes in. You need to alter either the quotation or the carrier sentence a little, to make a smooth connection. Any of the following would do:

- The Chief Examiner in his report said: "I have noted an improvement in standards this year."
- The Chief Examiner in his report said that he noted "an improvement in standards this year."
- The Chief Examiner in his report said that he "note(s) an improvement in standards this year."

The second and third sentences show how you can cut the quotation back a little to make it blend in. In the third sentence a small detail has also been added, in brackets, to make it run smoothly. The brackets show that it wasn't part of the original words.

(c) *Use one of the standard systems for referencing, to show the reader where the quotation came from.* You must indicate where it comes from in order to avoid plagiarism. It also allows your readers to go to the source, if they want to follow it up. There are two standard ways of referencing:

  (i) footnotes. With footnotes, you don't actually mention the author or book after the quotation. Instead you put a number (1, 2, 3 and so on) after each quotation on the page, and at the bottom of the page explain where each one came from. So in your text you'd say:

> . . . The Chief Examiner in his report said that he "noted an improvement in standards this year"[1]. This was cause for encouragement after last year's disappointing figures.

And at the bottom of the page you'd have a note:
1. L. Lloyd 'The Report of the *Chief Examiner SWEG* ', 1989 p 2.
Other references on the same page would be numbers 2, 3, 4 and so on.
(ii) Author–date (running references). With the author–date system you give a passing reference to the source, immediately after the quotation, but it is very brief:

> . . . The Chief Examiner in his report said that he "noted an improvement in standards this year" (Lloyd, 1989: p 2). This was cause for encouragement after last year's disappointing figures.

A running reference like this has just the author's surname, the book's date of publication, and the number of the page from which the quotation came. It does not give full details about the source, because it would interrupt the flow too much. The full details would, however, appear in the bibliography.

# Bibliography

A bibliography is a list of the books you've read or consulted in the business of writing the essay.

While you are writing, you'd make a rough list of all the publication details, as they came up. Then as the very last thing, you rearrange the list into alphabetical order by the authors' surnames.

Beale, C. *Living in Asia* (Asbath Books, 1985)
Dent, R. *The culture of India* (UPC Publishing, 1976)
Evans, R. *The economics of the Third World* (Beechcroft Press, 1989)

As you see, the author's surname is what decides the order, not the author's initial, or the first word of the book's title, or even the date of publication.

Bibliographies are written up in a slightly different way for footnotes and for running references. The bibliography above is written to go with footnotes. The bibliography below is written to go with running references. It puts the date of publication immediately after the author's name:

Beale, C. (1985) *Living in Asia* (Asbath Books)
Dent, R. (1976) *The culture of India* (UPC Publishing)
Evans, R. (1989) *The economics of the Third World* (Beechcroft Press)

Apart from where the date appears, there are no other differences.

# Book titles

When you write down the titles of books, you want to make them stand out from the ordinary words around. In essay writing you usually underline them, though publishers often put them in italics.

Writers often give capital letters to the main words of book titles, especially when the titles appear individually in the middle of a discussion. Again it helps to make them stand out. But when the titles appear in a bibliography or list of some kind, there is no need for a lot of capital letters. Many writers give a capital only to the first word of the title, and to any proper names which appear after it. All other words are in lower case. This is what has been done in the bibliographies we were looking at before. It is the normal practice in library lists, and the easiest one to use consistently.

# A to Z
# guide to writing
# and language

# Aa

**a**

This is one of the two shortest words in our language. In grammar it is called an <u>indefinite article</u>, and contrasts with the <u>definite article</u> *the*. See **indefinite articles** and **definite articles**.

**a** or **an**? Which do you use?

The general rule is that you use **an** only when the word following begins with a vowel sound. So we write:

an artist   an engineer   *but*   a doctor   a teacher

It is important to check whether the first sound is really a vowel or a consonant. With *hour* it is in fact a vowel (*ow*), hence *an hour*. With *union* it is a consonant (*y*), hence *a union*.

For more about this, see **an**.

**a-**

This prefix means "without" or "lacking", as in

amoral (without moral values)
atheist (someone without a faith in God)

The prefix <u>a-</u> becomes <u>an-</u> before words beginning with a vowel, for example <u>an</u>aerobic. See **an-**.

The meaning of <u>a-</u> often seems close to that of the negative prefixes <u>in-</u>, <u>im-</u> and <u>non-</u>. Note however the difference between *amoral* (without moral values), and *immoral* (against moral values). See **in-/im-** and **non-**.

## -a (as a singular ending)

Singular words ending in <u>-a</u>, such as *dogma*, *formula*, *stigma* and *vertebra*, are often borrowings from other languages. *Formula* and *vertebra* are from Latin, while *dogma* and *stigma* are from Greek. As they become part of the English language, they tend to take an <u>-s</u> for their plurals like most English nouns. However, those which are technical words often keep their foreign plurals as well, for example *formulae* and *stigmata*, and these are the ones used in scientific writing. In ordinary writing they would be *formulas* and *stigmas*.

## -a (as a plural ending)

The plurals of some of our words are formed with -a, for example, *bacteria, criteria, phenomena* and *strata*. Some of these (*bacteria, strata*) come from Latin, and their -a ending is their Latin plural. In the singular (if you ever had to use it) they are written *bacterium, stratum*. (See **-um**.) A few other words with -a plurals (*criteria, phenomena*) are from Greek. Note that in the singular they are *criterion, phenomenon*.

Because all these words are plural, the words in agreement with them are normally plural. But with *data* and *media* you may have a choice. For more about this, see **data, media, agreement,** and **collective nouns**.

Note that the word *agenda* always takes a singular verb in English. See **agenda**.

## abacus

The plural of this word may be spelled **abacuses** or **abaci**. For more about words like this, see **-us**.

## abbreviations

are shortened forms of words. There are two main types of abbreviation, with different punctuation rules:

1  abbreviations that consist of the first one or more letters of the full word or words. For example:

| p. | page | vol. | volume |
|---|---|---|---|
| cont. | continued | p.a. | per annum |
| BBC | British Broadcasting Corporation | Mon | Monday |
| Rev | Reverend | NUT | National Union of Teachers |

2  abbreviations that start with the first letter of the full word and end with its last letter. These are called **contractions**. For example:

| hcp | handicap | rd | road |
|---|---|---|---|
| vb | verb | figs | figures |
| Dr | Doctor | Mr | Mister |
| Fr | Father | Assn | Association |

### When do you use a full stop?

Contractions (type **2** above) never have a full stop. This applies whether or not the contraction begins with a capital letter.

Abbreviations like type **1** above do have a full stop if they begin with a lower-case letter. Those that begin with a capital letter also used to have full stops, but nowadays the tendency is to leave the stops out. So we write *cont.* with a full stop for *continued* but *Mon* without a stop for *Monday*.

Acronyms, such as *NATO*, do not have stops either. See **acronyms**.

Note that *a.m.* and *p.m.* can also be written without stops (*am* and *pm*), although they are not contractions. See **a.m.** and **p.m.**

There is one group of lower-case abbreviations which never have stops. They are the units of measurement. For example:

km   kilometre or kilometres
kg   kilogram or kilograms
ha   hectare or hectares

For other standard units, see APPENDIX C.

See **geographical terms** for compass points and geographical abbreviations.

For a list of common abbreviations, see APPENDIX B.

## -ability

This ending makes nouns out of adjectives ending in -able:

probable *becomes* probability
available             availability
capable               capability

See **-able/-eable**.

## ablative case

This case is used in Latin and some other languages, but not in English.

When you put a word into the ablative case, it means "by", "with" or "from" that word.

For example, you use an o to show the ablative in the Latin word *facto*. In the phrase *ipso facto*, this then means "by that same fact".

For more about cases in English, see **case**.

## -able / -eable

The ending -able is often used to make adjectives from verbs. So *teachable* is formed from *teach*.

Words ending in -e normally lose the -e before -able is added to them. Thus:

note *becomes* notable
argue             arguable

But when the word ends in -ce or -ge, the -e is needed to keep the c as an s sound, and the g as a j sound. So

trace    *becomes* traceable
manage              manageable

See **-e, -able/-ible**.

## -able / -ible

Both spellings fit the pronunciation, but which do you use? Overall there are more with -able. You could use -able with any new words not covered in the dictionary, for example, *confessable, contactable*.

Note that if you are adding -able to a word ending in -ce or -ge, you should keep the -e before the ending: *traceable, bandageable*. See also **-able/-eable**.

The words ending in -ible have mostly been borrowed straight from Latin. The following list includes those which you are most likely to use:

| | | |
|---|---|---|
| accessible | gullible | negligible |
| admissible | horrible | ostensible |
| audible | incomprehensible | perceptible |
| combustible | incorrigible | permissible |
| compatible | incredible | plausible |
| comprehensible | indelible | possible |
| contemptible | indestructible | reducible |
| convertible | inexhaustible | reprehensible |
| credible | infallible | repressible |
| digestible | inflexible | responsible |
| divisible | intangible | sensible |
| edible | intelligible | submersible |
| eligible | invincible | susceptible |
| fallible | invisible | tangible |
| feasible | irresistible | terrible |
| flexible | legible | visible |

### abridgement / abridgment

These are equally good spellings. See **-ment**.

An abridgement is a shortened version of a book. See **summary**.

### abseil

Note that e comes before i in this word. See **i before e**.

### abstract

This is a brief written statement giving the important points of a piece of academic work. See **summary**.

### abstract nouns

You use **abstract nouns** when writing about ideas, feelings and other things that you can't touch, hear, see, taste or smell. *Geography*, *love*, *golf*, *rudeness*, *lightness* and *flying* are all abstract nouns. As you can see, abstract nouns can refer to many different kinds of things.

Compare this with **concrete nouns**.

### accede

See **exceed/accede**.

### accelerator

Note the ending of this word. See **-ator**.

### accents

An accent can be:
1 the way someone speaks a language, for instance, *with an Irish accent*.
2 one of the extra marks used in writing some languages. They show that certain letters in a word have to be pronounced in a special way.

Sometimes foreign words which we have borrowed are written with their accents and sometimes without. For example, the

---

**Accents**
acute ´
cedilla ¸
circumflex ^
grave `
háček ˇ
tilde ~ ˇ
umlaut ¨

French borrowing *chateau* can be written *château* or *chateau* in English, and the German *Fräulein* can be written with or without the umlaut when used in English.

Other foreign borrowings like *hotel*, *debris* and *suede* have now been in the English language for such a long time that they have lost their accents altogether.

The accents which are most likely to be lost are those which occur on the last letter of a word. These accents tend to stay only if they are needed to make a distinction between the borrowed word and an existing English word. For example, if you leave the accent off the borrowed French word *exposé* (pronounced *ex-po-zay*) you're left with the English word *expose*. If you're not sure whether to include an accent or not, check with the dictionary.

### accept / except

These words sound the same but mean different things.

To **accept** something is to take or get it.

**Except** means "excluding or leaving out":
*Everyone understood the joke except me.*

### acceptance

Note the ending of this word. See **-ance/-ence**.

### accessible

Note the ending of this word. See **-able/-ible**.

### accusative case

See **objective case**.

### acetic / ascetic

These words look similar but have different meanings.

**Acetic** has to do with vinegar or acid, and we pronounce it *a-see-tic*.

**Ascetic** describes the lifestyle of monks, nuns, hermits and others like them. They are strict about the way they live and deny themselves pleasures. We pronounce it *a-set-ic*.

### ache

Drop the e when you add -ing to this verb:
*Her ears were aching after the concert.*
For more about words like this, see **-e**.

### -acious / -aceous

These endings sound exactly the same, and both show that the word is an adjective. But they are used with different kinds of words.

The ending -acious comes on many ordinary words, such as:

| | | |
|---|---|---|
| audacious | capacious | gracious |
| pugnacious | spacious | vivacious |
| voracious | | |

Note that the -aci part of these words is in fact part of the stem or root of the word, and -ous has been added to that. For more information see **-ous**.

The ending -aceous is a whole suffix, which comes on scientific words, particularly in botany. For example:
 farinaceous  (containing flour or grain)
 herbaceous  (like a herb or annual plant)
 rosaceous  (like a rose)

## acknowledgement / acknowledgment

These are equally good spellings. See **-ment**.

## acreage

This word is a little unusual because it keeps the e of **acre** before adding -age. (Compare *dosage* from *dose*.) The spelling helps to show that the middle syllable is pronounced. It doesn't follow the general pattern of words ending in -e. See **-e**.

## acronyms

are words which have been formed by joining together the first letters from a set of other words. Words like this have no stops between the letters.

Acronyms can be pronounced as a single word:
 NATO  N(orth) A(tlantic) T(reaty) O(rganisation)
 UNICEF  U(nited) N(ations) I(nternational) C(hildren's) E(mergency) F(und)
 SWAPO  S(wapo)-W(est) A(frica) P(eople's) O(rganisation)

Sometimes only the first letter of an acronym is written as a capital, and the rest of the letters are in lower case. For example:
 Nato  Unicef  Swapo

There are other abbreviations in which we pronounce each letter separately. These are sometimes called acronyms too for convenience:
BBC  B(ritish) B(roadcasting) C(orporation)
RCN  R(oyal) C(ollege of) N(ursing)
COD  C(ash) O(n) D(elivery)

Some acronyms have been accepted so fully into the English language that they are no longer spelled with capital letters to set them apart:
radar  ra(dio) d(etecting) a(nd) r(anging)
laser  l(ight) a(mplification by) s(timulated) e(mission of) r(adiation)
scuba  s(elf) c(ontained) u(nderwater) b(reathing) a(pparatus)

## active verbs

The most common way of writing a sentence is to have the subject doing the action of the verb. When this happens the verb is called an **active verb**:
 *Kate put her surfboard on the roofrack.*
In this sentence, *put* is an active verb because Kate, the subject of the sentence, is carrying out the action.

Even though they're called "active", these verbs don't necessarily involve movement. For example, both *paddled* and *waited* are active verbs in the following sentence:

> She <u>paddled</u> her board past the breakers and <u>waited</u> for a good wave.

Active verbs contrast with <u>passive verbs</u>, in which the subject is acted on by the action of the verb.

> Kate <u>fell</u> off the board and <u>was dumped</u> by a wave.

In this sentence, *fell* is an active verb and *was dumped* is a passive verb. See **passive verbs**.

**Active verbs** are said to be in the **active voice**.

### active voice

This is a grammatical term which describes how a subject is related to its verb. For examples, see **active verbs**.

### actor

An actor is someone, either male or female, who acts in a play. The word "actress" to describe a female actor is not used as much nowadays as it has been in the past. For more information, see **non-sexist language**.

### acute

See **chronic/acute**.

### acute accents ( ´ )

An acute accent is a mark used in writing French, Spanish, Greek and other languages. It shows certain vowels have to be pronounced in a special way.

In French, an acute accent over an é means that it should be pronounced *ay*, to rhyme with *day*. For example, the word *début*, meaning "first public appearance", is pronounced *day-boo*.

In other languages, such as Spanish and Greek, acute accents are used to show that a vowel is stressed.

For more about accents in English, see **accents**.

### AD / BC

We use **AD** and **BC** to show where the time we are writing about occurs within our dating system.

Our method of dating events is based on whether they occurred before or after the birth of Jesus Christ. When our dating system was first worked out, the year in which it was thought Christ was born was named AD 1 (the letters AD stand for the Latin words *anno domini* which mean "in the year of our Lord"). Although the year of Christ's birth is now believed to be different, we still use AD 1 as the starting point in our dating system and we count the years backwards or forwards from it.

AD written next to a number shows the number of years that have passed since AD 1. The year before AD 1 is 1 BC. There is no year "0" in our dating system. BC stands for the words "before Christ" and refers to any of the years before AD 1.

Note that you count backwards from AD 1 to work out a "BC" date. In that way, if, for example, you are writing about the year 50 BC, you are referring to the time 50 years before AD 1. If you are writing about the period between 50 BC and AD 20, you are writing about a time period lasting 70 years.

**How you write dates**

When you use the letters AD or BC, note that you don't put stops between them (see **abbreviations**). You usually write BC before and AD after the numbers showing the date:

*Alexander the Great died in 323 BC.*

*The Battle of Hastings took place in AD 1066.*

For more information, see **dates**.

## adaptor

Note the ending of this word. See **-er/-or**.

## addresses

For information about writing addresses on letters, see APPENDIX E.

## adjectival clauses

are clauses which act like adjectives. See **clauses**.

## adjectival phrases

are phrases which act like adjectives. See **phrases**.

## adjectives

You use **adjectives** to describe a noun in more detail:

*the snake*
*the square snake*
*The only snake in existence that is square.*

Adjectives are one of the major word classes.

An adjective doesn't have to come immediately before the noun it is describing:

*a square snake*          *George is a good surfer.*
*The snake is square.*    *George's surfing is good.*

In fact, a few adjectives can only come straight after the noun they're describing:

*bargains galore*
*president elect*

And some others can only come after a verb:

*The snake is awake.*
*The zoo-keeper is asleep.*

**Using adjectives in writing**

You can use adjectives to make very precise descriptions of things, but they are also useful for showing how you feel about something or how you judge it:

*The wave was large, curling and crystal clear.*
*George said it was unreal.*
*But Kim thought it was an uncatchable wave.*

The first example is an impersonal, precise description of a wave. The second sentence shows how George felt about the wave, and the third shows how Kim judged or assessed it.

### Comparing with adjectives

Adjectives can change their form to show how two or more things compare. You can use an -er ending with some adjectives to compare two things:

*Which of the two snakes is longer?*

You can add -est to some adjectives to compare three or more things:

*the longest snake in the world*

With adjectives of more than two syllables you can't add -er or -est. Instead, you use more or most before the adjective to show the comparison:

*Which of the two snakes is more beautiful?*
*Which is the most beautiful snake in the world?*

The ending -er and the word more are used to form what is called the comparative degree of an adjective. Most and -est form the superlative degree.

For more information, see **degrees of comparison**.

### Adjectives that never make comparisons

Some adjectives do not have a comparative or superlative. For example, you can't be *more first* in a race than someone else, you can't be the *deadest* corpse in the morgue, and one pot can't be *more iron* than another. When an adjective (like *first*, *dead* or *iron*) describes something that is complete, perfect or absolute it can have no degrees of comparison.

## administrator

Note the ending of this word. See **-ator**.

## adopted / adoptive

These words are both about **adoption** but they have slightly different meanings.

When people **adopt** a child, they become its **adoptive** parents.

You can describe the child as either their **adopted** child or their **adoptive** child.

## advantageous

Note that the -e at the end of **advantage** remains when you add -ous. For more about words like this, see **-ce/-ge**.

## adverbial clauses

are clauses which act like adverbs. See **clauses**.

## adverbial phrases

are phrases which act like adverbs. See **phrases**.

## adverbs

You use **adverbs** to say something extra about a verb, adjective, or another adverb. Many of them end in -ly, though some common ones don't. Adverbs often answer questions like "How?", "Where?" or "When?" for verbs:

How? →
*Sherlock Holmes strode <u>rapidly</u> across the room.*

How? —————————→
*He could see the traces of tobacco <u>well</u> through his magnifying glass.*

Where? →
*He could tell that the tobacco was grown <u>locally</u>.*

Where? —————→
*Holmes looked for Watson, but he had gone off <u>somewhere</u>.*

←—When?
*He <u>immediately</u> rang the police.*

↙When?
*They <u>soon</u> came.*

Each of the underlined words in these examples is an adverb, including the common words *well* and *soon* which don't end in -ly.

You can see that adverbs may come before or after the word they describe, and that they may appear next to that word or quite a distance away.

Adverbs may also strengthen or weaken an adjective or adverb (see **intensifiers** and **hedge words**):
*The murderer kept <u>very</u> quiet in the bushes outside the window.*
*He was <u>really</u> scared.*
*He was <u>fairly</u> certain that Holmes was on to him.*

Some adverbs look just like adjectives:
*The murderer knew he had to move <u>fast</u>.* (adverb)
*There was a <u>fast</u> train to London in five minutes.* (adjective)

But when the adverb is not the same as the adjective, it cannot be used instead of the adjective. For example, *well* is the adverb that relates to the adjective *good*, so *good* is not generally used as an adverb:
*He made a <u>good</u> getaway and was soon sitting in the train beside a tall quiet man.* (adjective)
*But the man was Holmes, who smiled and said: "These handcuffs will fit you <u>well</u>."* (adverb)
NOT *"These handcuffs will fit you <u>good</u>."*

## adversary

Note the ending of this word. See **-ary/-ery/-ory**.

## advertise

This is the usual spelling of this word. You may see it spelled **advertize**, as it's sometimes spelled this way in the USA. For more about words like this, see **-ise/-ize**.

## advertisement

The most common pronunciation of this word has *tis* rather than *tize* in the middle. If you use the common pronunciation, the spelling may seem surprising. Actually it's quite regular. Like most verbs ending in -e, it keeps the -e before adding -ment. See **-ment**.

For suggestions on designing and writing advertisements, see WRITING WORKSHOP p 54.

## advice / advise

This pair is one of a group of words where the noun ends in -ce and the verb ends in -se:

*I'll advise him, but you give him your advice too.*

Note that the verb **advise** is never spelled with the -ize ending. See **-ise/-ize**.

See **-ce/-se** for more about words like this.

## adviser / advisor

**Adviser** is the better spelling to use because the word is a simple extension of the verb **advise**. It is like many new words based on modern verbs, for example, *advertiser*, *promoter* and *trainer*, which give a name to the performer of a particular kind of action.

The spelling **advisor** is probably written by people who are thinking of the word **advisory**.

For more about words like this, see **-er/-or**.

## advisory

Note the ending of this word. See **-ary/-ery/-ory**.

## -ae-

Some of our more technical words, like *encyclop(a)edia*, *h(a)emorrhage* and *pal(a)eolithic*, have spellings which are slowly changing. They come from Latin and Greek, as shown in the syllable which has traditionally been spelled with -ae-. But in ordinary usage now the same syllable is often spelled with just -e-. Thus *hemorrhage* appears in today's newspapers, while it is still *haemorrhage* in medical books. In the USA such words are spelled with -e- in any kind of writing, and the trend may well develop here. Already we accept that *medieval* and *pedagogy* are correct without the -ae- that they used to have.

So there is nothing at all wrong with spellings such as:

| | | | |
|---|---|---|---|
| archeology | encyclopedia | orthopedic | pedophile |
| hematite | hematology | hemoglobin | hemorrhage |
| hemorrhoids | hemophilia | anemia | leukemia |
| septicemia | toxemia | Paleocene | paleography |
| paleolithic | paleomagnetism | Paleozoic | |

Note that the syllable from which -ae- is disappearing is in the middle of all these words. When -ae- appears at the beginning of a word, as in *aeon* and *aesthetics*, it usually remains.

Note that the ae in words like *aerobics* and *aerosol* is part of the prefix aero-. It never loses the a. See **aero-**.

### aeon / eon

These are equally good spellings. See **-ae-**.

### aero-

This prefix comes from a Greek word meaning "air" and is used to begin a whole group of words which have something to do with air. It is used in words like *aeroplane, aerobics* and *aerogram*.

The spelling <u>aer-</u> is used instead of <u>aero-</u> if a vowel is the next letter in the word, as in *aerial* and *aerate*.

Note that in the UK we use the spelling *aeroplane* rather than *airplane* which is used more in the USA. We do, however, use the word *airport*.

### affect / effect

These words sound the same and are rather alike in meaning. The big difference is that **affect** is usually a verb and **effect** is usually a noun:
> *Heat affects ice by turning it to water.*
> *The effect of the warm weather is to make me sleepy.*

### affixes

Many long words, and some short ones, have a root or core element, and some smaller "extras" added to it which we call **affixes**. They may be either in front of the root, as in <u>undress</u>, or after it, as in <u>dressing</u>. Those in front are called **prefixes**, and those which come after are called **suffixes** or endings. English has many more suffixes than prefixes. A word may have several suffixes attached to it, but usually only one or two prefixes.

For more about this, see **prefixes** and **suffixes**.

> How many prefixes and suffixes are there in
> antidisestablishmentarianism?

### age

As with other verbs ending in <u>-e</u>, we usually drop the <u>e</u> when <u>-ing</u> is added to **age**:
> *His cares and worries are aging him very quickly.*

For more about words like this, see **-e**.

### -age

This ending makes abstract nouns out of other words. You'll find it in words like:

| | | | | |
|---|---|---|---|---|
| breakage | coinage | dosage | drainage | frontage |
| postage | shrinkage | storage | wastage | wreckage |

Words ending in -<u>age</u> often come to mean something specific as well. Some, like *dosage* and *milage*, refer to an amount of something (medicine, and distance). Others, like *corkage* and *postage*, refer to the payment for something. Still others refer to the result of something, such as *breakage* and *wreckage*.

When -age is added to a word ending in -e, the -e is usually dropped. You see it in *dose/ dosage, store/ storage, waste/ wastage*. The most important exception is *acreage*. It has a special reason for keeping the -e in the middle — to show that it has three syllables.

For more about words ending in -e, see **-e**.

## agenda

is a singular word in English, and the verb and pronoun we use when referring to it should also be singular:

> *The agenda for the meeting was very long. It took us the whole day to work through it.*

For more information, see **agreement**.

## aggravate

This verb nowadays usually means "irritate or annoy":

> *The children aggravated the teacher by banging the lids on their desks.*

It has also kept its original meaning of "make worse":

> *The chaos was aggravated by an electrical power failure throughout the country.*

## aggressor

Note the ending of this word. It is -or, not -er, because it was borrowed straight from Latin. See **-er/-or**.

## agreement

In a piece of writing or in speech some words are linked in special ways. Subjects and their verbs are linked. So are nouns or pronouns, and the pronouns that refer to them. They show this connection by **agreement**.

> **1** *Look out! A bull is behind you.*
> **2** *Crikey! Three more bulls are over there.*

In these sentences the subjects and verbs agree in number. Example 1 has a singular subject, *a bull*, so the verb, *is*, must be singular. Example 2 has a plural subject, *three more bulls*, so the verb, *are*, must be plural.

> **3** *Try and shoo them out the field.*
> **4** *The gate's stuck. I can't open it!*

In example 3 the speaker is referring to all the bulls so she uses the plural pronoun *them*. The second speaker is talking about one door so he uses the singular pronoun *it*.

### Agreement with collective nouns

When you use collective nouns, such as *herd, class, flock* and *family*, they can be thought of as either singular or plural. Your choice depends on whether you are thinking of them as a single unit or whether you are thinking of the individuals who make up the group.

> **5** *Oh, no! A whole herd is coming through that hole in the fence!*
> **6** *Quick! Try and get them back out!*

In example 5 the *herd* is thought of as one thing, so it takes the singular verb *is coming*. However, in example 6 the speaker wants to get every single bull out. He is thinking of them as many individuals so he uses the pronoun *them*, even though that pronoun still refers to the *herd*.

### Agreement when the subject consists of several words
When you have a number of subjects joined by the word *and*, as in example 7, you use the plural of the verb.

    **7** *Jamie and Mr Benson are hiding behind the tree.*

But when you use most other joining words or phrases (like *with* in example 8), things are different. The nouns that follow such words are not part of the subject, and so they don't affect the agreement of the verbs.

    **8** *The leader with twenty other bulls is after them!*

Other phrases that act in this way are *together with*, *as well as* and *in addition to*.

### Beware!
Sometimes the subject is so far away from the verb that we forget how the agreement should be.

    **9** *The colour of our school uniforms and badges are making the bulls angry.*

Example 9 is wrong because the subject (*the colour*) is singular, and so the verb should be the singular *is*, not the plural *are*.

### Agreement with everyone
Even though pronouns like *everyone* are singular, you can often use the plural pronoun *they* with them.

    **10** *Everyone knows they should be careful with the clothes they wear. It's very easy to alarm a bull.*

This used to be frowned on, but it's common in speech, and is used more and more in writing. It avoids having to choose between the singular pronouns *he* and *she* when you either don't know or don't wish to specify the sex of the person you're referring to.

Other pronouns like this are *everybody*, *anybody*, *anyone*, *somebody*, *someone*, *no-one* and *nobody*.

See **non-sexist language** and **they**.

Some nouns, like *data* and *media*, raise special questions of agreement. For more about these, see **-a (as a plural ending)**, **data** and **media**.

## -aim / -ain
Verbs which end in -aim and -ain often change their spelling (and pronunciation) a little when they become nouns. For instance:

    exclaim   *becomes*   exclamation
    explain             explanation

This happens because the nouns have not been used as long as the verbs in English. The nouns have come straight from Latin, whereas the verbs have been altered during centuries of use in English.

At least the differences in spelling go with the differences in stress. The longer spellings -claim and -plain get strong stress, while the shorter spellings -clam- and -plan- get weaker stress.

Exactly the same kinds of changes occur with:

acclaim     acclamation
declaim     declamation
exclaim     exclamation
proclaim    proclamation

And there are changes to spelling when:

maintain  *becomes*  maintenance
sustain              sustenance

ordain    *becomes*  ordinance
abstain             abstinence

### ain't

This is an informal contraction. See **be**.

### air / heir

These words sound the same but mean different things.

**Air** is what we breathe.

An **heir** is a person who inherits something.

### aisle / isle

These words sound the same but have different meanings.

An **aisle** is a narrow passageway left clear for people to walk through, as in a supermarket or a hall.

An **isle** is a small island. This is an old-fashioned word, but you will still find it in some place names, as in the *Isle of Wight*.

### -al

This ending makes nouns out of verbs in English, for example:

arrive    – arrival
dismiss   – dismissal
survive   – survival

It also turns English nouns into adjectives:

culture   – cultural
parent    – parental
nature    – natural

Some of our adjectives ending in -al were borrowed ready-made from Latin, and can work as either adjectives or nouns in English:

animal    capital    liberal
oval      official   rival

Make sure you know when a word really ends in -al, rather than -el or -le, which sound exactly the same, for example, *cable*, *label*, *herbal*. When in doubt, check your dictionary. Note that with *principal* and *principle* the ending makes a different meaning. See **principal/principle**.

## algae

Although this word is most often used to refer to masses of **alga**, we usually use it as if it were <u>singular</u>. When we do, then the verb and pronoun we use with it must also be singular. For example:

> There <u>is</u> algae in our swimming pool and <u>it</u> has turned the water green.

This is so even though the word is technically a plural word.

## allegory

An **allegory** is a story in which the characters and events stand for something or someone else.

For example, you could make up a story about a person called John Bull who represents the United Kingdom. If he was drawn into a fight with someone from a different country, this could be an allegory of the UK going to war. John Bull might strike gold in the Welsh mountains, meaning the UK had a boom period in its economy.

Allegory is a good way of making general or abstract themes more personal.

## alliteration

is the repetition of the first letter of a word in the word or words following it. For example:

> Peter Piper picked a peck of pickled peppers.

Here the letter <u>p</u> is repeated at the beginning of almost every word.

**Alliteration** is often used in poetry but it can produce a good effect in prose as well.

## allot

Add another <u>t</u> when you add the verb endings <u>-ed</u> and <u>-ing</u> to this word to form **allotted** and **allotting**:

> The first settlers were allotted a piece of land along the river.

But don't add a <u>t</u> when you add <u>-ment</u>:

> They grew wheat on their allotments.

See **doubling of last letter**.

## all ready

See **already/all ready**.

## all right

See **alright/all right**.

## all together

See **altogether/all together**.

## allude to / elude

These words sound similar but have different meanings.

When you **allude to** a person or thing, you speak of them in passing. Note that **allude** is always followed by **to**.

If you **elude** someone, you escape or avoid them.

## allusion / illusion

These words sound similar but have different meanings.

An **allusion** is a passing mention of something, often made while speaking about something else:
*Your allusion to the moon in your poem about swimming was hard to understand.*

An **illusion** is something that seems to be true but isn't:
*I thought the puppet was really speaking but it was an illusion.*

Make sure you don't confuse *illusion* with *delusion*. See **delusion/illusion**.

## -ally

For most adjectives that end in -ic, you add -ally to make the adverb, instead of just -ly. So *drastic* becomes *drastically*, and *realistic* becomes *realistically*.

Many of the adjectives that end in -ic have had another spelling ending in -ical at one time or another in the history of English. As well as *geographic* there is *geographical*, and there is *economic* as well as *economical*.

So in fact the adverbs from these words have been formed in the normal way, by adding -ly to the -ical ending: *geographically*, *economically*.

In some cases this is no longer clear because the -ical spelling for the adjective has fallen out of use. We no longer write *organical* for *organic*, *fantastical* for *fantastic*, or *romantical* for *romantic*, but those spellings were common when the adverbs *organically*, *fantastically* and *romantically* were formed.

There are also a few cases where there never was an -ical spelling: *drastic* and *realistic*, for example. The adverbs formed from these words simply followed the form of the others, and were spelled with -ally.

Note that there is only one commonly used adjective ending in -ic to which you add just -ly to make the adverb: *public*, *publicly*.

## a lot

These are two separate words and are never spelled as one:
*He ate a lot of candy floss at the school fete.*

## already / all ready

**Already** means "earlier or beforehand":
*Most of the guests have already left the party.*

If a group of people are **all ready** to do something, each one is prepared or ready:
*The musicians were all ready to start playing.*

## alright / all right

**Alright** means "satisfactory or okay". There's no need to spell it out as two full words when their meanings don't really help in understanding the word. It is just like *already* and *altogether*.
*"Are you alright?" the rescuer called to the child at the bottom of the cliff.*

**All right** can mean:

1 everything is correct:
   *She was amazed to find her answers to the science exam were all right.*
2 the same as **alright**.

## altar / alter

These words sound the same but have different meanings.

An **altar** is a table used in religious services.

If you **alter** something, you change it.

## alternate / alternative

These two adjectives are closely related, but they have different meanings.

**Alternate** refers to every second (or every other) thing in a series:
   *We'll sing alternate verses of the hymn.*

The word **alternative** describes a choice between options:
   *The signpost showed alternative routes over the mountains.*
Note that **alternative** used to be limited to a choice between just two options. Nowadays it can apply to two or more.

## altogether / all together

**Altogether** means "completely" or "in all":
   *The picnic was altogether spoiled by the weather.*
   *Our four concert tickets amounted altogether to thirty pounds.*

**All together** is used when a lot of things are grouped close to each other:
   *The sporting goods were all together in one section of the shop.*

## aluminium / aluminum

Both these spellings are used to refer to the same metal, but the endings are different.

**Aluminium** is the spelling used in the UK and **aluminum** is the way it is spelled in the USA.

It is interesting to note that the word was originally spelled **aluminum** even in the UK because it was the metal made from **alumina**. It was changed by the British in the early 1800s to make it conform with the other metals, like *calcium*, *potassium* and *sodium*, all ending in -ium.

## am

This is a form of the verb *to be*. See **be**.

## a.m.

This abbreviation is used when writing the time (*6.30 a.m.*), if you want to show that it is 6.30 in the morning.

The letters **a.m.** stand for the Latin words *ante meridiem*, which mean "before noon". They are often written without full stops (*6.30 am*).

For more information, see **abbreviations**.

## ambiguity

Writers usually want their meaning to be clear to the reader, so it is a pity when it seems **ambiguous** and can be taken in more than one way:

*The eggs of the hens were collected as soon as they had been laid by the farmer.*

**Ambiguity** can be avoided once you are aware of it. Often, changing the order of things will help:

*The eggs of the hens were collected by the farmer as soon as they were laid.*

## amoeba

For more about the spelling of this word, see **-oe-**.

The plural may be spelled **amoebas** or **amoebae**. For more about the plurals of words like this, see **-a (as a singular ending)**.

## among

See **between/among**.

## among / amid

These words both mean "in the middle of", but you use them with different kinds of nouns.

**Amid** nowadays seems rather poetic and even old-fashioned. But it can go with any kind of noun, whether it is

a count noun (a noun which refers to things that can be counted): *amid the trees*

or

a mass noun (a noun which refers to things that can't be counted): *amid the forest*

For more about these nouns, see **count nouns** and **mass nouns**.

**Among** only goes with count nouns. We can say *among the trees*, but not *among the forest*. Instead we have to say something like "in the middle of the forest".

**Amongst** is another way of spelling **among**, used more in literary styles of writing than elsewhere.

## amoral / immoral

These words both have moral as their base word, and have very similar meanings.

**Amoral** is used to describe someone who doesn't know or doesn't care about the difference between good and bad or right and wrong.

**Immoral** describes someone who knows the difference but who chooses to act in a way which is bad or wrong.

## ampersand (&)

is the name given to the character & which means "and". For more information, see **"and" sign**.

## an

When do you use **an** rather than **a** in front of a word?

The general rule is that you use **an** only when the following word begins with a vowel sound. So we write:
*an apple  an onion*     but     *a pear   a radish*

It is important to check whether the first sound is really a vowel or a consonant. With *hour* it is actually a vowel (ow), hence *an hour*. With *union* it is really a consonant (y), hence *a union*.

The trickiest cases are words beginning with h, such as *history* and *hotel*. Traditionally such words were said without the consonant sound at the beginning, and so *an (h)istory book* and *an (h)otel* sounded right and were in keeping with our general rule. But the h's have since been brought back into *history, hotel* and the like. The logical thing now is to use **a** rather than **an** in front of them, as most people do. But the tradition dies hard, especially with long words such as *habitual, hallucination, heroic, historical, hypothesis,* and *hysterical,* which don't stress the first syllable. There is no need for you to continue the tradition.

## an-

This Greek prefix means "not or without". You'll find it in
    anarchy  (the state of being without government)
    anaerobic  (lacking or surviving without oxygen)
The prefix is really a form of the prefix a-. It has been specially modified to go before words beginning with a vowel. You see this when you compare
    anaerobic  (an- aerobic)
with
    amoral  (a- moral)
For more about this, see **a-**.

## anaemic / anemic

These are equally good spellings. See **-ae-**.

## anaesthetic / anesthetic

These are equally good spellings. See **-ae-**.

## anagrams

An **anagram** is a word made up by rearranging the letters from another word. For example, if you start with the word *dance* you could, from the same set of letters, make up the word *caned.* If you are clever at this kind of thing you can manage more than just one word. There was a fashion for turning people's names into anagrams that revealed something about them. For example, an anagram of *Florence Nightingale* is *Flit on, cheering angel.*

---

**Anagram puzzle**
How many words can you make from:
    POST
    BEARS
    EARNED
    STREAMING?

---

## analogy

To make an **analogy** you liken one thing to another. Often the first thing is unfamiliar, and to explain something about it you draw an analogy with something more familiar.

For example, you could liken the heart to a pump to explain its function in sending blood around the body.

### analysis

The plural is spelled **analyses** with the last syllable pronounced like *seas*. For more about words like this, see **-is**.

### analyse / analyze

These are two possible spellings of this word. See **-yse/-yze**.

### -ance / -ence

These endings are both used to make nouns. They sound exactly alike, so pronunciation is no guide to correct spelling.

Noting which letter comes before the ending will help you to get many -ence ones right.

| | | | |
|---|---|---|---|
| *-cence* | innocence | magnificence | reticence |
| *-gence* | diligence | intelligence | negligence |
| *-ience* | convenience | experience | (im)patience |
| *-lence* | pestilence | turbulence | violence |
| *-quence* | consequence | eloquence | sequence |
| *-scence* | adolescence | convalescence | obsolescence |

Beyond these groups you could test whether the ending should be -ance or -ence by pronouncing related words which can often give you a clue. To get *tolerance* right, think of *tolerate*, and to get *difference* right, think of *differentiate*.

But some of these words are just a law unto themselves. For example: *existence, insistence, persistence,* but *assistance, resistance.* If you have trouble with them, a dictionary will always help.

### -ancy / -ency

To decide whether the ending should be spelled -ancy or -ency, see **-ance/-ence**. The general patterns described there also apply to words ending in -ancy/-ency.

### and

Is it wrong to begin sentences with **and**?

Not really, though it's better not to begin a lot of sentences with **and**. If you use **and** (or any other word) again and again at the start of your sentences, it gets very monotonous.

But now and then you may want to link a point from one sentence with the beginning of the next sentence, and **and** is very handy for this. For example:
  *She was extremely good at sport. And she was intelligent...*
It is something we often do when speaking, to add a separate but closely related point to whatever went before. There's nothing wrong with using it occasionally in writing.

As with *but*, some people argue that because **and** is a conjunction, it must link items inside the sentence. Yet its power to link things certainly reaches across from one sentence to the next. See also **link words**.

### "and" sign (&) (&) (  )

The "and" signs **&** and *&* are usually found only in titles and company names. People often use    for "and" when they're making rough notes, but it shouldn't appear in the final version.

## angel / angle

These words look similar but have different meanings.

An **angel** is a messenger of God. We pronounce it *ayn-jel*.

An **angle** is the point where two lines or surfaces meet. We pronounce it *ang-gle*.

## -ant / -ent

These endings are both used to make adjectives and a few nouns. Because they sound the same, it's not easy to know how to spell them.

You can often pick the -ent ones by checking the letter before the ending. For example:

| | | | |
|---|---|---|---|
| *-cent* | adjacent | complacent | (in)decent |
| *-gent* | cogent | intelligent | urgent |
| *-ient* | ancient | efficient | (dis)obedient |
| *-lent* | equivalent | insolent | silent |
| *-quent* | eloquent | (in)frequent | subsequent |
| *-scent* | adolescent | convalescent | obsolescent |

If your word isn't covered by these groups, try saying related words to see if they offer any clues. For example, the problem with *accident* is helped by *accidentally*, and *observant* by *observation*.

## Antarctic

is spelled with a c in the middle of the word.

It is spelled with a capital letter when you are using it as a noun (the **Antarctic**) which refers to the continent or zone. The continent is also called **Antarctica**.

When it is used as an adjective it is often spelled without the capital if the following noun is not strictly connected with the South Pole:
*Sydney has had almost antarctic weather in the last couple of days.*

## ante- / anti-

These two prefixes sound the same but they mean different things.

Ante- means "before", so you find it in words like *antenatal* (before birth) and *antedate* (to exist before something else).

Anti- means "the opposite of" or "opposed to", so you find it in words like *anticlimax* and *anticyclone*, or *antinuclear* and *antisocial*.

## antenna

The plural is spelled **antennae** when we are writing about the feelers found on the heads of some animals (particularly insects):
*Crickets have very long sensitive antennae.*
But when we are writing about radio or television aerials, the plural is spelled **antennas**:
*Television antennas can sometimes be very dangerous to install.*

For more about words like this, see **-a (as a singular ending)**.

### anti-

See **ante-/anti-**.

### anticlimax

See **climax**.

### antonyms

**Antonyms** are pairs of words with opposite meanings, such as *quick* and *slow*, *hot* and *cold*, *dead* and *alive*, *buy* and *sell*. Although they mean the opposite, antonyms always have a common denominator between them, such as:

speed (for *quick* and *slow*)
temperature (for *hot* and *cold*)
life (for *dead* and *alive*)
exchange of goods (for *buy* and *sell*)

Antonyms contrast with **synonyms**.

### any

This word can be used with both plural and singular verbs, pronouns and nouns. This is because it can refer to a whole group or an individual member of it:
*If any of the boys are available, they can come.*
*If any of the boys is available, he can come.*

### anyone / anybody

For information on how to use verbs and pronouns with these words, see **agreement**.

### apartheid

Note that e comes before i in this word. See **i before e**.

### apex

The plural of this word is usually spelled **apexes**. You may also find it spelled **apices**. For more about words like this, see **-x**.

### apostrophes (')

There are two reasons why we use **apostrophes**:

1 to show that something has been left out of a word: *they've gone*
2 to show ownership: *Gavin's hang-glider*

1 We use an apostrophe to show that we have left a letter (or sometimes more than one letter) out of a word or phrase:

| it's | it is | all's well | all is well |
| she'll | she will | John'll | John will (*or* shall) |
| I've | I have | might've | might have |

These are called contractions. They are quite common in speech, but usually avoided in formal writing.

2 We use an apostrophe when we want to show that something belongs to a person or thing.
(a) When a word is singular, whether it already ends in an s or not, we add an apostrophe and then an s at the end of the word:
*The bike's wheel came loose.*
*Here is Chris's dog.*

(b) When a word is <u>plural</u>, if it already ends in an <u>s</u>, we simply add an apostrophe at the end of the word, not an <u>s</u> as well:

*All the girls' fathers came to the meeting.*

(c) When a word is plural but does <u>not</u> end in an <u>s</u>, we add an apostrophe and then an <u>s</u> as well:

*The children's playground was unsafe.*

Note that apostrophes are often not used in the titles of institutions, organisations and so on:

Boys High School
Citizens Advice Bureau

### Its and it's

A tricky point to remember is that *it's* is short for *it is*, whereas *its* (without an apostrophe) shows ownership.

*The dog wagged its tail.*
*It's raining cats and dogs.*

One way of remembering this is to remind yourself that *its* is a pronoun like *her* and *his*, and they don't have apostrophes for ownership.

### Beware!

Never use an apostrophe with ordinary plural words. For example, you wouldn't write *Banana's for sale*. But when letters are used as words, we use apostrophes to avoid confusion and to make the text easier to read:

*Dot the i's and cross the t's.*

## apparatus

Whether we are writing about one piece of equipment or several, this word usually remains in the <u>singular</u>. You may, on rare occasions, see the plural form of the word (**apparatuses**).

Although the word can refer to one or several things, we tend to use it as if it were singular. When we do, the verb and pronoun we use with it must also be singular:

*The apparatus <u>is</u> set out ready for the experiment. Be careful not to move <u>it</u>.*

## appearance

Note the ending of this word. See **-ance/-ence**.

## appendix

The plural may be spelled either **appendixes** or **appendices** when you're referring to the sections of writing at the back of a book.

When you are using the word in a medical or anatomical way, the plural is spelled **appendixes**.

For more about words like this, see **-x**.

## apt

See **likely/liable/apt/prone**.

## aquarium

The plural may be spelled **aquariums** or **aquaria**. For more about words like this, see **-um**.

## aqueduct

is spelled with an e̲ in the first part of the word even though some other similar words, such as *aqualung* and *aquamarine*, are spelled with an a̲.

## -ar

This ending is found with two groups of English words:

**1** a special group of common nouns:

| | | | | | |
|---|---|---|---|---|---|
| altar | beggar | burglar | bursar | calendar | cellar |
| collar | dollar | grammar | hangar | liar | molar |
| pedlar | pillar | scholar | vicar | | |

The ones to note particularly are:

beggar   burglar   hangar   liar   pedlar

You might expect those to be -er words because they are related to familiar verbs. For more about that large group of words, see **-er/-or**.

**2** a sizable group of rather academic adjectives:

angular circular   jocular   perpendicular

as well as some more familiar ones

lunar   polar   solar   stellar

Note that some of these words also work as nouns in English.

## arc / ark

These words sound the same but mean different things.

An **ark** is a vessel like the one that Noah and the animals lived in during the Flood, as the story is told in the Bible.

An **arc** is a curved line. Note that **arc** is also a verb. It can mean "to move in a curve", or "to form a spark".

When you add the endings -ed and -ing, you have a choice – you can add a k̲ or you can leave it out:

arced     arcked
arcing    arcking

For more about this, see **-c/-ck-**.

## archaeology / archeology

These are equally good spellings. See **-ae-**.

## archipelago

The plural is spelled **archipelagos** or **archipelagoes**.
For more about words like this, see **-o**.

## are

This is a form of the verb *to be*. See **be**.

## aren't

This is a contraction of *are not*. See **contractions**.

## argument

You drop the e̲ from **argue** when you add -ment. It's an exception to the general rule. See **-ment**.

## armadillo

The plural is spelled **armadillos**. For more about words like this, see **-o**.

## articles

See **definite articles** and **indefinite articles**.

## -ary / -ery / -ory

These endings can all sound alike, but there's usually only one way to spell them. The original reasons for using one ending or the other are no longer obvious. You should check in the dictionary if you are not sure which one to use.

How do you remember the difference between *stationary* and *stationery*? See **stationary/stationery**.

## as

This word has more than one meaning, and you often need to make clear which one you intend.
*We came home as the wind was rising.*
In this sentence, it isn't clear whether the wind was <u>the reason why</u> people returned, or just something that happened <u>when</u> they returned. **As** is a conjunction which can express either cause or time (or comparison). In our example the meaning could be made clear by using either
*because* (if you are thinking about the reason)
or
*when* (if you are thinking about the timing of events).

In a novel this ambiguity might be useful. But if you were writing up a scientific experiment, it would be important to sort the matter out. **As** is best avoided in factual and argumentative writing.

See also **like/as**.

## ascetic

See **acetic/ascetic**.

## aspect

In English, verbs can show that the action is either *continuous* or *complete*. This difference is known as **aspect**.

**Continuous** aspect is shown by ending the verb with <u>-ing</u>, and by preceding it with a form of the verb *be*:
*I was walking.*
*I am eating.*
The **continuous** aspect is also known as the **imperfect** aspect.

If the action is complete, we can use the **perfect** aspect. This is shown by using the past participle of the verb (with an <u>-ed</u> or <u>-en</u> ending for most verbs) preceded by a form of the verb *have*:
*I have walked.*
*I have eaten.*

If the verb is neither continuous nor perfect, it is called a **simple** verb:
*I walked.*
*I eat.*

## assent / ascent

These words sound the same but mean different things.

**Assent** has to do with permission:
*I assent to your proposal.*
*The proposal got my assent.*

An **ascent** is a journey up, usually up a mountain:
*Sir Edmund Hillary made the first ascent of Mount Everest.*

## assessor

Note the ending of this word. See **-er/-or**.

## assistant

Note the ending of this word. See **-ant/-ent**.

## assonance

is the repetition of the same vowel sound in words for a special effect.
Say you've written this sentence in a story:
*Joe took a long time to drive home.*
If you want, you can create a feeling of slowness by using
**assonance**. You might try to use as many words as you can
with the long, slow "oh" sound:
*Joe drove home so slowly.*

You can make effective use of assonance in both poetry and prose.

## assure

See **ensure/insure/assure**.

## astronaut

is spelled with an <u>o</u>, not an <u>a</u>, in the middle of the word. Think
of *astro<u>no</u>my*.

## astronomy / astrology

These subjects both have to do with the stars but there is a difference.

**Astronomy** is the science of the stars and planets, in which they
are identified and described as closely as possible. Remember
that -<u>nomy</u> is a word part meaning "naming".

**Astrology** is a study which assumes that heavenly bodies have an
influence on human beings, and tries to explain what that effect is.

## ate

This is the past tense of **eat**:
*I eat meat today but I ate bread last week.*

## -ate

The -<u>ate</u> ending appears on many verbs, and a few adjectives
and nouns.

Some examples of verbs are in the list below:

| | | |
|---|---|---|
| assimilate | communicate | concentrate |
| contaminate | demonstrate | fabricate |
| fascinate | frustrate | hesitate |
| inflate | intimidate | moderate |
| originate | regulate | separate |
| stimulate | translate | violate |

Many of these verbs have nouns related to them. For example:

| | | |
|---|---|---|
| demonstrate | demonstrator | demonstration |
| regulate | regulator | regulation |
| translate | translator | translation |

The nouns in the second column are ones that describe a person by their actions, while those in the third column are abstract nouns. Both types of noun give you alternative ways of expressing something. For example:

> *The students were demonstrating about student loans.*
> *The demonstrators were protesting about the new student loan scheme.*
> *The demonstration was about the new student loan scheme.*

Most of the verbs ending in -ate come to us from Latin, and this is why the nouns ending in -ator are spelled that way (and not -ater). For more about this, see **-ator**.

The adjectives and nouns ending in -ate are also Latin borrowings, but they have fewer relatives in English than the verbs.

Some of the adjectives are:

affectionate    desolate    inanimate    separate    passionate

The nouns are of three kinds:

1 words which describe a particular office or body, such as *consulate*, *electorate* and *syndicate*
2 words which refer to someone by their office or status, such as *curate*, *graduate* and *magistrate*
3 words used in chemistry to describe salts or esters, such as *acetate*, *nitrate*, *phosphate* and *sulphate*

## -ation

This is the ending of many abstract nouns in English.

Some, like *education* and *meditation*, are related to verbs ending in -ate. (See **-ate**.) Others, like *civilisation* and *organisation*, are related to verbs ending in -ise. (See **-ise/-ize**.) A few, like *identification* and *justification*, are related to verbs ending in -ify. (See **-ify/-efy**.)

For more about these words, see **-ion**.

## -ative

This is the ending of a number of adjectives, such as:

| | | |
|---|---|---|
| affirmative | conservative | consultative |
| creative | generative | representative |

Some of them can also be used as nouns. They are usually related to abstract nouns ending in -ation, for example:

| | |
|---|---|
| affirmative | affirmation |
| conservative | conservation |

The meaning of the noun (and the way it is pronounced) is often slightly different from the adjective, however.

## -ator

This is the ending of many words that name a person or thing through the action they perform. You'll see it in words like:

calculator    creator    demonstrator    educator    investigator

You'll notice:
1 Most of these words are quite long – they have at least three syllables, and usually more.
2 All of them contain a verb which would end in -ate, except that the -e has been dropped in the usual way before a suffix beginning with a vowel. (See **-e**.) So *calculat(e)* becomes *calculator*, and so on.

These -ator words are the largest group which do not have -er in the last syllable. For more about this, see **-er/-or**.

## audible

Note the ending of this word. See **-able/-ible**.

## audience

Whenever you begin to write, it's important to think about your audience – that is, the reader or readers who will look at your writing.

For one thing, most people write better when they are conscious of really communicating with someone.

Secondly, it will help you to decide what information to put in, because you'll have some idea about your reader's interests. Naturally you'll leave out the heavy stuff if you're writing for younger children. And you'd feel free to talk about complicated things when writing for adults.

Thirdly, your sense of audience will help you to decide what sort of language to use in your writing. Your style when writing for your friends tends to be informal. But when you're writing for a general adult audience, for example in essays or a letter to a newspaper, it's an opportunity to use more formal language.

For more about this, see WRITING WORKSHOP p 28.

## auditor

Note the ending of this word. See **-er/-or**.

## auditorium

The plural of this word is usually **auditoriums**, though you may also see it spelled **auditoria**. For more about words like this, see **-um**.

## aunty / auntie

These are equally good ways of spelling this word.

For more about words like this, see **-ie/-y**.

Note the spelling of **Aunty**, a nickname sometimes given to the British Broadcasting Corporation.

## aural / oral

These two words are similar but one is to do with the ear and the other is to do with the mouth.

An **aural** test is one which tests your hearing. The first syllable rhymes with *door*.

An **oral** exam is one in which you speak your answers. **Oral** rhymes with *moral*.

## auto-

is a Greek prefix meaning "on its own". You'll find it in:
automatic   (working on its own)
automobile (a vehicle which moves on its own, that is,
                without animals to pull it)

The prefix also means "for or by oneself", as in:
autobiography (the story of one's life, by oneself)
autocratic      (taking all power for oneself)
autograph      (a signature by oneself)
autopsy         (examination of a dead body, but literally
                "inspection with one's own eyes")
Note that in *autobus* and *automotive*, the first part of the word is
a shortened form of *automobile*.

## autobiography

An autobiography is a biography written by the person whose
life story is being told. The value of an autobiography is that it
is a first-hand account of events. Its usefulness, however, can
depend on how much the person is willing to reveal.

## automatically

Note the ending of this word. See **-ally**.

## auxiliary verbs

We use **auxiliary verbs** all the time in speaking and writing, to
help make a complete verb. Here are some examples:
*I can make pavlovas.*
*I am making one now.*
*Who will eat my pavlova?*

Auxiliaries are used with other verbs for extra shades of meaning.
We can use them to show if something is possible or allowable:
*I can eat the pavlova.*
*I could eat the pavlova.*
*I may eat the pavlova.*
*I might eat the pavlova.*

We can use auxiliaries to show when something happens (in the
future, present or past tense):
*I will eat the pavlova.*
*I am eating the pavlova.*
*I have eaten the pavlova.*

Here are some examples of other uses of auxiliaries, including
the forming of questions and negatives:
*Do you like pavlova?* (question)
*I do like pavlova.* (emphasis)
*I should finish my pavlova.* (obligation)
*Did I eat the pavlova?* (question)
*You like pavlova, don't you?* (question negative)
*I don't like pavlova anymore.* (negative)

Auxiliaries are often contracted with pronouns and the word *not*.
For example:
*I will not eat*   – *I'm eating*        *I will eat*      – *I'll eat*
*I had eaten*     – *I'd eaten*         *I will not eat* – *I won't eat*

### avenge

See **revenge/avenge**.

### average / mean / median

These words all have to do with maths but there are some differences.

The **average** of a set of numbers is what you get when you add them all together, and then divide the sum by however many numbers there are. So the average of 2, 5, 8 and 9 is 6:

$(2 + 5 + 8 + 9) \div 4 = 6.$

**Mean** is often used as another name for the **average**.

The **median** is the middle number in a given set of numbers. So the median of 1, 3, 5, 20 and 50 is 5. But the median of 1, 3, 5 and 20 is 4. When you have an even number of numbers, the median is halfway between the two middle ones.

Look up your dictionary for other meanings of these three words.

### avocado

Note that there is no <u>d</u> in the first syllable of this word.

The plural is spelled **avocados**. For more about words like this, see **-o**.

### awe

See **oar/or/ore/awe**.

### awesome

Keep the <u>e</u> at the end of **awe** when you add <u>-some</u>:
 *The view from the top of the mountain was awesome.*
For more about words like this, see **-some**.

### awful

Drop the <u>e</u> from **awe** when you add <u>-ful</u>. It's an exception to the general rule. See **-e**. See also **-ful**.

### axe / ax

These are equally good spellings for this word. **Axe** is the usual spelling in the UK, and **ax** in the USA.

This spelling difference disappears when you add endings, so it is **axes, axed** and **axing** everywhere in the world:
 *They keep axing my favorite television shows.*

### axis

The plural is spelled **axes**, with the last syllable sounding the same as *seas*. For more about words like this, see **-is**.

# Bb

## b as a silent letter

The letter b̲ is written but not sounded at the end of a set of words, including *bomb, comb, crumb, dumb, lamb, numb, plumb, thumb, tomb* and *womb*.

Note that when words like these take the suffixes -e̲d̲ or -i̲n̲g̲, the b̲ remains silent. (Think of *comb* — *combing*.) But when the suffix makes it into a new kind of word (for instance, *crumb* — *crumble*), the b̲ is sounded.

Other words with a silent b̲ are *debt, doubt* and *subtle*. They came into English from French without any b̲, and only centuries later was it added to their spelling, but it has never been pronounced. The b̲ was added because of the way the words were written in Latin.

For more about this, see **silent letters**.

## backformation

Many words in English are built up from other, shorter ones. So *originate* comes from the shorter word *origin*. Sometimes the reverse happens. For example, *gravitate* actually comes from the longer word *gravitation*. English had already borrowed *gravitation* from Latin, and *gravitate* was "invented" from it. This invention is called backformation. A number of well-known English words have been formed in this way, such as *burgle* from *burglar, diagnose* from *diagnosis, grovel* from *grovelling*, and *resurrect* from *resurrection*.

When they are first invented, backformations are often thought to be colloquial and therefore not suitable for formal writing. Some of them, like the ones listed above, become acceptable. Some, like *buttle* from *butler*, were always intended as jokes and remain so. And others, such as *habitate* from *habitation*, where there is already the word *inhabit*, are thought to be incorrect.

## backward / backwards

For information about this pair of words, see **-ward/-wards**.

98

### bacteria

This is a <u>plural</u> word. The singular is spelled **bacterium**.
*Some bacteria cause infectious diseases.*
*A bacterium is a micro-organism.*
See **-a (as a plural ending)**. See also **germ/bacterium/virus**.

### bail / bale

These words sound the same but have different meanings.

The word **bail** in its legal sense is the money left with a court to ensure that the accused person comes back for trial. To **bail** someone out means "to help someone get out of trouble". **Bail** in its cricketing sense is part of a wicket.

The word **bale** can refer to a large bundle of goods, such as *a bale of wool*.

The word may be spelled **bale** or **bail** when it is used with *out* to mean either "to remove water from a boat with a bucket", or "to jump from a plane with a parachute".

### ball / bawl

These words sound the same but have different meanings.

A **ball** is a round object, or a formal dance.

When people **bawl** they cry noisily.

### ballot

Note that you don't add another <u>t</u> at the end of this word before you add endings like -<u>ed</u> or -<u>ing</u>. So it's *balloted* and *balloting*.
See **doubling of last letter**.

### ballad

A **ballad** is a simple poem, usually with short repeated stanzas and a strong rhythm. It often tells a folk story that is heroic or romantic, and is sometimes set to music. Linked to the ballad is a type of music piece called a **ballade**.

### banquet

Note that you don't add another <u>t</u> at the end of this word when you add the endings -<u>ed</u> and -<u>ing</u> to form **banqueted** and **banqueting**:
*We banqueted on the richest foods imaginable.*
See **doubling of last letter**.

### barbecue

The usual spelling of this word is **barbecue**. You may also find it spelled **barbeque**. In advertisements it even appears as **BBQ**.

### bare

See **bear/bare**.

### base / bass

These words sound the same but they have different meanings.

The **base** is the bottom of anything, or a centre of operations where things are organised.

A **bass** is the lowest voice, singer or instrument in a group. Note that **bass** with this meaning rhymes with *case*. When **bass** rhymes with *lass*, it means a type of fish.

## basically

Note the ending of this word. See **-ally**.

## basis

The plural is spelled **bases** (pronounced *bay-seez*).
For more about words like this, see **-is**.

## bass

See **base/bass**.

## bastard

When writing historical or biographical essays, you may have a proper reason to use this word, to show that someone was an illegitimate member of a family. For example:
*William the Conqueror was a bastard son of the Duke of Normandy.*

But in rough or casual talk, the word is used very off-handedly. It gets applied to all kinds of people, whether the speaker feels friendly or hostile towards them. This kind of usage is not recommended in your essay writing.

## bath / bathe

These two related words look similar but have different meanings.

You have a **bath** when you wash your body in water. You do this in a **bath**. You **bath** your dog if you wash him in the **bath**.

**Bathe** means "to wash something, or soak it in order to clean it":
*We must bathe that nasty cut.*
It also means "to have a swim". You can also use it as a noun:
*We had a quick bathe in the sea.*

## bawl

See **ball/bawl**.

## bazaar / bizarre

These words sound the same but they have different meanings.

A **bazaar** is a market where you can buy a variety of goods.

**Bizarre** means "very strange":
*She looks bizarre wearing that red and green wig.*

## BC

See **AD/BC**.

## be

The most common verb in English is the verb **to be**. It appears in several different forms, and some of them look quite different from **be**:

| *Present* | *Past* |
|---|---|
| (I) **am** | (I, he, she, it) **was** |
| (we, you, they) **are** | (you, they) **were** |
| (he, she, it) **is** | |
| **being** (*present participle*) | **been** (*past participle*) |

The verb **to be** can act on its own, or together with other verbs. That is, it can be a main verb or an auxiliary verb:

*She is a doctor.* (main verb)
*They were here last week.* (main verb)
*He was walking to the beach.* (auxiliary verb)
*You are coming on Friday.* (auxiliary verb)

The present and past forms, except for *am*, often form contractions with the word *not*. For example:

| | | |
|---|---|---|
| *is not* | becomes | *isn't* |
| *are not* | becomes | *aren't* |
| *was not* | becomes | *wasn't* |
| *were not* | becomes | *weren't* |

You shouldn't contract *am not* to *amn't*. Instead, *am* contracts with *I* to become *I'm not*. Note that you should avoid using *ain't* unless you're writing down ungrammatical speech or dialogue.

## beach / beech

These words sound the same but they have different meanings.

A **beach** is the sandy or pebbly shore of a river, sea or lake.

A **beech** is a kind of tree.

## bean / been

These words sound the same but they are very different in meaning.

A **bean** is a vegetable.

**Been** is the past participle of the verb **be**:
*I have been sick.*
*Have you been waiting long?*

## bear / bare

These familiar words sound the same but have different meanings.

Someone is **bare** when they are naked.

**Bear** refers to a large furry mammal.
It can also mean "to carry or support something":
*The kings came bearing gifts.*
*I can't bear your weight any longer.*

Look up your dictionary for other meanings.

## beat / beet

These words sound the same but have different meanings.

A **beet** is a kind of vegetable.

A **beat** is a regular rhythm, such as a heartbeat or the beat of music. It is also a verb with many meanings:
*Beat the eggs.*
*This yacht can beat them in the race.*
*The cruel man beat his horse.*

## beautiful / beautify

Note that for both of these words you change the y at the end of <u>beauty</u> to an <u>i</u> before you add <u>-ful</u> or <u>-fy</u>. For more about words like this, see **y→i**.

## beech

See **beach/beech**.

## been

See **bean/been**.

## beet

See **beat/beet**.

## beggar

Note the ending of this word. See **-ar**.

## beige

Note that <u>e</u> comes before <u>i</u> in this word. See **i before e**.

## belief

The plural is spelled **beliefs**. This word doesn't follow the general pattern for plurals of words ending in <u>-f</u>. For more about words like this, see **-f/-v-**.

## benefit

Note that you don't add another <u>t</u> at the end of this word when you add the endings <u>-ed</u> and <u>-ing</u> to form **benefited** and **benefiting**:

*He benefited greatly from the extra swimming training.*
See **doubling of last letter**.

## berry / bury

These words sound the same but they have different meanings.

A **berry** is a small juicy fruit.

When we **bury** something we put it in the ground and cover it with earth.

## berth

See **birth/berth**.

## beside / besides

These two words are similar but they are normally used in different ways.

If something is **beside** something else, it's next to it:
*Look at that huge shaggy dog standing beside your bike.*

**Besides** means "as well as":
*What do you want for tea besides fish?*

## between / among

These words are similar in meaning but they are sometimes used in different ways.

If there are only two things or people, you should use **between**. **Among** is never used for only two:

*There was a fight between Luke and Elisabeth over the last cake.*
NOT
*There was a fight among Luke and Elisabeth over the last cake.*

When you are talking about more than two people or things, you can use **among** or **between**:

*Share the lollies among all the kids.*
*A war broke out between the four countries.*

## between you and me

*Just between you and me, that teacher's out of his tree.*
It is a mistake to say *between you and I*. *Me* is the correct word to use because it is the object of the preposition *between*. (*Me* should always be used for the object, and *I* for the subject.) For more about this, see **case**.

## bi-

This prefix means "two" or "twice", as in *bicycle, bifocals, bilateral, bilingual* and *biweekly*. Technical words in science, such as *biped, bivalve, bicarbonate* and *bisulphide* are also formed with it. As the examples show, it needs no hyphen.

When it precedes a time word as in *bimonthly*, bi- is ambiguous. Does it mean every two months, or twice a month? To prevent ambiguity, writers have to make it clear which they mean:

*The magazine comes out every two months.*

See also **biannual/biennial**.

## biannual / biennial

These words look similar but mean different things. They both begin with the prefix bi- which can mean "twice" or "two".

Something is **biannual** if it takes place twice a year.

Something is **biennial** if it happens every two years.

## bias

Note that you don't need to add another s at the end of this word when you add the endings -ed and -ing to form **biased** and **biasing**:

*The tennis coach was biased against left-handers.*
See **doubling of last letter**.

## bibliography

A **bibliography** is a list of books and other publications on a particular subject. You often have one at the end of an essay to show which books you've consulted. How to compile and present a bibliography is explained in WRITING WORKSHOP p 64.

## biennial

See **biannual/biennial**.

## bight

See **bite/bight/byte**.

## -bility

For information about this ending, see **-ability** and **-ity**.

## billet

Note that you don't add another <u>t</u> at the end of this word when you add the endings <u>-ed</u> and <u>-ing</u> to form **billeted** and **billeting**:
*Our family billeted two boys from the touring soccer team.*
See **doubling of last letter**.

## billion

In the UK, this word now means "one thousand million" and is written 1 000 000 000. The older meaning of one million million (written 1 000 000 000 000) is disappearing. However people's uncertainty about **billion** means they usually avoid it if the number matters. In finance and statistics, they write the number out in figures, as we have done. In maths and science, they use $10^9$ or $10^{12}$.

## biography

A **biography** is a written account of a person's life. Biographies are factual in that the writer cannot invent the major events of someone's life, but they present the story in a readable and interesting way. To do this a biographer tries to get so close to the subject that it is possible to say exactly what that person thinks and feels. This can be done easily when the subject is still alive and cooperates with the biographer. But when the person is dead it requires a lot of imagination.

An **autobiography** is a biography written by the person whose life story is being told. See **autobiography**.

## biologically

Note the ending of this word. See **-ally**.

## biro

The plural is spelled **biros**. For more about words like this, see **-o**.

## birth / berth

These words sound the same but they have different meanings.

A **birth** is the beginning of a life.

A **berth** is the bunk or room where a traveller sleeps on a ship or train. It can also be the space for a ship to tie up at a dock.

## bite / byte

These words sound the same but they have different meanings.

A **bite** is a mouthful of something, or a wound made using teeth or something similar.

A **byte** is a unit of information stored by a computer.

### bivouac

The plural of this noun is spelled **bivouacs**.

Add a <u>k</u> to the verb when you add the endings <u>-ed</u> and <u>-ing</u> to form **bivouacked** and **bivouacking**:
*The troops bivouacked in the forest for two weeks.*
For more about words like this, see **-c/-ck-**.

### bizarre

See **bazaar/bizarre**.

### blanket

Note that you don't add another <u>t</u> at the end of this word when you add the endings <u>-ed</u> and <u>-ing</u> to form **blanketed** and **blanketing**:
*The mountains were blanketed in snow.*
See **doubling of last letter**.

### blasé

This word has been borrowed from French. The acute accent over the <u>e</u> shows that the last syllable is pronounced to rhyme with *day*.

Words like this tend to gradually lose their accent as they become more settled into English. So it's quite possible that we'll soon see this word written just **blase** (without any accent).

For more about accents in English, see **accents**. See also **acute accents**.

### blew

See **blue/blew**.

### block / bloc

These words sound the same but mean different things.

A **bloc** is a group of countries united by similar political systems:
*The Soviet Union leads the communist bloc.*

A **block** is commonly a solid lump of something, such as wood or concrete. For other meanings check your dictionary.

### bloody

Obviously enough, this word has something to do with **blood**. So in "bloody clashes with rebel soldiers", the word really means that blood was shed and violent things happened. If this is the point you want to make with the word, it's fair enough to use it in writing.

But in speaking, **bloody** is often used very loosely when there is certainly no blood around. The speaker just wants to stress or intensify a point, as in:
*It was bloody cold out there.*

Some speakers make a monotonous habit of using the word like this. For writers, there is no need. There are plenty of other ways to stress your point. See **intensifiers**.

## blue / blew

These words sound the same but have different meanings.

**Blue** is a color.

**Blew** is the past tense of **blow**:
*The wind blew the blue banners down.*

## boar

See **bore/boar/boor/Boer**.

## board / bored

These words sound the same but mean different things.

To be **bored** is to feel no interest in something. Wood has been **bored** when a hole has been made through it with a drill.

A **board** is commonly a long piece of wood. To **board** a bus is to get on it. **Board** has many other meanings as well. Check your dictionary.

## boarder

See **border/boarder**.

## boat / ship

People sometimes refer to a **ship** as a **boat,** and quite often it doesn't matter. But there is a rough distinction made on the basis of size. **Ships** are big and **boats** are small, and a rule-of-thumb guide is that a **ship** carries a **boat**. Yet submarines — even quite large nuclear submarines — are referred to as **boats**.

## boatswain

See **bosun/boatswain**.

## Boer

See **bore/boar/boor/Boer**.

## bolder / boulder

These words sound the same but mean different things.

**Bolder** means "more bold". It is the comparative of **bold**. The superlative is **boldest**:
*Frank is a bold boy in class, but Jack is bolder.*

A **boulder** is a large rock.

## bony

Drop the <u>e</u> from the end of **bone** when you add <u>-y</u>:
*The witch had long, thin, bony fingers.*
For more about words like this, see **-e**.

### book titles

How to set out book titles, and where to put capital letters in them, is explained in WRITING WORKSHOP p 64.

### boor

See **bore/boar/boor/Boer**.

### booty / bootee

These words sound the same but mean different things.

**Booty** is treasure stolen from the enemy in war.

A **bootee** is a knitted shoe for a baby.

### border / boarder

These words sound the same but mean different things.

A **boarder** is commonly a student at a boarding school.

A **border** is the edge of something, like a boundary line separating one country from another.

### bore / boar / boor / Boer

These words sound the same but mean different things.

A **bore** is either a tedious and uninteresting person, or a hole made by drilling.

A **boar** is a male pig.

A **boor** is a person who lacks manners and refinement.

A **Boer** is a South African of Dutch origin.

### bored

See **board/bored**.

### born / borne

These words sound the same but mean different things.

To be **born** is to be brought into this world. It is to go through the process of birth:
> *The baby was born yesterday.*
> *to be born blind*
> *a born fool.*

To be **borne** is to be carried. It is the past participle of **bear**, to carry, which has a past tense **bore** and past participle **borne**:
> *The leaf was borne away by the wind.*

### bosun / boatswain

These are equally good ways of spelling this word.

The spelling **boatswain** shows that it is a combination of two words: *boat* and *swain* (which is an old word meaning "boy" or "servant").

**Bosun** is closer to the way the word is pronounced.

## both / each

The basic thing to remember about these two words is that **both** takes a plural verb and **each** takes a singular verb:

*Both parents <u>are</u> invited to speech day.*
*Each bead on my necklace <u>is</u> made of ivory.*

With **both** you group together the two elements that go to make a whole, whereas with **each** you pick out one item in a set and look at it as an individual case. That is why **both** takes the plural verb and **each** takes the singular.

Note: **both...and...**
When you want to stress the likeness or contrast between two things in the same sentence, you use **both** before the first one, and **and** before the second:

*I am both happy and sad to be leaving school.*
*Both the apple and the orange are good to eat.*
*I will both do my homework and listen to the radio.*

## bough

See **bow/bough**.

## bought / brought

These two words sound similar but have different meanings.

**Bought** is the past form of the verb **buy**:
*I bought some lollies at the shop.*

**Brought** is the past form of the verb **bring**:
*I brought the lollies home before I ate them.*
Remember the two <u>r</u>'s go together, **b<u>r</u>ought** and **b<u>r</u>ing**.

## boulder

See **bolder/boulder**.

## boundary

Note the ending of this word. See **-ary/-ery/-ory**.

## bow / bough

These words can sound the same but they have different meanings.

A **bough** is a branch of a tree.

A **bow** is the bending movement you make to indicate respect.

Note that **bow** with this meaning is pronounced to rhyme with *cow*. When **bow** rhymes with *so*, it's a different word, as in *bow and arrow* or *a bow in your hair*.

## boy / buoy

These words sound the same but mean different things.

A **boy** is a male child.

A **buoy** is a marker which floats on water.

## bracket

Note that you don't add another t at the end of this word when you add the endings -ed and -ing to form **bracketed** and **bracketing**:

*The similar words were bracketed together.*

See **doubling of last letter**.

## brackets

are used in writing to include a thought or expression which may not be necessary, but which explains the topic further or adds interest to it. For example:

*London (the capital of England) is famous for its theatres.*
*My uncle (who's just turned 93) used to be a top-ranking tennis player.*

Commas or dashes may be used instead of brackets. In the two examples above, you could change the brackets to commas or dashes without changing the meaning. But brackets seem to separate information more than commas or dashes. See **commas** and **dashes**.

### Brackets with other punctuation

If the sentence should have a punctuation mark where the brackets are, then include it after the brackets. Otherwise, there is no need for other punctuation marks with the brackets.

The example below would need a comma after *skateboard* if the brackets weren't used, so you should still include it, but put it after the closing bracket. That way you're not separating related bits from one another:

*Daniel grabbed his skateboard (which he had recently painted), jammed his money into his pocket and took off with his friend.*

If the words inside the brackets need punctuation of their own, just follow the normal punctuation rules:

*Although my schoolbag was so brightly coloured (green with purple stripes, would you believe?), I couldn't find it in the giant pile of bags near the door.*

### Other types of brackets

Round brackets (or **parentheses**) are also used to enclose a number or letter which is introducing items in a list.

*The apparatus needed for this experiment includes:*
*(a) a bunsen burner*
*(b) a burette*
*(c) litmus paper*

Square brackets [ ] are used in writing to include something which is not meant to be read as part of the text:

*"Felicity, you'll have to hurry if you're going to the party," called Anne as she [Anne] closed the door.*

If you want to use one set of brackets inside another, square brackets can be used inside round brackets to avoid confusion:

*Patrick and Ben were meant to be going to the party too, but they had to look after Louis (their cousin down from Evesham [a town in Worcestershire] for a few days) because he was too young to be left alone.*

Square brackets can also be used to include additional information like:
*[turn to back of book for solution]*
*[continued on p 7]*

Two other special types of brackets are:
**braces** { }
**angle brackets** / /

### break / brake

These words sound the same but mean different things.

You can **break** a glass when you drop it, you can **break** your leg, you can take a **break** from work — **break** has many meanings. Check your dictionary.

A **brake** is a device for stopping a wheel going round.

### breath / breathe

These words are related but they mean different things.

**Breath** is a noun meaning "a puff of air":
*There was not a breath of wind.*

To **breathe** is the verb. It means "to draw air in and out of your lungs":
*It is so stifling I can't breathe.*

### brethren

This is an old-fashioned plural of **brother**. It has an old English plural ending -en, which is also seen in *children* and *oxen*.

Note that these days **brethren** is most often used to refer to the members of a religious group:
*The brethren have gathered in the meeting hall to praise the Lord.*

### bridal / bridle

These words sound the same but mean different things.

**Bridal** relates to a bride or a wedding:
*the bridal veil; the bridal feast.*

A **bridle** is part of a horse's harness.

### bring

This is one of those verbs in English which form their past tense in an unpredictable way. Although **bring** sounds like *ring* and *sing*, its past forms are quite different. You can't say *I brang* or *I brung*. Instead, it should be
I **bring**    I **brought**    I have **brought**

Don't confuse *brought* with *bought*: *bought* is the past tense of *buy*. See **bought/brought**.

### brooch / broach

These words sound the same but mean different things.

A **brooch** is an ornament which people pin to their clothes.

To **broach** a subject is to introduce or mention it for the first time:
*It's time to broach the small matter of the washing up.*

## brother-in-law

The plural is spelled **brothers-in-law**.

The possessive is **brother-in-law's**: *my brother-in-law's wife*.

## brought

See **bought/brought**.

## budget

Note that you don't add another t at the end of this word when you add the endings -ed and -ing to form **budgeted** and **budgeting**. See **doubling of last letter**.

## buffalo

The plural may be spelled **buffalos** or **buffaloes**. For more about words like this, see **-o**.

**Buffalo** may also be used collectively:
*There are a lot of buffalo up north.*
See **collective nouns**.

## buffet

Note that you don't add another t at the end of this verb when you add the endings -ed and -ing to form **buffeted** and **buffeting**:
*Strong winds buffeted the First Fleet.*

See **doubling of last letter**.

When **buffet** is used in this sense it is pronounced to rhyme with *rough it*. When it is pronounced so that the -et rhymes with *day*, it is a different word. You'll find it in *buffet dinner* or *kitchen buffet*.

## buoy

See **boy/buoy**.

## bureau

The plural of this word may be spelled **bureaus** or **bureaux**. For more about words like this, see **-e(a)u**.

## burglar / burglary

Note that both these words have -ar in them, though you might expect them to have -er. For more about words like this, see **-ar**.

## burned / burnt

The past form of **burn** is spelled both **burned** and **burnt** in the UK. The choice is yours. If you use **burned**, you bring it into line with the past form of most other English verbs. For more on this, see **-ed/-t**.

## burst

This word is spelled the same way whether it is present or past:
*If we burst in now, we'll catch them red-handed.* (present)
*They burst into the room and found only the TV switched on.* (past)
For more about verbs like this, see **past forms**. See also **bust/burst**.

## bury

See **berry/bury**.

## bus

The plural is spelled **buses**.

When **bus** is used as a verb, double the s when you add -ed and -ing — **bussed, bussing**.

## business / busyness

These words are both related to **busy** but mean quite different things.

**Business** refers to your occupation or profession:
*I am in the business of selling books.*

**Busyness**, pronounced *busy-ness*, refers to the state of being busy:
*The busyness of people in the city is bewildering to people in the country.*

## bust / burst

These words look similar and they can mean the same thing.

To **burst** is to split or break open:
*The sausages have started to burst and splatter all over the oven.*
*My budgerigar has burst my balloon.*
Note that this word stays the same for its past forms and doesn't add -ed to make *bursted*. So don't get it confused with **busted**.

**Bust** is an informal word meaning "break":
*Did you bust my pink balloon?*
*He busted my new headphones.*
Although the word is often used this way in speech, you should avoid it in your essays.

## but

It is not wrong to begin a sentence with **but**. People often do it, and there is nothing wrong with it grammatically. However, it would be better not to start too many sentences this way in a single piece of writing. For more about the matter, see **and** and **link words**.

Some speakers use **but** at the end of a sentence as a way of softening its impact for the listener:
*I'll still send them a card, but.*
This is very colloquial. There are other ways of softening a statement in writing. See **hedge words**.

## but / butt

These words sound the same but mean different things.

**But** is a conjunction meaning "however".

**Butt** is the end of something such as a rifle or a cigarette.

## buy

See **by/buy/bye**.

## by-

This prefix means "near to", as in *bypass, byplay* and *bystander,* or "secondary", as in *by-election, byname* and *byproduct.* More and more the hyphen is left out of such words.

## by / buy / bye

These words sound the same but have different meanings.

**By** means "near or close to something":
*The table is by the door.*
**By** has many other meanings and you should look it up in your dictionary.

To **buy** something is to pay money for it so that it becomes yours:
*I would like to buy a yacht.*

A **bye** in sport is when your team doesn't have to play in a particular round of a contest.

## byte

See **bite/byte**.

# Cc

## -c / -ck-

The letter c stands for a *k* sound in some words, such as *picnic*, and for an *s* sound in others such as *nice, icing* and *racy*.

If we added an ending such as -ed, -ing or -y straight after a c, it would look as if the word was said with an *s* sound. (Think of how you would pronounce *paniced* if it were a real word.) To make it clear that it still has a *k* sound, we add on the letter k before the ending.

Here are some examples of words in which -c becomes -ck-:

| colic | – | – | colicky |
| bivouac | bivouacked | bivouacking | bivouacker |
| mimic | mimicked | mimicking | mimicker |
| panic | panicked | panicking | panicky |
| picnic | picnicked | picnicking | picnicker |

Note: short words such as *arc* and *zinc* do not always add a k before endings, especially in technical writing. See **arc/ark** and **zinc**.

## cache

See **cash/cache**.

## cactus

The plural of this word may be spelled **cactuses** or **cacti**. For more about words like this, see **-us**.

## cafe / café

These are equally good ways of writing this word.

**Cafe** came into English from French, where it is always written with the acute accent over the e: **café**. In French, as in English, this shows that the fé is pronounced *fay*.

This word has become so widely known in English that it is no longer necessary to use the foreign accent to show this special pronunciation. So it is quite common nowadays to see the word written **cafe**.

For more about accents in English, see **accents**. See also **acute accents**.

## cagey / cagy

These are equally good ways of spelling this word. For more about words like this, see **-y/-ey**.

## calculator

Note the ending of this word. See **-ator**.

## caldron

See **cauldron/caldron**.

## calendar

Note the ending of this word. See **-ar**.

## calf

The plural is spelled **calves**. For more about words like this, see **-f/-v-**.

## calibre / caliber

These are equally good ways of spelling this word.

**Calibre** is the usual spelling in the UK, whereas **caliber** is the usual spelling in the USA. For more about words like this, see **-re/-er**.

Note that when you are writing about the **calibre** of a gun, you are describing the diameter of its bore, not the weight of the gun.

## callous / callus

These words sound the same but mean different things.

A **callous** person has lost all tender feelings of pity or sympathy.

A **callus** is a piece of your skin which has grown thick and hard.

One word is related to the other. A **callous** person is someone whose character has been hardened with rough treatment until they don't feel things anymore.

## calve / carve

These words sound the same but have different meanings.

To **calve** is to produce a calf:
*The cow calved in the early hours of the morning.*

To **carve** the meat is to cut it up into slices.

## cameo

The plural is spelled **cameos**. For more about words like this, see **-o**.

## can / may

**Can** and **may** have slightly different meanings, though they often overlap.

**Can** means "is able":
*It can fly faster than the speed of sound.*

**May** means
1 "it's allowed":
*You may turn the TV on if you've finished your homework.*
2 "it's possible":
*It may rain tomorrow.*

In conversation, this difference is often ignored:
*You can go to the beach.*
This sentence could mean either that you are able to go to the beach, or that you're allowed to.

In questions, **can** can also take on the first meaning of **may**. For example:
*Can I go to the beach?*
In this question, you are probably asking whether you are allowed to go to the beach. But note that some people feel it is more polite to ask:
*May I go to the beach?*

**Can** and **may** are modal verbs. See **modal verbs**.

## cancel

For information about whether to double the l when you add -ed, -ing or -ation, see **-l-/-ll-**.

## cannon / canon

These words sound the same but have different meanings. The number of n's makes the world of difference.

A **cannon** is a kind of large gun.

A **canon** can be either a church official or a church law.

## canoe

Keep the e at the end of this word when you add -ing or -ist: **canoeing, canoeist**.

But drop the e from **canoe** when you add -ed: **canoed**.

For more about words like this, see **-e**.

## canon

See **cannon/canon**.

## can't

This is a contraction of the word **cannot**. See **contractions**.

## canvas / canvass

These words sound the same but mean different things.

**Canvas** is a special type of material for tents and sails, among other things.

To **canvass** a group of people is to go round the group, one by one, asking each person their opinion.

### capacitor

Note the ending of this word. See **-er/-or**.

### capital / Capitol

The **Capitol** could refer to a temple in ancient Rome, or the United States Congress building in Washington DC.

A **capital** city is the chief city of a country or state. It is the seat of government.

### capital letters

are the large-sized letters used at the beginning of a sentence or as the first letter of a proper name. Capital letters are also called upper-case letters. Some are just larger versions of the lower-case letter, like *O, o*. Others are different in their shape as well as being larger in size. For example *Q, q* and *R, r*.

Capitals are used in the titles of books, films, plays, and so on. The following are the types of words which are spelled most commonly with a capital letter:

**1** the names and titles of specific people, organisations and institutions:

| | |
|---|---|
| Sir Robin Day | British Broadcasting Corporation |
| Lady Diana | York University |
| Mr Joe Williams | World Health Organisation |
| Ms Mary Jones | Lloyds Bank |
| John Smith | Royal College of Nursing |

See also **abbreviations**, **acronyms** and **forms of address**.

**2** the names of places, whether they are countries, states, or suburbs:

| | |
|---|---|
| Italy | United States of America |
| Fremantle | Brisbane |
| Kew | Tasmania |
| Liverpool | |

See also **geographical terms**.

**3** national and ethnic names, and the names of religious and language groups:

| | |
|---|---|
| Buddhist | Chinese |
| Fijian | English |
| Negro | Christian |
| Aboriginal | Swahili |

**4** the names of historical periods or events, as well as the names of holidays or ceremonies:

| | |
|---|---|
| the Second World War | Queen's Birthday |
| the French Revolution | Christmas Day |
| the Renaissance | Ramadan |

Note that geographical and other names often lose their capital letters when they are shortened:

> *The Second World War ended in 1945. This war ruined most of the countries in Europe.*

*Second World War* becomes just *war* if that word is used on its own.

*The River Thames is a tourist attraction. Many pleasure
cruisers travel up and down the river in summer.*
*River Thames* becomes just *river*; however, if you shortened it to
*the Thames*, the capital letter would be retained.

The general rule is that the capital letters are abandoned when
you shorten the name to just the common noun in it. See
**common nouns**.

Compare **lower case letters**.

## Capitol

See **capital/Capitol**.

## capsize

In **capsize** the -ize can never be spelled -ise. The word came
into English from Spanish with the -ize built in. See **-ise/-ize**.

## carat

See **carrot/carat/caret**.

## carcase / carcass

These are two possible spellings for the same word meaning "a
dead body".

Note, however, that in farming there is a distinction.
A **carcase** is an animal body prepared for human food at an
abattoir. A **carcass** is any dead body.

## cardinal numbers / ordinal numbers

**Cardinal numbers** are those such as 23, 7, 2, 16, and so on,
which show you how many things or people there are in a
particular set or group:
  *The band consisted of 6 people.*
or
  *They played to an audience of 25 000.*

**Ordinal numbers** are those such as 15th, 3rd, 2nd, 98th, and so
on, which show you the order in which things occur in a
particular set, not the total number of things in the set:
  *He came 15th in the race.*

For information on how to write and punctuate numbers in
essays, see **numbers**.

## caret

See **carrot/carat/caret**.

## cargo

The plural of this word may be spelled **cargos** or **cargoes**. For
more about words like this, see **-o**.

## carol

For information about whether to double the l when you add
-ed, -ing or -er, see **-l- / -ll-**.

## carpet

Note that you don't add another t at the end of this word when you add the endings -ed and -ing to form **carpeted** and **carpeting**:

*They even carpeted the floor of their tree-house.*

See **doubling of last letter**.

## carrot / carat / caret

These words sound the same but have different meanings.

A **carrot** is a kind of vegetable.

**Carat** is a measurement used to express the fineness of gold and the weight of gemstones:

*My watch is ten carat gold.*

A **caret** is the omission mark you use in writing ( ) to show where something has been added in.

## carve

See **calve/carve**.

## case

This is a grammatical term that refers to the way various parts of a sentence relate to each other:

*The girls have to choose the four dishes for Jane's party.*

In this sentence, *the girls* is the subject of the verb (the girls are doing the choosing), and you can say *girls* is in the **subjective case**. Similarly, *the four dishes* is the object of the verb (the dishes are being chosen), and you can say *dishes* is in the **objective case**. (See **subject** and **object**.) And since in some sense the party belongs to *Jane*, you can say that *Jane's* is in the **possessive case**.

The possessive case is the only one of the three that causes a change to the noun – it always has 's or s' on the end. Nouns in the subjective and objective cases don't look any different from each other.

In most English pronouns, though, all three cases are clearly distinguished:

| Subjective | Objective | Possessive |
|---|---|---|
| *Singular* | | |
| I | me | my (mine) |
| you | you | your (yours) |
| he, she, it | him, her, it | his, her (hers), its |
| *Plural* | | |
| me | us | our (ours) |
| you | you | your (yours) |
| they | them | their (theirs) |

Because most of the pronouns differ, you have to be careful in writing to select the right one for the job. For example, pronouns have to be in the objective case if they're the object of a verb:

*Karen picked him and me for the team.*     RIGHT
*Karen picked he and I for the team.*     WRONG

Because the pronouns here tell you who was picked (not who did the picking), you use the objective pronouns *him* and *me*.

**Case with prepositions**

Prepositions (words like *between, in, under, onto*) have to be followed by nouns and pronouns in the objective case.

between *you and me*      RIGHT
between *you and I*       WRONG

You'll sometimes hear other names for these three cases when you're studying other languages:

*nominative*  for **subjective case**
*accusative*  for **objective case**
*genitive*    for **possessive case**

Other languages may have extra cases that don't appear in English. See **ablative case**, **dative case**, and **vocative case**.

## cash / cache

These words sound the same but mean different things.

**Cash** is money, particularly in the form of notes or coins.

A **cache** is a hidden store of provisions or weapons:
*The smuggler had a cache of supplies and guns in the woods.*

## casino

The plural is spelled **casinos**. For more about words like this, see **-o**.

## cast / caste

These words sound the same but mean different things.

A **caste** is a group of people in a society set apart from the rest in some way:
*The untouchables are the lowest caste in Hindu society.*

The **cast** of a play are the people who play the various roles in it.

## caster / castor

These are equally good ways of spelling this word.

It is more common for the small wheels set under a piece of furniture to be **castors**. And it is more common for the sugar to be **caster** sugar. Nevertheless, both spellings are used for both meanings.

## catalogue / catalog

These are equally good ways of spelling this word. **Catalogue** is the usual spelling in the UK, and **catalog** the usual spelling in the USA.

Note that **catalogue** keeps the u when you add -ed and -ing: **catalogued, cataloguing**. But with **catalog** you may choose whether to add a u or not before the verb endings: **cataloged** or **catalogued**, and **cataloging** or **cataloguing**.

For more about words like this, see **-gue/-g**.

## caterpillar

This is a tricky word to spell, because you don't hear the r in the middle when you say the word.

Also note the ending of the word. See **-ar**.

### caught / court

These words sound the same but have different meanings.

Two common types of **court** are the *tennis court* and the *law court*.

**Caught** is the past form of **catch**:
*He threw the ball and I caught it.*

### cauldron / caldron

These are equally good ways of spelling this word. **Cauldron** is the more common in the UK, although **caldron** is closer in spelling to the original Latin word.

### the cause of something was due to . . .

It is not necessary to say all of this because **was due to** repeats the point made by the phrase **the cause of**. So don't write:
*The cause of his terror was due to the large spider that sat down beside him.*
It is enough to say either:
*The cause of his terror was the large spider that sat down beside him.*
or:
*His terror was due to the large spider that sat down beside him.*

For more information about unnecessary repetition, see **tautology**.

### caw

See **core/caw/corps**.

### -ce / -ge

When c̲ is followed by e̲, it sounds like an *s*, as in *race*. And g followed by e usually sounds like a *j*, as in *rage*. (Think how they would sound without the e̲.) Words which end in -e̲ normally drop that letter before adding an ending. This is what happens to -ce̲/-ge̲ words before -e̲d̲ and -e̲r̲ are added, as in *raced* and *racer*, *raged* and *rager*. (We don't write them *raceed*, *raceer*.)

The -e̲ is also dropped before -i̲ng̲, -i̲sm̲, -i̲st̲ and -y̲, as in *raging*, *racism* and *racy*. (The last three examples show how both i̲ and y̲ work like e̲, to make c̲ sound like an *s* and g sound like a *j*.)

But the e̲ is kept on -ce̲/-ge̲ words whenever the ending is -a̲ble̲, -fu̲l̲, -me̲nt̲ or -o̲us̲. For example:

traceable      (*not* tracable)
peaceful       (*not* peacful)
arrangement    (*not* arrangment)
courageous     (*not* couragous)

The e̲ is needed to keep the c̲ sounding like an *s* and the g sounding like a *j*.

For more about this spelling pattern, see **-e**.

Note that a handful of words ending in -ce̲ take -i̲ble̲ rather than -a̲ble̲, for example, *forcible* and *reducible*. See **-able/-ible**.

## -ce / -se

A few pairs of words like *practice* and *practise* end in -ce when they are nouns, and -se when they are verbs. For example:

*I do my trombone practice at midnight.* (noun)
*I practise my trombone at midnight.* (verb)

Other pairs which behave in the same way in the UK are *licence/license*, and *advice/advise*. You'll notice with the second pair that the different spellings go with slightly different sounds (*advice* rhymes with *nice* and *advise* rhymes with *size*). So if you have trouble with *practice/practise*, think of *advice/advise*, and you should get it right.

Note **1**  The nouns *defence*, *offence* and *pretence* are normally spelled *defense*, *offense* and *pretense* in the USA.

Note **2**  In the USA *practice* is used for spelling both the noun and verb. Perhaps this is because Americans avoid -ise spellings in other words. See **-ise/-ize**.

## -cede / -ceed / -sede

These three sets of letters are exactly alike in sound, but they belong with different verbs.

-sede is found in just one word: *supersede*, meaning "to replace someone or something".

-ceed is only found in *exceed*, *proceed* and *succeed*.

-cede is the spelling in all other verbs, including *concede*, *intercede*, *precede*, *recede* and *secede*.

The different spellings can make an important difference in meaning. Make sure you know *precede* (to go before) and *proceed* (to continue).

## cedilla ( ̧ )

A **cedilla** is a mark placed under the letter c in languages such as French and Portuguese, to show that the c should be pronounced like an *s*, not a *k*. For example, the French word *garçon* (boy) is pronounced with an *s* sound in the middle.

The **cedilla** comes into English with French words we have borrowed, for example, *façade*.

For more about accents in English, see **accents**.

## ceiling / sealing

These words sound the same but mean different things.

The **ceiling** of a room is above your head.

**Sealing** comes from the verb **seal**, to close or fasten tightly:
*I am sealing the jam jars with wax.*

## cell

See **sell/cell**.

### cellar / seller

These words sound the same but have different meanings.

A **cellar** is an underground room for storing goods like wine. For more about this word's ending, see **-ar**.

A **seller** is someone who sells things.

## Celsius

This is the scale of temperature used in the metric system. Its abbreviation is a capital C, written after the figure and the degree sign. It does not have a full stop:

*100°C is the boiling point of water.*
*At 0°C water freezes.*

The scale in the imperial system formerly used in the UK is the **Fahrenheit** scale. The conversion formulas for these scales are as follows:

$$°C = 5/9 \times (°F - 32)$$
$$°F = (9/5 \times °C) + 32$$

Another name for the Celsius scale is the **Centigrade** scale, though this name is no longer used in scientific writing.

### censor / sensor

These words sound the same but mean different things.

A **censor** is a person who is appointed to examine films, plays, news reports and the like, to see whether they are suitable for the general public.

A **sensor** is something that detects changes in heat, light and moisture.

For more about the -or ending of these words, see **-er/-or**.

### cent / sent / scent

These words sound the same but have different meanings.

A **cent** is one-hundredth of a dollar.

**Sent** is the past form of the verb **send**:
*He sent me this postcard.*

A **scent** is the smell that flowers and perfume have.

### center

See **centre/center**.

### centi-

This prefix comes from a Latin word meaning "hundred" and is used to begin a whole group of words which have something to do with the word *hundred*.

In *centipede* it refers to a set of 100.

In metric units like *centilitre*, *centigram* and *centimetre* it means "one-hundredth", that is, 1/100.

See also **number prefixes**.

## Centigrade

See **Celsius**.

## centimetre

**Centimetre** is the standard spelling in the UK. The symbol for **centimetre** is **cm**, without a full stop.

**Centimeter** is the usual spelling in the USA.

For more information on metric units and measures, see APPENDIX C. For more about the spelling, see **-re/-er**.

## centre / center

These are equally good ways of spelling this word. **Centre** is the usual spelling in the UK. **Center** is the way the word is usually spelled in the USA.

When you add -ed or -ing to **centre** you drop the -e: **centred**, **centring**.

For more about words like this, see **-re/-er**.

## centuries

For information on how to refer to centuries in your writing, see **dates**.

## cereal / serial

These words sound the same but mean different things.

**Cereal** is grain, such as wheat or rice. A **cereal** is the breakfast food made from this.

A **serial** is a story you get one part at a time at regular intervals.

## chairperson / chairman / chairwoman

The non-sexist word **chairperson** is often used to refer to the person who controls a meeting or a committee. The ending -person applies equally to both men and women.

**Chairman** is the traditional name for this person, but because it ends in -man it seems to favor men.

**Chairwoman** is the feminine alternative to **chairman**, but it has never been used very much. It does not solve the problem of finding a word that refers to both men and women.

An alternative solution is to find a completely different word for the position — *moderator, convener* and *the chair* have all been offered as suggestions.

See **non-sexist language**.

## chamois / shammy

We pronounce **chamois** *sham-mee* (to rhyme with *clammy*) when we are referring to the soft leather used for cleaning. **Shammy** is an easier way of spelling this kind of **chamois** because the spelling matches the pronunciation.

We pronounce **chamois** *sham-wah* (to rhyme with *car*) when we are talking about the antelope with this name. The word came into English from French, and this is how the French say it.

### changeable

Note that you keep the e at the end of **change** when you add -able. For more about words like this, see **-able/-eable**.

### channel

For information about whether to double the l when you add -ed or -ing, see **-l-/-ll-**.

### chapters

Most books, both fiction and non-fiction, are divided up into parts called **chapters**. Each chapter describes a particular stage of a story or history, or a separate unit of information in a textbook.

Chapters allow writers to present their material in manageable steps, and they show readers where they can take a break in their reading.

### charted / chartered

These words sound the same but they are quite different verbs.

**Charted** is the past form of **chart**, meaning "to draw or show an area of land or water on a map".

**Chartered** is the past form of **charter**, meaning "to hire a vehicle for private use".

### chassis

This word is spelled the same way whether it is singular or plural. The singular is pronounced *shaz-ee* and the plural is pronounced *shaz-eez*.
*The chassis of my poor old car is full of rust.* (singular)
*The chassis of modern cars are designed with the help of computers.* (plural)

### chastise

This is one of the few words ending in -ise that cannot also be spelled with -ize. It is always spelled **chastise**. For more about words like this, see **-ise/-ize**.

### cheap / cheep

These words sound the same but mean different things.

Goods are **cheap** if they don't cost very much.

Chickens and other small birds **cheep**.

### check / cheque

These words sound the same but mean different things.

**Check** can have several meanings:
*I think I know, but I'll do a check for you.*
*This drug will check the course of the disease.*
*Our new uniform has a check pattern.*

A **cheque** is a money order that you write to your bank on a special form, instructing them to pay a specific amount to someone. **Check** is the way this word is spelled in the USA.

## cheep

See **cheap/cheep**.

## chemically

Note the ending of this word. See **-ally**.

## chemical symbols

There is a list of chemical elements and their symbols at
APPENDIX D.

## child

The plural is spelled **children**.

There are now only two other words in English like this:
*brethren* and *oxen*. In old English many words made their plural
with -en.

## childish / childlike

These words both come from **child** but they have different
meanings.

We say that someone's behavior is **childish** when we consider it
silly or not appropriate to their age.

We call someone or something **childlike** if they have some of the
qualities of children, such as innocence and frankness.

## chilly / chilli / Chile

These words sound the same but have different meanings.

A **chilly** breeze makes you feel cold. If someone gives you a
**chilly** look, you know they feel unfriendly towards you.

A **chilli** is a type of small hot capsicum. We also spell this **chili**.

**Chile** is a republic in the south-west of South America.

## chimney

The plural of this word is spelled **chimneys**. For more about
words like this, see **-ey**.

## chisel

For information about whether to double the l when you add
-ed or -ing, see **-l-/-ll-**.

## chlorophyll

This is the usual spelling for this word. You may find it spelled
**chlorophyl** because it is sometimes spelled this way in the USA.

## choral

See **coral/choral**.

## chord

See **cord/chord/cored**.

## chronic / acute

These two words do not mean the same thing. In fact they are opposites when they refer to disease.

A **chronic** illness is one that continues for a long time:
*She suffers from chronic depression.*
*The child is a chronic asthmatic.*

An **acute** illness is brief and severe:
*I had an acute attack of appendicitis and was rushed to hospital.*

## chronologically

Note the ending of this word. See **-ally.**

## chute

See **shoot/chute.**

## cider / cyder

These are equally good spellings for this word, though **cider** is closer to the original French word. For more about words like this, see **i/y.**

## cipher / cypher

These are equally good spellings. See **i/y.**

## circumflex (ˆ)

A **circumflex** is a mark placed over a vowel in languages such as French and Portuguese. It can tell you something about how the vowel is pronounced, and also about the word's history.

In French, the circumflex usually shows that the vowel sound is slightly longer. Often it also means that a letter has dropped out from the spelling. Commonly, the letter left out was s̲. So French words like *hôtel* and *fête* are words which used to be spelled with an s̲ (*hostel* and *feste*).

For more about accents in English, see **accents.**

## cite

See **sight/site/cite.**

## classic / classical

These two words look similar but have different meanings.

Something is **classic** if it is very good or outstanding in its class:
*There were some classic catches at the cricket today.*
Some people also use **classical** in this sense.

But **classical** has other meanings. In the worlds of art, music and literature, it means having an established reputation. So the music of Mozart and Beethoven is *classical music.* **Classical** also means "connected with the ancient world of Greece and Rome".
*Homer and Virgil are classical authors.*
In this last sense, you will sometimes find the word **classical** with a capital C.

## clauses

A **clause** is the most important unit in the structure of a sentence. Whatever else is there, the sentence must have a **clause**. And the clause always contains a verb with a subject. This is how it differs from a **phrase**. For example:

| | |
|---|---|
| *on the corner* | phrase |
| *standing on the corner* | phrase |
| *I was standing on the corner* | clause |

Only the third example has a complete verb (*was standing*), with its subject (*I*), and therefore it is the only one that is a clause.

There are two major types of clause: **main clauses** (also called **principal clauses**) and **dependent clauses** (also called **subordinate clauses**).

### Main clauses

A main clause makes a complete message on its own. In fact, a main clause can stand on its own as a sentence:

*I was standing on the corner.*

### Dependent clauses

A dependent clause does not make a complete message by itself. That is, it cannot stand as a sentence on its own:

*While I was standing on the corner...*

There are three major types of dependent clause: adjectival clauses, adverbial clauses and noun clauses. You can tell from their names that they are clauses that do the work of adjectives, adverbs and nouns.

In the following examples you can see how the clauses replace the word in each part of speech. Notice that the clauses give you the chance to add in extra information:

| | |
|---|---|
| *the <u>winning</u> horse* | *the horse <u>that won this race</u>* |
| adjective | adjectival clause |
| *they came <u>late</u>* | *they came <u>after it had started</u>* |
| adverb | adverbial clause |
| *he said his <u>farewell</u>* | *he said <u>that he was going now</u>* |
| noun | noun clause |

**Adjectival clauses** normally begin with pronouns like *who, whom, whose, which* and *that*. These are all <u>relative</u> pronouns:

*The car <u>which hurtled past</u> was green.*
*The banana <u>that was thrown out</u> struck me.*
*The driver <u>who threw the banana</u> was my uncle.*

**Adverbial clauses** answer the questions "when?" "where?" "how?" or "why?":

*<u>After he threw the banana</u> he laughed.*  When? (adverbial clause of time)
*He drove round the corner <u>where I couldn't see him</u>.*  Where? (adverbial clause of place)
*<u>As an eagle swoops on its prey</u> I hurtled after him.*  How? (adverbial clause of manner)
*I slipped over <u>because a banana peel lay on the gutter</u>.*  Why? (adverbial clause of reason)

**Noun clauses** usually explain what people are thinking, feeling or saying:

> *I suspect that I have a broken leg.*
> *I hope my uncle enjoyed his supper.*
> *He says that bananas are good for you.*
> *I know what you're going to say.*

For more about the way clauses work, see **adjectives**, **adverbs** and **nouns**.

## clayey

Because **clay** already ends in a y, you have to add -ey and not just -y to make it into an adjective:

> *The soil in this area is very clayey.*

For more about words like this, see **-y**.

## cliché / cliche

These are equally good ways of writing this word. This is a word borrowed from French and in the French spelling there is an acute accent over the e. Although words like this gradually lose their accent when they become settled into English, it is helpful to use the accent to show that the last syllable is pronounced to rhyme with *day*.

For more about accents in English, see **accents**. See also **acute accents**.

## clichés

**Clichés** are phrases which are used too often in the same situation, and sooner or later seem tired and uninspired. If you say somebody is "as old as the hills" you are using a **cliché**.

Clichés help people to say something on the spur of the moment. They are often used by politicians, teachers and others who have to speak in public without preparing every word. If you were writing a parody of the way such people talk, you might bring in a lot of their clichés.

Because clichés are such well-worn expressions, they cannot give much precision to a serious discussion. It is better to avoid them in essay writing. See **variety in writing**.

---

**Spot the clichés!**
"Unaccustomed as I am to public speaking, I stand before you tonight as one who has known just how hard it is to get blood out of a stone. But on this historic occasion, as the winds of change blow through, I am reminded of the many individuals who have sweated it out here over the nitty gritty."

---

## climatic / climactic

These adjectives sound and look similar but they are formed from different nouns.

**Climatic** has to do with the **climate** of a place:
*The climatic conditions made it hard to survive.*

**Climactic** has to do with a **climax**, which is the highest point or most important part of anything:
*The climactic scene of the film is when the hero rescues his fair maiden from the jaws of a giant ant.*

## climax

In some kinds of writing you can try to make an effect by building an argument or a mood step by step. There is an element of suspense in this which has to be released, and so there needs to be some event which everything that has gone before builds up to. This is called the **climax**.

There is nothing worse than setting out on the build-up to a climax and then letting it peter out unresolved. This creates what is called an **anticlimax** which leaves the reader feeling very dissatisfied. However, sometimes an anticlimax can be deliberately introduced for comic effect. For example:
*In the old house all was dark. The window rattled and the candle in my hand flickered and nearly went out. I could hear my breath going in and out. The door opened slowly. Then Mum came in and put the light on and we all went to bed.*

## cloth / clothe

These two words are related but mean different things.

**Cloth** is a fabric made by weaving wool, cotton, silk or anything like this.

To **clothe** someone is to give them clothes to wear.

## co-

The prefix co- usually implies doing something jointly with someone else, as in:

co-author     co-pilot     co-producer
co-star       co-tenant    co-worker

In these new or newish words which describe people's roles, the co- needs a hyphen if it is liable to be misread with the second part of the word. *Co-worker*, without its hyphen, might perhaps be misread as *coworker*.

In older words where co- is the first element, the hyphen rarely appears. For example:
nouns such as *coeducation* and *cosine*
adjectives such as *coaxial* and *covalent*
verbs such as *coexist* and *coincide*

Hyphens are sometimes seen in *co(-)operate* and *co(-)ordinate*, although this is done less and less now.

A hyphen is usually used in short (four-letter) words formed with co-, such as *co-ed* and *co-op*, to ensure they are read as two syllables.

### coarse / course

These words sound the same but have different meanings.

**Coarse** is an adjective. We call someone **coarse** if their behavior is rude and offensive. We call a substance **coarse** if it has large rather than fine grains, as in *coarse sand*.

**Course** is usually a noun. A **course** is one part of a meal, as in *the main course*. A **course** is also the ground or stretch of water where a race is held. Look up your dictionary for other meanings of this word.

## cohesion

If your writing is to hang together, there must be **cohesion** from one sentence to the next. Without cohesion the sentences won't "add up".

One basic thing makes for cohesion in both speech and writing, and that is concentrating on the same topic. But to make the cohesion more obvious, we usually have linking words from sentence to sentence, which refer to the same (or a similar) thing. We may repeat words, or use pronouns, or synonyms or antonyms. All four are used in the following:

> The *rabbits* all grew enormously. In three months *they*'d become the size of *puppies*. *They* made other *rabbits* look tiny. *They* pursued unwary visitors like *foxes*, and dug super-*bunny* holes in the dust. Our *rabbits* were too big for the largest *animal* cages in the market. *This* made them hard to handle.

Apart from the nouns and pronouns which give cohesion, there are verbs (*grew*, *become*) and other words (*enormously*, *tiny*, *largest*). The word *size* also links up with that last group. As you see, there is often more than one word making the cohesive links between sentences. Most of this cohesion comes quite naturally when you are telling a story.

In essay writing, it is also important to make cohesive links from sentence to sentence, and then you may have to think harder about them, at least when revising your writing. In argumentative writing, conjunctions such as *but*, *thus* and *therefore* help to make a strong and cohesive line of argument.

See **link words**.

## collar

Note the ending of this word. See **-ar**.

## collective nouns

**A collective noun** groups a number of items under the one heading. The word *team*, for instance, brings together a number of individuals into the one group, as do the words *government*, *company* and *crowd*. Does this mean that *team* is a singular word or a plural? Which of the following should we say?

> *The team are...*

or

> *The team is...*

Both ways are possible in English. The thing to do is to decide whether you want to stress the <u>group</u> nature of the noun or the fact that it's a collection of <u>individuals</u>. For example:

*The team <u>is</u> at the top of the competition this season.*
*The team <u>are</u> agreed on their tactics for this match.*

There is another group of nouns that act rather like collectives. They are the names of fish and animals. For example:

*The fish <u>are</u> ready to eat.*
*The deer <u>are</u> grazing in the park.*

These are like collective nouns because the singular form can be used when you are writing about more than one item. However, you always use a plural verb with these nouns if you are writing about more than one item. If you say *the deer <u>is</u>,* you can only be referring to one deer.

### collector

Note the ending of this word. See **-er/-or**.

### colloquialisms

are expressions that you use when talking and chatting, or when you're not taking your written language too seriously. Examples are:

*He was <u>a whizz</u> at making pancakes.*
*They wanted to <u>buzz off</u> as soon as the meal finished.*

Such expressions have an informal character, and if you use them in writing, they give an informal flavor to it. You would probably use them when writing dialogue, but not in formal essays.

### colonel / kernel

These words sound the same but mean different things. One is a person and the other is a nut.

A **colonel** is an officer in the army.

A **kernel** is the hard centre of a nut or fruit.

### colons ( : )

We use the colon to show that we are going to explain, or give examples of, whatever we have just written. For instance:

*The kennels cared for a number of breeds of dog: terriers, spaniels, corgis, labradors, and German shepherds.*

In informal writing, a dash could have been used in the above example instead of a colon. See **dashes**.

Colons can be used before quoting someone's speech:

*The teacher said: "Sit down in that chair!"*

Instead of a colon, you can use a comma here, or you can leave out the punctuation altogether. See **quotation marks**.

### combustible

Note the ending of this word. See **-able/-ible**.

## comedian / comedienne

These used to be the masculine and feminine forms of the word. A **comedian** was a man, and a **comedienne** was a woman. Nowadays **comedian** is used for both men and women. You might come across **comedienne** in your reading, but try to avoid it in your own writing. See **non-sexist language**.

## comedy

A **comedy** is a theatrical work which is light and humorous and has a happy ending. It can be a play, film or TV show. The **situation comedies** that are very popular on TV are comedies in which the humor is derived from situations in ordinary life.

## comically

Note the ending of this word. See **-ally**.

## commando

The plural of this word may be spelled **commandos** or **commandoes**. For more about words like this, see **-o**.

## commands

can be expressed in various ways:

*Shut the door!*
*Would you shut the door?*
*The door needs shutting.*
*I wonder if you'd shut the door.*
*Could you shut the door, please?*
*I wonder if you might be able to shut the door?*

These are only some of the ways of expressing your wish for something to be done. The plain use of the imperative mood (*Shut the door!*) sounds too abrupt for most purposes. Turning the command into a request by using the interrogative mood (*Would you...*) makes it sound more polite, as does turning it into a statement (*The door needs...*).

Introductory phrases like *I wonder if*, and polite terms like *please*, make the commands even more gentle. Words like *could* or *might* (*Could you do that...*) are also helpful in making commands sound more like polite requests.

For more about the imperative mood, see **mood**.

## commas ( , )

You use a comma to separate one item from another within a list:

*Bob ran through the final checklist for the party: drinks, food, records and, of course, the birthday cake.*

You use a comma when you want to separate one section of a sentence from another to make it easier to read:

*Many of his guests were going first to the beach, then on to the party.*

You may also want to separate one section of a sentence from another, to ensure the reader doesn't misread words from one phrase to the next:

*All along, the beach was covered in bluebottles.*

Without the comma, this sentence would not work for the reader. It would seem to lack a subject.

Commas sometimes mark off a part of a sentence which adds more information. This may be a <u>phrase</u>, for example:

*The lifesavers scraped all the bluebottles, <u>large and small</u>, into a hole and covered them with sand.*

Or it may be a <u>clause</u>:

*This meant that all of Bob's guests, <u>who were already in their swimming costumes</u>, could race in for a quick swim before the party.*

Note that without the commas in the above example, the meaning of the sentence would be different. It would then mean that only those of Bob's guests who were already in their swimming costumes could have a swim.

For information about the use of commas in numbers, see **numbers**.

### comment / commentate

These words are linked but have different meanings.

To **comment** is to make a remark or criticism.

To **commentate** is to make running commentaries, or write them, as a way of earning a living. The people who do this sort of work are called **commentators**.

### commit

Add another <u>t</u> when you add <u>-ed</u>, <u>-ing</u> or <u>-al</u> to this word to form **committed, committing** and **committal**. But don't add a <u>t</u> when you add <u>-ment</u> to form **commitment**. See **doubling of last letter**.

### common gender

This is a term occasionally applied to nouns which are both masculine and feminine at the same time. While *boy* is always only masculine and *headmistress* is always only feminine, *student* is said to be **common** because it can refer to both males and females. For more information on this, see **gender**.

### common nouns

You use **common nouns** to refer to ideas and types of things. *Beauty, dog, skateboard* and *flying* are all common nouns. They contrast with **proper nouns**, like *George, England* and *Apollo 11*, which are names of individual things.

Common nouns are divided into two types: **concrete nouns** (like *dog* and *skateboard*) and **abstract nouns** (like *beauty* and *flying*).

See **proper nouns, concrete nouns** and **abstract nouns**.

### comparatives

See **degrees of comparison**.

### compare / compere

These words look similar but have different meanings.

When we **compare** things we look for the similarities and differences between them, or we show how they are similar:
*Don't bother to compare your new hairstyle with hers.*
*You can compare your eye to a camera.*

A **compere** is someone who introduces the acts in a show. We pronounce this word with a stress on the first syllable com-.

### compare / contrast

These words both have to do with setting two things up for consideration, but there is a difference.

To **compare** two things is to look at them to see whether they are alike or not.

To **contrast** two things is to show what they do not have in common.

### comparisons

In essays you may be asked to compare two things — two works of art, or pieces of literature, two historical events or characters, and so on. You can choose one of two ways to present your comparison, either point by point, or in block form. For example, if you were comparing the causes of World War I and World War II, you could write about all the causes of one, and then all those of the other. This would be a block comparison. Or, you could compare first, say, the economic causes of both, then the political, then the social, and so on. This would be a point-by-point comparison.

### compass points

See **geographical terms** to find out how to write compass points.

### compatible

Note the ending of this word. See **-able/-ible**.

### compere

See **compare/compere**.

### competitor

Note the ending of this word. It is -or, not -er, because it came straight into English this way. See **-er/-or**.

### complement / compliment

These words sound the same but are different in meaning. It is the choice of the i or the e that makes all the difference.

A **compliment** is a flattering remark:
*Her performance drew compliments from all her listeners.*
To **compliment** someone is to say something nice about them.
**Complimentary** is the adjective from **compliment**.

A **complement** is the bit that is required to complete a set or make up a whole:

*That tie is the perfect complement to your outfit.*

To **complement** something is to go with it to make up a complete whole:

*This stamp complements the ones in your collection — now you have the whole set.*

**Complementary** is the adjective from **complement**.

## complex sentences

A **complex sentence** is one which has at least one dependent clause in it, as well as a main clause.

*I can't tell you <u>because I can't remember</u>.*

In this sentence, *I can't tell you* is the main clause and *because I can't remember* is a dependent clause. (See **clauses**.)

Complex sentences contrast with **compound sentences** and **simple sentences**, which have only main clauses in them.

## complex words

are ones which have at least two separate parts, but only one part which can stand on its own. For example:

   *sausage/s    <u>surf</u>/ing    un/<u>scorch</u>/ed*

In these words, only the part underlined is capable of standing on its own. This part is sometimes called the **root** of the word. The parts added to it are **affixes**.

Complex words are always written as single words, with no space between the root and the affix(es). Compare these with **compound words**.

## compliment

See **complement/compliment**.

## composition

is the art or business of getting your ideas together for a piece of writing.

**Compositions** are the pieces of writing you produce, which may be either imaginative or factual, depending on the subject.

## compound sentences

A **compound sentence** is one which is made up of two or more main clauses:

*<u>I know that</u> and <u>he knows it too</u>.*

Both underlined parts of this sentence are main clauses.

Compound sentences contrast with **complex sentences**, which have at least one dependent clause in them, and with **simple sentences**, which have only one main clause.

## compound verbs

A **compound verb** is a verb that is made up of more than one word. The basic compound verb is made up of an auxiliary verb (like *am*) and a participle (like *talking*): *I <u>am talking</u>.*

Compound verbs can have more than one auxiliary:
*He has been talking.*
*We could have talked.*
*They will have been talking.*

When you make questions or negative statements, you usually use a compound verb:
*Are they talking?*
*Do they talk much?*
*They did not talk all day.*

Note that in the last two examples, the auxiliary verb *do* and the infinitive of the verb *talk* are used to form the compound verb.

See **auxiliary verbs**, **participles** and **infinitives**.

### compound words

are those with at least two separate parts, both of which can stand on their own. Examples are:
    car park     cliff-hanger     surfboard     sunbaking
Note that compound words can have affixes attached to them, like the -er in *cliff-hanger* and the -ing in *sunbaking*.

Some compound words are written as a single word, or with hyphens, particularly if they are verbs or adjectives. But quite a lot of compound nouns are written (like *car park*) with a space between their parts.

Compare **complex words**.

### compressor

Note the ending of this word. See **-er/-or**.

### comprise

This is one of the few words ending in -ise that cannot also be spelled with -ize. It is always spelled **comprise**. For more about words like this, see **-ise/-ize**.

### compromise

This is one of the few words ending in -ise that cannot also be spelled with an -ize ending. It is always spelled **compromise**. For more about words like this, see **-ise/-ize**.

### compulsory

Note the ending of this word. See **-ary/-ery/-ory**.

### computer

Note that this word ends with -er, though others from the same field, such as *calculator* and *tabulator*, are spelled with -or. For more about words like this, see **-er/-or**.

### computers in writing

Computers can help make writing, and especially revising, easier. Some ways of making the most of them are described in WRITING WORKSHOP pp 17–19.

### concerto

The plural of this word may be spelled **concertos** or **concerti**. For more about words like this, see **-o**.

## conclusions

At the end of an essay you need a firm **conclusion**. It should leave the reader in no doubt as to the purpose of your writing. For more about writing conclusions, see WRITING WORKSHOP p 48.

## concord

This is another name for **agreement**. See **agreement**.

## concrete nouns

You use **concrete nouns** when writing about things that you can touch, hear, see, taste or smell. *Dog, skateboard, bread* and *vice-captain* are all concrete nouns.

They contrast with abstract nouns, such as *beauty* and *flying*. See **abstract nouns**.

## condenser

ends with -er although similar words such as **capacitor** and **compressor** are spelled with -or. For more about words like this, see **-er/-or**.

## conditional

Some languages that you may study have what is called a **conditional** aspect of the verb. It expresses what may happen if certain conditions are true.

English doesn't have the conditional aspect, so we use certain conjunctions like *if* and *unless* to do the job. Clauses with these conjunctions can be called **conditional clauses**.
*If it rains, the barbecue's off.*
*You can't do that unless you've got a licence.*

## conductor / conductress

People used to distinguish between the men and the women who sold or collected tickets on a bus, tram or train, by calling the man a **conductor** and the woman a **conductress**. Nowadays we consider that it is the job that counts, not the sex of the person doing it, and so we refer to both men and women as **conductors**. You may come across **conductress** in your reading but don't use it yourself.

See **non-sexist language**.

## confer

This verb is spelled with -rr- in **conferred** and **conferring**. But **conference** has only a single r because of the difference in stress.

For information about the way stress affects words like this, see **doubling of last letter**.

## conferencing

is talking with your teacher and other students about what you've written. They can tell you what a reader would get from your writing. And it helps to show you what might need to be revised or edited. See WRITING WORKSHOP pp 5, 7 and 14.

## confident / confidant

These words sound almost the same but mean different things.

To be **confident** is to be sure of yourself, and quite certain of the outcome of what you do.

A **confidant** is a person in whom you **confide**:
*Some children find that a teacher can be a friend and confidant.*
You may sometimes see this word spelled **confidante**. This is because it came into English from French, where a **confidant** was a man, and a **confidante** was a woman. Nowadays, in English, we don't make this distinction and use the spelling **confidant** for both.

## conjugations

In languages which have a complicated verb system, **conjugation** is the name given to the set of forms that you have to learn for each verb.

In Latin, for instance, the following is the present tense conjugation of the verb *amare*, "to love":

| | | | |
|---|---|---|---|
| *amo* | I love | *amamus* | we love |
| *amas* | you (singular) love | *amatis* | you (plural) love |
| *amat* | he/she loves | *amant* | they love |

Note that the English verb has only two forms in the present tense (*love* and *loves*). Most of the work here is done by the pronouns (*I, you, he,* etc.). So conjugations are not an important part of learning English.

## conjunctions

You use conjunctions in your writing to join together words, phrases, clauses and sentences. *And, but, or, since, if* and *when* are examples of conjunctions.

There are two types of conjunctions, **coordinating** and **subordinating**.

**Coordinating** conjunctions join items of the same grammatical type:
*table and chair* (noun + noun)
*up the street or down the road* (phrase + phrase)
*He was tired but she was lively.* (main clause + main clause)
*She said she could dance all night. And she was right.*
(sentence + sentence)

**Subordinating** conjunctions connect items of different types, such as a main clause and a dependent clause:
*I went to the door* (main clause) *when I heard someone knocking* (dependent clause).

Subordinating conjunctions tend to express a closer logical tie between the items:

| | |
|---|---|
| *The weather's terrible and I won't go.* | **coordinator** |
| *The weather's terrible so I won't go.* | **subordinator** |

In the second sentence, *so* indicates that there is a link of cause and effect between the clauses, while in the first sentence that link is not actually stated.

For more about the function of conjunctions, see **link words**.

## conjurer / conjuror

These are equally good spellings. See **-er/-or**.

## connectable / connectible

These are equally good spellings. See **-able/-ible**.

## connection / connexion

These are equally good spellings. See **-ction/-xion**.

## connote / denote

These words both refer to meaning but in different ways.

If one thing **denotes** another then it is a sign or indication of it:
   *Your furrowed brow denotes your great anxiety.*
When you talk about a word denoting something, you mean that the word is a sign or symbol for something that exists in reality. The word "dog" **denotes** a furry creature that eats bones and goes "woof". This "woofing" creature is the **denotation** of the word "dog".

If a word **connotes** something then it calls to mind a certain feeling, mood or set of associations. **Connotations** of words are often very personal, because the emotional quality or colour that you attach to words comes from your own experiences:
   *For me, the colour purple connotes mystery and sadness.*
   *Racist words have bad connotations.*

## conqueror

Note the ending of this word. See **-er/-or**.

## conservation

See **conversation/conservation**.

## consistency

In spelling and punctuating your work, you have some freedom of choice as this book shows. The most important thing is to make sure you keep to the same choice consistently in any piece of writing.

So if you choose the spelling *recognise*, then you shouldn't switch to *recognize* halfway through an essay. And you should spell other words of this kind with *-ise* rather than *-ize* throughout your writing. (See **-ise/-ize** if you are in doubt about this.)

If you prefer to use double quotation marks in writing direct speech, don't suddenly switch to single quotation marks.

Consistency in spelling and punctuation is one of the things to check when revising your work.

## console

This word has two pronunciations and two meanings.

To **console** someone (with the stress on -sole) is to comfort them or cheer them up:
   *He tried to console me when I failed my exam.*

A **console** (with the stress on con-) is a control panel, especially of a computer.

Note that the word **consul** looks and sounds rather like **console**. But a **consul** is an official sent by a government to represent it in a foreign country.

## consonants

are all the letters in the alphabet except <u>a</u>, <u>e</u>, <u>i</u>, <u>o</u>, and <u>u</u> (the **vowels**). Sometimes <u>y</u> is used as a vowel instead of as a consonant, as, for example, in *rhythm*.

Note that the consonant letters you write don't always represent a sound. In some words they are silent. See **silent letters**.

You can usually tell from its sound which consonant begins a word. But if there's any doubt, see APPENDIX A.

## consul

See **console**.

## contagious / infectious

Both these words mean something similar, but there is a difference when you use them to describe a disease.

An **infectious** illness is one that can spread from one person to another:
*Influenza is an infectious disease but appendicitis isn't.*

A **contagious** disease is an **infectious** disease which is spread by contact, either by direct contact with the sick person or by indirect contact with their clothes or bedding.

But otherwise both **contagious** and **infectious** have a more general meaning of "catching":
*Her laughter was contagious and soon the whole room was giggling.*
*She has an infectious smile.*

## contemptible

Note the ending of this word. See **-able/-ible**.

## contemptible / contemptuous

These words are both related to **contempt**, but they mean different things.

**Contemptible** means "deserving to be treated with contempt". The person or thing that is despised is **contemptible**:
*His cruelty to the cat was contemptible.*

**Contemptuous** means "treating someone or something with contempt". The person who is doing the despising is **contemptuous**:
*The bullies were contemptuous of his attempts at football.*

## contents

Most readers want to know at the start what the contents of a book are, and how they are divided up. A table of contents is printed very close to the front of a book, after the title page and preface (if any), but before the introduction. It shows you how many chapters or sections there are, and usually gives the chapter headings, to tell you what topics are discussed in each one.

## continual / continuous

These words are very close in meaning and indeed are sometimes interchangeable, but there can be a difference.

Something is **continual** if it is more or less constant over a period of time, that is, if it happens again and again:

> *Your continual moaning is driving me mad.*

The implication here is not that you moan from the moment that you get up in the morning till the moment you go to bed. You do spend time on other things like eating and going to school. But you do moan an awful lot so that it is a constant factor.

Something is **continuous** if it goes on without a break. If your moaning had been **continuous** you would not have paused to eat or go to school. You would have just moaned all the time. **Continuous** lines go on and on without a break and **continuous** surfaces have no gaps or holes in them.

## continuous aspect

Verbs in English are said to be **continuous** or **perfect** in aspect. A verb like *was running* is continuous, while *have run* is the perfect form. For more information about this, see **aspect**.

## contra-

See **counter-**.

## contractions

When you drop letters from the middle of a word or phrase to make it shorter, you're using a **contraction**. There are two types of **contraction**.

1  One type of **contraction** is an abbreviation. If a shortened form of a word begins with the first letter of the word and ends with its last letter, it is a contraction. Some examples are:

> Dr    Doctor       Mr    Mister
> rd    road         rm    room
> hcp   handicap     cmdr  commander

Note that contractions do not have full stops. For more about this, see **abbreviations**.

2  The other type of **contraction** is where letters are dropped from a two-word phrase, joining the words together. The position of the missing letters is marked by an apostrophe. Examples of contractions are underlined in the following sentences:

> *It's raining today. (it is)*
> *We can't ride our horses. (cannot)*
> *The horses don't like getting wet. (do not)*
> *We should've gone yesterday. (should have)*
> *Rain's a pain sometimes. (rain is)*
> *Maybe it'll stop tonight. (it will)*
>   Note that *can't* is a contraction of this type even though *cannot* is only one word.

Contractions give an informal tone to your writing. This can be useful for some kinds of writing, but doesn't suit more formal styles such as essay writing.

### contralto

The plural of this word may be spelled **contraltos** or **contralti**. For more about words like this, see **-o**.

### contrast

See **compare/contrast**.

### convener / convenor

These are equally good spellings. See **-er/-or**.

### conversation

For information on **conversations**, see **dialogue**.

### conversation / conservation

These similar words have quite different meanings.

A **conversation** is a talk or discussion. Someone who enjoys conversation or is clever at it is called a **conversationalist**.

**Conservation** is the protection of nature or historic buildings. Someone who cares a lot about nature and wants it protected is called a **conservationist**.

### converse

This word has two meanings, with different pronunciations. One is a verb and the other can be an adjective or a noun.

**Converse**, pronounced with the stress on the -verse, is a verb meaning "to have a talk":
*We often converse about music.*

**Converse**, pronounced with the stress on con-, means "opposite" or "the opposite":
*I hold the converse view about pollution.* (adjective)
*I think the converse is true.* (noun)

### convertible

Note the ending of this word. See **-able/-ible**.

### conveyer / conveyor

These are equally good spellings. See **-er/-or**.

### coordinating conjunctions

See **conjunctions**.

### coral / choral

These words sound the same but mean different things.

**Coral** is the hard skeleton of small sea animals. The Great Barrier Reef is made of coral.

Music is **choral** if it is sung by a choir or a chorus.

### cord / chord / cored

These words sound the same but mean different things.

A **cord** is a kind of light rope.

A **chord** is a set of musical notes sounded together.

**Cored** is the past form of **core**, to remove the centre from a piece of fruit:
*I cored the apples before I cut them up.*

### core / caw / corps

These words sound the same but have different meanings.

A **core** is at the centre of something, like the **core** of an apple.

Crows **caw**, as do some other birds. They make a harsh unpleasant sound.

A **corps** is a unit of soldiers.

### cored

See **cord/chord/cored**.

### coronary

Note the ending of this word. See **-ary/-ery/-ory**.

### corps / corpse

These two words look similar but they are pronounced differently and have different meanings.

**Corps** is pronounced to rhyme with *door* and refers to a unit of soldiers.

A **corpse** is a dead body. It is pronounced to rhyme with *warps*.

### corrections

Making **corrections** is what every good writer does before publishing their work. No-one writes a perfect piece straight off! It is the essential business of revising your work — or Stage 3 of the writing process. See WRITING WORKSHOP pp 4–17.

### correspondence

Note the ending of this word. See **-ance/-ence**.

### cost / costed

These words are both possible past forms of the verb **cost**. But they do not mean the same thing.

We use the verb **cost** to give the price paid for something:
*My bikini cost me £25.*
*His rudeness has cost him the top job.*

If you want the word to mean "to estimate the price of something", then you use **costed**:
*She has costed the job and decided that it is too expensive.*

## could / might

**Could** is the past tense of **can**, and so it can mean "was able":
*I could climb a coconut palm when I was younger.*

**Could** is also used in polite questions and requests:
*Could you help me please?*

**Could** and **might** both mean that something is possible:
*If the weather is fine, they could go to the beach.*
*If the weather is fine, they might go to the beach.*

When the possibility is in the past, you could use **could have**, **might have** or even **may have**:
*I might have been near Central Station when it happened.*
*I could have been near Central Station when it happened.*
*I may have been near Central Station when it happened.*

**Could** and **might** are both **modal verbs**. See **modal verbs**.

## couldn't

This is a contraction of the words **could not**. See **contractions**.

## could've

When you say "could've" it may sound like the words "could of". In fact it is short for "could have", so **could've** is the correct way to write it. It is wrong to use **could of** because **could** is never followed by **of**. For more information, see **of/have** and **contractions**.

## council / counsel

These words sound the same but have different meanings.

A **council** is an assembly of local politicians:
*We pay our rates to Richmond Council.*
A person on a **council** is sometimes called a **councillor**.

**Counsel** is advice or guidance. The student **counsellor** is there as an adviser and offers **counsel** on a number of topics, particularly choice of subjects and career. The **counsellor** runs a **counselling** service.

For information about whether to double the l when you add endings to the verb **counsel**, see **-l-/-ll-**.

## counter-

is a prefix meaning "in opposition to", as in:

| | | |
|---|---|---|
| counteract | counterattack | counterbalance |
| counterblast | counterespionage | counterrevolutionary |

You'll see that all these examples are written as one word. This helps to distinguish them from expressions like *counter lunch*, which is a compound. The first part of that compound has nothing to do with the prefix counter-, and everything to do with the counter in a pub.

Note that counter- means the same as the prefix contra-. This isn't surprising when you realise that counter- is simply the French way of treating the Latin contra-.

## counterfeit

is a word whose spelling does not follow the i before e pattern. See **i before e**.

## count nouns

A **count noun** is a common noun that refers to things that can be counted. You can tell them fairly easily because nearly all of them have a plural form, and they can be used with words like *many*. Words like *rabbit*, *piano* and *letter* are count nouns:

| | | | |
|---|---|---|---|
| *rabbit* | *many rabbits* | *sixteen rabbits* | *a few rabbits* |
| *piano* | *many pianos* | *two pianos* | *several pianos* |
| *letter* | *many letters* | *a hundred letters* | *numerous letters* |

**Count nouns** contrast with mass nouns, which cannot be used with the word *many*. A word like *much* must be used instead:
*much butter      a large amount of rice*

See **mass nouns**.

## coup / coupé

These words look similar but mean different things.

A **coup**, pronounced to rhyme with *shoe*, is a plan carried out successfully and without warning:
*There was a military coup on the island and the government was overthrown.*

A **coupé** is a car with two doors, often with front seats only. You can write it with or without the accent over the final e. It is pronounced *coo-pay*, but you may sometimes hear it pronounced to rhyme with *loop*.

## course

See **coarse/course**.

## court

See **caught/court**.

## creak / creek

These words sound the same but have different meanings.

A **creak** is a sharp, rough or squeaking sound. To **creak** is to make this sound.

A **creek** is a small stream.

## credible

Note the ending of this word. See **-able/-ible**.

## credible / creditable / credulous

These three words are similar but they mean different things.

If you do something **creditable**, it brings honour or praise:
*The school's performance at the swimming gala was creditable.*

**Credible** means "believable":
*Their account of the UFO sighting was hardly credible.*

Someone is **credulous** if they believe things too easily, without good reason:
*You were pretty credulous to believe our story about the UFO.*

## credit

Note that you don't add another t at the end of this word when you add the endings -ed, -ing and -or to form **credited**, **crediting** and **creditor**. See **doubling of last letter**.

## creditable

See **credible/creditable/credulous**.

## creditor

Note the ending of this word. See **-er/-or**.

## credulous

See **credible/creditable/credulous**.

## creek

See **creak/creek**.

## crematorium

The plural may be spelled **crematoriums** or **crematoria**. For more about words like this, see **-um**.

## crescendo

The plural is spelled **crescendos**. For more about words like this, see **-o**.

## crisis

The plural of this word is **crises**, with the last syllable pronounced to rhyme with *seas*. For more about words like this, see **-is**.

## criteria

This is a plural word. The singular is spelled **criterion**:
> The *criteria* the committee used to select staff *were* very difficult to meet.
> The single *criterion* for membership of the club *was* the ability to make people laugh.

See **-a (as a plural ending)**.

## cruel

You double the l to make **crueller** and **cruellest**. See **-l-/-ll-**.

## crystal

Double the l when you make the words **crystalline** and **crystallise/crystallize**.

Note that you may see the spelling **crystalize**, because that spelling is sometimes used in the USA.

See **-l-/-ll-** and **-ise/-ize**.

## -ction / -xion

A handful of words may still be spelled with either **-ction** or **-xion**:

| | |
|---|---|
| connection | connexion |
| deflection | deflexion |
| genuflection | genuflexion |
| inflection | inflexion |
| reflection | reflexion |

But the forms with **-ction** are now more common, probably because there are common verbs to link them with. For example:

| connect | *with* | connection |
| reflect | *with* | reflection |

With *complexion* there's no other spelling, probably because we don't have a verb *complect*.

### cue / queue

These words sound the same but have different meanings.

A **queue** is a line of people or cars waiting in turn.

A **cue** is a signal in the theatre for certain words or actions to occur:
> *This music is your cue to enter.*

A **cue** can also be a long stick used to hit the ball in games like snooker.

### cultivator

Note the ending of this word. See **-ator**.

### cumquat

See **kumquat/cumquat**.

### cupful

The plural of this word is **cupfuls**. For more about words like this, see **-ful**.

### curable

Note that you drop the e from the end of **cure** when you add -able. See **-e**.

### curator

Note the ending of this word. See **-ator**.

### curb / kerb

These words sound the same but have different meanings.

When you **curb** something you control it or hold it back:
> *You must curb your desire for cream cake.*

A **kerb** is the line of concrete or stones at the edge of a road.

### current / currant

These words sound the same but mean different things.

A **currant** is a small seedless raisin.

**Current** has several important meanings:
> *The river's current is strong here.*
> *Turn off the current at the switch.*
> *This is a sample of our current research.*
> *Is this really the current fashion?*

### curriculum

The plural of this word may be spelled **curriculums** or **curricula**. For more about words like this, see **-um**.

**cursor**

Note the ending of this word. It is -or, not -er, because it was borrowed straight from Latin. See **-er/-or**.

**cursory**

Note the ending of this word. See **-ary/-ery/-ory**.

**cyder**

See **cider/cyder**.

**cymbal / symbol**

These words sound the same but have different meanings.

A musician strikes the **cymbals** together to make a loud ringing sound.

A **symbol** is a token, or character used to represent something:
*The dove is a symbol of peace.*
*The symbol for a heart is* ♥.

**cypher / cipher**

These are equally good spellings. See **i / y**.

**czar**

See **tsar/czar**.

# Dd

### dairy / diary

These words look similar but mean different things.

A **diary** is a book in which you write what happens each day.

A **dairy** farm is one where cows are milked.

### dam / damn

These words sound the same but have different meanings.

To **dam** a river is to block its course. When you add endings to **dam**, it becomes **dammed** or **damming**:

*The river was dammed at the narrowest point.*

To **damn** is to ruin with fierce criticism, as in *a damning report.* It also means to curse:

*He damned the weather and everything.*

### dashes ( — )

are punctuation marks which are used:

1 to mark off a part of a sentence which may not be necessary, but which explains the topic further or adds interest to it.
   In this case, dashes work the same way as commas or brackets:

   *The fashion parade lasted so long — about three hours — that Prince Charles fell asleep.*

2 to show an abrupt break or pause in the structure of a sentence:

   *And suddenly, at the end of the film she — but I won't spoil it for you by telling you the ending.*

3 instead of colons at the beginning of an informal list:

   *He emptied out the contents of his pencil case — a rubber, two pencils, a pencil sharpener and a stapler.*

See also **commas** and **brackets**.

### data

**Data** can mean one block of information, or many individual items. So you may use it as a singular or plural noun.

150

Whichever you choose, remember that the verb and pronoun you use should be in agreement:

*The data <u>was</u> analysed carefully and results were calculated on the basis of <u>it</u>.* (**data** as a <u>singular</u> noun)

or

*As the data <u>were</u> collected <u>they</u> were quickly classified.* (**data** as a <u>plural</u> noun)

See **agreement**.

Note that one piece of information is sometimes called a **datum** in technical language.

For more about words like this, see **-a (as a plural ending)**.

### dates

You need to use dates in many kinds of writing – letters, essays, science reports and even creative work.

**Days, months and years** There are several different ways of writing dates. Here is the simplest way to write out a date in full:

4 May 1996

You use numbers for the day and the year but spell out the month. The order is day, month, year. There is no need for commas or any other punctuation between the words. This style works well for every kind of writing. Figures are used even in essays and other work where you would normally spell out small numbers.

You may also find dates written in the style *4th May 1996* or *May 4th 1996*. Both of these are also correct. The main point, as in all writing, is to convey your information as clearly and concisely as possible.

Sometimes numbers alone are used to write dates. There are several ways to do this:

4.5.96      4/5/96
4.5.1996    4/5/1996

These are convenient because they are quick to write and take up less space. But they can be misleading. In the UK the first number means the day, the second means the month and the third the year. In the USA the first is the month and the second is the day. So in the UK we would read the examples as 4 May 1996 but Americans would read them as 5 April 1996.

This style is mostly used for forms or notebooks, and sometimes at the head of letters.

Another method is often used with computers. Here the year comes first, followed by the month, then the day. Numbers less than ten have a zero in front of them. So 4 May 1996 would be written like this:

1996–05–04

**BC and AD** These abbreviations are often written with dates. **BC** is used to show a date before year 1 in our dating system. It is normally written after the year.

*In 55 BC Julius Caesar invaded Britain.*

**AD** is used to show a date of year 1 or later. It normally comes before the year.

*The battle of Hastings took place in AD 1066.*

For more detail about these abbreviations see **AD/BC**.

**Centuries** A century is a period of 100 years. The first century AD covers the years 1 to 100, the second century 101 to 200, and so on. The number of the century is always one greater than the number of hundreds in the year. So if you are writing about the 1800s you are writing about the nineteenth century, and the 1900s are the twentieth century.

Similarly, the first century BC includes the years 1 BC to 100 BC, the second century BC is the years 101 BC to 200 BC, and the nineteenth century BC covers the 1800s BC.

Special note: Strictly speaking, 1900 is the last year of the nineteenth century, not the first year of the twentieth, and so on for all round hundred years. Nevertheless many writers would refer to 1900 as the first year of the twentieth century.

A capital C is sometimes used as an abbreviation for the word *century*, coming either before or after the number. Other shortened forms are shown below, but in essays it is usual to spell out all the words:

| | | |
|---|---|---|
| 18C | 18thC | 18th century |
| C18 | C18th | 1700s |
| C18th | | |

## dative case

The dative is a case used in some languages you may study (but not in English). It works like the indirect object in English. So in the following sentences *them* and *her* would be in the dative case:

*I gave them the presents.*
*I bought her the wetsuit.*

In other languages there are special endings on nouns and pronouns to show that they're in the dative case.

See **case** and **object**.

## daughter-in-law

The plural is spelled **daughters-in-law**. The possessive is **daughter-in-law's**: *my daughter-in-law's husband.*

## de-

This prefix indicates the taking away of something, as in *defuse* or *dethrone*, or else the reducing or lowering of something, as in *decentralise* or *devalue*. People often invent new words with it, some close to home:

| | |
|---|---|
| defrost | delouse |
| demist | deodorant |

and some more technical ones:

| | |
|---|---|
| deactivate | decontaminate |
| defoliate | demilitarise |

The prefix is not normally used with a hyphen, except in very short new words such as *de-ice*. Without the hyphen it could be misread as one syllable.

### dear / deer

These words sound the same but have different meanings.

A **deer** is a large grass-eating animal.

Someone or something is **dear** to you if you love them very much. Something you buy is **dear** if you pay a lot of money for it.

### debtor

Note the ending of this word. See **-er/-or**.

### deceased

See **diseased/deceased**.

### declension

In languages which have a complicated system of nouns, **declension** is the name given to the set of forms that you have to learn for each noun.

In Latin, for instance, each noun may appear in six different cases for both singular and plural. Though some forms are the same, you still have a lot of different forms to learn for each noun.

If you give the declension for an English noun, there are only two forms, each with a plural:

*dog* (singular) ⎱ subjective or objective case
*dogs* (plural) ⎰

*dog's* (singular) ⎱ possessive case
*dogs'* (plural) ⎰

So declensions are not an important part of learning English.

See **case**.

### deduce / deduct

These words look similar but mean different things.

To **deduce** something is to work it out by reasoning:
*I deduce that it is raining outside from the fact that your shoes are wet.*

To **deduct** something is to subtract it or take it away:
*I will deduct a pound from your pocket money.*

The noun form for both **deduce** and **deduct** is **deduction**.

### deductable / deductible

These are equally good spellings. See **-able/-ible**.

### deer

This word is usually spelled the same way whether it is singular or plural:
*The baby deer (who was barely able to walk) joined the three other deer resting near the river.*
Note, however, that you may sometimes see the plural spelled **deers**.

**Deer** is often used collectively:
*Deer are very timid animals.*
See **collective nouns**. See also **dear/deer**.

## defence / defense

These are equally good ways of spelling this word.

**Defence** is more common in the UK, and **defense** is the usual spelling in the USA.

Whenever this word is made into an adjective by adding -ive, it is spelled with an s not a c:
*The knight was wearing defensive armor.*

For more about words like this, see **-ce/-se**.

## defendant

Note the ending of this word. See **-ant/-ent**.

## defense

See **defence/defense**.

## defer

Add another r when you add -ed, -ing, or -al to this word: **deferred, deferring, deferral**. But don't add another r when you add -ence: **deference**.

See **doubling of last letter**. See also **differ/defer**.

## definite articles

The word *the* in English is called the **definite article**. It comes before a noun, and you use it when the noun has already been referred to, or when the noun is about to be identified. For example:
*Phil Collins released a new single last week. The record is already number one in the charts.*
*The rumour that you were leaving school . . .*

Definite articles contrast with the **indefinite articles** such as *a* and *an*, which imply that the noun is as yet unidentified.

## deflection / deflexion

These are equally good spellings. See **-ction/-xion**.

## degrees of comparison

Adjectives and adverbs can be given special endings to show when you are comparing one thing with others:

| | | |
|---|---|---|
| clean | cleaner | cleanest |
| fast | faster | fastest |

The -er form is known as the **comparative**, and you use it when you're comparing two things. The -est form is called the **superlative**, and it's used to compare more than two. The basic form without endings is called the **positive**.

Some adjectives and adverbs, especially those with two or more syllables, don't take these endings. We use *more* and *most* to do the job instead:

| | | |
|---|---|---|
| beautiful | more beautiful | most beautiful |

## deign

Note that e comes before i in this word. See **i before e**.

### delusion / illusion

These words are often confused, partly because they look and sound alike and partly because they both have to do with mistaken notions about reality.

An **illusion** is when our eyes deceive us about something. When a magician pulls a rabbit out of a hat, that is an **illusion**. It can also mean "a false impression", as when you have an **illusion** of freedom.

The word **delusion** suggests that your own beliefs and perceptions are distorted. If you think that you are Napoleon then you are suffering from a **delusion**. To have *delusions of grandeur* is to think that you are more important than you really are.

**Illusions** are usually fleeting things whereas **delusions** are often established over a long period of time.

### demonstratives

We use **demonstratives** in English to point out specific persons or things. There are only four, and all begin with <u>th-</u>:

this    that    these    those

They can act as either adjectives or pronouns.

> <u>*This*</u> *is what I mean.* (pronoun)
> <u>*Those*</u> *are the ones.* (pronoun)
> <u>*That*</u> *guitar* . . . (adjective)
> *Are* <u>*these*</u> *books yours?* (adjective)

They are important because they create links with other words in the text. For more information on this, see **cohesion** and **link words**.

### demonstrator

Note the ending of this word. See **-ator**.

### denominator

Note the ending of this word. See **-ator**.

### denote

See **connote/denote**.

### denouement

The **denouement** of a story is the moment when all the complications of the plot are resolved, all the loose ends tied up, all the mysteries explained. It usually comes after a big climax. You will find a clear example of a denouement in a detective story. There is always the chapter at the end after the villain is unmasked, in which all the mysterious events are explained.

### dependent / dependant

These are equally good ways of spelling this word, whether you are using the noun or the adjective. For more about words like this, see **-ant/-ent**.

### dependent clauses

Some clauses are not complete enough in themselves to form a sentence on their own. We call them **dependent clauses**. For more information, see **clauses**.

### depression / recession

When used in economics, these terms refer to similar circumstances, but there is a difference.

A **recession** is a downturn in the economy for a small period of time.

A **depression** is a downturn in the economy lasting for a long period of time. It is a major economic and social crisis.

### descendant / descendent

These are equally good spellings. See **-ant/-ent**.

### descriptive writing

With descriptive writing you can create a whole world for your reader − lively and colorful, or sinister and spine-chilling. It could be based on something you've actually seen, or you could invent it out of your imagination. Descriptions are important not only in creative and personal writing, but also in factual writing and reporting. See WRITING WORKSHOP pp 42−4 for an example.

### desert / dessert

These words look similar and can sound the same, but there are differences.

A **dessert**, pronounced with the stress on the second syllable, is a sweet dish served at the end of a meal.

A **desert**, with the stress on the first syllable, is an arid piece of land, often covered with sand:
*The Sahara is the most famous desert in the world.*

To **desert** someone, with the stress on the second syllable, is to leave them in the lurch:
*Don't desert me when I am in danger.*

If you get your **just deserts** then you get what you have justly earned either as reward or punishment:
*Don't worry, he is so nasty that eventually he will get his just deserts.*

### despatch

See **dispatch/despatch**.

### dessert

See **desert/dessert**.

### destructible

Note the ending of this word. See **-able/-ible**.

### detective story

See **thriller**.

### detector

Note the ending of this word. See **-er/-or**.

### detonator

Note the ending of this word. See **-ator**.

### develop

Note that you don't add another p at the end of this word when you add the endings -ed, -ing, -er and -ment: **developed, developing, developer, development.**

### device / devise

These words are pronounced differently but they work in the same way as *practice* and *practise*, that is, the -ice word is the noun and the -ise word is the verb.

**Devise** is the verb. To **devise** something is to contrive it or work it out:

*I will devise a way of going to the pictures this weekend.*

Note that this verb can never end in -ize. It is always spelled **devise**.

A **device** is a tool or implement, particularly one that has been cunningly contrived:

*This ingenious device can be used as both a CD player and a bottle opener.*

For more about words like this, see **-ce/-se**.

### devil

For information about whether to double the l when you add endings like -ed or -ing, see **-l-/-ll-**.

### dew / due

These words sound the same but have different meanings.

**Dew** appears as beads of water on the grass in the early morning.

Your **due** is what is owed to you:

*When the goodies are handed out you will get your due.*

**Due** also means "expected to arrive":

*The maths assignment is due on Friday.*

### diagnosis

The plural is spelled **diagnoses**, with the last syllable rhyming with *seas*. For more about words like this, see **-is**.

### diagnosis / prognosis

These are both medical terms, although they have more general meanings.

A **diagnosis** is a doctor's analysis of what is wrong with a patient:

*The doctor's diagnosis is that you have glandular fever.*

A **prognosis** is the next step that the doctor takes after making a **diagnosis**. It is an informed guess as to what course the illness will take:

*The doctor's prognosis is that you will have a fever for two weeks.*

## dial

For information about whether to double the l when you add endings like -ed or -ing, see -l-/-ll-.

## dialect

A dialect is a special variety of any language, one which is used in a particular region or by a particular group of speakers. We're most aware of it when listening to someone whose speech is different from our own (because it sounds American or Australian, say) – though British speech is really a dialect too.

A dialect has its own special features of accent and vocabulary, and sometimes grammar as well. All these things can make one dialect different from another, and, of course, the more differences there are, the harder it is for people of different dialects to understand each other. A Scottish dialect differs in accent, vocabulary and grammar from a southern British one, whereas a southern British dialect and Australian English do not differ much except in accent.

## dialogue

**Dialogue** is the exchange of words between two or more people. When reporting or writing dialogue, you always start a new line when a different person begins to speak:
*"Knock knock."*
*"Who's there?"*
*"Lettuce."*
*"Lettuce who?"*
*"Let us in and I'll tell you."*

When you write dialogue you usually want to make the speakers' words sound like real conversation. So you'll need to use the kind of language which goes naturally with talk, such as **contractions** and **colloquialisms**.

Some uses of dialogue are explained in the WRITING WORKSHOP.

## diary

See **dairy/diary**.

## dice

is really a *plural* word – the singular is spelled **die**. But we can use **dice** as a singular noun, and when we do the verb and pronoun we use with it must also be in the singular:
*This dice is black with white spots on it.*

## dictator

Note the ending of this word. See **-ator**.

## did

This is a form of the verb **to do**. See **do**.

## didn't

This is short for **did not**. See **contractions**.

### die / dye

These words sound the same but have different meanings.

To **die** is to exit from life.

To **dye** something is to colour it with a **dye** or colouring agent:
*I'm sick of my brown hair — I'm going to dye it black.*

### dieresis (¨)

A **dieresis** is the mark used when you want to show that two vowels side by side are pronounced separately. In English you might use it with names like *Chloë* and *Noël*. It is placed over the second of the two vowels.

Although it looks like an umlaut in German, its function is different, as we've seen. See **umlaut**.

The plural of **dieresis** is spelled **diereses**, with the last syllable rhyming with *seas*. See **-is**.

Note that you may also find this word spelled **diaeresis**. See **-ae-**.

### differ / defer

These words are similar but have different meanings.

To **differ** is to be different:
*This chair differs from that because it's plastic.*

To **defer** is to put off to another time:
*My exams have been deferred for another month.*
If you **defer to** someone's wishes, you do what they want rather than what you want.

### different to / from / than

You will see the word **different** followed by **to, from** and **than**.

**Different from** has traditionally been the form that people prefer:
*That kitten is different from the rest of the litter.*

**Different to** is often used as a perfectly acceptable alternative:
*Your uniform is different to mine.*

While **different than** is commonly used in speech, it is still discouraged in written work.

### digestible

Note the ending of this word. See **-able/-ible**.

### dike / dyke

These are equally good spellings. See **i/y**.

### diminish / minimise

These words have similar meanings but they are not exactly the same.

To **diminish** is to make or become smaller or less:
*You'll diminish our store of provisions if you eat so much.*

To **minimise** is to reduce something to the smallest possible amount:
*We must minimise what we eat each day if we hope to survive.*

## dinghy / dingy

These words look similar but they mean different things.

A **dinghy** is a small rowing or sailing boat. We pronounce this noun _ding-gee_.

Something is **dingy** if it looks dirty or shabby. We pronounce this adjective _din-jee_.

## dingy

See **dinghy/dingy**.

## direct object

See **object**.

## direct speech

When you want to record or write down what someone said, you can do it either directly or indirectly. With **direct speech** you would quote the words actually spoken, as in:

_The Minister said, "There's no such thing as society."_

The quotation marks show that these were exactly the words used. This is the most dramatic way to present speech, because it is written in the same direct way as it was uttered.

A less direct way of doing it is to write it as **indirect speech**:

_The Minister said that there is no such thing as society._

In this version there are no quotation marks because the Minister's remarks have been translated a little by the writer.

For more information, see **indirect speech**.

## dis-

This prefix indicates the opposite or undoing of the word it is joined to, as in:

disarm     disappear     disinfect     dislike     distrust

The meaning is clearest in words like these, which have been formed in modern English.

In words which were borrowed ready-made from Latin or French, such as:

disappoint     discriminate     discuss     display     distance

the prefix has been absorbed into the total meaning of the word.

Contrast the prefix _dys-_, which means "faulty" or "poor". It is found in technical words in medicine and psychology such as _dysfunction_, _dyslexia_ and _dysentery_.

## disastrous

Note that **disaster** loses its _e_ when you add _-ous_.

## disc / disk

**Disc** is the spelling we use when we are talking about a thin, flat, circular object, especially a gramophone record, or a part of the spine, as in _a slipped disc_.

**Disk** is the spelling we usually use when we are referring to the circular object used in computers for storing data. This is also called a **floppy disk** or a **diskette**.

Note, however, that the relatively new **compact discs** are not spelled with a _k_.

### discreet / discrete

These words look and sound similar but they have different meanings. Both come from a Latin word meaning "separated".

You are **discreet** if you are careful about what you say. Something is **discreet** if it does not draw attention to itself:
*The opera singer wore a dress of discreet elegance.*

We say that something is **discrete** if it is separate or distinct from other things.

### diseased / deceased

These words look similar but have different meanings.

If someone or something has a disease they are **diseased**:
*After years of smoking, my uncle's lungs are diseased.*

If someone is **deceased** they have died.

### disembowel

You have a choice whether or not to double the l when you add -ed or -ing to this word. See **-l-/-ll-**.

Note that when you add -ment, the l is never doubled:
**disembowelment**.

### dishevel

You have a choice whether or not to double the l when you add -ed or -ing to this word. See **-l-/-ll-**.

Note that when you add -ment, the l is never doubled:
**dishevelment**.

### disinterested / uninterested

The main part of these words is the same but they begin with different prefixes. They also mean different things.

A **disinterested** person is one who is free from bias and self-interest:
*A judge has to act as the disinterested controller of a court.*

**Uninterested** means "not interested" and is the opposite of **interested**:
*She was so uninterested in the proceedings that she left the courtroom.*

### disk

See **disc/disk**.

### dispatch / despatch

These are equally good ways of spelling this word. Choose whichever you like, but make sure you use the same spelling throughout your work.

### dispensary

Note the ending of this word. See **-ary/-ery/-ory**.

### distributor

Note the ending of this word. See **-er/-or**.

# ditto ( " )

**Ditto marks** are used to indicate that the word above them is to be repeated:

*George ate four potatoes.*
*Harry    "      "        "    .*

This means that Harry also ate four potatoes.

Some people disapprove of ditto marks in general writing, though their use can sometimes make tables easier to read. As with all writing, your use of ditto marks should be to make things as clear and simple for the reader as possible.

# divisible

Note the ending of this word. See **-able/-ible**.

# do

One of the most common verbs in English is the verb **to do**. It appears in several different forms, and some of them look quite different to **do**:

| *Present* | *Past* |
|---|---|
| (I, you, we, they) **do** | (I, you, he, she, it, we, they) **did** |
| (he, she, it) **does** | |
| **doing** (*present participle*) | **done** (*past participle*) |

You shouldn't use **done** without **has** or **have** before it, unless you're writing down ungrammatical speech or dialogue:

*Who done it?*     WRONG
*Who has done it?*     RIGHT
*Who did it?*     RIGHT

**Do** is also used as a modal verb (a type of auxiliary verb). We use it to form questions and negative statements:

They know.   *becomes*   <u>Do</u> they know? (question)
*and*   They <u>do</u> not know. (negative)

See **modal verbs**.

# doctor

Note the ending of this word. See **-er/-or**.

# documentary

A **documentary** is the factual presentation of an interesting topic for television, radio or film. There is usually some analysis of the important issues involved so that the audience have an informed overview of the subject. It is the equivalent of the feature article in journalism.

# doe / dough

These words sound the same but have different meanings.

A **doe** is the female of animals such as deer, rabbits and kangaroos.

**Dough** is a mixture of flour and water or milk which is baked to make bread or pastry. It is also an informal word for money.

# does

This is a form of the verb **to do**. See **do**.

# doesn't

This is short for **does not**. See **contractions**.

### domino

The plural of this word may be spelled **dominos** or **dominoes**. For more about words like this, see **-o**.

### donkey

The plural is spelled **donkeys**. For more about words like this, see **-ey**.

### donor

Note the ending of this word. See **-er/-or**.

### don't

This is short for **do not**. See **contractions**.

### dormitory

Note the ending of this word. See **-ary/-ery/-ory**.

### double negatives

There have been times in the history of our language when it was possible to stack up negative words in a sentence (like *no, not, never*) to emphasise your point. It is not possible to do that today in standard English — people will say that two negatives make a positive, as in maths:

*I haven't got no money.*

This sentence could be taken to mean that you <u>have</u> got some money!

Even words like *hardly* and *scarcely* are regarded as negatives:

*I can't hardly do it.*

Sentences like this are not acceptable in standard writing or speech (although there may be occasions when you want to include them in informal dialogue to indicate emphasis).

Note also that the use of double negatives can be quite deliberate in formal writing. It can give a quality of understatement to your writing:

*I was not unimpressed by the sight of Stonehenge at dawn.*

### doubling of last letter

Many words which end in a single consonant will double it before adding suffixes <u>beginning with a vowel</u> (or with <u>-y</u>). This is most common with verbs:

| | | | |
|---|---|---|---|
| chat | chatted | chatting | (chatter, chatty) |
| plan | planned | planning | (planner) |

But it also happens with adjectives:

| | | |
|---|---|---|
| sad | sadder | saddest |
| slim | slimmer | slimmest |

Though this is the general pattern, there is a let-out rule which we don't so often think about: If the vowel of the word is spelled with two letters (that is, it is a <u>digraph</u>) there is no need to double the final consonant. This is what happens in:

| | | | |
|---|---|---|---|
| float | floated | floating | (floater) |
| sweet | sweeter | sweetest | |

Things get a bit more complicated when the <u>base</u> word has two syllables. The let-out rule applies to words with a digraph:

| | | | |
|---|---|---|---|
| repeat | repeated | repeating | (repeatable) |

But when there's a single vowel in the last syllable, you have to ask whether it's stressed or not. Notice that the second syllable of *regret* has stronger stress than the first. That is why the t is doubled in *regretted* and *regretting*. But whenever a word has strong stress on the first syllable, we leave the final consonant alone before an ending. Think of *rocketed*, and how it differs from *regretted*.

This is why we double the:

| | | | | |
|---|---|---|---|---|
| t | *in* | admitted | *but not in* | audited |
| n | *in* | beginning | *but not in* | buttoning |
| r | *in* | deferred | *but not in* | differed |
| r | *in* | deterring | *but not in* | lettering |
| r | *in* | occurred | *but not in* | offered |

Check also:

| | | |
|---|---|---|
| conferred | *versus* | conference |
| preferred | *versus* | preference |
| referred | *versus* | reference |

So words which have their stress early are also let off from the general rule of doubling before endings. This is really a second let-out rule.

In fact this means that there is no need to double the last letter of the many words of two or more syllables which have begun to work as verbs in twentieth-century English. They include:

| | | | |
|---|---|---|---|
| balloted | bias(s)ed | budgeted | cordoned |
| focus(s)ed | galloped | marketed | zippered |

The simple spelling of the root, with no doubling of the last consonant, is normal in such words (apart from a little variation for the ones ending in s). The simple spelling makes the root clear, and has much to recommend it.

**Exceptions**: There are words of two syllables like those above which do not usually keep their simple spelling. A small set of exceptions are the words whose last syllable could stand on its own, like:

| | | |
|---|---|---|
| handicap | (*cap* . . .) | handicapped |
| program | (*gram* . . .) | programmed |
| kidnap | (*nap* . . .) | kidnapped |
| worship | (*ship* . . .) | worshipped |
| waterlog | (*log* . . .) | waterlogged |

The spellings with the double consonants are probably the result of writers thinking about what they would do with the last syllable if it were on its own. The tendency to "double" in such words is less strong in the USA than in the UK.

For information on whether to double the final l in words like *travel* and *cancel*, see **-l-/-ll-**.

**Final notes**:

1. Words which end in -c, such as *panic*, take a k (not another c) before -ed, -ing and the like. See **-c/-ck-**.

2. Words ending in -x never have that x doubled:

| | | |
|---|---|---|
| box | boxed | boxing |
| transfix | transfixed | transfixing |

### dough

See **doe/dough**.

### doughnut

is the usual spelling of this word. You may also find it spelled **donut**.

### downward / downwards

For information about this pair of words, see **-ward/-wards**.

### draft / draught

These words sound the same but mean different things.

A **draft** is a rough plan or piece of writing, or a letter instructing the bank to pay money. In the USA **the draft** is the forcing of people to join the armed forces.

A **draught** is a current of air or wind. It is also a rather old-fashioned word for a drink.

### drafting of essays

You draft an essay in three major steps or stages. See WRITING WORKSHOP p 4.

### draftsman / draughtsman

These words may be used interchangeably but many people use them to mean different things.

A **draftsman** is someone who writes legal documents.

In architecture and building, a **draughtsman** draws up sketches, plans or designs.

You might note that these words both end with the suffix -man. Nowadays this is thought to be a sexist ending because it favors men. You could use alternatives, such as
    *draftsperson/draughtsperson* or *drafter/draughter*.

See **non-sexist language**.

### drama

is the general name for literary works that are intended to be performed by actors. A play is a work of drama, and it can be written in prose or poetry.

The story of a play takes place entirely through the dialogue and action of the characters. So, unlike a novel or poem, a play doesn't usually allow the writer's own feelings or ideas to be expressed directly. See **dialogue**.

For more about the two major types of drama, see **comedy** and **tragedy**.

### dramatically

Note the ending of this word. See **-ally**.

### drastically

Note the ending of this word. See **-ally**.

### draught

See **draft/draught**.

## draughtsman

See **draftsman/draughtsman**.

## draw / drawer

These words sound the same but have different meanings.

A contest where neither side wins is a **draw**.

A **drawer** is the part of a cupboard or desk that slides in and out. **Drawers** can be a set of sliding containers, as in a *chest of drawers*. It can also be a rather old-fashioned word for underpants.

## dreamed / dreamt

These are equally good ways of spelling the past form of **dream**.
*I dreamed      I have dreamed*
*I dreamt       I have dreamt*
For more about words like this, see **-ed/-t**.

## drier / dryer

These are equally good ways of spelling this word, which comes from **dry**.

Both the adjective (meaning "more dry") and the noun ("something that dries") can be spelled **drier** or **dryer**. For more about words like this, see **y→i**.

## drily / dryly

These are equally good ways of spelling this word. For more about words like this, see **y→i**.

## drivel

For information about whether to double the l when you add endings like -ed or -ing, or -er, see **-l-/-ll-**.

## dryer

See **drier/dryer**.

## dryly

See **drily/dryly**.

## dual / duel

These words sound the same but have different meanings. The first is an adjective and the second a noun.

**Dual** has to do with two or having two parts:
*This computer game has dual controls.*
*The film has a dual purpose — to show you the Welsh landscape and to make you laugh.*

A **duel** is a fight or contest between two people using swords or pistols.

For information about whether to double the l when you add endings to the verb **duel**, see **-l-/-ll-**.

## due

See **dew/due**.

## duel

See **dual/duel**.

## duplex

The plural of this word is **duplexes**. For more about words like this, see **-x**.

## dwarf

The plural of this word may be spelled **dwarfs** or **dwarves**. For more about words like this, see **-f/-v-**.

## dye

See **die/dye**.

## dyeing / dying

These words sound the same but mean different things.

**Dyeing** is a form of the verb **dye**, meaning "to colour with a liquid":

*She is dyeing her hair purple.*

**Dying** is a form of the verb **die**, meaning "to stop living".

## dyke

See **dike/dyke**.

## dynamo

The plural of this word is spelled **dynamos**. For more about words like this, see **-o**.

## dys-

See **dis-**.

**-e**

Words that end in -e often lose this e when they become part of a longer word. It happens with all kinds of words.

The final -e disappears before an ending which begins with a vowel vowel (a, e, i, or o), or with y. Here are some common examples:

| | | | |
|---|---|---|---|
| not(e) | -able | *becomes* | notable |
| dos(e) | -age | | dosage |
| propos(e) | -al | | proposal |
| reserv(e) | -ation | | reservation |
| driv(e) | -er | | driver |
| simpl(e) | -er | | simpler |
| simpl(e) | -est | | simplest |
| fals(e) | -ify | | falsify |
| pressur(e) | -isation | | pressurisation |
| pressur(e) | -ise | | pressurise |
| styl(e) | -ish | | stylish |
| elit(e) | -ism | | elitism |
| typ(e) | -ist | | typist |
| immun(e) | -ity | | immunity |
| adventur(e) | -ous | | adventurous |
| choos(e) | -y | | choosy |

But when you add an ending which begins with a consonant, the e is kept. For example:

| | | | |
|---|---|---|---|
| hope | -ful | *becomes* | hopeful |
| shape | -ly | | shapely |
| measure | -ment | | measurement |
| rude | -ness | | rudeness |

This is why we spell *hopeful* with an e, and *hoping* without it, and why *closeness* has an e, but *closing* doesn't.

Note that there are a few small groups of words which keep the e, even when you add an ending beginning with a vowel:

1 Words ending in -ce and -ge keep their e before endings beginning with a and o. For example *trace*, *change* and *courage* have to keep their e, so that they still have an s sound as in *traceable*, or a j sound as in *changeable* and *courageous*.

See **-ce/-ge**.

168

**2** A few verbs ending in -inge keep their e before an ending with -i, for example *singeing, whingeing*. The reason with *singeing* is clear: without the -e it would be *singing*. With *whingeing* there is no such problem, and the spelling *whinging* is also used.

There is no reason for the -e in the following: *cringing* (from *cringe*), *hinging* (from *hinge*), *impinging* (from *impinge*), *tinging* (from *tinge*), *twinging* (from *twinge*).

None of these could be mistaken for another word.

**3** Words ending in -oe, such as *canoe*, *hoe*, and *toe* keep their -e before -ing, as in *canoeing*, *hoeing* and *toeing*. But they lose it, according to the general pattern, before -ed: *canoed*, *hoed* and *toed*.

**4** Words ending in -ue, such as *glue*, keep their -e before adding a -y, as in *gluey*. It is needed to make the second syllable. (Without it they would be *gluy*, and look as if they sounded like *buy*.) Before other endings such as -ed or -ing, the -e is dropped: *gluing*.

**5** The verb *dye* keeps its e before -ing (and becomes *dyeing*) to make it different from *dying* (from the verb *die*).

Special note: Words ending in -ie, for example *die*, *lie*, *tie* and *vie*, change in two ways when the ending is -ing. They drop their -e, and change i to y. Thus they become *dying*, *lying*, *tying*, *vying*.

See **i→y**.


## e as a silent letter

The letter e is written but not sounded in many English words, such as:

    love    some    freeze    tongue    discipline

It is often silent at the end of a word.

The e often shows that a previous vowel is pronounced long. For example, the e on *bite* makes the previous vowel different from the one in *bit*. It is exactly the same in:

| | | |
|---|---|---|
| rate | *compare with* | rat |
| mete | | met |
| robe | | rob |
| tube | | tub |

Once again, the e on the end of these words has no sound in itself.

But as words like *manageable* show, the -e also helps to indicate how neighboring sounds are pronounced. There it shows that the g before it sounds like *j*, but it has no sound itself.

For more about silent letters, see **silent letters**.


## each

See **both/each**.

## each / every / either / neither

All of these words are said to be singular words, so in formal writing you should say *each (of them) is* . . . or *each is* . . . and so on, not *each (of them) are* . . . or *each are* . . .

However, in speech and in informal styles of writing, these words are often treated as if they were plural:
*Each of the boys are getting paid.*

See **agreement**.

## -ean

This ending mostly appears on geographical adjectives, such as:
    Chilean    Crimean    European    Korean
Note that you stress the e in -ean when you say these words, and that there's an e in all the place names they build on (Chile, Crimea). This will help to remind you that they are -ean and not -ian.

## earn / urn

These words sound the same but have different meanings. The first is a verb and the second is a noun.

To **earn** is to receive something in return for working, or to deserve to get something.

An **urn** is a kind of vase. It is also a container with a tap, for heating water.

## -e(a)u

Words ending in -eu, like *adieu*, or -eau, like *plateau*, are borrowings from French. In French their plurals are *adieux* and *plateaux*, and the -x plurals are retained in English. Like most borrowed words, they are sometimes given English plurals with -s, and you may see the spellings *adieus* and *plateaus*.

## echo

The plural of this word is spelled **echoes**. This is one of the few surviving English nouns ending in -o which does not form its plural by simply adding -s. For more about words like this, see **-o**.

## ecology / environment

These words both have to do with the world around us, but they mean different things.

Your **environment** is everything that surrounds you:
*They grew up in a rural environment.*
It can also be the physical conditions of a place, such as weather, water, vegetation and buildings.

**Ecology** is the study of the relationship between living things and their **environment**.

## economic / economical

These words are related but they have different meanings.

**Economic** means "concerned with how the money, industry and trade of a place or group is organised":
*We are entering a golden age in British economic growth.*

**Economical** means "not wasteful":
*What an economical use of your time!*
You can also say *an economic use of time.*

Note that **economically** is the adverb for both **economic** and **economical**. See **-ally.**

## -ed

The ending -ed is often used to make the past form of a verb.
For example:

| | |
|---|---|
| climb | climbed |
| hose | hosed |
| part | parted |
| want | wanted |

In some cases (*parted* and *wanted*) it makes an extra syllable. In others (*climbed* and *hosed*) you just hear a *d* sound.

Some verbs form their past tense and past participle with different spellings. See **past forms**, **irregular verbs** and **-ed/-(e)n.**

For a small group of verbs, there are two possible ways of writing the past form. See **-ed/-t.**

Note: When we add -ed to words ending in an -a, -e, -i, or -o the result may look rather peculiar:

| | |
|---|---|
| mascara | mascaraed |
| cliche | clicheed |
| shanghai | shanghaied |
| tattoo | tattooed |

To avoid these strings of vowels, some writers use -'d instead of -ed:

mascara'd     cliche'd     shanghai'd     tattoo'd

The choice is yours.

## -ed / (-e)n

Some verbs have -ed for their past participle, others -n or -en.
For example:

| | |
|---|---|
| we like | we have liked |
| we know | we have known |
| we take | we have taken |

The ones with -n or -en are a shrinking minority.

Some verbs give you a choice between -ed and -en (or -n), for instance *proved* or *proven*, *showed* or *shown*. The -ed is the newer form, and it will probably take over in the end, because it is more regular. (See **regular verbs.**)

In a few cases, the different endings have different meanings. For instance, *melted* and *molten* (both from *melt*) are used with different things:
*The snow had melted.*
*The ore was molten.*
It's the same with *struck* and *stricken* (both from *strike*):
*The clock had struck.*
*He was stricken with guilt.*

See also **-ed/-t.**

burned *or* burnt
dreamed *or* dreamt
leaned *or* leant
leaped *or* leapt
learned *or* learnt
smelled *or* smelt
spelled *or* spelt
spilled *or* spilt
spoiled *or* spoilt

## -ed / -t

With a small group of verbs, you have a choice of endings when writing the past form. For example:

| | | | |
|---|---|---|---|
| burn | burned | *or* | burnt |
| dream | dreamed | | dreamt |
| spell | spelled | | spelt |

Sometimes the two spellings sound different:

| | | |
|---|---|---|
| dreamed | *rhymes with* | steamed |
| dreamt | *rhymes with* | tempt |

In spite of the difference in sound, there is no difference in meaning. So in writing you might as well use the -ed ending, because it is in keeping with the more regular pattern.

See also **past forms**.

## edible

Note the ending of this word. See **-able/-ible**.

## editing

is when you revise and check what you've written, as the final step in the writing process. You should review both your expression and the contents of the piece. Make sure it says things in a streamlined way, and without any distracting mistakes with words or grammar. There is a checklist for revising in WRITING WORKSHOP pp 14 and 16–17.

## editor

Note the ending of this word. See **-er/-or**.

## editorials

An editorial is a newspaper article in which the editor puts forward a point of view on an issue in the news. For more information about newspaper writing, see **journalism**.

## -ee

A word ending in -ee often makes a pair with another one ending in -er, for example, *employee/employer*. In these cases the -er word is the person who performs the action, like most -er or -or words. (See **-er/-or**.)

The -ee word is the person whom the action is done to or for, so its meaning is passive. The ending -ee has a passive meaning like this in *addressee, licensee, nominee* and *trustee*.

You will still find words ending in -ee which have an active meaning. That is, they refer to a person who performs an action rather than having it done to them. For example, *absentee, devotee, escapee* and *referee*. See also **escapee/escaper**.

## -eer

This suffix is found on a few nouns which refer to someone by whatever they work at. For example *auctioneer, engineer, mountaineer*.

## eerie / eyrie

These words sound the same (they rhyme with *cheery*) but they mean different things. The first is an adjective and the second a noun.

Something is **eerie** if it is strange and frightening:
*I crept into the twilight of that eerie cave.*

An **eyrie** is the lofty nest of a bird of prey. It can also be a house or castle built so high up that it is hard to reach.

## effect

See **affect/effect**.

## effeminate

See **female/feminine/feminist/effeminate**.

## e.g.

is an abbreviation of the Latin words *exempli gratia* and means "for example".

It is used just after a statement to introduce examples which explain the statement:
*Some dogs have long hair, e.g. collies, Afghan hounds, whereas others have short hair, e.g. boxers, bull terriers.*
See **Latin abbreviations**.

Note that you use full stops after both the letters e and g. See **abbreviations** for more detailed information about stops in abbreviations.

Also note that some people object to abbreviations like **e.g.** being used in essay writing. In a formal essay, you could either write it out in full: *for example,* or use an alternative phrase: *such as,* or *as in.*

## ego

The plural of this word is spelled **egos**. For more about words like this, see **-o**.

## either

See **each/every/either/neither**.

## either . . . or

The verb that follows the **either . . . or** construction agrees with only one of the alternatives, usually the first:
*Either this or that is the one you want.*
*Either you or I are going to come first.*
See **agreement**.

## elder / eldest / older / oldest

Whenever you mean "more old" or "most old", it's normal to use the words **older** and **oldest**:
*the older of the two monkeys*
*the oldest house in the street*
People used to use **elder** and **eldest** for relationships within the family. For example:
*my elder sister*
*his eldest son*
This use of **elder** and **eldest** is fading as more and more people use *my older sister* and *his oldest son* instead.

## electric

See **electronic/electric**.

## electrocute / electrify

**Electrocute** means "to kill by electricity". It does <u>not</u> simply mean "to get an electric shock".

**Electrify** means "to equip something for use with electricity":
*The railway line has been electrified.*
It can also mean "to thrill or excite someone":
*That newsflash is sure to electrify them.*
**Electrify** does <u>not</u> mean "to get an electric shock".

## electronic / electric

These words sound similar but mean different things.

Equipment which is **electronic** makes use of transistors or integrated circuits, as *an electronic calculator* does.

Something is **electric** if it works by **electricity**, like *an electric blanket*, or is produced by it, like *an electric shock*.

## electronically

Note the ending of this word. See **-ally**.

## elegant

Note the ending of this word. See **-ant/-ent**.

## elegy

An **elegy** is a sad poem. It used to be a mournful song written for a funeral, a lament for the dead. Then the poem on its own without the music was referred to as an **elegy**, and finally any poem on the theme of death could be given that name.

## elementary

Note the ending of this word. See **-ary/-ery/-ory**.

## elevator

Note the ending of this word. See **-ator**.

## elf

The plural is spelled **elves**. For more about words like this, see **-f/-v-**.

## eligible

Note the ending of this word. See **-able/-ible**.

## ellipsis ( . . . )

An **ellipsis** is a set of three dots used in writing to show that letters or words have deliberately been left out as the text was being copied from the original.

You can use an ellipsis
1 <u>within</u> a sentence:
    *An ellipsis is a set of three dots . . . to show that letters or words have been left out of the text.*
2 at the <u>beginning</u> of a sentence:
    *. . . Letters or words have been left out of the text.*
    Note that in this case you may have to put a capital letter on the first word after the ellipsis. This is because it may become the first word in a new sentence, whatever it was in the original.

**3** at the <u>end</u> of a sentence:

*An ellipsis is a set of three dots . . .*

Note that when the ellipsis comes at the end of a sentence, you don't add a full stop.

## elude

See **allude to/elude**.

## embryo

The plural of this word is spelled **embryos**. For more about words like this, see **-o**.

## emigrate / immigrate / migrate

These words all have to do with travelling from one place to another.

To **emigrate** is to <u>leave</u> your own country to live in another, but to **immigrate** is to <u>come</u> to live in a new country.

An **emigrant** <u>goes away</u> from a place (**emigration**) and an **immigrant** <u>comes into</u> a place (**immigration**).

When birds **migrate** they change their place of living at regular times each year. The journey of these **migratory** creatures is **migration**.

## eminent / imminent

These words sound similar but have different meanings.

We call someone **eminent** if they are important or have a high rank, as in *an eminent professor*.

Something is **imminent** if it is likely to happen at any moment:

*The flashes of lightning show that a thunderstorm is imminent.*

## emotive / emotional

These words are both related to **emotion**, but there is a difference.

An **emotive** speech is one which is intended to produce emotion in the audience.

An **emotional** speech is one in which the speaker is full of emotion.

## emperor

Note the ending of this word. It is -or, not -er, because it was borrowed straight from French. See **-er/-or**.

## emphasis

The plural of this word is **emphases**, with the last syllable pronounced like *seas*. For more about words like this, see **-is**.

## emphatically

Note the ending of this word. See **-ally**.

## employer / employee

These words look similar and are both used in a work situation, but they mean different things.

You are an **employer** if you are the boss and you pay people to work for you.

You are an **employee** if you work for an **employer** who pays your wages.

## en- / in-

This prefix makes a verb out of an adjective or noun, as in:
endanger (to put in danger)
enlarge (to make larger)
enrich (to make richer)
entitle (to give a title to)

The en- becomes em- before words beginning with b or p, as in *embitter, empower.*

## -en

This ending turns an adjective into a verb that expresses a process:

| | | |
|---|---|---|
| brighten | *means to make or become* | bright |
| darken | | dark |
| ripen | | ripe |
| straighten | | straight |

The -en also turns a few nouns into verbs:
frighten　　(give a fright to)
lengthen　　(give extra length to)
strengthen　(give strength to)
threaten　　(make threats to)

## enamel

For information about whether to double the l when you add endings like -ed, -ing or -er, see **-l-/-ll-**.

## encyclopedia / encyclopaedia

These are equally good spellings. See **-ae-**.

## enrol

For information about whether to double the l when you add endings like -ed or -ing, see **-l-/-ll-**.

## ensure / insure / assure

These words have the same -sure ending but mean different things.

To **ensure** is to make certain of something:
*I'm reminding you now to ensure that you return the book tomorrow.*

To **insure** is to arrange a guarantee that your property will be replaced if it is lost, stolen or damaged.

The most common meaning of **assure** is to tell someone something with certainty:
*They assure us that the roof is on.*

## enterprise

is one of a small group of words ending in -ise that cannot also be spelled with an -ize ending. It is always spelled **enterprise**. For more about words like this, see **-ise/-ize**.

## entomology / etymology

These words sound similar but have different meanings. Scientific words or words indicating "the study of something" often have the suffix -ology.

**Entomology** is the study of insects.

**Etymology** is the study of the history and derivation of words.

One way to remember this is that the <u>ent-</u> in **entomology** sounds a bit like *ant*, which is an insect.

## entrance

This word has two meanings, with different pronunciations. One is a noun and the other is a verb.

An **entrance** (with the stress on the <u>en-</u>) is a way in. Note that **enter** loses an <u>e</u> when <u>-ance</u> is added to form this noun. See **-rance**.

To **entrance** (with the stress on the <u>-trance</u>) is a verb meaning "to delight":
*The dancing horses will entrance the crowds with their skill.*

## entrée / entree

These are equally good ways of writing this word.

This is a word borrowed from French and in the French spelling there is an acute accent over the <u>e</u>. Although words like this gradually lose their accent when they become more settled into English, the accent helps to show that the last syllable is pronounced *ray*.

For more about accents in English, see **accents**. See also **acute accents**.

## envelope / envelop

These words look similar but the first is a noun and the second is a verb.

An **envelope** is a folded paper cover for a letter. We pronounce it with a stress on the first syllable <u>en-</u>.

To **envelop** is to wrap or cover someone or something:
*"Let me envelop you in my velvet cloak," said the prince.*
We pronounce it with a stress on the middle syllable <u>-vel-</u>, to rhyme with *develop*.

Note that you don't add another <u>p</u> at the end of **envelop** when you add <u>-ed</u>, <u>-ing</u> and <u>-ment</u>: **enveloped, enveloping, envelopment**. See **doubling of last letter**.

## environment

See **ecology/environment**.

## eon / aeon

These are equally good spellings. See **-ae-**.

## epics

An **epic** was originally a long narrative poem like Homer's *Iliad* or Milton's *Paradise Lost*. It had a big theme like war between nations, and characters who were somewhere between human beings and legendary figures.

The term was then transferred to other categories of creative writing and in particular to film-making. In this sense *Star Wars* is an **epic** film.

**Epic** gradually came to mean anything on a huge scale, so that we now talk about *an epic production* and even *an epic meal.*

## epilogue

An **epilogue** is the concluding part of a written work, especially a play. Originally it was a speech made by one of the actors at the end of a play to round it off. Often it summed up what the play was supposed to be about. Then people adopted the epilogue for other forms of writing, such as the novel, to serve much the same function – to tidy up any remaining details of the plot, to finish neatly, or to sum up what it was all about.

You also find this word spelled **epilog** because it is sometimes written this way in the USA. For more about words like this, see **-gue/-g**.

## equal

You have a choice whether or not to double the l when you add -ed or -ing to this word. See **-l-/-ll-**.

Note that when you add -ise, the l is never doubled: **equalise**.

## equator

Note the ending of this word. See **-er/-or**.

## equi-

This prefix means "equal". It is found in a number of technical words such as *equilateral* and *equidistant*. Equi- also appears in some more common words such as *equivalent*, where it is perhaps less obvious as a prefix.

## equilibrium

The plural of this word may be spelled **equilibriums** or **equilibria**. For more about words like this, see **-um**.

## -er

This word-ending marks the comparative form of adjectives and some adverbs: *older, faster*. See **degrees of comparison**.

## -er / -or

Both -er and -or are used to make words for the doer of an action. It can be the person or the thing that does the action. For example:

| | | | |
|---|---|---|---|
| preach | preacher | comput(e) | computer |
| elevat(e) | elevator | act | actor |

Although the endings mean and sound exactly the same, we rarely have any choice. *Conveyer/conveyor* is one of the few examples where we can choose: with most there is no option. Awkward as it seems, we must write:

| | | |
|---|---|---|
| computer | *but* | calculator |
| protester | *but* | demonstrator |

The -or is normally used with words ending in:

| | | |
|---|---|---|
| -at(e) | calculator | demonstrator |
| -it | auditor | creditor |
| -ut(e) | distributor | prosecutor |
| -ct | collector | instructor |

It would make things easier if all words ending in a -t took -or. This happens most of the time, but not always. It is true for *inventor*, but not *decanter*, for *investor*, but not *protester*. The -er words are ones created in Modern English, whereas the -or ones usually go back to Latin. This is clear in cases like *doctor*, *pastor* and *victor*, because there's no English verb in them. (We have no verb *to doct* or *to vict*, for example.)

The lack of a related English verb is often a clue to -or spellings. It works for ones such as *ambassador*, *emperor*, *juror*, *lessor*, *tailor* and *traitor*, all of which were borrowed straight from French. Note, however, the handful of French loanwords like *conqueror*, *governor*, *surveyor* and *survivor*, where we've borrowed the verb as well.

But when they are not French or Latin loanwords, such words just take -er, and this is the ending for vast numbers of them:

| baker | commander | dancer | driver | gambler |
| informer | meddler | printer | singer | sweeper |
| teacher | trainer | weaver | wrecker | writer |

If you are in doubt about any word like this, you should check it in a dictionary. But if the word is too new to be listed there, you are safe spelling it with -er.

Note: A handful of words like this are spelled with -ar, such as *beggar* and *liar*. See **-ar**.

### error

Note the ending of this word. See **-or/-our**.

### escalator

Note the ending of this word. See **-ator**.

### escapee / escaper

Both these words mean someone who escapes, usually from prison. You can use either one.

The -ee ending of **escapee** seems unusual because here it refers to the person who does something. But there are other words like it. See **-ee**.

The -er suffix of **escaper** is much older and follows the usual English pattern for making such nouns.

An **escapologist** is someone who has mastered the art of escaping from chains, ropes and other such things.

### eschalot

See **shallot/eschalot**.

### -ese

This ending is added to the names of countries or regions. It makes a word which refers to the language and culture of that region. For example:

| Japan | Japanese |
| Burm(a) | Burmese |
| Chin(a) | Chinese |
| Portug(al) | Portuguese |

When added to ordinary English words, it implies the typical language and style of a particular group. For example:

| journalese | *is the language of* | journalists |
| medicalese | | medical people |
| legalese | | lawyers |

Note that these words can imply that such styles of writing are unnecessarily difficult.

## Eskimo

The plural may be spelled **Eskimos** or **Eskimo**. For more about words like this, see **-o**.

Sometimes you will find this word spelled **Esquimau** (which is French), and then the plural is spelled **Esquimaux**.

## espresso / expresso

These are equally good ways of spelling this word. **Espresso** is the Italian form, **expresso** makes it more English.

The plural is spelled **espressos** or **expressos**. See **-o**.

## Esq

is an abbreviation for the word **Esquire**, which is a polite title put <u>after</u> a man's name, particularly in the addressing of letters. It's a form of address which is not used much these days. Most people now just use the title *Mr*. If you do use **Esq**, here are some points to remember:

**1** It comes <u>after</u> a man's <u>full</u> name.

**2** It doesn't have any full stop (see **abbreviations**).

**3** You don't use *Mr* as well as **Esq** — it actually takes the place of *Mr*. For example:

    *John Smith, Esq*

See also **forms of address**.

### -ess

See **feminine word endings**.

### essays

are written compositions in which you present information to the reader, or argue for a particular point of view.

How to write essays, and the writing process itself, is explained in the WRITING WORKSHOP.

### -est

This word-ending marks the superlative form of adjectives and adverbs: *oldest, fastest*. See **degrees of comparison**.

## etc.

is an abbreviation of the Latin words *et cetera* and means "and the rest". It is used at the end of a list of items to show that you could have written more, but you are just going to say "and the rest" to keep it short:

    *He packed his sun cream, hat, towel etc., into his beach bag.*

See **Latin abbreviations**.

Note that you use a full stop after **etc.** If **etc.** does not come at the end of a sentence, there is usually a comma after it too. See **abbreviations** for more detailed information about stops in abbreviations.

Also note that some people object to abbreviations like **etc.** being used in essay writing.

## -ette

This ending usually means "small" in English. This is its meaning in *cigarette*, *kitchenette* and *rosette*.

Other new words formed in the same way are:
  diskette  (a small computer disk)
  dinette  (a small dining area)

Note: Although -ette is a feminine ending in French, it is scarcely used this way in English. For more about feminine suffixes, see **feminine word endings**.

## etymology

See **entomology/etymology**.

## euphemisms

A **euphemism** is a word or phrase you use to avoid some other word or phrase which is considered vulgar or offensive in some way. Instead of saying *I'm going to the toilet*, you might say *I'm going to powder my nose* or *I'm going to see a man about a dog*. These are euphemisms.

What is considered offensive varies from one society to another or from one period of time to another. In the early 1800s men's trousers were referred to as *unmentionables*, but a century later there was no longer any need to blush at the mention of trousers, and the euphemism was transferred to women's underwear.

Nowadays we are generally more inclined to speak plainly, but there are still subjects that people avoid mentioning if they can. We should not fall into the trap of treating words as if *they* were the thing that we fear or hate. If there is a need to talk about such things we should say plainly what we mean without resorting to all kinds of elaborate euphemisms.

## every

See **each/every/either/neither**.

## everybody

See **everyone/everybody/everything**.

## every day / everyday

**Everyday** (one word) is an adjective meaning "having to do with ordinary or casual situations", as in *the everyday language of the playground*.

**Every day** (two words) is a phrase meaning "on each day".
  *In summer I go to the beach every day.*

## everyone / everybody / everything

All of these words have to be followed by a singular verb:
*everyone is . . .*
*everybody is . . .*
*everything is . . .*

A following pronoun, though, sometimes causes problems:
*Everyone has to do his or her best.*
The *his or her* construction is awkward, and for speech and most styles of writing it's acceptable to use a plural pronoun instead:
*Everyone has to do their best.*

See also **agreement** and **they/them/their/theirs/themselves**.

## ewe / you / yew

These words sound the same but have different meanings.

A **ewe** is a female sheep.

**You** is the person being spoken to.

A **yew** is an evergreen tree.

## ewes / use

These words sound the same but have different meanings.

**Ewes** is the plural of **ewe**, a female sheep.

To **use** is to employ something or put it into action for some purpose.

## ex-

This prefix meaning "out" or "outside" is built into many words we've inherited from Latin. For example:

| | |
|---|---|
| excavate | *(dig out)* |
| exclude | *(shut out)* |
| explode | *(burst out)* |
| export | *(sell overseas)* |
| external | *(outside)* |
| exoskeleton | *(having a skeleton outside the body)* |

When it is used to make new words in English, it means "former":
ex-manager     ex-president     ex-wife

With this meaning it is usually separated with a hyphen from the main word.

## exaggeration

Sometimes we exaggerate for dramatic effect. See **hyperbole**.

## exceed / accede

These words sound similar but mean different things.

To **exceed** is to go beyond something:
*Don't exceed the speed limit.*

To **accede** is to agree or consent to something:
*I accede to your demand for a new pair of sunglasses.*

## except

See **accept/except**.

### exclaim / exclamation

These words both have the idea of shouting out, and both really go back to the same Latin root. They differ a little in spelling because **exclaim** (the verb) comes to us via French, and **exclamation** (the noun) direct from Latin.

For more about words like this, see **-aim/-ain**.

### exclamation marks (!)

We use an exclamation mark when we write down an utterance to show that it has been said

**1** as a command:
> *Look out!*
> *Come here!*

**2** as an expression of pleasure, surprise, fright, or some other strong feeling:
> *Oh no!*
> *What a pity!*
> *How lovely!*

Note that if you are using an exclamation mark, you don't use a full stop as well.

If you have an exclamation which is also a question, the exclamation mark comes after the question mark:
> *You mean you're going to the party?!*

### exclamations

An **exclamation** is an expression of excitement, surprise, fear, or some other strong emotion. Often exclamations are short utterances, such as *Oh!, Aha!, Hooray!, Good heavens!* They can be sentences which have exactly the same word order as statements or questions, but which are identified as exclamations by the way you say them and by their exclamation mark in writing. For example:
> *That was some party!*
> *Did he ever go mad!*

Exclamations are part of spoken language and therefore turn up in any representation of dialogue. But they are not common in normal prose writing. In particular, the exclamation mark should not be used as a quick way of indicating the attitudes of the writer. For example:
> *In this permissive age children have been brought up to be quite independent!*

The way you <u>say</u> this would show whether you approve or disapprove of independence, but it is not clear in the written form. You need to spell out your attitude:
> *In this permissive age children have been brought up to be quite independent. To me this is a good thing.*

### exercise

This is one of the few words ending in <u>-ise</u> that cannot also be spelled with an <u>-ize</u> ending. It is always spelled **exercise**. For more about words like this, see **-ise/-ize**.

### exercise / exorcise

These words look similar but have different meanings.

To **exercise** your body or mind is to train or develop it through some activity.

To **exorcise** is to drive away evil spirits by prayers or a religious ceremony.

### exhaustive / exhausting

These words are both linked to **exhaust** but they mean different things.

**Exhaustive** means "thorough", as in *an exhaustive search*.

Something is **exhausting** if it is tiring or if it wears you out, as in *an exhausting day at school*.

### exhibiter / exhibitor

These are equally good spellings. See **-er/-or**.

### exorcise

See **exercise/exorcise**.

### expiry / expiration

These words are related and have similar meanings.

The **expiry** of something is its ending after a fixed period of time. We usually use it in relation to legal documents or agreements that are no longer valid at the end of that time:
*The date of expiry for my passport has gone by.*

We use **expiration** in formal writing to mean "the close of a period":
*The expiration of his academic career caused him great sorrow.*
**Expiration** can also be the action of breathing air out through your lungs.

### explain / explanation

These words both imply presenting something clearly for a reader or listener, and both are from the same Latin root. They differ because **explanation** has kept the Latin spelling, while **explain** has changed a little under the influence of the English word **plain** (meaning "clear").

For more about words like this, see **-aim/-ain**.

### explicit / implicit

These words are opposites.

Something is **explicit** if it is clearly and fully set out:
*The directions were so explicit that I managed to assemble the cupboard.*

Something is **implicit** if it is suggested or implied but not actually stated:
*We had an implicit agreement even though nothing was signed.*

It is the prefixes ex- and im- that make these words opposites. See **ex-** and **in-/im-**.

## export

See **import/export**.

## expose / exposé

These related words look similar, but mean different things and are pronounced differently.

To **expose** something is to uncover it.

An **exposé** is the publication of scandalous events that have been covered up. It is a French word, and the acute accent over the final e indicates that the last syllable is pronounced to rhyme with *day*.

Note that words like **exposé** gradually lose their accent over the -e as they become more settled into English. But you can see that the accent is particularly useful in this case because without it **exposé** would look exactly the same as **expose**. For more about accents in English, see **accents**. See also **acute accents**.

## expresso

See **espresso/expresso**.

## extendible / extendable

These are equally good spellings. See **-able/-ible**.

## extra-

This prefix means "outside" or "beyond". It is built into words such as *extraordinary* and *extraterrestrial*.

It usually becomes extro- in *extrovert* and *extroversion*. It does not take a hyphen.

Extra- is also used to intensify the meaning of a word, as in *extra-special*. Here it means "extremely". In words like this it is used with a hyphen.

## extro-

See **extra-**.

## -ey

The plural of most words ending in -ey is simply -eys. For example:

| journey | journeys |
| monkey | monkeys |

## eye

may be spelled **eyeing** or **eying** when you add -ing. But when you add -ed it drops the e and becomes **eyed**. For more about words ending in e, see **-e**.

## eyrie

See **eerie/eyrie**.

# Ff

## f / ph

These letters sound exactly the same in English, so you have to be careful when spelling with them. *Fight*, *flag* and *fun* must have f̲, and *elephant*, *photograph* and *telephone* must have p̲h̲.

In some languages, such as Italian and Spanish, the p̲h̲ in such words has been replaced by f̲, but not yet in English. The influence of Spanish in the Philippines means that a person from those islands is now called a *Filipino*. The only English word in which p̲h̲ has changed to f̲ is *fantasy* (which used to be *phantasy*).

## -f / -v-

There is a small group of words with one syllable, ending in -f̲, or -f̲e̲ (like *loaf* and *wife* ) whose -f̲ changes to -v̲ in the plural. In fact you use -v̲e̲s̲ for the plural:

| | | | | | |
|---|---|---|---|---|---|
| calves | elves | halves | knives | leaves | loaves |
| lives | sheaves | shelves | thieves | wives | wolves |

But some words which used to belong to this group can now be spelled either -f̲s̲ or -v̲e̲s̲ in the plural:

| | | |
|---|---|---|
| dwarves | *or* | dwarfs |
| hooves | | hoofs |
| rooves | | roofs |
| scarves | | scarfs |
| wharves | | wharfs |

For the plural of other words ending in -f̲ (or -f̲f̲, or -f̲e̲), you just add -s̲. For example:

| | | | | | |
|---|---|---|---|---|---|
| beliefs | carafes | chefs | chiefs | cliffs | cuffs |
| giraffes | griefs | gulfs | handkerchiefs | proofs | puffs |
| reefs | skiffs | staffs | strifes | turfs | waifs |

## facade / façade

These are equally good ways of writing this word.

This is a word borrowed from French, and in the French spelling there is a cedilla under the c̲. Words like this gradually lose their accent as they became more settled into English, though it may be helpful to use the accent to show that the c̲ is pronounced like an s̲ not a k̲.

For more about accents in English, see **accents**. See also **cedilla**.

### facility / faculty

These words look similar but are very different in meaning.

A **faculty** is one of the five senses. To have all your **faculties** is to be in full possession of all your mental powers.

The **facility** with which you do something is the ease and grace with which you do it. **Facilities** are also those things which make life easier in some way:
> *The school has very good facilities — a library, a swimming pool, a tennis court, a sports ground, and a hall.*

### faction

See **fraction/faction**.

### factor

Note the ending of this word. It is -or, not -er, because it was borrowed straight from Latin. See **-er/-or**.

### factory

Note the ending of this word. See **-ary/-ery/-ory**.

### factual writing

is writing in which you present facts or information to the reader. Many essays in history, geography, economics and social studies are really factual writing. The information in them is what most people would agree on, so there's no need to argue about it. Factual essays are different therefore from argumentative ones, where you do have to argue and debate the material you're presenting.

There are samples of factual and argumentative writing in the WRITING WORKSHOP pp 47–9.

### faculty

See **facility/faculty**.

### Fahrenheit

This is the scale of temperature in the imperial system of measures, which is now almost entirely phased out in the UK. Its abbreviation is a capital F, written after the figure and degree sign. It does not have a full stop:
> *212°F is the boiling point of water.*
> *At 32°F water freezes.*

For more information, see **Celsius**.

### fair / fare

These words sound the same but mean different things.

A **fare** is the money you pay for a ticket on a bus, train, or the like.

A **fair** is a carnival. For other meanings of **fair** look up your dictionary.

### fallible

Note the ending of this word. See **-able/-ible**.

### falsetto

The plural of this word is spelled **falsettos**. For more about words like this, see **-o**.

### fantasy

is a style of writing in which the subject matter, the characters and the world in which they live are imaginary. Stories about fairies and creatures from space are fantasy. The opposite is **realism**.

Note that this word can be written either **fantasy** or **phantasy**, although the spelling **phantasy** is fading away in modern English. For more about words like this, see **f/ph**.

### farce

A **farce** is a short play intended to make people laugh. The humor comes from a far-fetched situation. A situation that is **farcical** is ludicrous and absurd.

The word **farce** comes from the Latin for "stuffing", the point being that originally farces were short pieces of comedy inserted as padding into religious services.

### fare

See **fair/fare**.

### farther

See **further/farther**.

### fatal / fateful

These words are both linked to **fate** but have different meanings.

A **fateful** action is one which has inevitable consequences, usually unpleasant:
  *On that fateful day I ran away from home.*

**Fatal** can mean the same as **fateful**:
  *That was the fatal moment when I stole the box of sweets.*
But more commonly it means "causing death":
  *The wound was fatal and he died a few days later.*
You speak of **fatalities** at an accident referring to the number of people who have died.

### fate / fete

These words sound the same but mean different things.

Your **fate** is your destiny.

A **fete** is a kind of fair to raise money for a school or church or the like. Note that this can also be written **fête**. See **fete/fête**.

### fateful

See **fatal/fateful**.

### father-in-law

The plural of this word is spelled **fathers-in-law**. The possessive is **father-in-law's**: *my father-in-law's daughter.*

## fauna

is a collective noun and refers to a group of animals from a particular area:

*The fauna in outback Australia is adapted to a desert climate.*

If you are writing about a number of different groups from different areas, the plural may be spelled **faunas** or **faunae**. See **-a (as a singular ending)**. See also **collective nouns**.

Don't confuse this word with **flora** which refers to the plants of a particular area. Remember, **fauna** sounds like *fawn*, which is an animal, whereas **flora** sounds like *flower* or *floral*.

## faze / phase

These words sound the same but mean different things.

A **phase** is a period of time in which something happens. If you **phase in** something, you do it in stages.

To **faze** someone is to worry them or cause them some uneasiness:
*The boxer's reputation fazed his opponent even before they got into the ring.*

## feasible

Note the ending of this word. See **-able/-ible**.

## feat

See **feet/feat**.

## feces / faeces

These are equally good spellings. See **-ae-**.

## feet / feat

These words sound the same but mean different things.

You stand on your two **feet**.

A **feat** is an achievement or an accomplishment, usually something difficult to do:
*It was quite a feat to scale the face of that cliff.*

## feign

Note that e comes before i in this word. See **i before e**.

## fell swoop

**One fell swoop** is one of the few phrases in which the adjective **fell** survives. It is an old-fashioned word meaning "destructive" or "deadly". Because it is such an unusual word people confuse it with *foul* and say **one foul swoop**, which tries to make sense of this phrase.

## female / feminine / feminist / effeminate

These words are all related in meaning but there are important differences.

You use the word **female** when you just wish to identify the sex of a person or an animal. A woman is female.

A person who is **feminine** has the attributes which are traditionally linked to the female sex, such as gentleness, kindness, or frailty. A man or a woman could be described as having feminine characteristics. **Feminine** is also used as the adjective from **female**, as in *feminine endings of words* and *the feminine sex*.

A **feminist** is someone who believes that women should have the same rights and opportunities as men. Note that **feminist** and **feminine** do <u>not</u> mean the same thing.

A man is described as **effeminate** when he is thought to have too many characteristics that are regarded as feminine. You would not describe a woman as **effeminate**.

## feminine gender

The pronouns *she, her* and *hers* are said to be **feminine** in gender because they refer to females, while *he, him* and *his* are said to be masculine, because they refer to males. Some pairs of nouns, too (like *prince* and *princess*), can be said to have gender.

This kind of gender is called **natural gender** because it depends on whether the thing or person being referred to is male or female. In some languages you may learn, though, there is what is called **grammatical gender**. For more information see **gender**.

## feminine word endings

There are some words in English where we can recognise at a glance that the person spoken about is a woman. This is because the word has an ending which clearly identifies this.

**-ess** is the most common feminine word ending in English. For example:

   god/goddess    actor/actress

These days, however, we are less inclined to attach the -ess ending to words. There is no need to turn *editor* into *editress*, or even *poet* into *poetess*, and it seems preferable to use neutral words for a person's job or position. In work situations where equal pay for men and women and equal promotion opportunities count, it is best to describe the job that someone is doing, not the gender of the person doing it. So if a job was advertised for a poet, then men and women would both apply. To advertise for a poetess would be regarded as discriminatory and not allowed by law.

There are, however, groups in the community who are more conservative and traditional in their thinking and who would themselves prefer to distinguish between the male and female form of a word. As with all your writing, you should be careful to make your writing suit the nature of your audience.

In zoology, the feminine ending does serve a useful purpose. It distinguishes the male and female of animals, as with *lion/lioness* and *leopard/leopardess*. It doesn't work for all animals, of course, because some species have different names for male and female, as with *doe/hart*, *vixen/fox* and *goose/gander*.

**-ix** is a feminine word ending which comes into English from Latin, and is therefore attached only to words which we have borrowed from Latin. It is not common and is rapidly disappearing, partly because of the move to non-sexist language and partly because the ending itself does not seem as natural to us as the English ending -ess. So there is no need to use the word *aviatrix. Aviator* does quite well for either a man or a woman. The only area of language in which this ending still survives is in law, with *testatrix* (a female witness) or *executrix* (a female executor of a will).

**-ienne** is a feminine word ending which comes to us from French. It has appeared in a very small number of words like *comedienne, tragedienne* and *equestrienne,* but it is no longer fashionable to use it. *Comedian, tragedian,* and *equestrian* will do very well for either sex.

See **non-sexist language.**

## feminist

See **female/feminine/feminist/effeminate.**

## fete / fête

These are equally good ways of writing this word.

This is a word borrowed from French, and in the French spelling there is a circumflex over the first e to show that there used to be an s following it (*feste*). Words like this gradually lose their accent as they become settled into English, which is why **fete**, without the accent, is more common these days.

For more about accents in English, see **accents.** See also **circumflex.**

See also **fate/fete.**

## fetus / foetus

These are equally good spellings. See **-oe-.**

## fewer / less

Both of these words have to do with "a smaller quantity".

Many people use *less* on every occasion, and never use *fewer* at all.

In careful writing though, **fewer** should be used with nouns that refer to things you can count (count nouns), and **less** with nouns that refer to things that aren't countable (mass nouns):

*fewer chairs       less water*
*fewer people       less butter*

See **count nouns** and **mass nouns** for other words that behave in the same way.

## fiancé / fiancée

These words sound the same and are closely related, but there is a difference. A **fiancé** is a man who is engaged to be married. A **fiancée** is a woman who is engaged to be married.

These are French words, and in French they are spelled with acute accents, though in English you will often find them written without accents: **fiance, fiancee.**

Words like this gradually lose their accent when they become more settled into English, though it is helpful to use the accent to show that the last syllable is pronounced *say*.

For more about accents in English, see **accents**. See also **acute accents**.

### fiasco

The plural of this word may be spelled **fiascos** or **fiascoes**. For more about words like this, see **-o**.

### fibre / fiber

These are equally good spellings for this word. **Fibre** is the usual way of spelling this word in the UK. It is usually spelled **fiber** in the USA. For more about words like this, see **-re/-er**.

### fiction

Writing can be divided into two broad categories – **fiction** and **nonfiction**. Most fiction is made up or invented to entertain the reader, while non-fiction is factual and can be informative or present a point of view.

Fiction can be written in many ways – as poetry, prose or drama. The most popular form of fiction prose writing is the novel. There are many different kinds of novel. See **western**, **thriller**, **romance** and **science fiction**.

Some suggestions about how to write fiction are given in the WRITING WORKSHOP pp 40–2.

### figuratively

See **literally/figuratively**.

### figures of speech

A **figure of speech** is a form of expression or a technique of writing which creates a special effect. You may use visual images to link ideas and convey meaning. This is called imagery, and is a way of making your writing more colorful and interesting. See **similes**, **metaphors**, **symbolism** and **personification**.

You can also create sound effects in your writing to add to the meaning. See **alliteration**, **assonance**, and **onomatopoeia**.

### Filipino

A **Filipino** is someone from the Philippines. **Filipino** is also sometimes used as an adjective to describe something relating to the Philippines.

You can tell that **Filipino** and **Philippines** are related words because, although they begin with different letters, their pronunciation is similar.

The F spelling of **Filipino** has come from Spanish, an important language in the Philippines' history. The Ph spelling of the country's name is the English version.

Sometimes you might hear the word **Filipina** used to refer to a woman or girl from the Philippines. The feminine -a ending is also from Spanish.

## final / finale

These words are linked but different in meaning.

A **final** is the last in a series.
*I'm playing in the final of the local chess tournament tomorrow.*

A **finale** is the concluding part of a performance. It originally referred to the last part of a musical performance so it always has a theatrical feel. It rhymes with *Bali*.
*She rattled off the names of all the Prime Ministers of the UK and for a finale listed all the members of the present cabinet.*

## finite verbs

All verbs have forms which are called **finite**. For example, *run, runs* and *ran* are finite forms of the verb *to run*.

You can tell that a verb is finite if it sounds correct when you place a subject (like *I, they* or *the dog*) in front of it.

So because *I run* and *the dog ran* sound correct, *run* and *ran* are finite verbs. *I to run* and *I running* sound wrong, which is how you can tell that *to run* and *running* are not finite verbs.

Note that verbs made up of two or three words (compound verbs) can also be finite verbs. For example, when you add a subject like *I* to *am running*, it sounds correct: *I am running*. So *am running* is a finite verb.

*I been running* does not sound correct, so *been running* is not a finite verb. But *I have been running* does sound correct, so *have been running* is a finite verb.

Compare this type of verb with **infinitives, auxiliary verbs** and **participles**.

## fiord / fjord

These are equally good ways of spelling this word. **Fiord** is the more natural English spelling, whereas **fjord** is the Norwegian spelling.

## fir / fur

These words sound the same but mean different things.

A **fir** is a kind of tree.

**Fur** is hair on an animal.

## fireman / firefighter

**Firefighter** is now the preferred word for a person who fights fires. It is replacing **fireman** since it allows for the possibility that both men and women can do this job.

## first person

*Scenes of violent death leave <u>me</u> unmoved. But <u>we</u> were quite unprepared for the sight that greeted <u>us</u> as <u>I</u> opened the door to <u>my</u> office.*

A story such as this, which is told from the narrator's point of view, using such pronouns as *I, we* and *me*, is said to be in the **first person**.

See **person** for more about this grammatical term. See also WRITING WORKSHOP pp 26 and 29 for information about the use of the first person in essays.

### fish

The plural of this word may be spelled **fishes** or **fish**.

When it is used as a collective noun for a <u>group</u> of fishes, it is often spelled **fish**:
*a tankful of tropical fish*
See **collective nouns**.

### fjord

See **fiord/fjord**.

### flair / flare

These words sound the same but mean different things.

A **flare** is a kind of light, usually short-lived and very bright.

To have a **flair** for something is to display a natural talent for doing it:
*She has a real flair for acting and entertains everyone with her imitations.*

### flamingo

The plural of this word may be spelled **flamingos** or **flamingoes**. For more about words like this, see **-o**.

### flammable / inflammable

There used to be just one word, **inflammable**, which referred to something which was likely to burst into flames. The <u>in-</u> of this word meant "into". But people confused it with <u>in-</u> meaning "not", as in *insoluble* (not soluble). And so there was confusion about the label **inflammable**. Did it mean "bursting into flames" or "not bursting into flames"?

Because this confusion was dangerous it was decided to drop the label **inflammable** and invent a new word, **flammable**, about which there could be no mistake. So while you may still find the old word **inflammable** in its original meaning, it is now replaced by **flammable**. Something which doesn't burn is therefore <u>not</u> **flammable**.

### flare

See **flair/flare**.

### flaunt / flout

These words look similar but they mean quite different things.

To **flaunt** something is to put it on show, often with the intention of making others envious. It rhymes with *haunt*:
*She flaunted her new bike before her friends at school.*

To **flout** a rule is to deliberately ignore it. It rhymes with *stout*:
*You have flouted the school rule that you must wear a tie.*

### flaw

See **floor/flaw**.

### flea / flee

These words sound the same but have different meanings.

A **flea** is a tiny biting insect.

To **flee** is to run away to escape danger.

### flee

See **flea/flee**.

### flew

See **flu/flue/flew**.

### flexible

Note the ending of this word. See **-able/-ible**.

### flier / flyer

These are equally good ways of spelling this word. For more about words like this, see **y→i**.

### floor / flaw

These words sound the same but mean different things.

A **flaw** is a fault or defect.

The **floor** of a room is what you walk on.

### flora

is a collective noun and refers to a group of plants from a particular area:

> *The flora in a coastal area has to be able to withstand salt as well as sun.*

If you are writing about a number of different groups from different areas, the plural may be spelled **floras** or **florae**.

See **-a (as a singular ending)**. See also **collective nouns**.

Don't confuse this word with **fauna** which refers to the animals of a particular area. Remember, **flora** sounds like *flower* or *floral*, whereas **fauna** sounds like *fawn*, which is an animal.

### flounder / founder

These words are similar but have different meanings.

To **flounder** is to do something clumsily and with great difficulty.

A boat **founders** if it fills with water and sinks.

### flour / flower

These words sound the same but have different meanings.

A **flower** is the blossom of a plant.

**Flour** is the powder made from grinding wheat or some other grain.

When Dr Johnson wrote his dictionary in 1755, he gave **flower** with both these meanings. The flower of grain was the edible part of it. But at some point in the 1700s the two meanings became established with different spellings.

## flout

See **flaunt/flout**.

## flu / flue / flew

These words sound the same but mean different things.

**Flu** is the shortened form of **influenza**.

A **flue** is a passage made for air or gases:
*The fire won't burn because the flue in the chimney is blocked up.*

**Flew** is the past tense of the verb **fly**:
*The startled birds flew out of the tree.*

## flyer / flier

These are equally good spellings. See **y→i**.

## focus

The plural of this word may be spelled **focuses** or **foci**. For more about words like this, see **-us**.

Note that when you add the endings -ed and -ing to the verb **focus** you may write it with a single s (**focused, focusing**), or with a double (**focussed, focussing**). See **doubling of last letter**.

## foetus / fetus

These are equally good spellings. See **-oe-**.

## fogy / fogey

These are equally good ways of spelling this word. If you choose **fogy**, the plural is spelled **fogies**. If you choose **fogey**, the plural is spelled **fogeys**. For more about words like this, see **-y/-ey**.

## for / four / fore

These words sound the same but have different meanings.

**For** is a preposition with a wide range of meanings. Look it up in your dictionary. Here is one example:
*This apple is for the teacher.*

**Four** is the number that comes after three.

**Fore** is in the phrase **come to the fore** meaning "to come to the front of everything else". It is also what golfers shout when they are warning someone that a ball is coming and they are in danger of being hit by it.

## forbad / forbade

These are equally good ways of spelling this word, which is the past tense of **forbid**:
*I thought I forbad you to use my lipstick.*
*The council forbade the demolition of the old mill.*

## forcible

Note the ending of this word. See **-able/-ible** and **-ce/-ge**.

### fore- / for-

These prefixes sound exactly the same, but they mean different things.

<u>Fore-</u> means "before", and you'll find it in quite a lot of words, such as:

forecast     forerunner     foresee     foreshadow
forestall     foretaste     foretell     forethought

<u>Fore-</u> can mean something is before in time or place, and in *forearm*, *forecourt* and *forefinger* it means "being placed in front". Some <u>fore-</u> words refer to the person who is in charge, as in *foreman* and *forewoman*.

<u>For-</u> is a very old negative prefix which survives in just a few words, like *forbid*, *forget*, *forgo* and *forsake*. It isn't used nowadays to make new words.

Note: Make sure you can distinguish
forebear (ancestor)     *from*     forbear (put up with)
foregone (gone ahead)                   forgone (done without)

See also **forward/foreword**.

### foreign

Note that <u>e</u> comes before <u>i</u> in this word. See **i before e**.

### foreman / forewoman

You can either talk about a **foreman** when you mean a man, and a **forewoman** when you mean a woman, or you can avoid the problem entirely by calling them *supervisors* or *forepersons*. See **non-sexist language**.

### for ever / forever

These are equally good ways of writing these words. Choose whichever you like, but make sure you use the same one throughout your work.

### forewoman

See **foreman/forewoman**.

### foreword

See **forward/foreword**.

### foreword / preface

The **foreword** is a brief section at the front of a book, straight after the title page. The author may talk about how the book came to be written, explain the aims of the book, and give the names of people who helped in some way with it.

The word **preface** is used in the same way nowadays.

### forfeit

Note that <u>e</u> comes before <u>i</u> in this word. See **i before e**.

### for free

See **free/for free**.

### formal writing

Some of the differences between formal and informal styles of writing are explained and illustrated in WRITING WORKSHOP pp 28–31.

### formally / formerly

These words sound the same but mean different things.

**Formally** is the adverb from **formal**:
*We have to dress formally for the dinner tonight.*

**Formerly** is the adverb from **former** and means "previously" or "in the past":
*Now we can wear ordinary clothes to school. Formerly we had to wear school uniforms.*

### former / latter

These words can work together as a pair of pronouns. You use them when you wish to refer to two things or people that you have mentioned before. The **former** is the first of the pair and the **latter** is the second:
*Winston Churchill and Harold Wilson are two of the most popular prime ministers the UK has ever had. The former was a member of the Conservative Party, while the latter belonged to the Labour Party.*

In the sentence above, **the former** stands for *Winston Churchill* and **the latter** stands for *Harold Wilson*.

### formerly

See **formally/formerly**.

### forms of address

When you are writing someone's name you often use a title, such as *Mr, Ms* or *Sir*. This title gives some extra information or is a polite form of address. Most titles in common use are quite straightforward to use:

**Mr** stands for *mister*, and is the general title for a man: *Mr John Smith*.

**Master** is the title sometimes used for a boy. There is no abbreviation for this word: *Master George Fox*. This title is not used very often nowadays.

**Ms** is the general title for a woman. It is not an abbreviation and was invented fairly recently. *Ms* is the equivalent of *Mr*, since it does not indicate whether the person is married or not: *Ms Jane Smith*.

**Mrs** is pronounced "missus", and is the title for a married woman: *Mrs Martha Jones*. When writing the name of a married woman people sometimes use the husband's given name rather than the woman's: *Mrs Ian Jones*. This happens less often nowadays.

*Mrs* actually stands for *mistress*, which was the title used for married women in earlier centuries.

**Miss** is the title used for a girl or woman who isn't married: *Miss Wendy Ho*. This title is being used less frequently nowadays.

Some titles indicate a profession or a degree in education. For example, **Doctor** is a title used for someone who practises medicine or who has the university degree of PhD (Doctor of Philosophy). Such titles replace the ordinary titles such as *Ms*, *Mr* and *Miss*. You refer to someone as *Dr Jones*, not *Dr Mrs Jones*.

**Esq** stands for *esquire*, and is written without a full stop. Nowadays it means almost exactly the same as *Mr* so you only need one title, either *Mr* or *Esq*, for a man. For more information, see **Esq**.

## formula

The plural of this word may be spelled **formulas** or **formulae**. For more about words like this, see **-a (as a singular ending)**.

## fort / fought / forte

**Fort** and **fought** sound the same but have different meanings.

**Fought** is the past tense of the verb **fight**:
*They fought well in the last war.*

A **fort** is a building guarded by armed soldiers.

Your **forte** is something which you do particularly well:
*Making minestrone was his forte.*
Note that **forte** does not have the same pronunciation as **fort** and **fought**. The te is pronounced *tay*.

## forth / fourth

These words sound the same but mean different things.

**Forth** is rather old-fashioned and means "forwards":
*Go forth and conquer the world.*
It also survives in the phrase **and so forth**.

**Fourth** is the next number after third.

## forty

See **four/forty**.

## forward / foreword

These words have very similar pronunciations but they are quite different in meaning.

To go **forward** is to go ahead or to advance.

A **foreword** is an introduction in a book. It is the word you say before the book begins. See **foreword/preface**.

## forward / forwards

For information about this pair of words, see **-ward/-wards**.

## fought

See **fort/fought/forte**.

## foul / fowl

These words sound the same but mean different things.

**Foul** means "filthy" or "repulsive".

A **fowl** is a bird, especially a chicken.

## founder

See **flounder/founder**.

## four

See **for/four/fore**.

## four / forty

Note that **four** loses its <u>u</u> for **forty** and **fortieth**, but keeps its <u>u</u> for **fourteen**.

## four-letter words

A **four-letter word** is an informal name for a swear word. It is a euphemism — that is, a harmless name for something considered bad. It came about because some of the most common swear words have four letters in them. It now refers to a swear word of any length.

It is now used also as a joke to refer to things you may wish to show are as offensive as swear words. The joke is particularly good when the word does in fact have four letters. For example:

*Work is a four-letter word.*

## fourth

See **forth/fourth**.

## fowl

See **foul/fowl**.

## fraction / faction

These words sound similar but mean different things.

A **fraction** is a part of a whole number, or a small piece or amount of something:

*¼ is a fraction.*
*Open the window a fraction.*

A **faction** is a small group of people within a larger group, who hold a different opinion to that of the larger group.

## fractions

In mathematics there are several ways to write fractions:

proper fraction     1¼
improper fraction     ⁵/₄

Fractions can also be written as decimals or percentages:

decimal fraction     0.75
percentage     75%

When you use fractions in any other kind of writing it is normal to spell out the fraction rather than use figures:

*Almost one-third of the class came late.*
*Forty per cent of teachers are bald.*

Note that when you write out proper or improper fractions you always use hyphens:

four-fifths     one-ninth     three-quarters

## frankfurt / frankfurter

These are equally good ways of spelling this word. Another less common way of spelling it is **frankforter**.

Note that if you are writing about the city in West Germany, the spelling is **Frankfurt**.

## frantically

Note the ending of this word. See **-ally**.

## free / for free

If something is **free**, you can have it or use it without paying for it:

*The biscuits were free.*
*Win a fabulous free gift by entering this contest.*

In these sentences **free** is an adjective.

You do something **for free** if you do it without being paid:

*She said she'd babysit for free.*

You get something **for free** if you get it without having to pay:

*I got the pen for free.*

In these sentences **for free** is a phrase used as an adverb. People used to frown on the use of **for free** and say that it was wrong. Nowadays so many people use it that it is becoming more acceptable.

## free verse

**Free verse** is poetry which doesn't have a fixed pattern of rhyme or rhythm. The poet is free to have lines of any length. This is the beginning of a poem called "The Galloping Cat" by the poet Stevie Smith:

Oh I am a cat that likes to
Gallop about doing good
So
One day when I was
Galloping about doing good, I saw
A Figure in the path; I said:
Get off! (Be-
cause
I am a cat that likes to
Gallop about doing good)

## freeze / frieze

These words sound the same but mean different things.

To **freeze** is to turn to ice, or to feel very cold.

A **frieze** is a band around the top of a wall which is often decorated with a painted or sculpted pattern.

## freight

Note that e comes before i in this word. See **i before e**.

## fresco

The plural may be spelled **frescoes** or **frescos**. For more about words like this, see **-o**.

## fridge

This is a shortening of the word **refrigerator**.

The spelling has been adapted so that it is quite clear how the word should be said.

Sometimes you might see the abbreviation **frig**, which is straight from the middle of **refrigerator**. The problem with this spelling is that the pronunciation (the same as **fridge**) isn't obvious.

Note that *frigid*, meaning "cold", as in *Frigid Zone*, is never spelled with a d before the g.

## frieze

See **freeze/frieze**.

## frolic

This word can be a noun or a verb.

The plural of the noun is spelled **frolics**.

When you add the endings -ed and -ing to the verb, you add a k: **frolicked**, **frolicking**. For more about words like this, see **-c/-ck-**.

## fuel

For information about whether to double the l when you add endings like -ed or -ing, see **-l-/-ll-**.

## -ful

This ending is often used to turn a noun into an adjective, as when *peace* becomes *peaceful*. As you might expect, it means "full of", but note that it only has one l. Many common words are formed with it:

| | | | |
|---|---|---|---|
| careful | cheerful | delightful | doubtful |
| faithful | forgetful | graceful | harmful |
| hopeful | joyful | skilful | powerful |
| thankful | thoughtful | truthful | wonderful |

The ending -ful is also used in common measurements of volume:

| | | | |
|---|---|---|---|
| cupful | handful | mouthful | spoonful |

Here again, it only has one l.

Note that for the plural, you just add -s to the end of these words. For example:

| | | | |
|---|---|---|---|
| cupfuls | handfuls | mouthfuls | spoonfuls |

## fulcrum

The plural of this word may be spelled **fulcrums** or **fulcra**. For more about words like this, see **-um**.

## fulfil / fulfill

These are equally good ways of spelling this word. **Fulfil** is the usual way it is spelled in the UK, whereas **fulfill** is more common in the USA.

## full stops ( . )

You use a **full stop** at the end of a sentence except where a question mark or an exclamation mark is needed:

*The dog bit the man.*

Sometimes, if you are reporting a conversation, you may use a short phrase which, although it is not a sentence, can make sense on its own and can have a full stop:

*"Which hat do you like?"*
*"This one."*

*"Did you see him?"*
*"No."*

Full stops are used in some abbreviations. See **abbreviations** for a full explanation.

Note that a full stop can also be called a **period**.

## funeral / funereal

These words look similar but have different meanings. The first is a noun and the second an adjective.

A **funeral** is a service held to honor someone who has died.

Something **funereal** is like a funeral, usually meaning "dismal or gloomy".

## fungus

The plural of this word may be spelled **funguses** or **fungi**. For more about words like this, see **-us**.

Note that if you want to talk about a mass of fungus, you use the singular:

*The tree was covered with fungus.*

Here, **fungus** is a mass noun. See **mass nouns**.

But if you want to talk about several individual ones, use the plural (**funguses** or **fungi**):

*There are two funguses near my front door.*

## funnel

For information about whether to double the l when you add endings like -ed or -ing, see **-l-/-ll-**.

## fur

See **fir/fur**.

## furore / furor

These are equally good ways of spelling this word. **Furore** is the usual spelling in the UK. **Furor** is more commonly used in the USA.

Note that both **furore** and **furor** are pronounced to rhyme with *you roar.*

### further / farther

People have tried to make distinctions between these two words but in fact they are just different ways of spelling the same word. In the UK the more popular spelling seems to be **further**:

*I can go no further down the track.*
*I will give you no further advice.*

The superlative is either **furthest** or **farthest**.

### future tense

In English we show that the action of a verb takes place in the future by using words such as *will* and *shall* (modals) and *tomorrow* and *soon* (adverbs of time):

*He <u>will</u> come.*
*He comes <u>tomorrow</u>.*

In many other languages the future tense is indicated by a change to the ending of the verb.

See **tense** for further information.

# Gg

## g as a silent letter

The letter g can be silent in many words. It is not sounded when it comes before n̲ at the start of a word, as in:

gnarled    gnash    gnat    gnaw    gnome    gnu

It is also silent before n̲ and m̲ at the end of words like:

sign    align    malign    paradigm    diaphragm

Note however that the g is no longer silent when these words become part of another word, as when *sign* is developed in *signature*, or *malign* into *malignant*.

The letter g is usually silent when it is combined with h̲, either in the middle or at the end of a word, as in *daughter* and *dough*. For more about this, see **gh** and **silent letters**.

## gaberdine / gabardine

These are equally good ways of spelling this word which can mean "a type of cloth" or "a long, loose cloak worn in the Middle Ages".

**Gaberdine** is probably more common, but the spelling **gabardine** actually reflects more accurately the Medieval English word it comes from, which meant "pilgrimage". Presumably the cloaks were worn while travelling on pilgrimages.

## gait

See **gate/gait**.

## galleon

See **gallon/galleon**.

## gallery / galley

These words look similar but have different meanings.

A **gallery** is a room or building where you can see paintings and sculptures.

A **galley** is a long low ship propelled by oars. It is also the kitchen in a ship or an aeroplane.

Remember that the plural of **gallery** is **galleries** but the plural of **galley** is **galleys**. See **y→i** and **-ey**.

## gallon / galleon

These words look similar but mean different things.

A **gallon** is a measure of liquid in the imperial system of measurement, equal to about 4.5 litres.

A **galleon** is a large sailing ship.

## gallop

Note that you don't add another p to this word when you add the endings -ed, -ing, or -er to form **galloped**, **galloping** and **galloper**. See **doubling of last letter**.

## gallows

This word is usually the same for both singular and plural:
*Butch became very nervous when he noticed the townspeople building a gallows.* (singular)
*The whole gang was uneasy when they saw that several gallows had been built.* (plural)
But you may also see the plural spelled **gallowses**:
*They were very relieved when a movie crew arrived and started to film some actors slowly walking towards the group of gallowses.*

## gamble / gambol

These words sound the same but mean different things.

To **gamble** is to play a game in which you risk losing something, usually money.

To **gambol** is to jump about in play, the way children and lambs do.

## gaol

See **jail/gaol**.

## gaol / goal

These words look similar but have different meanings.

**Gaol** is another spelling for **jail**, the place where criminals are imprisoned.

A **goal** is what you aim the ball at, in games such as football and basketball.

Whatever you aim towards can be your **goal**:
*His goal is to write dictionaries.*

## gas

This word can be either a noun or a verb.

To make the plural of the noun, you just add the -es ending.
*Many different gases are used for experiments in the science lab.*

But when you add the endings -es, -ing, and -ed to the verb ("to kill with a poisonous gas"), you double the s:
*The mad scientist gasses twenty rats a day in his experiments.*
*We caught him just as he was gassing some yesterday.*
*The animal liberationists say the mad scientist should be gassed.*

Note that some people don't treat the noun and the verb differently, so you may see the plural with a double s and the verb forms with just one s.

## gate / gait

These words sound the same but mean different things.

You close a **gate** to block the way.

Your **gait** is the way you walk.

## gay

As long ago as 1935 the adjective **gay** was being used to mean "homosexual".

Nowadays this is accepted by most people as standard. This usage also extends to the noun, although this is mainly reserved for male homosexuals:

*Gays and lesbians attended the march.*

Homosexuals adopted the word as an acceptable or positive alternative to words of abuse like "poofter", "queer" and "pansy".

While this is understandable, it has made people reluctant to use the word **gay** in its original meaning of "cheerful" or "bright". They feel that they may be misinterpreted. This can certainly happen with literature written before World War II. Remember that if an author writing then refers to *a gay young man*, it most probably means that the man is full of youthful good cheer.

Some writers call this process "contamination" because they feel that a non-offensive word has been tainted through its usage and has acquired unpleasant overtones. This depends on your viewpoint.

The meanings of words can change dramatically over time.

## gelatine / gelatin

These are equally good ways of spelling this word. For more about words like this, see **-ine/-in**.

## gender

Nouns in some languages are divided into groups such as feminine, masculine and neuter. These different groups, or **genders**, are distinguished by their different endings or by the words that are allowed to go with them. When you learn these nouns you have to learn what group they fall into and what endings they have.

Even though these groups are often described by the labels *masculine, feminine* and *neuter*, sex has very little to do with it.

For instance, the French word for "moon", *la lune*, is feminine gender, while "sun", *le soleil*, is masculine. The genders are shown by the accompanying words *la* (the feminine form of "the") and *le* (the masculine form of "the"). In German, interestingly enough, the genders for these two words are reversed: "moon" is a masculine noun and "sun" is feminine.

Gender in English is restricted to forms of the pronouns *he, she, it* and their varying forms. This is said to be an example of **natural gender** rather than **grammatical gender**: that is, it depends on whether the thing or person being referred to is male, female, or neither.

**Common gender** is a term sometimes used to refer to a particular kind of natural gender: when the noun stands for both male and female. The noun *student* can be said to be common gender, for example.

### generator

Note the ending of this word. See **-ator**.

### genes

See **jeans/genes**.

### genetically

Note the ending of this word. See **-ally**.

### genitive case

See **possessive case**.

### genius

When you're writing about exceptionally clever or creative people like Einstein and Mozart, the plural of **genius** is spelled **geniuses**. This follows the normal English pattern for making plurals — simply add -es (or -s).

Another, more unusual **genius** is a sort of spirit or demon. The plural in this case is spelled **genii** and is pronounced *jean-ee-eye*. **Genius** came into English from Latin, and **genii** is the Latin plural.

For more about words like this, see **-us**.

### genius / genus

These words look similar but mean different things.

A **genius** is a very talented or clever person.

A **genus** in biology is one of the main subdivisions of a family of animals or plants.

### genre

**Genres** are the different forms or types of writing that we recognise.

At their broadest, genres are the different forms and styles of poetry, prose and drama. But we also recognise genres within each of these. Within prose, there are genres of both fiction and non-fiction. And within non-fiction, we might distinguish between the genres of biography, essay, journal, letter and so on, because of the different form and presentation of each. Going still further, we could say that there were different genres of essay, such as the personal, reflective, factual and argumentative kinds. The differences at this level are more a matter of style and approach than of form. Several genres of prose are illustrated and discussed in WRITING WORKSHOP pp 35–60, including journal, narrative, essay, science report, news report and letter.

## gentle / genteel / Gentile

These words look similar but have different meanings.

A **gentle** person is kind and patient. A **gentle** thing is not rough or violent. For example: *a gentle breeze, a gentle tap on the shoulder.*

We say someone is **genteel** if they are very polite and careful in their manners, speech and behavior.

Anyone who is not Jewish, especially a Christian, may be referred to as a **Gentile**. We can spell this word with or without a capital letter.

## genus

The plural of this word is spelled **genera**. For more about words like this, see **-us**.

See also **genius/genus**.

## geographical terms

There are two main areas to consider when writing geographical terms: when to use capital letters, and when and how to use abbreviations.

1 **Capitals** should be used whenever the geographical term is part of the name of a place:

| | |
|---|---|
| Murray River | Bass Strait |
| Mount Kosciusko | Cape York Peninsula |
| Cradle Mountain | the Great Barrier Reef |
| the Great Dividing Range | Reedy Creek |
| the Pacific Ocean | Gibson Desert |
| Lake Eyre | Dodge City |

Note however that if the word *river* appears before the name it does not have to have a capital: *the river Nile* and *the River Nile* are both correct.

A capital is never used when the geographical term is simply describing a place and is not part of its name:

| | |
|---|---|
| the Victorian mountains | Darwin's harbour |
| the Sydney city skyline | the South Australian deserts |

2 **Abbreviations** No full stops are used in geographical abbreviations since they all begin with a capital letter. Check the list in APPENDIX B for the abbreviations of common geographical terms and compass points. Compass points can be abbreviated as capitals or in lower case. Either way they don't have full stops.

Note that in ordinary essay writing it is generally better to avoid abbreviations and spell out all words in full. This makes it easier for the reader. Abbreviations are best kept for writing where space has to be saved, such as maps, tables and lists.

However the abbreviations for some countries have become so well known that they are sometimes used in ordinary writing. *USSR* is almost always used instead of the full spelling, and *USA* often appears as a noun. *US* and *UK* are also commonly used, both as nouns and adjectives:

*We visited the US last year.*
*They're playing the UK top 40.*

For a general description of abbreviations, see **abbreviations**.

## geranium

The plural of this word is spelled **geraniums**. For more about words like this, see **-um**.

## germ / bacterium / virus

These words all refer to the cause of a disease.

A **germ** is an everyday term that nonscientists might use to describe a bacterium or virus which causes an infectious illness.

A **bacterium** is a single-celled micro-organism. Some **bacteria** cause infectious diseases and others take part in the process of fermentation or rotting.

A **virus** is a strand of genetic material (DNA or RNA). It reproduces by infecting living cells and undermining their cellular structure so as to make more virus. As viruses do not use up energy it is debatable whether they are living things or merely complicated biochemical molecules.

## gerunds

The -ing form of verbs, the present participle, is often used as a noun. When this happens, the participle can be called a **gerund**:

*I love jogging.*
*Does my whistling annoy you?*

Compare these two sentences:

*He gets really annoyed at my whistling.*
*He gets really annoyed at me whistling.*

Some people argue that the second example isn't correct because if *whistling* is a noun it has to have the possessive pronoun, *my*, rather than *me* in front of it. Except in the most formal writing, though, both are acceptable.

## get

This is among the commonest verbs in English, though more so for speakers than writers. When talking, we use it almost as often as the auxiliary verbs *be, have* and *do*. We often use **get** instead of the verb *be* in expressions such as:

*My brother is getting married on Saturday.*
*My brother is being married on Saturday.*

The second sentence sounds rather formal. It has what we call the passive form of the verb. (See **passive verbs**.)

In conversation, we also use **get** instead of the more formal become:

*My parents get angry when I mention money.*
*My parents become angry when I mention money.*

Among its other uses, **get** often replaces other more specific verbs, such as: *buy, borrow, fetch, obtain* and *prepare*, again when a speaker isn't trying to be too formal. In these cases **get** is working as a main verb, not an auxiliary.

People sometimes worry about **get** appearing too often in writing. It may indeed be a pity if it is overused as a main verb in writing which is supposed to be precise and formal. (If you are looking for alternatives to **get**, a thesaurus would help you to find some.) But if you're aiming at an informal style, **get** is quite natural.

## gh

This is the most notorious pair of letters in English spelling. In some words they have no sound at all, and in others they make an *f* sound. Together with either <u>au</u> or <u>ou</u> they can be pronounced in at least eight different ways.

| | | |
|---|---|---|
| bough | *which rhymes with* | now |
| dough | | sew |
| through | | you |
| bought/caught | | port |
| cough | | off |
| laugh | | staff |
| tough | | stuff |
| thorough | | -urra |

Note that at the beginning of a word, like *ghost*, <u>gh</u> just sounds like <u>g</u>.

## ghetto

The plural of this word may be spelled **ghettos** or **ghettoes**. For more about words like this, see **-o**.

## gigantically

Note the ending of this word. See **-ally**.

## gilt / guilt

These words sound the same but mean different things.

**Gilt** is the gold or other material used to decorate precious objects like vases.

**Guilt** is the feeling you have when you've done something wrong.

## gipsy / gypsy

These are equally good ways of spelling this word. For more about words like this, see **i/y**.

## glacier / glazier

These words look similar but have different meanings.

A **glacier** is a large area of ice which moves slowly down a valley or mountain.

A **glazier** is someone who fits glass into windows.

## gladiator

Note the ending of this word. See **-ator**.

## glazier

See **glacier/glazier**.

## glean / gleam

These words look similar but mean different things.

To **glean** something is to gather it slowly and bit by bit:
*They must glean more information about their ancestors.*

To **gleam** is to shine, the way chrome or polished wood does.

# glossary

**Glossaries** are lists of technical terms or foreign words, with explanations of their meanings. They are often printed at the back of textbooks.

# glue

Note that the noun **glue** keeps its e before -y is added to make the adjective **gluey**. If it didn't, the word would be *gluy*, and would seem to have only one syllable, like *buy*. For more about words like this, see **-e**.

The past form of the verb is **glued**.

When you add -ing it's more common to drop the e (**gluing**) but you will sometimes see it with the e (**glueing**).

# go

One of the most common verbs in English is the verb **to go**. It appears in several different forms:

| Present | Past |
|---|---|
| (I, you, we, they) **go** | (I, you, he, she, it, we, they) **went** |
| (he, she, it) **goes** | |
| **going** (*present participle*) | **gone** (*past participle*) |

One of the most common functions of the verb **to go** is to help to indicate future time in English:
> *I'm going to be sick.*
> *They are going to look pretty silly.*

**Going to** is often written in dialogue as **gonna** or **gunna**.

Note that you don't use **went** straight after *have*, *has*, *had* or *having* unless you're writing down ungrammatical speech or dialogue:
> *He should have went yesterday.* WRONG
> *He should have gone yesterday.* RIGHT
> *He went yesterday.* RIGHT

# goal

See **gaol/goal**.

# God / god

Having a capital letter for this word makes a difference to its meaning.

**God** is the name for the supreme maker and ruler of the universe. Those who believe in such a being (for example Jews, Christians, and Muslims) use a capital letter, both for the word God and for connected pronouns like *He* and *His*. Those who don't, often use lower case.

A **god** is a supernatural being who is worshipped because of his power to control human affairs and the world of nature. Many nations have their own group of **gods**:
> *Thor is the ancient Scandinavian god of thunder.*

We call something like money a **god** if we pay too much attention to it.

### goddess

A **goddess** is a female god. The -ess ending indicates the feminine. For more about words like this, see **feminine word endings** and **non-sexist language**.

### goes

This is a form of the verb **to go**. See **go**.

### good / well

These two words are different parts of speech — **good** is an adjective, and **well** is the adverb that relates to it. So, generally, **good** belongs with nouns and **well** with verbs, as in the following sentences:

*You did a good job.* good + noun
*You did it well.* verb + well

We do not say
*You did a well job.* or *You did it good.*

There are, however, common expressions using **good** as an adverb that are generally accepted:
*That sounds good.*
And there's a distinction in meaning between
*You're looking well.* (a comment on health)
and
*You're looking good.* (a comment on looks)

Note that even though **goodly** looks like the adverb from **good** (because of its -ly ending), it is actually an old-fashioned adjective meaning "good".

### goodbye / good-bye

These are equally good ways of writing this word, but **goodbye** is more common. It is a shortening of the expression *God be with ye*.

### goose

The plural of this word is spelled **geese**.

### gorilla / guerilla / griller

These words sound the same (or similar in the case of **griller**) but have different meanings.

A **gorilla** is the largest kind of ape.

A **guerilla** is a member of a small band of soldiers that makes surprise raids and attacks on the enemy. This may also be spelled **guerrilla**.

A **griller** is the part of a stove or kitchen appliance which cooks meat by direct heat.

### gossip

Note that you don't add another p to this word when you add the endings -ed, -ing, or -er to form **gossiped**, **gossiping**, and **gossiper**. See **doubling of last letter**.

### got / gotten

These are both past forms of the verb **get**, though they are used in slightly different ways.

**Got** is the past tense, as in:
> *She got hungry and he got a pizza on the way home.*

It is used this way by English speakers everywhere in the world.

Although you may occasionally see **gotten** in your reading, it is more commonly used in the USA than in the UK.

## got to

This is a common way of saying that someone must do something:
> *I've got to make some lamingtons.*
> *The school's got to raise money for computers.*

The two words are often run together as they are said, and so they're sometimes written as **gotta**. But this spelling is only used in writing that is meant to look colloquial. More formal ways of saying **I've got to** are:
> I have to     I ought to     I must     I should

## governor

Note the ending of this word. See **-er/-or**.

## graceful / gracious

These words are both related to **grace** but they mean different things.

A movement or shape is **graceful** if it is elegant or attractive to look at.

Someone or something is **gracious** if they show kindness and courtesy, as in *a gracious hostess* or *a gracious act of hospitality.*

## graffiti

This noun often takes a singular verb in English:
> *The graffiti at the university is always about sex these days.*

You may also find it with a plural verb:
> *In the good old days, the graffiti were mainly about politics.*

**Graffiti** comes from Italian, and in that language it is a plural noun. Its singular is **graffito**. You might sometimes hear English speakers using **graffito** to refer to a single item of graffiti, but this is very unusual.

## grammar

Every language works by a system of rules which we call **grammar**. The rules affect the way words work, and how they are combined into phrases and sentences.

People know the grammar of their own language without thinking about the rules. Still it's useful and interesting to know something about grammar, so you can talk about language.

For more about the details of English grammar, see **parts of speech, phrases, clauses** and **sentences**.

## Grand Prix

This term has been borrowed from French. Its plural may be spelled in various ways:

| | |
|---|---|
| Grand Prixs | (*Prixs* rhymes with *freeze*) |
| Grands Prix | (*Prix* rhymes with *free*. Don't pronounce the s in *Grands*.) |
| Grand Prix | (*Prix* rhymes with *free*) |
| Grand Prixes | (*Prixes* rhymes with *freeze*) |

## granny / grannie

These are equally good ways of spelling this word. For more about words like this, see **-ie/-y**.

## graphically

Note the ending of this word. See **-ally**.

## grate / great

These words sound the same but mean different things.

A **grate** is a frame of metal bars for holding burning wood or coal in a fireplace. To **grate** is to rub on something making a rough sound:

*Don't let the chalk grate on the board.*

To **grate** cheese or something similar is to rub it into small pieces against the hard rough surface of a kitchen **grater**.

**Great** has a number of important meanings. The most common are "large", as in *a great crowd of people*, or "very good" as in *a really great film*. Look up your dictionary for other meanings of this word. Note that the other forms of **great** are **greater** and **greatest**.

## grave accent ( ` )

The grave accent is used in languages such as French and Italian to show that a vowel is altered in some way. In Italian it shows that the vowel is stressed. In French it is used mostly with e to show that it sounds like the vowel of *met* (rather than *mate*). See **accents**.

It is also used sometimes in English in the editing of poetry, to show that the last part of verbs ending in -ed should be pronounced as a separate syllable. For example *crossèd* would be pronounced as two syllables rather than just one, as you would normally say it. Putting the accent over the e shows how the poet originally intended the word to be pronounced, and is important for the rhythm and rhyme of the poem.

## gray

See **grey/gray**.

## grease / Greece

These words can sound the same but they have different meanings.

The noun **grease** rhymes with *peace*. It is melted animal fat, or any fatty or oily substance like this. The verb **grease** rhymes with *sneeze*. It means "to put **grease** on something":

*Grease the pan before you pour in the batter.*

### great

See **grate/great**.

### grey / gray

This word can be spelled in both these ways, though **grey** is the usual spelling in the UK, and **gray** is more common in the USA.

### grievance

Note the ending of this word. See **-ance/-ence**.

### grill / grille

These words sound the same but mean different things.

A **grill** is a meal, mainly of meat, which has been cooked under a **griller**. To **grill** is to cook meat by direct heat in this way. It can also mean "to question someone harshly and closely".

A **grille** is a screen of metal bars for a window, gate or the front of a motor car.

### griller

See **gorilla/guerilla/griller**.

### grisly / grizzly

These words sound the same but have different meanings.

Something is **grisly** if it is horrible or frightening, as in *a grisly murder*.

Something is **grizzly** if it is greyish in color, as in *a grizzly head of hair*.

The **grizzly bear** is a ferocious bear from North America. Its fur is not always grey — the name is actually a respelling of **grisly**.

### groan / grown

These words sound the same but have different meanings.

To **groan** is to make a low sad sound, often because you are in pain.

**Grown** is a past form of **grow**, to increase in size.

### grovel

For information about whether to double the l when you add endings like -ed or -ing, see **-l-/-ll-**.

### grown

See **groan/grown**.

### guarantee / warranty

When these words have to do with a person's legal rights as a buyer of goods, they mean almost the same thing.

A **guarantee** is a formal declaration in writing by a maker of goods. It says that the goods are of good quality, and promises to repair or replace them if they are found to be faulty within a certain period of time.

A **warranty** has several important legal meanings. One of these is "a manufacturer's written promise as to the extent that defective goods will be repaired or replaced". You usually receive a **warranty** rather than a **guarantee** with second-hand goods such as cars. These are valid for a specified period of time, often three months.

Look up your dictionary for other meanings of these words.

## -gue / -g

These are two ways of spelling the ends of words like:

analog(ue)  catalog(ue)  dialog(ue)  monolog(ue)  travelog(ue)

The shorter forms are standard in the USA, whereas we usually use the longer forms in the UK. The chief exception is *analog(ue)*, which is often spelled with the short form, probably because it is the usual spelling for computers.

## guerilla

See **gorilla/guerilla/griller**.

## guidance

Note the ending of this word. See **-ance/-ence**.

## guilt

See **gilt/guilt**.

## gullible

Note the ending of this word. See **-able/-ible**.

## guttural

If something is **guttural** it has something to do with your throat. It is spelled with -ur in the middle, and not -er, though you can't tell this from the pronunciation. This may be easier to remember if you know that **guttural** comes from the Latin word *guttur* meaning "throat", and not from the English word *gutter*. It has nothing to do with "gutter language".

## gymnasium

The plural of this word may be spelled **gymnasiums** or **gymnasia**. For more about words like this, see **-um**.

## gypsy / gipsy

These are equally good ways of spelling this word. For more about words like this, see **i/y**.

# Hh

### h as a silent letter

The letter <u>h</u> is written but not sounded at the beginning of a few words, such as *heir*, *hour*, *honour* and *honest*. The <u>h</u> is still silent when prefixes are added: *dishonour, dishonest*.

Some speakers also make the <u>h</u> silent at the beginning of words like *herb*, *history*, *historical* and *hotel*, but the habit is becoming less common. (*Habit* itself once had a silent <u>h</u>.) The trend has been to put <u>h</u> back at the beginning of words, perhaps because of the fear of "dropping <u>h</u>'s". However the trend has certainly not touched *heir*, *hour*, *honour* and *honest* yet. For more about this, see **an**.

At the end of words such as *rajah* and *verandah*, the <u>h</u> is silent, and may be left off the spelling altogether.

Note that <u>h</u> can also be silent when it is paired with <u>g</u>. See **gh**.

For more information about silent letters, see **silent letters**.

### háček (ˇ)

This is an accent shaped like a small <u>v</u> that is used in writing Slavic languages such as Czech and Croatian. It usually appears above consonants, and changes the way the letter would be said if it did not have an accent.

For example, the word *háček* itself has the accent above the <u>c</u>. In Czech, from which this word comes, the <u>c</u> is normally pronounced as an <u>s</u>. With the háček it is pronounced like the <u>ch</u> in *cheese*.

The háček appears only very rarely in English writing, mainly when a proper noun from a Slavic country is used (as for example with the former Czech leader *Alexander Dubček*).

For more about accents in English, see **accents**.

### had

This is a form of the verb **to have**. See **have**.

## hadn't

This is a short form of **had not**. See **contractions**.

## had've

Occasionally you'll hear people say phrases like these:
*If I had have gone . . .*
*If I had've gone . . .*
These are irregular versions of:
*If I had gone . . .*
The *have* serves no useful purpose in such a phrase, so it's better not to use it in your writing.

Some people even write (or say) *had of*, which makes even less sense than the original mistake. *Could of* and *should of* are similar mistakes. Avoid all three.

## haiku

**Haiku** is a form of Japanese verse, usually containing just seventeen syllables. In such a short poem the object is to capture the essence of a mood or an idea. The following is a translation of a haiku by the Japanese poet Basho:
On a withered bough
A crow alone is perching;
Autumn evening now.

## hair

If you are writing about hair there are some points to note.

You simply use **hair** if you are writing about a single bunch or mass of hair:
*My hair is red.*
*She cut off a whole handful of hair.*
Here **hair** is a singular noun, because although there are many hairs they are thought of as one mass. **Hair** used in this way is a mass noun.

If you want to stress the particular strands of hair, you use the plural **hairs**:
*Oh no! Three hairs in my beard are turning grey.*
*She cut some long hairs from her fringe.*

For more information, see **mass nouns**.

## hair / hare

These words sound the same but mean different things.

**Hair** is what grows on your head.

A **hare** is a rabbit-like animal.

## half

The plural of this word is spelled **halves**. For more about words like this, see **-f/-v-**.

## half of

There is often disagreement over whether *half of* is followed by a singular or a plural verb. Should we say
*Half of X is . . .*
or
*Half of X are . . . ?*

The answer is simple: it depends on the number of *X*. If *X* is singular, so is the verb that follows:
*Half of my apple <u>is</u> gone.*

If X is plural, so is the verb:
*Half of my apples <u>are</u> gone.*

## hall / haul

These words sound the same but have different meanings.

A **hall** is a large assembly room.

To **haul** something is to drag it along. A **haul** is something you grab or drag in:
*We went fishing and got a good haul of whiting.*

## halo

The plural of this word may be spelled **halos** or **haloes**. For more about words like this, see **-o**.

## handicap

You add an extra p to make the words **handicapped**, **handicapping**, and **handicapper**. For more about words like this, see **doubling of last letter**.

## hangar / hanger

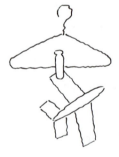

These words sound the same but have different meanings.

A **hangar** is a large building in which aeroplanes are kept.

A **hanger** is something on which you hang your clothes, as in *coathanger*.

## hanged / hung

Both these words are past forms of the verb **hang**. The difference lies in whether you are hanging a person or a thing.

To hang a person is a method of execution. It takes the past form **hanged**.
*He was hanged for drug trafficking.*

To **hang** some<u>thing</u> takes the past form **hung**:
*The Union Jack was hung from our balcony.*

## hanger

See **hangar/hanger**.

## hard / hardly

**Hard** is both an adjective and an adverb. In the following sentence it is an adjective:
*This is a hard bench I'm sitting on.*
In this sentence, however, it is an adverb:
*We worked hard all day.*

**Hardly** is a special negative adverb commonly used with *any*:
*There are hardly any flowers in the garden.*
Because **hardly** functions as a negative it does not need another negative as well. The following is wrong:
*There are hardly no flowers in the garden.*

In the same way, *without hardly* is considered to be illogical. You can walk away *with hardly* a backward glance, but it makes no sense to walk away *without hardly* a backward glance. *Almost without* is the more logical expression to use:
*He walked away almost without a backward glance.*

For more information, see **double negatives**.

Note that when **hardly** is the first word in the sentence, the second word is always an auxiliary verb:
*Hardly had he walked away . . .*

## hard sell

Advertisers, and other persuaders, may choose to address you either directly or indirectly. When their approach is direct and insistent, and seems to pressure you into responding, it is **hard sell** advertising. The less direct approach, which relies on enticing you in more subtle ways, is **soft sell**. Both hard sell and soft sell advertisements are to be seen in WRITING WORKSHOP pp 54–5.

## hare

See **hair/hare**.

## harebrained

This word means "reckless or crazy". It originated in the idea that reckless behavior was typical of a **hare**.

You may sometimes find this word spelled **hairbrained**. This spelling suggests that people have heard the word and assumed it has something to do with hairy brains. Although this mistakes the word's true origin, the spelling has been around now for over 300 years.

## hart

See **heart/hart**.

## has

This is a form of the verb **to have**. See **have**.

## hasn't

This is a short form of **has not**. See **contractions**.

## haul

See **hall/haul**.

## have

One of the most common verbs in English is the verb **to have**. It appears in several different forms:

| *Present* | *Past* |
| --- | --- |
| (I, you, we, they) **have** | (I, you, he, she, it, we, they) **had** |
| (he, she, it) **has** | |
| **having** (*present participle*) | **had** (*past participle*) |

The verb **to have** can work both on its own (as a *main verb*), or it can combine with other verbs (as an *auxiliary verb*):
> *I have an apple.* (main verb)
> *I have returned.* (auxiliary)

**Have** often forms contractions with *not*. For example:
| has not | *becomes* | hasn't |
| have not | | haven't |
| had not | | hadn't |

**Have** also combines with *to*, as a substitute for *must*, to express a need or a duty:
> *I have to go now.*

A common error is to write *of* instead of **have**. See **had've**.

## haven't

This is a short form of **have not**. See **contractions**.

## he / him / his / himself

These personal pronouns are all third person, masculine and singular.

**He** is in the <u>subjective</u> case (it is the subject of a verb):
> *He was walking down the street.*

See **subjective case**.

**Him** is in the <u>objective</u> case:
> *A dog bit him.*

See **objective case**.

**His** is the personal pronoun in the <u>possessive</u> case. It is sometimes called a possessive adjective:
> *The dog bit his leg.*

**His** is also the possessive pronoun:
> *This dog was more vicious than his.*

**Himself** is the reflexive pronoun:
> *He rubbed himself on the leg.*

For more information, see **case, personal pronouns, possessive pronouns** and **reflexive pronouns**.

## heading / headline

**Headings** are the titles given to chapters, or sections and subsections of them, which tell you what subject is about to be discussed. For example:
| *The discovery of Australia* | (chapter heading) |
| *Early Dutch explorers* | (subheading) |
| *The French push* | (subheading) |
| *Captain Cook and the transit of Venus* | (subheading) |

**Headlines** are the brief statements at the top of a newspaper article or editorial. They tell you the main thrust of the item reported underneath. They often read like abbreviated sentences:
> *Minister warns on govt leak*
> *Guests shot at barbecue*

Headlines are printed in larger type than the article itself, and often in a different typeface.

## heal / heel

These words sound the same but mean different things.

To **heal** someone is to cure them of a disease.

Your **heel** is the rounded back of your foot.

## hear / here

These words sound the same but mean different things.

You **hear** sounds with your ears.

If you are **here**, in this place, you are not there in that place.

## heard / herd

These words sound the same but have different meanings.

A **herd** is a mob of cattle.

**Heard** is the past form of the verb **hear**:
*Don't shout. I heard you the first time.*

## heart / hart

These words sound the same but have different meanings.

The **heart** is one of the vital organs of the body, and its function is to pump blood.

A **hart** is a male deer.

## he'd

This is a short form of **he had** or **he would**. See **contractions**.

## hedge words

are words like *rather, quite, somewhat, possibly,* used to soften the impact of a statement:
*The show went well until the set collapsed.*
*The show went quite well until the set collapsed.*
Without the word "quite", you get a strong or bald contrast between the two parts of the sentence. With "quite" added, the first part is softened, and the statement becomes an understatement, with its own more subtle effect.

Hedge words are also useful if you're not sure how strongly you can assert something:
*The author gives a rather sketchy account of federation.*

But be careful not to use hedge words too often in your writing. It quickly becomes noticeable if you "hedge" every second statement.

**Hedge words** contrast with **intensifiers**.

## heel

See **heal/heel**.

## heifer

Note that e comes before i in this word. See **i before e**.

### height

Note that e comes before i in this word. See **i before e**.

**Height** is the noun from the adjective **high**. The word *heighth* is no longer used in English.

Many nouns which come from adjectives of measurement are formed with a -th: *width* from *wide*, *length* from *long*, *depth* from *deep*, *breadth* from *broad*. The word *heighth* was once a common spelling which followed this pattern, but the only correct spelling nowadays is **height**.

### heir

See **air/heir**.

### heir / heirloom

Note that e comes before i in these related words. See **i before e**.

### he'll

This is a short form of **he will**. See **contractions**.

### herd

See **heard/herd**.

### here

See **hear/here**.

### hereditary / heredity

These words are linked — **hereditary** is the adjective from the noun **heredity**.

**Heredity** is the biological process by which characteristics are handed down from one generation to another:
*Heredity determines that you are short and I am tall.*

Something is **hereditary** if it is passed on from parent to child:
*Your tallness must be hereditary — your father's over 200 cm tall!*

### hero

The plural of this word is spelled **heroes**. This is one of the few surviving English nouns ending in -o which does not form its plural by simply adding -s. For more about words like this, see **-o**.

### hero / heroine

A **hero** is someone who has done something very brave. It can also be the person (usually a man or boy) who has the main part in a book, film or play.

A **heroine** is always a woman or girl who has done something brave, or who has a leading role in a story.

Nowadays it is the thing achieved that is most important and not the sex of the person who does it. This is why it is common to find both women and men referred to as **heroes**, although you will also find **heroine** used for women.

For more about this subject, see **non-sexist language**.

### heroin / heroine

These words sound the same but mean different things.

**Heroin** is a drug.

A **heroine** is a female hero:
*She was proclaimed a heroine for rescuing the kitten.*

### he's

This is a short form of **he is** or **he has**. See **contractions**.

### hetero-

This prefix means "different" or "other", as in:
heterogeneous   (of a different kind or kinds)
heterosexual    (attracted to the other sex)

Hetero- is a less common prefix than its opposite number homo-.
See **homo-**.

### hew / hue

These words sound the same but have different meanings.

To **hew** wood is to chop it up into pieces.

**Hue** is another word for "colour":
*This fabric is of such a pretty hue.*

### hiccup / hiccough

These are equally good ways of spelling this word.

**Hiccup** indicates how the word is pronounced, while **hiccough** is closer to the origin of the word.

### him / hymn

These words sound the same but mean different things.

A **hymn** is a religious song.

**Him** is a form of the pronoun **he**:
*I saw him going down the street.*

### hindrance

Note that the verb **hinder** loses its e when you add -ance: **hindrance**. For more about words like this, see **-rance**.

### hinge

The past form of this verb is spelled **hinged**.

When you add -ing you may drop the -e or not — the choice is yours. **Hinging** and **hingeing** are equally good spellings.

For more about words like this, see **-e**.

### hippopotamus

The plural of this word can be spelled **hippopotamuses** or **hippopotami**. For more about words like this, see **-us**.

### hire

See **rent/lease/let/hire**.

## historic / historical

Both these words are linked to **history** but they mean different things.

**Historic** means "memorable". A **historic** occasion is one felt to be important in history.

A **historical** event is one that really happened and is part of history.

## historical / hysterical

These words sound similar but have different meanings.

**Historical** is an adjective from **history**:
*The letters your grandfather wrote from Gallipoli are of historical interest.*

**Hysterical** is the adjective from **hysteria**:
*The child was hysterical with fright and kept screaming.*

## hoard / horde

These words sound the same but have different meanings.

A **horde** is a large group of people or animals.

A **hoard** is a secret supply collected over some period of time:
*I have a private hoard of biscuits in my room.*

## hoarse / horse

These words sound the same but mean different things.

A **horse** is a four-legged animal that neighs.

If your voice is **hoarse**, then it sounds rough and distorted:
*He spoke in a hoarse voice because his throat was sore.*

## hoe

When you add the verb endings -ed and -ing to this word, the spellings are **hoed** and **hoeing**. See **-e**.

## hole / whole

These words sound the same but mean different things.

You can have a **hole** in your pocket or dig a **hole** in the ground.

Something is **whole** if it is complete or entire:
*I have a whole packet of biscuits to myself.*

## holy / wholly / holey

These words sound the same but mean different things.

A **holy** person is saintly and good.

**Wholly** means "entirely":
*I am wholly committed to this new project.*

Something is **holey** if it is full of **holes**:
*Your socks are so holey it's a wonder they don't fall apart.*

## home / hone

These two entirely unrelated words tend to be confused in the phrase **home in on** something, meaning "to focus on or target something".

To **hone** is to sharpen something, such as a knife. There is no such phrase as *hone in on*.

## homo-

This prefix means "same", as in:
homogenise     (to mix so that all parts are alike)
homonym       (same word)
homosexual    (attracted towards the same sex)

Homo- is the opposite of hetero-. See **hetero-**.

## homographs

See **homonyms**.

## homonyms

are sets of words which have the same sound or the same spelling.

So *sail* and *sale* are different words with the same sound. And *row* is an example of how different words can have exactly the same spelling. It can be:
row (quarrel) which rhymes with *how*
*or*
row (a line) which rhymes with *so*

These two types of homonyms have different names. You can call those like *sail/sale* **homophones** (the word is made up of homo-, meaning "same" and -phone, meaning "sound"). Those like *row/row* are called **homographs** (made up of homo-, meaning "same" and -graph, meaning "writing"). The difference in sound or spelling usually means that the words have different origins, though they overlap in modern English.

English has a large number of homophones, and not just pairs, but triplets and even quadruplets. For example:

| | | | |
|---|---|---|---|
| cite | site | sight | |
| flew | flu | flue | |
| holy | holey | wholly | |
| meet | meat | mete | |
| you | ewe | yew | |
| right | rite | write | wright |

Many English homonyms are discussed and illustrated in this book.

## homophones

See **homonyms**.

## hone

See **home/hone**.

### honorary / honourable

These words are both linked to **honour**, but they have different meanings.

An **honorary** position is an unpaid one you take purely for the **honour** it confers on you.

An **honourable** person is one who has a sense of **honour** and who acts accordingly. An **honourable** action is one which is in accordance with that sense of **honour**.

### -hood

This is a suffix from Old English. It means "the state or condition of" (as in *childhood* and *likelihood*), or "a group of" (as in *priesthood* and *sisterhood*). So it has nothing to do with capes, crooks, car bonnets or even Robin Hood!

### hoof

The plural of this word may be spelled **hoofs** or **hooves**. For more about words like this, see **-f/-v-**.

### hopefully

**Hopefully** is often used to mean "I hope that". For example:
*Hopefully the flood waters will subside by tomorrow.*
This could have been phrased as follows:
*I hope that the flood waters will subside by tomorrow.*

Some people consider that the first example really means that the flood waters were "full of hope", and that therefore the sentence is illogical. But logic does not always apply to idiomatic expressions. Most people use **hopefully** in speech to mean "I hope that", and an increasing number are using it this way in their writing. There seems no point in avoiding such a useful idiom which has gained wide acceptance, but be aware that some people will still object quite strongly to it.

### horde

See **hoard/horde**.

### horrible

Note the ending of this word. See **-able/-ible**.

### horror

Note the ending of this word. See **-or/-our**.

### horse

See **hoarse/horse**.

### however / how ever

**However** means the same as *but* and *nevertheless*, and is used in the same way:
*I am going out now. However, I will come back.*
*I am going out now. But I will come back.*
*I am going out now. Nevertheless, I will come back.*

**However**, followed by an adjective indicates that you are being deliberately imprecise:

*A stick of 10 cm, 20 cm or however long it is . . .*

**However many** and **however much** are used in the same vague way:

*However many people attend the dance, we will still have it in the hall.*

**How ever** is an emphatic version of **how**:

*How ever did you do it?*

### hue

See **hew/hue**.

### human / humane

**Humane** is linked to **human** but means something rather different.

A **humane** person has the qualities of kindness, thoughtfulness and sympathy for others that we expect a good human being to have.

A **human** quality is one that is typical of human beings:

*It is only human to put off worrying about things until it is too late.*

### hung

See **hanged/hung**.

### hyena / hyaena

These are equally good spellings. See **-ae-**.

### hymn

See **him/hymn**.

### hyper- / hypo-

These two prefixes are the same for the first three letters, and sound much the same in English, yet their meanings are almost opposite.

Hyper- means "excessively" or "too much", as in:

| | |
|---|---|
| hyperactive | (excessively active) |
| hypercorrect | (too much concerned with what is correct) |
| hypersensitive | (oversensitive) |

Hypo- means "under" or "at a low level", as in:

| | |
|---|---|
| hypodermic | (under the skin) |
| hypothermia | (abnormally low body temperature) |

Make sure you distinguish these prefixes in the following examples:

| | |
|---|---|
| hypercritical | (excessively critical) |
| hypocritical | (pretending, speaking under a guise) |

### hyperbole

**Hyperbole** is the use of exaggeration for emphasis. For example:

*I've told you a million times before not to do that!*

This is of course an exaggeration. The speaker has not told you a million times, but probably only a few times.

## hyphens (-)

are punctuation marks used to link words which should be read together.

**Hyphens** often link the two parts of a compound, as in *baby-sitter, icy-cold* and *(to) cold-shoulder.*

With adjective and verb compounds (like *cold-shoulder* and *icy-cold*) the hyphen has an important role to play in making sure that both parts are read in the right grammatical "slot" in the sentence. Compare the following sentences:

*With icy cold turkey soup, it was a queer meal.*
*With icy-cold turkey soup, it was a queer meal.*

If the hyphen is missing, you're not sure at first which word "cold" goes with. It's the same in these examples:

*They will cold shoulder anyone from outside.*
*They will cold-shoulder anyone from outside.*

The hyphen helps to show that "cold" is part of a compound verb.

With noun compounds the hyphen is usually less important:

*The baby sitter did the washing up.*
*The baby-sitter did the washing up.*

The compound won't suffer from misreading whether there is a hyphen there or not.

Hyphens can also help to keep apart the two parts of a compound or complex word, which would otherwise be misread. You may be puzzled or misled by the following:

sealegs      shakeout      reice      coop

But with hyphens, their meaning is plain:

sea-legs      shake-out      re-ice      co-op

For more information, see **complex words** and **compound words.**

**Hyphens and wordbreaks**. Hyphens are also used when we divide a word at the end of a line, because the whole word won't fit in. The hyphen shows that the rest of the word is on the next line. See **wordbreaks.**

Note that hyphens are the punctuation mark we use within words. The similar but longer mark we use in punctuating sentences is the **dash**. See **dashes.**

## hypo-

See **hyper-/hypo-**.

## hypothesis

The plural of this word is spelled **hypotheses**, with the last syllable pronounced to rhyme with *seas*. For more about words like this, see **-is**.

## hysterical

See **historical/hysterical**.

## I / me / my / mine / myself

These personal pronouns are all first person and singular.

**I** is in the <u>subjective</u> case (it is the subject of a verb):
> *I sent Tony to the office.*

See **subjective case**.

**Me** is in the <u>objective</u> case:
> *Maria sent me to the office.*

See **objective case**.

**My** is the personal pronoun in the <u>possessive</u> case. It is sometimes called a possessive adjective:
> *Take my bag.*

**Mine** is the possessive pronoun:
> *That bag is mine.*

**Myself** is the reflexive pronoun:
> *I hurt myself.*

The question of whether to use **I** or **me** crops up in some common expressions. Should you say *between you and me* or *between you and I*? Remember that **I** must be the <u>subject</u> of a verb. Since in this expression it is not, you should use **me**:
> *between you and me.*

For more information, see **case, personal pronouns, possessive pronouns** and **reflexive pronouns**.

## i before e

As the old rhyme says:
> <u>i</u> before <u>e</u> except after <u>c</u>
> when it sounds like *ee.*

Some of the many words that follow this rule are:
> achieve    believe    chief    grief    piece    siege

The rule also covers words such as:
> ceiling    deceive    deceit    perceive    receive    receipt

With these words you get <u>e</u> before <u>i</u> because of the <u>c</u>.

It also shows why other words do not come under the rule — because the letters do not sound like *ee*. For example:

in *Fahrenheit* and *height* they sound like *eye*.
in *abseil, freight, vein* and *weight* they sound like *ay*.
in *leisure* they sound like the vowel of *met* and *set*.
in *their* they sound like *air*.
in *weir* and *weird* they sound like *eer*.
in *conscience* they sound like the vowel schwa (see **schwa**).

The most common exceptions to this rule are *seize* and *Sheila*, and chemical words like *caffeine, codeine* and *protein*. Others which <u>may</u> be exceptions for you are *either* and *neither*. It depends on whether you say them with an *ee* sound or like *eye*.

### i / y

A few English words can have either <u>i</u> or <u>y</u> as their second letter:

| | | |
|---|---|---|
| cider | *or* | cyder |
| cipher | | cypher |
| dike | | dyke |
| gipsy | | gypsy |
| pigmy | | pygmy |
| silviculture | | sylviculture (forest culture) |
| siphon | | syphon |

In the UK the trend is to use <u>i</u> in all of them, though some writers still prefer to use <u>y</u> in *gypsy* and *pygmy*. Their reason with *gypsy* may be that they think of them as coming from *Egypt*, and therefore the word must have <u>gyp</u> in it. In fact, the gipsies originally came from northern India.

In the USA, some other words are also spelled with <u>i</u> rather than <u>y</u>:

| | | |
|---|---|---|
| silvan | *rather than* | sylvan |
| sirup | | syrup |
| tire (on a wheel) | | tyre |

### i → y

The letter <u>i</u> changes to <u>y</u> in a few words when you add *-ing*. For example, <u>die-</u> becomes <u>dy-</u> in *dying*. Like most words ending in *-e*, it loses the <u>e</u> before adding *-ing*. If the <u>i</u> were not changed to <u>y</u>, it would then become *diing*.

The same changes happen with two other words. *Vie*, meaning "compete", becomes *vying*, and *tie* becomes *tying* — whenever it means "bind" or "link". But when *tie* means "to get an equal score", it keeps both the <u>i</u> and the <u>e</u> in *tieing*:

*The Swans and the Magpies keep tieing every time they play.*

### -ian

This is a very common ending for both nouns and adjectives. You'll find it in common nouns such as:

barbarian   civilian   electrician   grammarian   guardian
historian   librarian   magician   musician   vegetarian

As you can see, many of these words refer to particular kinds of people and their jobs.

The -ian ending also appears in geographical adjectives such as:

| | | | |
|---|---|---|---|
| Austrian | Australian | Belgian | Canadian |
| Indian | Panamanian | Persian | Tasmanian |

Note that the place names built into these words usually have an i in them:

Austrian *from* Austria

Indian *from* India

They never have an e. (Compare **-ean**.)

Note that *Britain* is not an adjective, and is <u>not</u> spelled *Britian*.

Note also that -ian sounds just the same as -ion, but the -ion words are almost always abstract nouns. See **-ion**.

## -ic / -ics

The suffix -ic is the ending of many adjectives — as common as *basic* and as rare as *eclectic*. The list below shows you some of them:

| | | | | | |
|---|---|---|---|---|---|
| automatic | authentic | chronic | civic | classic | comic |
| dogmatic | domestic | dramatic | dynamic | electric | graphic |
| horrific | optic | poetic | public | spastic | toxic |

Like other adjectives, they may be made to work as nouns, and get plural endings as a result. You've probably seen words like *classics, dynamics, graphics,* and the like. When used in sentences they normally take plural verbs:

*The computer graphics <u>are</u> out of this world.*

Note that words like these are also the names of subjects at school and in education, for example, *economics, linguistics, optics, physics,* and *technics*. When these words are used as the name of a subject area they take a <u>singular</u> verb:

*Economics <u>is</u> an exhausting subject.*

## I'd

This is short for **I had** or **I would**. See **contractions**.

## idealistically

Note the ending of this word. See **-ally**.

## idioms

An **idiom** is a special way that a group of people say or write something. It can be a term applied to a language as a whole, or to a dialect, or a jargon. By the idiom of the people we mean popular speech, or the vernacular. The idiom of the computer world is the special jargon we associate with computer experts.

In particular, an idiom is a phrase that is commonly accepted as the right way of expressing a particular idea. Idiom in this sense is a form of expression which is often not meant to be taken literally or analysed grammatically. This is why idioms are so difficult for people who are learning the language. Idioms have to be recognised as a whole unit and they seem to break all the rules. For example, *the spitting image* is not an image that is spitting but an exact likeness.

Sometimes a phrase is idiomatic simply because it has become an accepted way of saying something, rather like a cliché, and it would now seem odd to tamper with the phrase in any way. For example, *to all intents and purposes* is quite grammatical and can be analysed for its literal meaning. It is an idiom because it is an accepted phrase. To change it to, for example, *to all intentions and purposes* or *to all plans and purposes,* would seem very odd to your reader or listener.

**Idiomatic** English is a term used to describe the English of someone who has a good command of the language and who knows all the accepted expressions and idioms.

## idiotically

Note the ending of this word. See **-ally**.

## idle / idol

These words sound the same but mean different things.

You are **idle** if you are doing nothing.

An **idol** can mean a statue of a god or the object of someone's admiration, love or worship, such as a **pop idol**.

## i.e.

This abbreviation means "that is". The letters stand for the Latin words for this expression, *id est*.

You use **i.e.** when you are explaining something in more detail:
*Her letter was addressed to the whole school, i.e. the headmaster, the teachers and all the students.*
*The ice-cream cost him all his pocket-money, i.e. 50p.*

Note that full stops are normally used after each letter and that **i.e.** is not usually followed by a comma.

For more information, see **Latin abbreviations**.

## -ie / -y

Some of the words we use in informal talk are really abbreviations with a special ending added. For example, *pressie* is *present* cut back to the first syllable, with -ie then added on. *Aussie* takes the first syllable of *Australian,* doubles the s, and adds -ie.

People of all ages are very fond of these informal words, and will often invent them on the spur of the moment. But many are established and used everywhere, like the following:
| | | | |
|---|---|---|---|
| bickie | Chrissie | ciggie | cossie |
| hottie | pressie | sickie | trannie |

Some of these words have been around, and written down, for decades. They are just as likely to be spelled with -y as -ie. For example:
| | | |
|---|---|---|
| cabbie | *or* | cabby |
| hippie | | hippy |
| junkie | | junky |
| kiddie | | kiddy |
| tellie | | telly |

Ones that refer to members of the family are actually most often written with -y. For example:

aunty    daddy    granny    hubby    mummy    nanny

But in all such cases, it doesn't matter if you use -ie or -y, because the words themselves are informal. You use them because you want to create a friendly relaxed style, and one which doesn't fuss about the details.

However, note that there is a handful of words where the ending -ie or -y makes a different meaning. They are:

bogie    (railway wagon)        bogy    (something you fear)
bootie   (baby's shoe)          booty   (loot)
caddie   (golfer's assistant)   caddy   (tea container)

## -ienne

See **feminine word endings**.

## if

is one of the conjunctions of English. It suggests that what follows is not to be taken for granted, and that it may or may not be true or about to happen:

*If I have the money, I'll come to aerobics.*

As this example shows, it is used to begin dependent clauses, that is, clauses that cannot stand on their own. Together with the main clause, **if** often sets up a condition for doing something. See **conditional**.

You may see **if** followed by a special form of the verb known as the subjunctive. See **subjunctive**.

*If I were a rich man, I'd build a big house . . .*

Now that there are so few subjunctive verb forms left in English, it is quite normal to use ordinary verb forms with if:

*If I was a rich man, I'd build a big house . . .*

## -ify / -efy

We use both these endings on verbs, and as they sound the same, it is hard to tell which it should be. Overall, -ify is far more common, and the following list shows you only a handful of the words with it:

amplify    beautify    clarify    classify
fortify    gratify     petrify    purify

People often invent new words with -ify on the same pattern:

*We decided to pot-plantify the bathroom.*

The -efy ending is only found with four words:

liquefy    putrefy    rarefy    stupefy

But *liquefy* is also being spelled *liquify* these days, no doubt because of the word *liquid*. It would not be surprising if *putrefy* and *stupefy* begin to be spelled with -ify too, if people think of *putrid* and *stupid* when writing them. *Rarefy* could go either way, because of *rare* and *rarity*.

## I'll

This is short for **I will** or **I shall**. See **contractions**.

## illusion

See **allusion/illusion**. See also **delusion/illusion**.

## illustrator

Note the ending of this word. See **-ator**.

## im-

See **in-/im-**.

## I'm

This is short for **I am**. See **contractions**.

## imagery

is the technique through which a writer creates pictures in the reader's mind to make the words more vivid. Most poetry and poetic prose relies a great deal on imagery.

The two main types of imagery are **metaphors** and **similes**. In a metaphor you say that something <u>is</u> something else:
*A wave is a sea horse tossing its mane.*

In a simile you say that something is <u>like</u> something else:
*A wave is like the mane of a horse.*

Images work best if they refer to something that the reader is familiar with and has actually seen. So the example given above works because most people have seen a horse. If you had written that a wave was like the hide of a yak your reader probably wouldn't get any picture from that at all, because few would have seen a yak.

See **similes**, **metaphors** and **figures of speech**.

## imaginary / imaginative

These words are both linked to **imagine** but they mean different things.

Something is **imaginary** if it is produced by imagining, that is, if it is made up or fanciful:
*My young sister has an imaginary friend that she talks to all the time.*

An **imaginative** person is good at imagining things. If something is **imaginative** then it shows that someone with a good **imagination** thought it up.

## immigrate

See **emigrate/immigrate/migrate**.

## imminent

See **eminent/imminent**.

## immoral

See **amoral/immoral**.

## immorality / immortality

These words look similar but mean entirely different things.

**Immorality** is wicked behavior.

**Immortality** is the power to live forever.

### imperative

The **imperative** is one of the three moods of verbs in English grammar. See **mood**. See also **commands**.

### imperfect aspect

This is another name for the **continuous aspect** of verbs. For more information, see **aspect**.

### imperial measures

This is a system of weights and measures which used to be used in the UK. It is now considered old-fashioned. Nevertheless you may still come across imperial measures in your reading.

The most common units and their symbols are as follows:

| Length | Mass | Volume | |
|---|---|---|---|
| inch (in) | ounce (oz) | fluid ounce | (fl oz) |
| foot (ft) | pound (lb) | pint | (pt) |
| yard (yd) | ton | gallon | (gal) |
| mile | | | |

For more about how to write measurements, see APPENDIX C.

### impersonal writing

is writing which does not show the character of the writer. The personality of the writer is not expressed either through the words or between the lines. The style of government writing is often deliberately impersonal, because the writers have to express the official view rather than any of their own.

In some kinds of essays, and in science writing, you may be encouraged to write in an impersonal way, because personal views are not thought to be relevant to the subject. For ways of developing a more impersonal style, see WRITING WORKSHOP pp 28–31.

### impersonator

Note the ending of this word. See **-ator**.

### implicit

See **explicit/implicit**.

### imply / infer

To **imply** something is to suggest it without actually stating it. For example, the two statements *London is in England* and *Chelsea is a district in London* imply a third — *Chelsea is in England*.

To **infer** something is to work it out from the information provided or from what has been said by other people.

When the great detective states confidently that the man before him is a plumber he has drawn an **inference** from the facts that the man has mud on his shoes and that he arrived in a truck which advertised Wilson's Plumbing.

You can make an **inference** which is not correct. For example, the man might have dirty shoes because he is a gardener and he just borrowed the truck from his friend, Mr Wilson, the plumber. Appearances can be deceiving.

Sometimes we make statements which are not clear and which allow for misinterpretation. There is not much room for error or confusion in the statements about Chelsea and London, but we are not always so precise. So it is possible for others to **infer** things from what we say which we did not mean to **imply**. The **implication** may or may not have been there.

### import / export

Both these words relate to trade.

To **import** goods is to bring them <u>into</u> a country.

To **export** goods is to send them <u>out of</u> a country.

You can remember them from the prefixes <u>im-</u> meaning "into" and <u>ex-</u> meaning "out of ".

Of course whether it is in or out depends on your point of view, that is, which country you take as your starting point. Let us take, for example, trade between the UK and America. If I am an Englishman in England and I am selling goods to America, then I am exporting them. But if I am an American receiving them in America, then those goods are being imported.

### impossible

Note the ending of this word. See **-able/-ible**.

### impostor

Note the ending of this word. See **-er/-or**.

### improvise

This is one of the few words ending in <u>-ise</u> that cannot also be spelled with an <u>-ize</u> ending. It is always spelled **improv<u>ise</u>**. For more about words like this, see **-ise/-ize**.

### in- / im-

These prefixes can mean either "not" or "in", depending on what word they appear in.

1 The meaning "not" is the commoner one in modern English, helping to make many negative words. You'll find you usually know the opposite word as well.

| | |
|---|---|
| inaccurate | (accurate) |
| incredible | (credible) |
| incorrect | (correct) |
| indefinite | (definite) |
| inexperienced | (experienced) |
| infertile | (fertile) |
| insecure | (secure) |
| intolerant | (tolerant) |
| invalid | (valid) |

The prefix im- means the same, but is used before b, m and p:
imbalance    immovable    impossible

The same negative prefix appears as il- before l, and ir- before r:
illegal      illegible
irregular    irrelevant

Curiously, it changes to ig- in *ignoble*, probably because of words like *ignore* and *ignorant*. But this does not happen before any other words beginning with n, such as *numerable*, which becomes *innumerable*.

2 The prefix in- (also im-/il-/ir-) actually meant "in", "on", "into", or "towards", in both Latin and Old English. These are the meanings it has in words from Latin such as:
incline   include   inflame   immigrant   impress
invest    income    inland    inroad      insight

Because we know the words, there is usually no problem about the meaning of the prefix in them. The one case which has caused difficulty is *inflammable*. Its prefix is actually an example of the second meaning ("in" or "into"), but it could be misunderstood as the first (negative) one. The consequences of misunderstanding could be dangerous (or even explosive). Most people now use *flammable* instead, to avoid trouble. See **flammable/inflammable**.

See also **en-/in-** and **in-/un-**.

## in- / un-

Both un- and in- can have negative meanings, and in a few words it doesn't matter which you use. But the general rule is that un- goes with English words, whether old or recently formed, while in- goes with words borrowed from Latin, or formed on the Latin model. This is why we have:
unable   *but*   inability
unjust   *but*   injustice

The adjectives *able* and *just* were part of the English language centuries ago, whereas the nouns *inability* and *injustice* were borrowed from Latin more recently.

It also helps to explain why we have, for example:
uncompleted       *but*   incomplete
undigested                indigestible
undiscriminating          indiscriminate

The words with un- also have English verb endings (-ed, -ing) showing that they have been formed in modern English.

The un- prefix is also used with words that already begin with in-:
uninformative    uninquisitive    unintelligible

It would be confusing to spell them with in- (for example, *ininformative*).

The words from Latin which usually have in- are:
words ending in  -ent   *such as*   infrequent
                 -ate               inadequate
                 -ial               inessential
                 -ible              indestructible
                 -ive               inexpensive

The following may be written with either <u>un-</u> or <u>in-</u>:

| | |
|---|---|
| unadvisable | inadvisable |
| unconceivable | inconceivable |
| uncontrollable | incontrollable |
| uncontrovertible | incontrovertible |
| undecipherable | indecipherable |
| undefinable | indefinable |
| undistinguishable | indistinguishable |
| unescapable | inescapable |

The only case where <u>in-</u> and <u>un-</u> make a different meaning is:

| | |
|---|---|
| inhuman | (brutal) |
| unhuman | (supernatural) |

See also **non-**.

### inaccessible
Note the ending of this word. See **-able/-ible**.

### incense
This word has two meanings, with different pronunciations. One is a noun and the other is a verb.

**Incense,** pronounced with a stress on the <u>in-</u>, is a substance which gives off a sweet smell when burned. It is a noun.

**Incense,** pronounced with a stress on the <u>-cense</u>, is a verb meaning "to make someone angry":
*His rude remarks about the British incense me.*

Note that this word has an <u>-se</u> ending whether it is a noun or a verb.

### incinerator
Note the ending of this word. See **-ator**.

### incisor
Note the ending of this word. See **-er/-or**.

### incite / insight
These words sound similar but they have different meanings.

To **incite** someone to do something is to stir them up so that they will take action. The word is pronounced with the stress on the second syllable <u>-cite</u>.

An **insight** is an intuition or sudden understanding that you have. The word is pronounced with the stress on the first syllable <u>in-</u>:
*Her books reveal an insight into the problems of growing up.*

### incorrigible
Note the ending of this word. See **-able/-ible**.

### incredible
Note the ending of this word. See **-able/-ible**.

### incubator
Note the ending of this word. See **-ator**.

## indefinite articles

The **indefinite articles** in English are *a* or *an* for singular nouns, and *some* for plural nouns or mass nouns:

*I want a banana and an apple for lunch.* (singular)
*There are some apples in the bowl.* (plural)
*There is some butter in the dish.* (mass)

*Some* is optional – it can be left out before plural nouns or mass nouns:

*There are apples in the bowl.* (plural)
*There is butter in the dish.* (mass)

You use an **indefinite article** in front of a noun that has not been referred to before in your writing. The **definite article** (*the*), on the other hand, comes before nouns that have already been referred to or which are clearly identified:

*Where are the apples you promised?*

For more information, see **a, an** and **definite articles**.

## indelible

Note the ending of this word. See **-able/-ible**.

## indent

Paragraphs often begin with the first line at a little distance from the margin, while the next lines go right out to the margin. The space left at the start of the first line is called an **indent**.

Sometimes a whole paragraph is indented, particularly when it is a long quote. The indentation shows that this section of writing is not part of the written work but has been taken from someone else's work.

Note that there are two styles of letter writing, one of which uses indents (open form) while the other doesn't (blocked form). See APPENDIX E.

## indestructible

Note the ending of this word. See **-able/-ible**.

## index

Many books have an index at the back to help readers find what they're looking for in the book. It is an alphabetical list of the items, people, places, and so on which are discussed or referred to in the book. It tells you the numbers of all the pages they are mentioned on. Compare this with **contents**.

The plural of this type of index is **indexes**, though you might sometimes see the rarer spelling **indices**.

In maths, an index is the little number which shows how many times another number has to be multiplied by itself. For example, in $10^4$ (10 to the power of 4, which means $10 \times 10 \times 10 \times 10$) the **index** is $^4$.

The plural of **index**, when you use it with this meaning, is generally **indices**. For more about the plurals of words like this, see **-x**.

## Indian

The word **Indian** could refer to a native of India, or a native of North or South America. While context often makes it clear which type of Indian you are talking about, it is sometimes useful to use the term **American Indian** or **Amerindian** for a member of the aboriginal race of America, and keep **Indian** for a native of India.

In writing about colonial America, American Indians are sometimes referred to as **Red Indians**.

Of course in the phrase **cowboys and Indians**, the presence of the cowboys makes it clear that you are not in India.

## indicative

The **indicative** is one of the three moods of verbs in English grammar. See **mood**.

## indicator

Note the ending of this word. See **-ator**.

## indigestible

Note the ending of this word. See **-able/-ible**.

## indirect object

Compare these sentences:
*Buy your friend the book.*
*Give me the book.*
The phrases *your friend* and *me* are **indirect objects**, and *the book* is the **direct object**.

**Indirect objects** can always be replaced by a phrase beginning with *to* or *for*:
*Buy the book for your friend.*
*Give the book to me.*
In a sense, this object is only "indirectly" acted upon by the verb. For more information on this, see **object**.

## indirect questions

**Indirect questions** are those which are reported rather than quoted directly.
*"Why are you doing that?" he asked.* (direct question)
*He asked me why I was doing that.* (indirect question)
Notice that in the indirect question, there is a shift of tense. The reported question is moved into the past tense to match the main verb in the sentence (*asked*). Note also that there is no question mark in the indirect question.

For more information, see **indirect speech**.

## indirect speech

is speech which is reported from the angle of a witness, rather than in the actual words used by the speaker. For example, when a masked man says to his assistant:
*"You get the keys of the safe."* (direct speech)
it might be reported as:
*The masked man told his assistant to get the keys of the safe.*
(indirect speech)

You can see the small but quite important differences. The indirect speech of the report puts it all into the past tense, making it narrative rather than drama. ("Says" becomes "told".) The word "told" also shows the reader that what the man said was a kind of command. Indirect speech gives you the gist of what was said, but does not claim to tell you the actual words. That's why there are no quotation marks in indirect speech.

For more discussion of this, see **direct speech**.

Note that another name for **indirect speech** is **reported speech**.

### indivisible
Note the ending of this word. See **-able/-ible**.

### indoor / indoors
These words both mean "inside (the house or building)" but **indoor** is the adjective and **indoors** is the adverb:
*My indoor plants always die.* (adjective)
*Let's go indoors to have dinner.* (adverb)

### industrial / industrious
These words look similar but have different meanings.

Something is **industrial** if it has to do with manufacturing goods, as in *industrial waste* or *an industrial worker*. A nation is said to be **industrial** if it has many industries that manufacture goods.

You are **industrious** if you work hard, as in *an industrious student*.

### -ine / -in
The ending -ine is used with a number of adjectives. You see it in *genuine, marine* and *feline*, to name only a few. As those examples show, it has more than one pronunciation:

| *in* genuine | *it rhymes with* | basin |
|---|---|---|
| marine | | seen |
| canine | | sign |

The names of some household chemicals can be spelled either -ine or -in (unless you are writing in science, where the difference is important):

| gelatine | *or* | gelatin |
|---|---|---|
| glycerine | | glycerin |
| lanoline | | lanolin |
| nicotine | | nicotin |
| saccharine | | saccharin |

In these examples, the -ine spelling rhymes with *seen*, and the -in spelling rhymes with *basin*.

In chemistry, -ine is used for alkaloids and organic bases, and -in for neutral substances, so you don't have any choice about which ending to use.

### inedible
Note the ending of this word. See **-able/-ible**.

### ineligible
Note the ending of this word. See **-able/-ible**.

### inexhaustible

Note the ending of this word. See **-able/-ible**.

### infallible

Note the ending of this word. See **-able/-ible**.

### infectious

See **contagious/infectious**.

### infer

Add another r at the end of this word when you add -ed or -ing to form **inferred** or **inferring**. Note that the stress is on the second syllable. But **inference** has only a single r because of the difference in stress — the stress has moved to the first syllable.

For information about the way stress affects words like this, see **doubling of last letter**.

See also **imply/infer**.

### inferno

The plural of this word is spelled **infernos**. For more about words like this, see **-o**.

### infinitives

The **infinitive** form of a verb is the one that's thought of as the *basic* form. When we speak of the verb *to be*, the verb *to jump*, the verb *to dream* and so on, we are using the infinitive to identify each of them. Sometimes it appears without the *to* before it. In the following sentences, the underlined verbs are all infinitives.

> *I want to go home.*
> *She asked them to buy the album.*
> *Did you hear me say I hate to miss the bus?*

See also **split infinitives**.

### inflammable

See **flammable/inflammable**.

### inflections

are the endings which add a grammatical meaning to particular classes of words, especially nouns and verbs. Some languages, such as German and Latin, have a great many different inflections on their words, while English has only a few.

The main ones for English nouns are:

| | |
|---|---|
| -s | (plural) |
| -es | (plural) |
| -'s | (possessive) |

The main ones for English verbs are:

| | |
|---|---|
| -s | (present, 3rd person singular) |
| -ing | (continuous) |
| -ed | (past) |

The main ones for English adjectives are:

| | |
|---|---|
| -er | (comparative) |
| -est | (superlative) |

See also **affixes, case, number, aspect, tense** and **degrees of comparison**.

### inflexible

Note the ending of this word. See **-able/-ible**.

### informal language

is language which has a lot of colloquial words and phrases in it. It may also have some of the loose grammar that spoken language has.

While it is fine to use informal language in informal situations, it is not good to use it in formal writing such as essays. For example, in conversation you might refer to your *trainers* but in formal writing you would refer to *training shoes*. In conversation you might talk about *shooting off* but in formal writing you would *leave* or *depart*. In factual writing, informal language would rarely have a place, but in fictional writing it can help to set a scene or give you a feel for a character.

See **slang, taboo words, four-letter words** and **swear words**.

### informal writing

There's a world of difference in style between:
*Good morning, sir.*
and
*Hi ya!*
The first is a very formal style, the second **informal**. We use the formal style when we are on our best behavior, and want to show that we have a respectful and serious approach. At other times, we may want to be more relaxed and casual in communicating, and then the informal style is definitely the one to use.

In writing too, it is possible to be either formal or informal. Essay writing in school subjects such as history and geography is usually rather formal. But if you are doing creative or personal writing, you can choose the level of formality to suit your purpose.

For more information about this, see WRITING WORKSHOP pp 26–31.

### -ing

This ending can be added to any English verb, such as *cook* (*cooking*), *run* (*running*), and *talk* (*talking*). It means that the action is continuous and goes on without limits. (It is used for the continuous aspect of the verb. See **aspect**.)

Words ending in -ing are often used as adjectives:
*What with barking dogs, blaring transistors and whining chainsaws, my Sunday was less than peaceful.*
They also serve as nouns:
*What with the barking of dogs, blaring of transistors, and the whining of chainsaws, my Sunday was less than peaceful.*

These adjectives and nouns with -ing endings suggest busy action, because of their strong connection with a verb. For more information on this, see **gerunds**.

Note that there is never a hyphen between the verb and -ing, except in the case of *to-ing and fro-ing*. Without the hyphen they would look like words of one syllable (*toing* and *froing*).

Some nouns ending in -ing have begun to lose their link with the verb they came from. They refer more to events and materials than actions. For example:

| sitting (of parliament) | wedding | bedding |
| clothing | icing | mooring |

A few have moved so far in this direction that they are usually plural:

diggings    earnings    findings    innings    savings

## inhuman / inhumane

These words look similar and perhaps the difference between them is just a question of degree.

To be **inhumane** is to be cruel or unkind:

*Drowning cats is an inhumane way of killing them.*

**Inhuman** behaviour is behaviour that you would not believe that human beings could exhibit:

*The treatment of the Jews in Nazi concentration camps was inhuman.*

## initial

For information about whether to double the l when you add endings like -ed or -ing, see **-l-/-ll-**.

## initials

For information about shortening names to their initials, see **abbreviations** and **acronyms**.

## innings

Although this word ends in -s, it can be a singular noun as well as a plural:

*One innings is all you play in a one-day match.* (singular)
*Three innings have been played so far.* (plural)

## innovation

An **innovation** is something new or different:

*The microcomputer is a marvellous innovation for essay writers.*

Since **innovation** means "something new", it is quite unnecessary here to describe it as "new". To say that something is a "new innovation" would be an example of what is called tautology. See **tautology**.

## innuendo

The plural of this word may be spelled **innuendos** or **innuendoes**. For more about words like this, see **-o**.

## inquiry / enquiry

You can use either of these spellings for this word. But note that **enquiry** is often used as a formal word for "a question" and **inquiry** for "an investigation", as in *a government inquiry*. For more about words like this, see **en-/in-**.

## insight

See **incite/insight**.

## insignia

**Insignia** means "badges or special marks of a position someone holds". This noun can take a plural or a singular verb:

*The mayor's insignia are so heavy and elaborate that she rattles when she walks.* (plural)

*The insignia of that airline is an eagle flying through a cloud.* (singular)

It is an interesting word because in Latin it is actually a plural noun whose singular is **insigne**. Some people use **insigne** in English when they are referring to a single badge of office, but this is very rare.

## inspector

Note the ending of this word. See **-er/-or**.

## install

This verb loses an l when -ment is added to form the noun **instalment**.

Note that it keeps the -ll- in the verb forms **installed** and **installing**, and in the noun **installation**.

You may also see the spellings **instal** and **installment**, although these are very rare.

## instants / instance

These words sound the same but mean different things.

**Instants** is the plural of **instant**, meaning "moment":

*For several instants I couldn't breathe.*

An **instance** is a particular example of something happening:

*This was just one instance of injustice.*

## instructor

Note the ending of this word. See **-er/-or**.

## instrumental case

If you do something by means of a particular object, that object is the "instrument" of the action. For example:

*They fastened the door with a padlock.*

*She cut the tape with scissors.*

In these sentences, *padlock* and *scissors* are the instruments used to carry out particular actions. Some grammar books would say that they are examples of the **instrumental case**.

In English the instrumental case is shown by *with* (or *by means of*) going in front of the object which is the instrument. In other languages the instrumental case is shown by special inflections on nouns. See also **case** and **inflections**.

## insulator

Note the ending of this word. See **-ator**.

## insure

See **ensure/insure/assure**.

## intelligent / intellectual

Although you need to be **intelligent** to be an **intellectual**, these words have different meanings.

An **intelligent** person is someone who has the power to reason and learn and think things out.

An **intellectual** person spends a lot of time studying and thinking.

## intensifiers

An **intensifier** is a word used to emphasise others, and give extra weight and attention to them.

The most common all-purpose intensifier is *very*, which can be used to underscore the point, whether you want to say something is *great* or *ghastly*:

*a very exciting movie*
*a very upsetting movie*

The word *very* can be used in all styles of writing, both formal and informal. But like any word, you don't want to overdo it or it becomes obvious. Some alternatives which can also be used are:

extremely    most    particularly    remarkably    really

Some of the intensifiers we use a lot in speech are less suitable for writing, such as:

awfully    incredibly    terrifically

They have a rather casual flavor to them, which is out of place in more formal writing.

## inter- / intra-

The prefix inter- means "between or among". It is built into many words we've borrowed from Latin, such as:

intercept    interjection    intermediate    interpret

It has also helped to make many words in modern English:

interaction    interface    interlock
international    interplay    interview

The meaning "between" is clearest in words such as:

intercontinental    interstate    intertribal

The prefix intra- means "inside", but it has mostly been used in words created in science and government. For example:

intracranial    (inside the skull)
intramural    (inside the walls of the institution; in-house)

These two prefixes make all the difference in pairs such as:

interstate    (between the states)
intrastate    (within the state)

## interjections

An **interjection** is a short exclamation expressing emotion. *Oh!*, *wow!* and *great!* are examples of interjections. For more information, see **exclamations**.

## interpretive / interpretative

These words mean the same thing. **Interpretive** has been formed from the verb **interpret**, while **interpretative** comes from the noun **interpretation** and is what is called a backformation. Some people would disapprove of it for this reason. They argue that there already is a perfectly good word (**interpretive**) and we don't need to invent another. However, **interpretative** is widely used and is listed in most dictionaries.

See **backformation**.

## interrogative pronouns

Many questions are introduced by the words *who, whom, which, whose* and *what*. In such questions, these words are **interrogative pronouns**:

*Who can come?*
*Whom do you want?*
*Which is the one?*
*Whose is that?*
*What do you want?*

They all stand in for nouns, so they're **pronouns**. And they all identify what follows as a question, so they're **interrogative** words.

For more information on the various types of pronouns, see **pronouns**. See also **that/which/who/whom/whose**.

## into / in to

There is quite a difference in meaning between these two sentences:

*She walked in to dinner.*
*She walked into the dinner.*

In the first example the **in** and **to** are separate because *in* connects with *walked* while *to* connects with *dinner. She walked in* is one main idea of the sentence and *to dinner* is another.

In the second example *into* connects as a whole with *the dinner. Into the dinner* is one main idea of the sentence, and *she walked* is the other.

So it's important to think about how these words connect with the other parts of the sentence they're in, when deciding whether to use **into** or **in to**. Note that **into** is a preposition, while **in** is an adverb in the phrase **in to**.

## intra-

See **inter-/intra-**.

## intransitive verbs

Verbs can be **transitive** or **intransitive**. You can usually tell which by asking the question *"what?"* or *"who?"* after the verb. If there is no answer, the verb is **intransitive**. If there is an answer, the verb has a direct object and it is **transitive**:

*After a while the train stopped.* (intransitive)
*The driver stopped the train.* (transitive)

When you ask "stopped what?" in the first sentence, there is no answer. So *stopped* in this sentence is **intransitive**. When you ask "stopped what?" in the second sentence, the answer is "the train", so *stopped* in this sentence is **transitive**, with *the train* as its object.

Note that the answer to the question *"who?"* or *"what?"* has to be a noun or an expression that acts as a noun:

*I walked for miles with my dog.*
*I walked him for miles.*

In the first sentence *for miles* is an adverbial phrase, which does not act as a noun. It does not really answer the question *"what?"*, so *walked* here is intransitive. In the second sentence *him* is a pronoun, which acts like a noun, and <u>does</u> answer the question *"who?"*, so *walked* is transitive here.

Note that there are many verbs like *walk* and *stop* which can be either transitive or intransitive, depending on the sentence they're in. There are also some verbs which can only be one or the other. *Talk, proceed* and *degenerate*, for example, are always intransitive. *Assure, brandish* and *bring* are some that are always transitive.

For more information, see **object**.

### intrigue

Note that the <u>e</u> is dropped when you add the verb endings <u>-ed</u> and <u>-ing</u> to form **intrigued** and **intriguing**. For more about words like this, see **-e**.

### introductions

**Introductions** should tell readers what to expect as they read on. At the start of a novel or narrative you need to know something about the characters and the situation they're in. (For more about this, see WRITING WORKSHOP p 42.)

In the introduction to an essay, you need to tell the reader what topic you are going to discuss, so that it is clear <u>why</u> you are presenting the points that follow. The best introductions also say something to make the topic sound interesting, so that the reader is keen to read on. For more about essay introductions, see WRITING WORKSHOP pp 46 and 48.

### invalid

This word has two meanings, with different pronunciations. One is an adjective and the other is a noun.

**Invalid**, pronounced with the stress on the <u>-val-</u>, is an adjective meaning "not valid or correct":
*Your credit card is invalid because you did not sign your name.*

An **invalid**, pronounced with the stress on the <u>in-</u>, is someone in such a poor state of health that they need to be looked after or nursed. It is a noun.

### invaluable

See **valuable/invaluable/valueless**.

### inverted commas ( " " or ' ' )

are better known as **quotation marks**. For more on how to use them, see **quotation marks**.

### investigator

Note the ending of this word. See **-ator**.

### investor

Note the ending of this word. See **-er/-or**.

### invincible

Note the ending of this word. See **-able/-ible**.

### invisible

Note the ending of this word. See **-able/-ible**.

### -ion

This is the most common ending for abstract nouns. Some of the words you'll find it in are:

| | | | |
|---|---|---|---|
| adaptation | adoption | assertion | combustion |
| communion | competition | completion | confession |
| conclusion | decision | detention | distribution |
| expulsion | inspection | motion | recession |

Many such words were borrowed ready-made from Latin (or French), but they do have other relatives in English. For example:

| | | | |
|---|---|---|---|
| conclusion | (conclude) | decision | (decide) |
| detention | (detain) | expulsion | (expel) |
| motion | (move) | recession | (recede) |

The verbs in brackets are a little different in form, but their meaning is similar.

### ion / iron

These words sound the same but mean different things.

You **iron** your clothes with an **iron**.

An **ion** is a small particle of matter with an electric charge.

### -ious

is the ending of many of our longer adjectives. For example:

| | | | |
|---|---|---|---|
| ambitious | glorious | gracious | harmonious |
| industrious | oblivious | rebellious | religious |

For more about them, see **-ous**.

### iron

See **ion/iron**.

### irony

is a form of humour in speech or writing in which what you say is the opposite of what you actually mean.

In plays or stories you can use what is called **dramatic irony**. This is where the <u>characters</u> respond to what is happening at face value, but the <u>audience</u> or <u>reader</u> understands what is really going on.

In the story of Little Red Riding Hood the little girl says to her grandmother, "Oh Grandmamma, what big ears you have! What big eyes you have!" The reader knows that Grandmamma is not really Grandmamma but the wolf, so there is dramatic irony in this conversation.

The climax comes when Red Riding Hood says "What big teeth you have!" and the wolf replies "All the better to eat you with!". There can be no misunderstanding this. Little Red Riding Hood is at last let in on the knowledge that the reader has had for some time, that her grandmother is a wolf and wants to eat her.

Sarcasm is a form of irony used to make fun of someone. On the surface it says to someone else "You're okay" but underneath it says "You're an idiot".

"What an athlete!" you might say to a friend who has just tripped over. "What style! What grace!" You mean, of course, just the opposite. When you are just kidding, sarcasm can be friendly, but when the intention is to make fun of someone, sarcasm can be cruel.

## irregular verbs

Some of the most common verbs in English form their different tenses in an unpredictable way. The majority of verbs (**regular verbs**) add -ed to give both the past tense and the past participle. For instance, *to walk*:

> *I walked* (past tense)
> *I have walked* (past participle)

Any verb which does not use this method of creating its past participle and its past tense is known as an **irregular verb**.

An example of an irregular verb is *to draw*, where the past forms are:

> *I drew*      not   *I drawed*
> *I have drawn*   not   *I have drawed*

Another example is the verb *to hit*, which doesn't change at all for its past tense and past participle:

> *I hit the ball so hard it broke the window.*
> *I have hit it so many times my arm's sore.*

| Some irregular verbs | | | | | |
|---|---|---|---|---|---|
| begin | began | begun | ride | rode | ridden |
| bite | bit | bitten | ring | rang | rung |
| blow | blew | blown | rise | rose | risen |
| break | broke | broken | see | saw | seen |
| drink | drank | drunk | shake | shook | shaken |
| drive | drove | driven | sing | sang | sung |
| eat | ate | eaten | sink | sank | sunk |
| fall | fell | fallen | speak | spoke | spoken |
| fly | flew | flown | swim | swam | swum |
| forget | forgot | forgotten | take | took | taken |
| freeze | froze | frozen | tear | tore | torn |
| give | gave | given | throw | threw | thrown |
| go | went | gone | tread | trod | trodden |
| hide | hid | hidden | wear | wore | worn |
| know | knew | known | write | wrote | written |

### irrelevant / irreverent

These words are similar but have different meanings.

You are **irreverent** when you make fun of something that ought to be revered or taken seriously.

A comment is **irrelevant** when it is unnecessary, superfluous and of no account.

### irresistible

Note the ending of this word. See **-able/-ible**.

### irresponsible

Note the ending of this word. See **-able/-ible**.

### irreverent

See **irrelevant/irreverent**.

### is

This verb is part of the verb **to be**. For more information, see **be**.

### -is

This is the ending of a number of words we've borrowed from Latin and Greek, such as:

axis    basis    genesis    hypothesis    neurosis    thesis

They make their plurals by changing the -is to -es. So the plural of

| axis | *is* | axes |
| basis | | bases |
| genesis | | geneses |
| thesis | | theses |

Although these special plurals look exactly like ordinary English plurals, the last syllable is pronounced like *seas*.

Note that in writing you can't tell apart the plural of *axe* (*axes*) and *axis* (*axes*), or the plural of *base* (*bases*) and *basis* (*bases*).

### -isation / -ization

As with -ise/-ize, you can choose either of these spellings:

civilisation    *or*    civilization
organisation    *or*    organization

Both are equally good. But your choice should match up with whatever you do with **-ise/-ize**:

If you write *civilise*, you should use *civilisation*.
If you write *organize*, you should use *organization*.

The argument for using -ise/-isation is given under **-ise/-ize**.

### -ise / -ize

Many words can be spelled with either **-ise** or **-ize** at the end:

| civilise | *or* | civilize |
| emphasise | | emphasize |
| hypnotise | | hypnotize |
| organise | | organize |
| realise | | realize |
| recognise | | recognize |

For the sake of consistency, you should decide to use either -ise or -ize in all such words.

In the past, people have sometimes argued for one spelling or the other in a particular word because of its history. But the arguments are never clear-cut, and it is simpler to spell all one way or the other. Still, there are one or two points to note.

1 If you choose -ise, you can use it in every case except *capsize*. (See **capsize**.) It is the only exception.

2 If you choose -ize, as most Americans and some British people do, you have to remember quite a large number of exceptions. There can, for example, be no -ize in:

| | | | |
|---|---|---|---|
| advise | chastise | comprise | compromise |
| demise | devise | despise | enterprise |
| exercise | improvise | revise | surprise |
| supervise | televise | | |

Because there are so many words which must take -ise, it is easier to use -ise everywhere.

## -ish

We use the ending -ish to make adjectives out of nouns:

| | | | |
|---|---|---|---|
| childish | feverish | girlish | prudish |
| selfish | sheepish | stylish | |

They express the particular character or style of something.

This ending is also added to adjectives to make words with a tentative meaning:

bluish     (sort of blue)
largish     (rather large)
latish     (a bit late)
reddish     (sort of red)
thinnish     (rather thin)

The tentative or approximate meaning is also found in words relating to time:

*It'll be tennish before they're back.* (about ten o'clock)

## -ism

This ending appears on words which describe a particular philosophy or way of life. For example:

| | | |
|---|---|---|
| communism | cynicism | idealism |
| imperialism | impressionism | marxism |

In a special subgroup of words, -ism is used to mean a particular idiom or expression of language. For example:

Americanism     (an American expression)
archaism     (an old-fashioned expression)
colloquialism     (an expression used in casual conversation)
legalism     (an expression used in law)

## -ist

Words ending in -ist refer to a particular attitude or commitment. For example:

| | | | |
|---|---|---|---|
| alarmist | capitalist | conservationist | defeatist |
| escapist | extremist | humanist | materialist |
| opportunist | racist | sexist | socialist |

They may be used as adjectives or nouns.

Some words like these are nouns which describe a person's job, or their particular expertise. For example:

artist            botanist            cartoonist        dentist
economist     harpist              herbalist          novelist
organist        physiotherapist   tobacconist      typist
ventriloquist

As job titles, they can all apply to both men and women. There is nothing sexist about them.

## it

is the pronoun we use to refer to things or animals:

*As the sun rose, it raised their hopes.*

*The spider is very tidy. It wraps its prey in neat packages.*

Note that **its** is the possessive form of **it**, without any apostrophe. (See **its/it's**.)

Because **it** never refers to people, it is sometimes called the impersonal pronoun. In fact, it can be used to avoid mentioning people at all. Compare these two sentences:

*The staff all agreed to abolish the cane.*

*It was agreed that the cane should be abolished.*

In the second version there is no sign as to who did what. It is as if the agreement took place without human intervention! **It** doesn't stand as a pronoun for anything at all there. It is just a "dummy" subject for the sentence. It helps to keep people out of the subject role, and to create an impersonal style.

For more about writing in the impersonal style, see WRITING WORKSHOP pp 29–31 and 32.

## italics

are a special sloping form of print, with the letters slightly slanted. They contrast with our normal upright form of print, which is called roman. The words printed below show you the difference between italics and roman:

*manned space flight*     (italics)
manned space flight     (roman)

Italics are used for words that the writer wants to show are somehow different from their neighbours in the regular line of print. They may be foreign words, like *Rakete* (German for "rocket"), or the particular name of something, like the *Challenger* spacecraft, for example, or the title of a book or film such as *Dogs in Space*.

Italics cannot be properly shown with your handwriting, or on many typewriters. Instead, writers underline the word or words which they would like to have **italicised** (put into italics).

## it'd

This is short for **it had** or **it would**. See **contractions**.

## it'll

This is short for **it will**. See **contractions**.

## its / it's

**It's** is short for **it is**: *it's wet*. See **contractions**.

**Its** is the special possessive form of **it**, and never has an apostrophe: *The dog chewed its bone*.

Just remember that for this pair of words you only use an apostrophe when you leave something out – the i of *is* in **it is**.

## -ity

The most common words ending in -ity are nouns with a related adjective. For example:

| | |
|---|---|
| brutality | brutal |
| fatality | fatal |
| inferiority | inferior |
| salinity | saline |
| simplicity | simple |
| sincerity | sincere |
| vanity | vain |

New words ending in -ity are often formed from adjectives ending in -able or -ible. For example:

| | |
|---|---|
| capable | capability |
| liable | liability |
| possible | possibility |
| responsible | responsibility |

Notice how with these -ity words there are two changes from the adjective:

**1** an i is inserted between the b and the l.
**2** the final e is dropped before -ity.

For more about words ending in -e, see **-e**.

## -ive

This is the ending of many adjectives. You'll find it in words like:

| | | | |
|---|---|---|---|
| active | aggressive | attentive | attractive |
| collective | competitive | conclusive | creative |
| decisive | exclusive | impressive | persuasive |
| possessive | productive | representative | subversive |

Most of them have partners – nouns or verbs or both – which you can use to help vary your writing. For example:

| | | |
|---|---|---|
| aggressive | aggression | |
| attractive | attraction | attract |
| competitive | competition | compete |
| creative | creation | create |
| exclusive | exclusion | exclude |

So the same idea could be expressed as:
*There was plenty of competition in the class.*
*There was a competitive spirit in the class.*
*The students were competing with one another.*

## I've

This is short for **I have**. See **contractions**.

## -ix

See **feminine word endings**.

# Jj

### jail / gaol

These are equally good ways of spelling this word.

**Jail** is the most natural spelling for the pronunciation.

Both **jail** and **gaol** are very old spellings in English, going back to the medieval English spellings *jaiole* and *gayole*.

### jam / jamb

These words sound the same but mean different things.

**Jam** is a sweet spread made from fruit.

A **jamb** is part of a door frame.

### janitor

Note the ending of this word. See **-er/-or**.

### jargon

is the language of specialists and experts. It is used by professionals (like teachers and doctors), tradespeople (like plumbers and carpenters) and in sports and recreations. You could speak of the *jargon of chemistry*, the *jargon of hairdressing* or the *jargon of cricket*. Any specialised activity needs its own jargon to describe the details of what goes on there.

Most people apply the word **jargon** to specialised language they don't understand, and to express their dislike of it.

### jeans / genes

These words sound the same but have different meanings.

**Jeans** are trousers made of denim or other strong material.

**Genes** are the units in your body which are responsible for passing on physical characteristics, like blue eyes, from parents to their children.

257

## jewellery / jewelry

These are equally good spellings for this word.

**Jewellery** is the usual spelling in the UK.

**Jewelry** is the usual spelling in the USA.

Note also that **jeweller** is the usual spelling in the UK for someone who works with jewels. The usual US spelling for this word is **jeweler**.

See **-l-/-ll-**.

## journalese

is the language and style typical of journalists' writing. Because they have to write a lot in a short time, they tend to recycle clichés, and their reporting is often rather predictable. How often does a news report speak of a "war-torn" country, or of "a snap decision" by a minister? If you are writing a newspaper article yourself, you might want to use some **journalese**, but it is a pity to use it in other kinds of writing.

## journalism

is a form of nonfiction writing for newspapers. There are two main types of journalistic writing – the news report (which presents the facts) and the feature article (which provides some discussion and interpretation of the facts). An example of a news report is reproduced in WRITING WORKSHOP p 53.

## journals

A **journal** is a record of what happens day by day. Travellers and explorers write journals to make sure their experiences don't get forgotten, and as a source of information for others. Journals are therefore more likely to be written as public documents than are **diaries**. A sample of a famous journal is reproduced in WRITING WORKSHOP p 38.

Students are quite often asked to keep their own journals, for daily practice in writing. The more you try to put your thoughts down on paper, the easier it becomes. In your journal you can experiment with words, and try out different ways of saying something – without having to worry about what marks it will score.

A **journal** is also the name for a specialist magazine that comes out regularly, for example, the *Journal of Applied Science*.

## journey

Note that you keep the y at the end of this word when you add -s, -ed or -ing: **journeys, journeyed, journeying**.

## judgement / judgment

These are equally good ways of spelling this word. See **-ment**.

## junkie / junky

These are equally good spellings for this noun, which is an informal word for a drug addict. For more about words like this, see **-ie/-y**.

# Kk

### k as a silent letter

The letter k̲ is not sounded when it comes before n̲ at the beginning of a word. You'll find it in words like:

knee  kneel  knife  knight  knit
knob  knock  knot  know  knuckle

They are all very old English words, and over the centuries the k̲ in them has gradually disappeared from the pronunciation. You might wonder why we don't just drop the k̲ from the spelling too. But it helps to make:

knight  *different from*  night
knit                        nit
knot                        not

and so on.

For more about silent letters, see **silent letters**.

### Kelvin scale

This is a scale of temperature in which zero is $-273.16°C$. Its symbol is K, without a full stop:

*O°K equals $-459.69°F$.*

Compare this scale with **Celsius**.

### kerb

See **curb/kerb**.

### kernel

See **colonel/kernel**.

### kerosene / kerosine

These are equally good ways of spelling this word.
Choose whichever spelling you like, but make sure you use the same one throughout your work.

### key / quay

These words sound the same but mean different things.

A **key** is most often a small, specially shaped piece of metal that can open a lock. For other meanings of this word look up your dictionary.

A **quay** is a wharf where ships load or unload passengers and cargo.

## kidnap

Add another p to this word when you add -ed, -ing or -er to form **kidnapped**, **kidnapping**, and **kidnapper**.

In the USA, the p is not always doubled, so you might see the spellings **kidnaped**, **kidnaping**, and **kidnaper**.

See **doubling of last letter**.

## kidney

The plural of this word is spelled **kidneys**. For more about words like this, see **-ey**.

## kilo-

This prefix means "one thousand" or "one thousand times". It is used to form units of measurement. For example:

kilogram   1000 grams
kilometre   1000 metres
kilojoule   1000 joules

Note that in computer technology, a *kilobyte* is actually 1024 bytes, not 1000.

## kilometre

**Kilometre** is the conventional spelling in the UK. The symbol for **kilometre** is **km**, without a full stop.

You may sometimes find this word spelled **kilometer**, which is the usual spelling in the USA.

For more information on how to write measurements, see APPENDIX C.

For more on the spelling, see **-re/-er**.

## kimono

This word comes from Japan. Its plural is spelled **kimonos**. For more about words like this, see **-o**.

## kind of / kinds of

When you are using **kind** as a noun to mean "sort", remember that it is a singular noun. This is especially important when you use it with a collective noun such as *people*, *team*, and *crowd*, which stands for a group of things taken as a whole.

So while it is correct to write *this kind of fruit*, it is wrong to write *these kind of fruit*.

If you want to talk about more than one type of fruit, you should use **kinds of**, as in *these kinds of fruit*.

## knead

See **need/knead**.

### kneeled / knelt

These are equally good spellings for the past forms of the verb
**kneel**:

I kneeled    I have kneeled
I knelt      I have knelt

For more about words like this, see **-ed/-t**.

### knew

See **new/knew**.

### knife

The plural of this word is spelled **knives**. For more about words
like this, see **-f/-v-**.

### knight

See **night/knight/nite**.

### knit / nit

These words sound the same but have different meanings.

To **knit** is to make something out of long strands of wool, using
a pair of long needles.

A **nit** is the egg or young of an insect, such as a louse, living in
human hair.

### knitted / knit

These are equally good spellings for the past forms of the verb
**knit**:

I knitted    I have knitted
I knit       I have knit

Both spellings can be used for the adjective.

**Knitted** is usually used when writing about wool:
   *He knitted her a beautiful woollen jumper.*
   *It was a knitted tea-cosy.*

**Knit** is usually used for things other than wool:
   *His forehead was knit in concentration.*
   *We were a closely knit group.*

For more about words like this, see **-ed/-t**.

### knot

See **not/knot**.

### know

See **no/know**.

### knowledgeable

Note that you keep the e at the end of **knowledge** when you
add -able to form this word.

For more about words like this, see **-able/-eable**.

### kumquat / cumquat

These are equally good spellings for this word. Choose
whichever you like, but make sure you use the same spelling
throughout your work.

# Ll

## l as a silent letter

The letter l is not sounded when it comes after a or o, and before f, k or m. It happens in words like:

| | | | |
|---|---|---|---|
| almond | alms | calf | calm |
| chalk | folk | half | palm |
| psalm | qualm | salmon | stalk |
| talk | walk | yolk | |

It is also silent before d in *could*, *should* and *would*. In fact there shouldn't be an l in *could*. It wasn't there in Old English, and has got into the spelling by mistake.

For more about silent letters, see **silent letters**.

## -l- / -ll-

When a word ends in l, do you have to double the l before adding endings that begin with a vowel? Which should we choose?

| | | | | |
|---|---|---|---|---|
| equaled | *or* | equalled | marvelous | *or* | marvellous |
| reveled | | revelled | medalist | | medallist |
| totaled | | totalled | modeling | | modelling |
| trialed | | trialled | tranquiliser | | tranquilliser |

According to the general rules for doubling the last letter, they should all have one l, because there's no stress on the syllable which ends in l. (See **doubling of last letter**.)

In the USA, such words are normally written with just one l. It helps to show the difference in stress between, say, *reveled* and *rebelled*. In British spelling, the words ending in l get double l (-ll-), whatever the stress, before most endings. Even so, we don't double l before -ise. For example:

equalise  formalise  legalise  socialise  vandalise

When you put *equalled* beside *equalise*, or *totalled* beside *totalisator*, it seems inconsistent.

Writers need a consistent policy on -l-/-ll-, especially when new words are being created all the time. What do you do with the following words?

chanel(l)ed  initial(l)ed  pencil(l)ed  spiral(l)ed  tunnel(l)ed

If you go for -ll- you are safely within traditional British spelling. If you use -l- you're in line with standard American spelling.

## label

For information about whether to double the l when you add endings like -ed, -ing, or -er, see **-l-/-ll-**.

## laboratory

Note the ending of this word. See **-ary/-ery/-ory**.

## laconically

Note the ending of this word. See **-ally**.

## laden / loaded

These words are sometimes both thought to be past forms of the verb **load**. In fact this is not so, but many of their meanings are the same.

**Laden** is the past form of the verb **lade**. Except in this past form, **lade** is quite a rare word in English. It has basically the same meaning as the verb **load** ("to put on or take on a load"), but with a stronger sense of unpleasant burden:

*The truck was heavily laden with iron girders.*
*I felt laden with too many responsibilities.*

**Loaded** is the past tense of **load**. It can be used anywhere where **laden** is used. It can also be used in some senses of **load** where **laden** cannot be used:

*The gun was loaded when she fired.*

## lady / woman

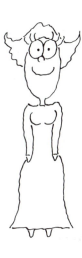

People used to save the title **lady** for women of the upper classes. In a class-conscious society it was important to know who was from the "best" families and who was part of the common herd. Nowadays the distinction is not so important and the term **lady** refers either to a woman who has good manners and is very polite, or simply to any woman.

This genteel term has, however, turned up in efforts to deal with a new problem. Many occupations have names which do not indicate the gender of the person doing the job. And so where, for example, a doctor or a plumber is a woman, some people are tempted to indicate gender by such clumsy expressions as *a lady doctor* and *a lady plumber*. In most cases like this the fact that the person is female is irrelevant. It is their occupation that is important. For more information, see **non-sexist language**.

## laid / lain

These words are similar in meaning, but there is an important difference. They are the past forms of different verbs. See **lay/lie**.

## lama / llama

These words sound the same but mean different things.

A **lama** is a Buddhist priest or monk.

A **llama** is a native animal of South America related to the camel and used for carrying loads.

## lame / lamé

These words look similar, but mean different things and are pronounced differently.

**Lame** means "crippled".

**Lamé** is a type of fabric. It is a French word, and the acute accent over the -e indicates that the last syllable is pronounced *may*.

Note that words like **lamé** gradually lose their accent as they become more settled into English. But you can see that the accent is particularly useful in this case because without it **lamé** would look exactly the same as **lame**. For more about accents in English, see **accents**. See also **acute accents**.

## lane / lain

These words sound the same but have different meanings.

A **lane** is a narrow road, or a strip of road marked out for a single line of vehicles.

**Lain** is a past form of the verb **lie**:
*She felt refreshed after she had lain down for half an hour.*

## lanoline / lanolin

These are equally good spellings. See **-ine/-in**.

## larva

The plural of this word is spelled **larvae**, with the last syllable pronounced to rhyme with *see*. For more about words like this, see **-a (as a singular ending)**.

## larva / lava

These words sound the same but mean different things.

**Lava** is molten rock from a volcano.

A **larva** is the young of an insect.

## larynx

The plural of this word may be spelled **larynxes** or **larynges**. For more about words like this, see **-x**.

## lasso

The plural of this word may be spelled **lassos** or **lassoes**. For more about the plural of words like this, see **-o**.

When you add -ed and -ing to the verb, the spelling is **lassoed** and **lassoing**.

**Lasso** has a strange spelling for its pronunciation (*lass-oo*), because it came into English from Spanish. The original Spanish word is *lazo*.

## later / latter

These words look similar but have different meanings.

**Later** is one of the forms of **late**:
*Dinner will be later than usual.*
*I'll go to a later session of the film.*

**Latter** refers to the second thing mentioned out of two (as opposed to *former*):
*I prefer the latter of the recipes you read out.*
See also **former/latter**.

## Latin abbreviations

Some of the most common abbreviations used in English actually come from Latin words and phrases. Abbreviations like *e.g.*, *i.e.*, *a.m.* and *p.m.* all stand for Latin phrases.

Latin abbreviations are used in three main areas. Some examples of each are given below:

### 1 General

e.g.   short for *exempli gratia*, which means "for example". See **e.g.**

etc.   short for *et cetera*, which means "and the rest". See **etc.**

i.e.   short for *id est*, which means "that is". See **i.e.**

Note that when you are writing an essay, it's more appropriate to write what you mean out in full, rather than using abbreviations like these. Instead of *e.g.* you could use *such as* or *for example*. For *etc.*, phrases like *and so on* and *and the like* are useful. The best thing to use instead of *i.e.* is *that is*.

### 2 Time

a.m.   short for *ante meridiem*, which means "before noon".

p.m.   short for *post meridiem*, which means "after noon".

c. *or* ca   short for *circa*, which means "about" or "approximately".

AD   short for *anno domini*, which means "in the year of our Lord". For information on how to use AD and BC in your writing, see **dates** and **AD/BC**.

### 3 Footnotes

ibid.   short for *ibidem* which means "in the same place".

loc. cit.   short for *loco citato*, which means "in the place or passage already mentioned".

op. cit.   short for *opere citato*, which means "in the work already mentioned".

See APPENDIX B for more examples of Latin abbreviations we commonly use.

For general information about writing abbreviations, see **abbreviations**.

## latitude / longitude

These words both have to do with plotting a point on the earth's surface.

**Latitude** is the distance (measured in degrees) by which a point on the earth is north or south of the equator.

**Longitude** is the distance (measured in degrees) by which a point on the earth is east or west of Greenwich in England. Note that this word should not be pronounced or spelled as if it had an extra t (*longtitude*).

## latter

See **later/latter**. See also **former/latter**.

## lava

See **larva/lava**.

## law / lore

These words sound the same but mean different things.

The **law** is a set of rules made by a government or a ruler.

**Lore** is learning or knowledge about a particular subject, as in *the lore of herbs*.

## lay / lie

The past forms of these verbs are often confused.

**Lay** is a verb meaning "to put down". It always needs an object – you lay <u>something</u> somewhere. It's an irregular verb, with *laid* as its past form:

| | |
|---|---|
| *I now lay my heart before you.* | (present) |
| *I laid the table last night.* | (past) |
| *I had laid the old map open on the desk.* | (past participle) |

**Lie** is another irregular verb, meaning "to be or rest in a flat position". It never has an object – you just lie <u>somewhere</u>. Its past tense is **lay**, and its past participle **lain**:

| | |
|---|---|
| *Every day I lie in the sun for a while.* | (present) |
| *I lay down for a sleep this morning.* | (past) |
| *I had lain in the sun for an hour.* | (past participle) |

**Lie** is also a verb meaning "to tell an untruth". Its past forms are regular: **I lied, I have lied**.

## leach

See **leech/leach**.

## lead / led

**Lead** means two things. Firstly, it can be a heavy bluish-grey metal used to make things such as pipes and petrol. This **lead** rhymes with *fed*. Secondly, it is a verb meaning "to guide". This **lead** rhymes with *feed*.

**Led** is the past form of the verb **lead**:
*She led them up the garden path.*

## leaf

The plural of **leaf** is **leaves**:
*The leaves are falling from the trees.*
*The leaves of my book are turning yellow with age.*

When **leaf** is used as a verb, it keeps its -f when you add -s, -ed or -ing:
> *A speed-reader quickly leafs through a book.*
> *I leafed through the magazine in the waiting room.*
> *I've stopped reading — I'm just leafing through.*

For more about words like this, see **-f/-v-**.

### leak / leek

These words sound the same but have different meanings.

A **leak** is a hole or crack that lets liquid or gas in or out accidentally.

A **leek** is a vegetable that is related to the onion.

### leaned / leant

These are equally good ways of spelling the past forms of the verb **lean**:
> I leaned    I have leaned
> I leant     I have leant

For more about words like this, see **-ed/-t**.

### leant / lent

These words sound the same but have different meanings.

**Leant** is a past form of the verb **lean**, to rest against or on something for support:
> *He leant his head on my shoulder.*

The word **lent** is the past form of the verb **lend**, to let someone use something of yours for a short time.

Note that **Lent** (with a capital L) is the period of forty days before Easter. Some people fast during this time in memory of Christ's fast in the wilderness.

### leaped / leapt

These are equally good spellings for the past forms of the verb **leap**:
> I leaped    I have leaped
> I leapt     I have leapt

For more about words like this, see **-ed/-t**.

### learn / teach

These words have to do with the gaining or giving of knowledge and they should not be confused.

To **learn** is to gain knowledge of or master a particular thing. You yourself can *learn Italian* or *learn the saxophone*, but you cannot *learn someone else Italian* or *learn someone else the piano*. Instead we say that you *teach someone Italian* or *teach someone the piano*.

### learned / learnt

These are equally good ways of spelling the past forms of the verb **learn**:
> I learned   I have learned
> I learnt    I have learnt

For more about words like this, see **-ed/-t**.

## lease

See **rent/lease/let/hire**.

## leased / least

These words sound the same but have different meanings.

**Leased** is the past form of the verb **lease**, to give or have the use of something in return for rent:
*I leased my car.*
*We have leased this office space for many years.*

**Least** means "smallest":
*Which teacher gives you the least amount of homework?*

## led

See **lead/led**.

## leech / leach

These words sound the same but mean different things.

A **leech** is a small worm that sucks the blood of humans or animals.

When soil is **leached**, chemicals are washed out of it by the passage of water.

## leek

See **leak/leek**.

## legend

The legend on a map explains the meaning of any symbols and colours that have been used. It is the key to understanding the map. For example, if the map presents land forms, the legend would tell you what the colours mean in terms of metres above sea level. It may have symbols for forests or marshes, which are also explained in the legend.

## legends

See **myths/legends**.

## legible

Note the ending of this word. See **-able/-ible**.

## leisure

Note that e comes before i in this word. See **i before e**.

## lend / loan

It is usual to use **lend** as a verb, and **loan** as either a noun or a verb:
*My father won't lend me his new sports jacket.*
*I asked him so nicely for a loan of it.*
*I'd loan him mine if I owned one.*

In casual talk you will often hear people use **lend** as a noun:
*He said he'd give me a lend of his red sports car instead.*

## lent

See **leant/lent**.

### leper / leprosy / leprous

Note that the second e̲ in **leper** is dropped to spell the name of the disease, **leprosy**, and the adjective **leprous**, meaning "having leprosy".

### less

See **fewer/less**.

### -less

is an ending meaning "without" or "lacking". It often contrasts with the ending -ful:

| careless | careful | lawless | lawful |
|----------|---------|---------|--------|
| fearless | fearful | merciless | merciful |
| harmless | harmful | restless | restful |
| hopeless | hopeful | | |

But note that some pairs like these don't make perfect opposites:

doubtless    (unquestionably)
doubtful    (full of doubt, uncertain)

shameless    (lacking a sense of shame, blatant)
shameful    (regrettable)

### less / lesser

These related words are similar in meaning but are used in different ways.

**Less** means "not as much":
*I use less salt than you.*
*Her research has received less attention than it deserves.*

**Lesser** means "smaller than another":
*The judge sentenced him for the lesser crime of manslaughter.*

### lessen / lesson

These words sound the same but mean different things.

To **lessen** is to become or make **less**:
*The pain should begin to lessen soon.*

A **lesson** is the time a student or a class spends learning one subject.

### lesser

See **less/lesser**.

### lesser / lessor

These words look similar but mean different things.

We describe one thing as **lesser** than another if it is smaller in any way:
*He chose the lesser of two evils.*

A **lessor** is someone who owns property and leases it to someone else. Note that **lessor** ends in -o̲r̲, not -e̲r̲. This is because it came into English straight from French. For more about this, see **-er/-or**.

### let

See **rent/lease/let/hire**.

### letters

When you write a letter, the style and contents are affected by the person, or the institution, you're writing to. It may be very personal, or very impersonal. Several different kinds of letters are shown in WRITING WORKSHOP pp 56–8.

Business letters may be set out in either <u>open</u> or <u>blocked</u> format. There are diagrams of both in APPENDIX E.

### levee / levy

These words sound the same but have different meanings.

A **levee** is a natural or a man-made bank of earth and sand beside a river.

A **levy** is a fee or a tax which has to be paid.

### level

For information about whether to double the <u>l</u> when you add endings like <u>-ed</u>, <u>-ing</u>, or <u>-er</u>, see **-l-/-ll-**.

### levy

See **levee/levy**.

### liable

See **likely/liable/apt/prone**.

### liar / lyre

These words sound the same but have different meanings.

A **liar** is someone who tells lies.

A **lyre** is a stringed musical instrument like a harp, used in ancient Greece.

### libel / slander

These legal words have similar meanings but there is an important difference.

**Slander** is a <u>spoken</u> statement which damages someone's reputation or good name.

**Libel** is a <u>written or printed</u> statement which damages someone's reputation. For information about whether to double the <u>l</u> when you add <u>-ed</u>, <u>-ing</u>, <u>-er</u> or <u>-ous</u> to **libel**, see **-l-/-ll-**.

### licence / license

**Licence** is a noun and **license** is a verb:
> *I can get my driver's licence next year.*
> *The government wants to license all television sets.*

The adjective **licensed** comes from the verb **license**:
> *Is it a licensed restaurant?*

The noun **licensee** also comes from the verb **license**:
> *Who is the licensee of this hotel?*

Note that, in the USA, both the noun and the verb are spelled **license**.

For more about words like this, see **-ce/-se**.

## licorice / liquorice

These are equally good ways of spelling this word. **Licorice** is the spelling that is closest to the word's original spelling in English, *lycorys*, which was used in medieval times.

People began to use the spelling **liquorice** because they thought licorice had something to do with *liquor*, but in fact this is not so. A further development from this mistaken notion is the spelling **liquorish**.

In older writing you might also find the word **lickerish**. This is pronounced the same as **licorice** but is quite a different word. It means "greedy" or "lustful".

## lighted

See **lit/lighted**.

## lightning / lightening

These words look similar but mean different things.

**Lightning** is the sudden flash of light in the sky caused by electricity in the air during a thunderstorm.

**Lightening** is a form of the verb **lighten**, to make less dark, or to make less in weight:
*I've been lightening the paint but it's still too red.*

## likable / likeable

These are equally good spellings. See **-able/-eable**.

## like / as

In traditional grammar **like** is a preposition, used to introduce a noun or something standing for a noun. So we would write:
*She acts like a witch.*

**As** is a conjunction and we use it to link a new clause with one already there:
*She acts as witches do.*

These two sentences mean the same thing.

Nowadays people use **like** in many cases when it is formally wrong because it sounds better than **as**:
*She acts like witches do.*
Here **like** is acting as a conjunction which people used to think was wrong.

This is an example of a word taking on a new role in grammar. For more about words that do this, see **transfer of classes**.

## likeable / likable

These are equally good spellings. See **-able/-eable**.

## likely / liable / apt / prone

These four words can all be used to express the probability of something happening, but there are differences between them.

**Likely** is best used for a particular probability:
*She is likely to pass this maths exam.*

**Apt** is better used for general rather than specific probability:
*She is apt to speak her mind.*

**Liable** and **prone** are often used to indicate an unpleasant outcome:
*You are liable to get a parking fine if you stay there.*
*She is prone to hay fever in spring.*

So remember to consider what sort of probability you want to write about and choose the word that serves your purpose best.

## limericks

A **limerick** is a type of humorous verse of five lines. It was named after Limerick in Ireland because originally this sort of verse was part of a song with the refrain "Will you come up to Limerick?" Here is an example:

There was an old lady from Ryde
Who ate green apples and died.
The apples fermented
Inside the lamented
And made cider inside her inside.

## link words

Any good piece of writing will connect and develop ideas from one sentence to another. The connecting links in these chains of ideas are often **link words**. They may seem small and unimportant, if you look at the lists below. However, they can do a great deal to make your writing cohesive.

(Some of the link words in the paragraph you've just read are *these, they, if* and *however*.)

Link words include:
1  this     that     these     those     (**demonstratives**)
2  he   she   it   his   him   her   hers   its   they   them
their   (third person **pronouns**)
3  although   and   as   because   but   if   nor   or   since
so   when   while   yet   (**conjunctions**)
4  also   besides   consequently   furthermore   hence
however   likewise   nevertheless   next   otherwise
neither   similarly   still   then   therefore   thus
(connective **adverbs**)

All these words, and others like them, make links with something already mentioned. The demonstratives and pronouns link up with things and people named earlier. The conjunctions and connective adverbs link ideas and statements with each other, either within a sentence, or from one sentence to the next.

See also **cohesion**.

## liquefy / liquify

These are equally good spellings for this word. See **-ify/-efy**.

## liqueur / liquor

These words look similar but refer to different types of alcoholic drink.

**Liquor** is any strong alcoholic drink distilled from wine, such as brandy, or from grain, such as whisky.

A **liqueur** is a type of sweet **liquor**.

## liquidator

Note the ending of this word. See **-ator**.

## liquify

See **liquefy/liquify**.

## liquor

See **liqueur/liquor**.

## liquorice

See **licorice/liquorice**.

## lists

When you first make a list of things, it's often a bit rough and ready. You may be just brainstorming ideas, and the order and the wording in the list doesn't matter at all. (See WRITING WORKSHOP p 6.)

But when you want to present a list in an essay or report, it needs to be tidy. Here are some points to check. Make sure:
- the items are all alike    (and all deserve their place in the list)
- the wording of each item    (if one begins with <u>the</u>, then they
  is like the others    all should)
- the punctuation and    (all with a dash, or number in
  layout are the same for    front; all in capitals, or in lower
  each item    case; all with a full stop, or
  comma, or nothing after them)

A list like this makes it easy for readers to run their eye straight down it, and it presents things in the clearest way.

The list of books which makes a <u>bibliography</u> is presented in a special way. See WRITING WORKSHOP p 64.

## lit / lighted

These are equally good ways of spelling the past forms of the verb **light**, although **lit** is more common.
| I lit | I have lit |
| I lighted | I have lighted |

For more about words like this, see **-ed/-t**.

## literally / figuratively

These words have opposite meanings.

If you take something **literally** then you take it at face value. So, for example, if someone offered "to lead you up the garden path", you would follow them.

If someone is speaking **figuratively**, then they are giving words an abstract or imaginative meaning rather than the ordinary one. So, for example, if someone says "you're being led up the garden path" then they mean that you're being deceived.

## literary / literally

These words look similar but they have different meanings.

**Literary** means "relating to books or literature", as in *literary criticism*. A **literary** person has a knowledge or love of literature.

A common meaning of **literally** is "actually or without exaggeration":
*There were literally thousands of ants swarming in the kitchen.*

## literary style

Writers can create special literary effects through the style in which they cast their ideas. You choose the style to suit the particular point you want to get across, or the kind of world you want to create. For more about these styles, see **allegory**, **fantasy**, **irony**, **parody**, **realism** and **satire**.

## litre

**Litre** is the conventional spelling in the UK. The symbol for **litre** is **l**, without a full stop.

You may sometimes see this word spelled *liter*, which is the spelling most often used in the USA.

For more on the spelling, see **-re/-er**. For more about metric measures, see APPENDIX C.

## livable / liveable

These are equally good spellings. See **-able/-eable**.

## llama

See **lama/llama**.

## load / lode

These words sound the same but have different meanings.

A **load** is something carried.

A **lode** is a geological word for a strip of minerals running along a joint in rocks.

## loaded

See **laden/loaded**.

## loaf

The plural of this noun is spelled **loaves**:
*We baked thirteen loaves of bread today: a baker's dozen!*

When **loaf** is used as a verb, it keeps its -f when you add -s, -ed or -ing:
*He just loafs around the house all day.*
*He loafed around the house all day yesterday.*
*He'll be loafing around the house all day tomorrow.*

For more about words like this, see **-f/-v-**.

## loan

See **lend/loan**.

## loan / lone

These words sound the same but mean different things.

A **loan** is the giving of something to be used for a short time and then returned to the owner:
  *Can I have a loan of your ruler?*
It can also be the thing lent, particularly if it's money, as in *a loan from the bank*.

**Lone** means "not with anyone", as in *a lone traveller*. It can also mean "standing apart", as in *a lone tree*.

## loan words

are words that English has borrowed from other languages, such as *ballet* (from French), *rodeo* (from Spanish) and *abseil* (from German). *Boomerang* is of course a loan word from an Aboriginal language. Though these words have come into English, they go on being used in the language from which they were borrowed, and in that way they are loans, rather than takeovers.

Loan words often bring with them unusual spellings, because the language they come from uses the letters of the alphabet a little differently from English. The "silent t" on *ballet* is one example.

## loath / loathe

These words are related but mean different things.

**Loath** means "unwilling" or "reluctant" and rhymes with *both*.
  *I'm loath to sack them.*

To **loathe** is to feel intense hatred and disgust for something or someone. This rhymes with *clothe*.

## lock / loch

These words sound the same but have different meanings.

A **lock** is used with a key for fastening doors and other things.

**Loch** is the Scottish word for a lake.

## locus

The plural of this word may be spelled **locuses** or **loci**. For more about words like this, see **-us**.

## logically

Note the ending of this word. See **-ally**.

## lone

See **loan/lone**.

## longitude

See **latitude/longitude**.

## loose / loosen

As verbs these words have slightly different meanings, though both are related to the adjective **loose**.

To **loose** is to set someone or something free. The opposite of this is *bind*:

*I don't think you should loose such a dangerous animal.*

This way of using **loose** is becoming less common than it once was. Nowadays it is more common in the form **let loose**, as in *to let the horses loose*.

To **loosen** something is to make it less tight. The opposite of this is *tighten*:

*I've eaten so much that I'll have to loosen my belt.*

The distinction between **loose** and **loosen** becomes less clear when we speak of loosing or loosening a knot. To loose a knot is to undo it, but to loosen a knot is to make it less tight. There isn't much difference between these two actions.

Note that **unloose** means the same as **loose**. It is *not* the opposite as you might expect from the **un-** at the beginning. This is an old-fashioned word and you will usually find it in sayings such as *unloose the dogs of war*.

**Unloosen** means the same as **loosen**, but it seems to be becoming more common than **loosen**:

*Why don't you unloosen your belt?*

## loose / lose

These words look similar but mean different things.

Something is **loose** if it is not fastened, as in *a loose end of a rope*. This word rhymes with *moose*.

When you **lose** something, you can't find it. This word rhymes with *chews*.

## loosen

See **loose/loosen**.

## loot / lute

These words sound the same but mean different things.

**Loot** is anything that has been stolen, often from an enemy in wartime.

A **lute** is an old-fashioned musical instrument with strings like a guitar.

## lore

See **law/lore**.

## lose

See **loose/lose**.

### loud / loudly

**Loud** can be used as an adjective and an adverb:
*What a loud voice you have!* (adjective)
*There's no need to shout so loud.* (adverb)

**Loudly** is only ever used as an adverb:
*There's no need to shout so loudly.*

### louse

If you're writing about the insects that sometimes infest people's hair, the plural is spelled **lice**. But if you're using **louse** to refer to a nasty, unpleasant person, the plural is **louses**.

### louvre / louver

These are equally good ways of spelling this word. **Louvre** is the usual spelling in the UK. In the USA, it is usually spelled **louver**. For more about words like this, see **-re/-er**.

### lovable / loveable

These are equally good spellings. See **-able/-eable**.

### lower case letters

**Lower case letters** are the opposite of *capital letters*. They are the small letters that make up most of your writing.

The name **lower case** comes from the printing industry. In older methods of printing, each letter was on a separate piece of metal, called a *type*. These pieces of type were all stored in boxes or cases in the printery. The boxes on the top held the capital letters. The boxes underneath held the others — they were in the <u>lower</u> case.

### lunar

Note the ending of this word. See **-ar**.

### lustre / luster

These are equally good ways of spelling this word. The usual spelling in the UK is **lustre**. **Luster** is the way this word is usually spelled in the USA.

For more about words like this, see **-re/-er**.

### lute

See **loot/lute**.

### luxuriant / luxurious

These related words have different meanings.

**Luxuriant** means "plentiful or growing strongly", as in *luxuriant plants* or *luxuriant hair*.

We say that something is **luxurious** if it is very comfortable, beautiful and expensive, as in *a luxurious hotel*.

**-ly**

is the ending we normally use to turn adjectives into adverbs:

| bright | + | ly | brightly |
| quick | + | ly | quickly |
| smiling | + | ly | smilingly |

A few of our adverbs don't have this ending, but they are the minority. See **adverbs**.

Quite a few adjectives already end in -ly, including the following:

| cowardly | deadly | frilly | friendly | heavenly |
| homely | kindly | leisurely | lovely | manly |
| motherly | orderly | sickly | silly | stately |
| ungainly | worldly | | | |

Of course, none of these can be turned into adverbs by adding -ly. It would be too awkward. Instead we use a phrase, for example *in a cowardly way*.

The -ly ending is the usual one for adjectives referring to intervals of time, or compass points.
For example:

| daily | fortnightly | hourly | monthly | nightly |
| quarterly | yearly | | northerly | southerly |

To turn these into adverbs we again use a phrase, for example: *every day, every fortnight, from the north.*

**lyre**

See **liar/lyre**.

**lyrics**

are most commonly thought of as the words that go with a song, but a poem can be described as a **lyric** even though it was never intended to be sung. Such poems are divided into sections called **stanzas** as if they were meant to go with a tune, and they are simple and personal in tone. The following is a stanza from a lyric poem by William Wordsworth:

I wandered lonely as a cloud
That floats on high o'er vales and hills,
When all at once I saw a crowd,
A host, of golden daffodils;
Beside the lake, beneath the trees,
Fluttering and dancing in the breeze.

## macaroni

In English **macaroni** is a <u>singular</u> noun, even when you are writing about lots of pieces of macaroni:

*They've made so much macaroni <u>it is</u> pouring out the kitchen window.*

This kind of noun is called a *mass* noun: a mass of macaroni is singular as well as just one piece. See **mass nouns**.

Sometimes, though, you will need a <u>plural</u> for **macaroni**, especially when you are writing about different types of macaroni. This plural is spelled **macaronis**:

*We make three macaronis at the factory: white, red and green.*

The word **macaroni** is borrowed from Italian, where it was once spelled *maccaroni* but is now spelled *maccheroni*. In English you may also see this word spelled **maccaroni**, with the double <u>c</u>.

## macramé

Note that this word has an acute accent over the final <u>e</u>. This shows that the word has come to us from French, where the last two letters would be pronounced *may*. In English, though, it is more usual to pronounce them like the word *me*.

The acute accent helps to show that there is this special pronunciation. But words with accents tend to lose them when they become better known in English. In the future you may well see this word written without the acute accent.

For more about accents in English, see **accents**. See also **acute accents**.

## madam

You use this word as a polite way to address a woman:

*Madam, your dress is on fire.*

If you are addressing more than one woman you can use either **madams** or **mesdames**, though it is more usual in such cases to use the word *ladies*.

**Madams** follows the normal English pattern for making plurals — simply adding <u>-s</u> (or <u>-es</u>).

**Mesdames** is the French form of the plural. As well as adding an s̲, the first part of the word changes. This is because the word was originally two words in French – *ma dame* – and the French make both these words plural – *mes dames.*

**Madam** is sometimes shortened to **ma'am**, but this form is mainly used for women in the USA and the Queen.

### made / maid

These words sound the same but have different meanings.

**Made** is the past form of the verb **make**:
  *I made a cake yesterday.*

A **maid** is a woman who tidies guests' rooms in a hotel.

### magically

Note the ending of this word. See **-ally**.

### magnet / magnate

These words sound similar but they have different meanings.

A **magnet** is something which attracts metals.

A **magnate** is an important and powerful person in business.

### maharaja / maharajah

These are equally good spellings for this word, a title for Indian princes. Choose whichever you like, but make sure you use the same spelling throughout your work.

For the plural, simply add -s̲: **maharajas, maharajahs.**

The female is called a **maharani,** which can also be spelled **maharanee.**

### maid

See **made/maid**.

### mail / male

These words sound the same but have different meanings.

To **mail** a letter is to post it. The **mail** is all the letters, parcels, and so on that are sent by post.

A **male** animal is of the masculine gender. A man is a male, and so is a boy.

### main / mane

These words sound the same but have different meanings.

The **main** thing is the most important thing.

A **mane** is long hair growing on the neck of an animal like a horse or a lion.

## main clauses

**Main clauses** always have a main verb in them. They can stand alone as a sentence, as in:

*I'm going home.*

When the main clause stands alone, as in the sentence above, it is known as a simple sentence. A main clause can also join with a dependent clause to form a longer sentence, as in:

*After we've had lunch, I'm going home.*

Another name for main clauses is **principal clauses**. See **clauses**.

## maintain / maintenance

The noun **maintenance** is related to the verb **maintain** in spite of the different spelling. For more about words like this, see **-aim/-ain**.

## main verbs

A **main verb** tells what action or process is or was taking place in a sentence:

*He sings softly.*
*We ate the cheese.*
*They were running.*

In these sentences *sings*, *ate* and *running* are **main verbs**. *Were* is different — it is an **auxiliary verb**. Its job is simply to join with *running* to make up a complete verb. *Running* on its own would not be enough.

For more information, see **auxiliary verbs**.

## maize / maze

These words sound the same but have different meanings.

**Maize** is another name for corn.

A **maze** is a confusing network of connecting paths or passages. It is another word for *labyrinth*.

## majestically

Note the ending of this word. See **-ally**.

## majority / minority

When you use **majority** and **minority** the verb will be either singular or plural depending on the sense you want to emphasise. This is the same as with words like *government*, *team* or *crowd* which refer either to a single unit or to a collection of individuals:

*A large majority of teachers was present.*
*A tiny minority of protesters were present.*

For further information, see **collective nouns**.

## male

See **mail/male**.

## mall / maul

These words can sound the same but actually mean different things.

A **mall** is a large shopping area, usually with the shops grouped around an open space for the public. This word can be pronounced to rhyme with either *ball* or *pal*.

The original meaning of **mall** derives from the old game of pall-mall in which a ball was driven through an iron ring with a mallet (a **mall**). Pall-mall came to be used for the alley where the game was played, hence the street Pall Mall in London. From there, **mall** came to mean a level shaded walk, a street or area with shops, hence its modern meaning.

To **maul** something or someone is to attack them savagely.
*The lion mauls a carcass.*
This word is always pronounced to rhyme with *ball*.

## man

This old English word is the first part of quite a lot of compounds and longer words. The following are a sample of them:

| | | | | |
|---|---|---|---|---|
| man-eating | manful | manhood | manhandle | manhole |
| manhours | manhunt | mankind | manly | man-made |
| manpower | man-sized | manslaughter | | |

The word **man** has two meanings:

1 an adult male
2 people in general

These two different meanings are not always recognised. In words like *manful, manhood* and *manly,* the first part clearly means "adult male". In others, such as *manhandle, manhunt* and *man-sized,* the word **man** seems to mean "adult male", because the whole word refers to something which normally involves men.

But in quite a lot of similar words, **man** is intended to mean "people in general". This is so in *man-eating, manhole, manhours, mankind, man-made, manpower, manslaughter,* etc. Man-eating tigers certainly don't limit their diet to adult males! And women help to make up the *manpower* which turns out *man-made* products in a given number of *manhours.* These words, like *mankind* itself, are intended to refer to people in general, not a single sex.

Still, it is easy enough to avoid words in which **man** may seem to be exclusive. For example, you could use:

the human race (*instead of* mankind)
workforce (*instead of* manpower)
artificial (*instead of* man-made)

Note that in words such as the ones below, the letters man- are the Latin root for "hand":

| | |
|---|---|
| manicure | manufacture |
| manoeuvre | manual |
| manuscript | manipulate |

They have nothing to do with either adult males or people at large.

For more about *man,* see **-man** and **non-sexist language**.

## -man

This old English word appears in the names of many job titles.
For example:

| | | | |
|---|---|---|---|
| alderman | businessman | chairman | draughtsman |
| fireman | foreman | linesman | newsman |
| ombudsman | policeman | postman | salesman |
| spokesman | sportsman | stockman | |

Though **man** can mean either "adult male" or "human being", it tends to be understood as "adult male" in such words. So they seem to exclude women from doing the job they refer to.

The difficulty can be avoided in one of two ways:
**1** by using an alternative term to cover both men and women.
For example:

| executive | *for* | businessman/woman |
|---|---|---|
| chairperson or chair | | chairman/woman |
| firefighter | | fireman/woman |
| supervisor | | foreman/woman |
| journalist *or* reporter | | newsman/woman |
| salesperson *or* assistant | | salesman/woman |
| competitor *or* athlete | | sportsman/woman |

**2** by using a parallel term with -woman, for example:

| businessman | businesswoman |
|---|---|
| chairman | chairwoman |
| policeman | policewoman |
| sportsman | sportswoman |

For more about this, see **non-sexist language**.

## manageable

Note the ending of this word. See **-able/-eable**.

## mandarin

A **mandarin** is a fruit like an orange. It can also be spelled **mandarine**.

A **mandarin** was a public official in the Chinese Empire.

When it has a capital <u>M</u>, **Mandarin** refers to the official language of China.

## mane

See **main/mane**.

## maneuver

See **manoeuvre/maneuver**.

## mango

The plural of this word may be spelled **mangos** or **mangoes**. For more about words like this, see **-o**.

## manifesto

The plural of this word may be spelled **manifestos** or **manifestoes**. For more about words like this, see **-o**.

## manikin / mannequin

These words can sound the same but they mean different things.

A **manikin** is a little man. It is also a model of the human body used for such study as anatomy. This word is sometimes spelled **manakin** or **mannikin**.

A **mannequin** is a person who models clothes. It is also another name for the dummy or model in the shop window. It can be pronounced the same as **manikin**, or with the last syllable pronounced *kwin*.

## manner / manor / manna

These words sound the same but have different meanings.

Your **manner** is the way in which you behave. If you have **good manners** you behave politely.

A **manor** is a mansion surrounded by a large estate.

**Manna** is the food which, in the Old Testament, miraculously fell from heaven to feed the Israelites in the desert.

## manoeuvre / maneuver

These are equally good spellings for this word. **Manoeuvre** is the usual spelling in the UK. **Maneuver** is the usual spelling in the USA. See **-oe-** and **-re/-er**.

## manor

See **manner/manor/manna**.

## mare / mayor

These words sound the same but have different meanings.

A **mare** is a female horse.

A **mayor** is the chief official of a local government.

## marijuana / marihuana

These are equally good spellings for this word, though **marihuana** is closer to the sound of the original Mexican Spanish word.

Choose whichever spelling you like, but make sure you use the same one throughout your work.

## marshal / martial

These words sound the same but mean different things.

**Martial** means "to do with fighting or war", as in *martial arts*. It comes from *Mars*, the name of the Roman god of war.

A **marshal** is an official like a sheriff. To **marshal** troops is to line them up in order.

For information about whether to double the l when you add -ed or -ing to **marshal**, see **-l-/-ll-**.

## marvel

You have a choice whether or not to double the l when you add -ed, -ing or -ous to this word. See **-l-/-ll-**.

## masculine gender

The pronouns *he*, *him* and *his* are said to be **masculine** in gender because they refer to males, while *she*, *her* and *hers* are said to be **feminine**, because they refer to females. Some pairs of nouns, too (like *prince* and *princess*), can be said to have gender.

This kind of gender is called **natural gender** because it depends on whether the thing or person being referred to is male or female. In some languages you may learn, though, there is what is called **grammatical gender**. For more information on this, see **gender**.

## mass nouns

contrast with **count nouns**. **Count nouns** refer to individual things that can be counted. **Mass nouns** refer to things that occur as a mass, and are not normally counted or used in the plural. As an example, *butter* is a mass noun. You don't usually say *two butters* — you just say *butter* or *some butter*.

For more information, see **count nouns**.

## masterful / masterly

These words are both linked to **master** but mean different things.

A **masterful** person is one who takes command of things.

To do something in a **masterly** way is to do it like an expert.

## mat / matt

These words sound the same but have different meanings.

A **mat** is a small floor covering.

**Matt** means "not shiny" or "unpolished". It is also spelled **matte** but this is most commonly an American spelling. There is, however, a variant spelling **mat** which is becoming increasingly popular.
  *The kitchen wall has a matt finish.*

## mathematically

Note the ending of this word. See **-ally**.

## matinee / matinée

These are equally good ways of writing this word.

The word originally came into English from French, where it is always written with an accute accent: **matinée**. This accent shows that the -nee is pronounced *nay*.

However the word has become so well-known in English that it is now most often written without the accent: **matinee**.

For more about accents in English, see **accents**. See also **acute accents**.

## matrix

The plural of this word can be spelled **matrixes** or **matrices**. For more about words like this, see **-x**.

## matt

See **mat/matt**.

## maul

See **mall/maul**.

## maxi-

comes from the Latin word meaning "greatest". The *maximum* is the greatest value on a scale, and it of course contrasts with the *minimum*, the smallest value.

Now **maxi-** and **mini-** are beginning to be used as prefixes, and as the opposite of each other. So *maxiskirt* is the opposite of *miniskirt*.

For more information, see **mini-**.

## maximum

The plural of this word may be spelled **maximums** or **maxima**. For more about words like this, see **-um**.

## may

See **can/may**.

## mayor

See **mare/mayor**.

## maze

See **maize/maze**.

## mean

See **average/mean/median**.

## means

When the word **means** is a noun with the sense "a way of achieving something", it can be treated as either a singular or a plural:
*A means of communication is vital.*
*Our means of transport were quite varied.*

When the word refers to money or other resources, it's always treated as a plural:
*They lived comfortably, because their means were considerable.*

## meat / meet / mete

These words sound the same but mean different things.

**Meat** is the flesh of animals.

To **meet** someone is to come across them, either by accident or by arrangement.

To **mete** out something is to dole it out or share it out:
*I will mete out suitable punishments for all you naughty children.*

## medal / meddle

These words sound the same but have different meanings.

A **medal** is a kind of badge, especially one given to someone to show that they have done something special.

To **meddle** is to interfere in someone else's business.

## media

This word is the Latin plural of the noun **medium**, and is used because the word originally came into English from Latin.

In this plural form, the word often refers to the various means of mass communication in our society, including radio, television and newspapers (the **mass media**). **Media** is now often thought of as a singular noun:

*What is the media doing about this?*

In the past, people regarded that as a mistake, because they knew it was a Latin plural. However, in English, it behaves like a collective noun and can take either a singular or plural verb. See **collective nouns**.

## median

See **average/mean/median**.

## medieval / mediaeval

These are equally good spellings. See **-ae-**.

## medium

There are two ways to spell the plural of this word: **mediums** and **media**. Both are widely used, although **media** cannot be used as the plural when **medium** means "a person who communicates with the supernatural". The special use of **media** in *mass media* is discussed under **media**.

But **mediums** can be used for every meaning of the word **medium**. For more about words like this, see **-um**.

## medley

The plural of this word is spelled **medleys**. For more about words like this, see **-ey**.

## meet

See **meat/meet/mete**.

## mega-

This means "very large".

In physical measurements, it has a precise value of "one million", or $10^6$ of the unit it is prefixed to. For example:

  megabyte   (one million bytes)
  megaton    (one million tons)
  megawatt   (one million watts)

But in other scientific and scholarly words, its meaning is just "impressively large". For example:

  megalith    (a very large stone, like those of Stonehenge)
  megaphone   (a device that amplifies voices, making them sound loud)

You'll also find mega- at the beginning of some new everyday words, like *megabucks* and *megadeath*, where it again just means that something works on a huge scale.

In informal talk you'll even hear it used instead of "very":

*It was a megatrendy party.*

Or as an exclamation: *Mega!*

This sort of usage is too informal for essay writing.

## melodrama

A **melodrama** is a kind of play in which the characters are exaggeratedly good and evil and have exaggerated emotions. In a typical melodrama the villain is diabolically wicked and the hero and heroine unbelievably virtuous. The plot is predictable in that the villain is always defeated by the hero in the end.

## memento

The plural of this word may be spelled **mementos** or **mementoes**. For more about words like this, see **-o**.

## memo

The plural of this word is spelled **memos**. The word is a shortening of **memorandum**. For more about words like this, see **-o**.

## memorandum

The plural of this word may be spelled **memorandums** or **memoranda**. For more about words like this, see **-um**.

## -ment

is an ending which makes nouns out of verbs. The list below contains some of them:

| | | | |
|---|---|---|---|
| agreement | amazement | amusement | announcement |
| arrangement | assessment | astonishment | confinement |
| development | embarrassment | engagement | enjoyment |
| establishment | excitement | government | improvement |
| investment | management | measurement | replacement |
| retirement | settlement | statement | |

Many of these words carry two kinds of meaning:
**1** the action of the original verb
**2** the thing which results from the action
You can see these different meanings in the following sentences:
*Reagan and Gorbachev reached agreement at the end of the day.*
*An agreement was signed by the parties.*

Words formed with -ment usually add it straight to the verb, as with

excite + -ment excitement
settle + -ment settlement

This is normal for any ending which begins with a consonant. (For more about words ending in -e, see **-e**.)

Note, however, that -ment words formed from verbs ending in -dge can be spelled in two ways:

| | | |
|---|---|---|
| abridgement | *or* | abridgment |
| acknowledgement | | acknowledgment |
| judgement | | judgment |

## merchandise

This is one of the few words ending in -ise that cannot also be spelled with an -ize ending. It is always spelled **merchandise**. For more about words like this, see **-ise/-ize**.

## metal / mettle

These words sound the same but mean different things.

**Metal** is a hard substance like gold, silver, copper or iron.

To be on your **mettle** is to be keyed up to do your very best. Something that tests your **mettle** is something that tests your courage or spirit.

A **mettlesome** horse is one that is spirited and lively.

## metamorphosis

The plural of this word is spelled **metamorphoses**, with the ending pronounced to rhyme with *sees*.

This is the Latin plural spelling, and is used because the word **metamorphosis** came into English from Latin.

For more about words like this, see **-is**.

## metaphors

A **metaphor** is a kind of word picture in which you replace the thing you want to describe with another image. For example, in the following sentence *the ball* is thought of as a rocket:
*She hit the ball so hard that it rocketed across the net.*
Compare the vividness of this sentence which uses a metaphor with the next sentence which doesn't:
*She hit the ball so hard that it sped across the net.*

A **metaphor** differs slightly from a *simile*. With a metaphor the image completely replaces the thing you are describing — the ball becomes a rocket. With a simile you have both the thing you are describing and the image, and you link them with a word such as *like* or *as*:
*The ball went like a rocket as it crossed the net.*
For more about this, see **similes**.

Metaphors are so basic to the way in which we use language that it has to be very plain prose indeed that does not rely on a word picture to convey a thought. Some metaphors are fresh and original, but others have been around for some time and are used so much that we don't notice them. See **clichés**.

## mete

See **meat/meet/mete**.

## meteoroid / meteor / meteorite

These words are linked but they do not mean the same thing.

A **meteoroid** is a mass of stone or metal travelling through space.

A **meteor** is a meteoroid which is passing through the earth's atmosphere and is thus heated up, seen from the earth as a fiery streak. It is commonly called a *shooting star*.

A **meteorite** is a meteoroid which has landed on the surface of the earth.

## metre / meter

These words sound the same but mean different things.

A **meter** is a measuring instrument, as in *gas meter* and *electric meter*.

A **metre** is a unit of length, equal to 100 centimetres. Its symbol is **m**, without a full stop. **Metre** is the conventional spelling in the UK, but you may sometimes find the spelling **meter** used for this word. This is the usual spelling in the USA. For more about measurements, see APPENDIX C. For more on the spelling, see **-re/-er**.

## -metre / -meter

These endings are used with different groups of words in the UK.

You use -metre in measurements of length, such as *kilometre* and *millimetre*. This is the conventional spelling in the UK. In North America, they are spelled *kilometer* and *millimeter*.

The ending -meter is used in the names of some measuring instruments, for example:

    altimeter    (measures altitude)
    barometer   (measures atmospheric pressure)
    hydrometer  (measures specific gravity of liquids)
    hygrometer  (measures humidity)
    pedometer   (counts numbers of steps you have walked)
    speedometer (shows the speed of a vehicle)
    thermometer (measures temperature)

The spelling -meter is also the one used in words for the rhythmic patterns in poetry, such as

    pentameter  (verse with five stress units per line)
    hexameter   (verse with six stress units per line)

Note, however, that the general word for a verse pattern is **metre**.

Note the difference between:

    micrometre  (a millionth part of a metre)
    micrometer  (an instrument for measuring minute distances)

For more information, see APPENDIX C.

## metric system

This is Europe's official system of measurements. The UK used to use the imperial system.

For information on the units of the metric system and their symbols, see APPENDIX C.

## mettle

See **metal/mettle**.

## micro-

This prefix means "minute or tiny", as in:

microprocessor (the tiny part of a computer system that does the actual processing)

microwaves (sound waves much smaller than those used for radio or TV transmission)

In physics, micro- means precisely a one-millionth part of the unit named, for example:

micro-ohm (one-millionth of an ohm)

microsecond (one-millionth of a second)

microvolt (one-millionth of a volt)

The opposite prefix in a physical system is mega-, meaning "one million times" the unit. So the *megavolt* contrasts with the *microvolt*.

In the life sciences and other fields of study, micro- simply means "very small in size or focus". For example:

microbe (a very small organism)

microclimate (the climate in a very small area)

microdont (an animal with small teeth)

micro-economics (the economics of small units)

micro-organism (a small organism)

microscope (an instrument for observing small things)

microstructure (structure on a very small scale)

A few words beginning with micro- have something to do with the *microscope* or microscopic work, such as *microbiology, microfilm, microphotography* and *microsurgery*.

## midwife

The plural of this word is spelled **midwives**.

Note that the noun **midwifery** does <u>not</u> have a double <u>f</u>.

For more about words like this, see **-f/-v-**.

## might

See **could/might**.

## might / mite

These words sound the same but mean different things.

A **mite** is a small insect.

**Might** is power: as in the phrases *with all your might* and *the might of the Roman Empire*.

## might've

is a short form of **might have**. See **contractions**. See also **of/have**.

## migrate

See **emigrate/immigrate/migrate**.

## mileage

Note that while the **mile** is not a unit in the metric system, there is no term from that system that covers the idea of mileage — if there were, it would be something like *kilometrage*. So **mileage** is still in common use.

For more about words like this, see **-age**.

### millennium

Don't forget to double the <u>n</u> as well as the <u>l</u>.

The plural of this word may be spelled **millenniums** or **millennia**. For more about words like this, see **-um**.

### milli-

This prefix means "a thousandth part" of any unit of measurement, as in *milligram*, *millimetre* and *millisecond*. It is part of our metric system. See APPENDIX C.

In biology, <u>milli-</u> means "roughly a thousand", in words such as *millipede*. This small crawling creature seems to have more legs than a *centipede* (hundred legs), though no-one would really claim that it had a thousand of them. Note that *millipede* is also spelled *millepede*. This second spelling helps to make it different from words which have the metric prefix.

### millimetre

**Millimetre** is the conventional spelling in the UK.

You may sometimes see this word spelled **millimeter**, which is how it is usually spelled in the USA. For more about the spelling, see **-re/-er**. For more about measurements, see APPENDIX C.

### mimic

Note that you add a <u>k</u> to make the words **mimicked** and **mimicking**, but don't use a <u>k</u> to make **mimicry**.

For more about words like this, see **-c/-ck-**.

### miner

See **minor/miner/myna**.

### mini-

is a new prefix, meaning "small in size". You'll find it in *mini-budget*, *minibus*, *minigolf*, *mini-series*, *miniskirt*, *mini-van* and other words.

Because <u>mini-</u> is still quite new, people often use a hyphen when writing words with it (for example, *mini-budget*, *mini-van*). But as the words and the prefix become more familiar, the hyphen tends to disappear.

<u>Mini-</u> can be used in contrast with <u>maxi-</u>. See **maxi-**.

### minimal / minimum

These words both have something to do with small amounts, but they have different meanings.

**Minimum** is a noun meaning "the least possible amount or quantity". Most nouns can be used as adjectives, so **minimum** can be used adjectivally. (See **transfer of classes**.) For example:

*The minimum time that you should spend on your homework is two hours.*

**Minimal** is an adjective meaning "so small that it is not worth noticing":

*You spent a minimal amount of time on your homework last night.*

## minimise

See **diminish/minimise**.

## minor / miner / myna

These words sound the same but have different meanings.

**Minor** means "lesser in size, extent, or importance" as in *a minor share* or *a minor weakness*. **Minor** has other meanings which you should look up in your dictionary.

A **miner** is a person who works in a **mine**. It is also an Australian bird, such as the **noisy miner**.

A **myna** is another kind of bird. It is also spelled **mynah** and comes from the Indian name for a starling.

## minute

This word has two meanings depending on its pronunciation.

When it is pronounced with the stress on the first syllable <u>min-</u>, it refers to the unit of time, a sixtieth part of an hour.

When it is pronounced with the stress on the second syllable, to rhyme with *beaut*, it means "very, very small".
*There was a minute scratch on the polished table.*

## mirror

Note the ending of this word. See **-or/-our**.

## mis-

This prefix means "bad or badly". It suggests that something is wrong with whatever word it is prefixed to. The list below shows you some of the many words with it:

| | | | | |
|---|---|---|---|---|
| misadventure | miscarry | misconduct | misdeed | misfit |
| misgivings | misguided | mishit | mislay | mislead |
| mismanage | mismatch | misnomer | misprint | misrepresent |
| misshapen | misspell | mistake | mistrial | mistrust |

One reason why there are so many **mis-** words is that it's really two separate prefixes that have merged into one:
1 <u>mis-</u> meaning "bad" from older English (which is the same as <u>miss-</u> in German)
2 <u>mes-</u> from French, which was originally *minus* (less) in Latin. Both meant that something had gone wrong, and so they merged in English.

## misled

This is the past tense of the verb **mislead**. You pronounce it with the first part sounding like *miss* and the second part rhyming with *red*: **I misled, I have misled**.

For more about the prefix of this word, see **mis-**.

## mite

See **might/mite**.

## moan / mown

These words sound the same but mean different things.

You **moan** with sorrow or pain.

**Mown** is a past form of the verb **mow**, meaning "to cut something off or down":
*Have you mown the lawn yet?*

## mobile

See **movable/mobile**.

---

> ### Some modal verbs
>
> can/could
> will/would
> shall/should
> may/might
> must
> need to
> ought to

---

## modal verbs

**Modal verbs** are a type of auxiliary verb. They combine with other verbs for three main purposes:

1 to indicate the future:
    *I will be late.*
2 to indicate how probable an event is:
    *I might be late.*
3 to distinguish between what you've got to do, what you're allowed to do and what you're able to do.
    *You must go in now.*
    *You may go in now.*
    *You can go in now — I've unlocked it.*

See also **auxiliary verbs**.

## model

For information about whether to double the l when you add endings like -ed, -ing, or -er, see **-l-/-ll-**.

## moderator

Note the ending of this word. See **-ator**.

## modifiers

are words or phrases that soften the impact of others. Compare these sentences:
    *That barbecue was a disaster. But the music was good.*
    *That barbecue was rather a disaster. But the music was quite good.*
The modifiers *quite* and *rather* make the second pair of sentences less strong in their judgements.

Modified statements are less powerful, but they give the speakers more room to move in their opinion.

If you are looking for other modifiers to use, see **hedge words**.

## Mohammed

See **Muhammad/Mohammed**.

## molar

Note the ending of this word. See **-ar**.

## mollusc

The usual spelling for this word is **mollusc**. You may sometimes see it spelled **mollusk**, which is how it is usually spelled in the USA.

## momentous / monumental

These words both have to do with <u>importance</u> but they have different meanings.

Something is **momentous** if it is very important at the moment:
*Will this momentous question ever be answered?*
We use **momentous** to refer to abstract nouns.

A work of art is **monumental** if it is large in size and great enough to have lasting value. We use **monumental** to refer to concrete nouns.

## momentum

The plural of this word may be spelled **momentums** or **momenta**. For more about words like this, see **-um**.

## money

**Money** usually stays singular even when you are writing about several pieces of money:
*I've got lots of money in my pocket.*
When it is used in this way **money** is a mass noun. For more information about this, see **mass nouns**.

**Money** does sometimes need to be plural, though. Usually this is when you are comparing different types or units of currency:
*The moneys of the world are many and varied.*

**Moneys** can also be spelled **monies**. For more about words like this, see **-ey**.

## monitor

Note the ending of this word. See **-er/-or**.

## monkey

The plural of this word is spelled **monkeys**. For more about words like this, see **-ey**.

## mono-

This prefix means "one" or "single". You'll find it in everyday words such as *monologue, monopoly, monorail* and *monotony*. It also appears at the beginnings of some technical words, for example:

| | |
|---|---|
| monocotyledon | (a plant whose seeds have just one section) |
| monogamy | (marriage to one other person) |
| monograph | (a single publication) |
| monolingual | (speaking just one language) |
| monotreme | (an animal with a single outlet hole for excretion and reproduction) |

It is also used in the names of chemicals, such as *carbon monoxide* and *monosodium glutamate*.

<u>Mono-</u> contrasts with <u>bi-</u> "two", in some pairs of words. For example:

| | |
|---|---|
| monogamy | bigamy |
| monolingual | bilingual |

But in chemistry and some areas of science, <u>mono-</u> contrasts with <u>di-</u>, also meaning "two". For example:

| | |
|---|---|
| monocotyledon | dicotyledon |
| monoxide | dioxide |

<u>Mono-</u> comes from Greek, and is the same in meaning as the Latin prefix <u>uni-</u>. See **uni-**.

## monologue

When one person speaks continuously (like a teacher, lecturer, or a radio announcer), the words they utter are **monologue**. As soon as they exchange words with other people, it becomes *dialogue*.

Most of what you write by way of essays, reports and reviews is monologue, because you are describing or explaining or arguing something continuously. But now and then you may be asked to script a dialogue, to give voice and words to two or more people on paper. It is a way of creating drama on paper. See **dialogue**.

## monumental

See **momentous/monumental**.

## mood

**Mood** is a term of grammar that is applied to verbs. In English, verbs can be **indicative** (making factual statements or asking questions), **imperative** (giving commands) or more rarely, **subjunctive** (expressing wishes or possibilities).

**Indicative mood**
*She is going.*  (statement)
*Are you going?*  (question)
**Imperative mood**
*Go on!*
**Subjunctive mood**
*I wish I were going.*

For more about the subjunctive mood, see **subjunctive**.

## moral / morale

These words look similar but they have different meanings.

A **moral** question is one that asks if something is right or wrong. A **moral** person is one who chooses to do the right thing. A **moral** is a lesson taught through a story or one you learn by experience.

Your **morale** is how you feel: high when you are in a cheerful and confident state of mind, and low when you feel sad or depressed. We pronounce this with a stress on the second syllable *-ale* (rhyming with *snarl*).

## more / moor / Moor

These words sound the same but have different meanings.

**More** is the opposite of **less**:
*I want more bananas.*

A **moor** is an open area of wild land. To **moor** a boat is to fix it in position with ropes or an anchor.

A **Moor** is an old-fashioned literary word for the dark-skinned Muslims who lived in North Africa and conquered Spain in the eighth century.

## more / most

Both these words can act as either a singular noun or a plural noun, depending on what they're referring to. So be careful to use the correct form of the verb with them:

*You've put in a lot of effort, but more [more effort] is needed.*
(singular)
*You've collected a lot of stamps, but more [more stamps] are
needed.* (plural)
*Is most of the pavlova eaten now?* (singular)
*Are most of the strawberries eaten now?* (plural)

### morning / mourning

These words sound the same but mean different things.

The **morning** is the first part of the day. **Morn** is an old-
fashioned word for **morning**.

Someone is in **mourning** if they are grieving over the death of
someone they love.

### mortar

Note the ending of this word. See **-ar**.

### Moslem

See **Muslim/Moslem**.

### mosquito

The plural of this word may be spelled **mosquitos** or
**mosquitoes**. For more about words like this, see **-o**.

### -most

is an ending used to mean "the extreme position". You'll find it
on words such as *foremost, innermost, outermost* and *uppermost*.
It also gets attached to the words for compass directions, such as
*northernmost* and *southernmost*.

One other example is the word *utmost*. It now usually means
"greatest", though once it meant "outermost". The link with
*outer* can still be seen in *uttermost*, which is the older way of
writing *utmost*.

### mother-in-law

The plural of this word is **mothers-in-law**. The possessive is
**mother-in-law's**: *my mother-in-law's daughter*.

### motif

The plural of this word is **motifs**. For more about words like
this, see **-f/-v-**.

### motto

The plural of this word may be spelled **mottos** or **mottoes**. For
more about words like this, see **-o**.

### mourning

See **morning/mourning**.

### mouse

When it's an animal, the plural of **mouse** is **mice**.

When it's a computer device, the plural of **mouse** is **mouses**.

The adjective from **mouse** can be spelled **mousey** or **mousy**.
For more about adjectives like this, see **-y/-ey**.

### moustache

The usual spelling for this word is **moustache**. You may sometimes find it spelled **mustache**, which is the spelling normally used in the USA.

### mouthful

The plural of this word is spelled **mouthfuls**. For more about words like this, see **-ful**.

### movable / mobile

These words both have to do with <u>movement</u> but they are used in different ways.

**Movable** objects normally stay in one place but can be moved from one place or position to another, as in *a movable screen* or *a movable wardrobe*.

We say that things are **mobile** if they can move freely or are designed to move easily:
*These mobile army tanks can be driven over any terrain.*
We say that people are **mobile** if they can move or travel about easily:
*He's not mobile yet after breaking both his legs.*
*I'm more mobile now that I've bought this car.*
We say that someone has a **mobile** face if their expression changes easily as their feelings change.

### movable / moveable

These are equally good spellings for this word. Note that while you may use either spelling in any writing, **moveable** is more common in legal writing. For more about words like this, see **-able/-eable**.

### mowed / mown

These are equally good spellings for the past participle of **mow**:
*I have mowed, I have mown.*

For more about words like this, see **-ed/-(e)n**.

### mown

See **moan/mown**.

### Ms

is a title that a woman may choose to put in front of her name. It is used to avoid mentioning whether she is married or not. **Ms** gives women a title equal to *Mr*, which refers to the man in question and not to his marital status. Because of this, **Ms** is also useful when you're writing to a woman whose marital status is unknown to you. But if you know that a woman prefers to be addressed as Mrs or Miss, it is polite to use the preferred title.

Note that **Ms** is not an abbreviation of some other word as *Mr* is of *Mister*, and it doesn't have a full stop after it.

For more information, see **non-sexist language**.

### mucus / mucous

**Mucus** is the noun, **mucous** is the adjective:
*They found some mucus in the rat's lung.*
*The mucous membrane was moist.*

### Muhammad / Mohammed

These are both correct spellings for the name of the prophet of Islam, though **Muhammad** is the one preferred by most Muslims.

The word comes from Arabic, a language which doesn't use the alphabet we use in English. For this reason a number of different versions of the spelling have been used in English. As well as the two already discussed you may find the spellings **Mahomet** and **Muhammed**. These two are less commonly used nowadays.

### multi-

is a Latin prefix meaning "many". You'll find it in new words like:

multicultural    multimillionaire
multinational    multistorey

**Multi-** is also built into some older words like:

multiply  (increase many times)
multitude  (a crowd of many people)

Compare **poly-**.

### muscle / mussel

These words sound the same but have different meanings.

Your **muscles** are the parts of your body which give it the ability to move.

A **mussel** is a type of shellfish that you can eat.

### musically

Note the ending of this word. See **-ally**.

### Muslim / Moslem

These are both correct spellings for this word, though **Muslim** is the spelling preferred by most Muslims themselves.

### mussel

See **muscle/mussel**.

### myna

See **minor/miner/myna**.

### myths / legends

These are two types of story handed down as part of folklore.

**Legends** are stories about extraordinary deeds that are supposed to have been performed by real people, or by fictional characters who might have been real people. For example, there are legends about early saints, like Saint Patrick, who is supposed to have rid Ireland of snakes. There are the legends of Robin Hood and King Arthur, who may or may not have been real people. And you could certainly write of the **legendary** deeds of Grace Darling, or even of the sporting heroes of the past.

**Myths** are stories about supernatural events. The characters in myths usually include gods and beings outside the ordinary natural world. Myths often explain the origins of things in this natural world, and so form the basis of many religions.

# Nn

### n as a silent letter

The letter <u>n</u> is written but not sounded in a few words, when it comes after <u>m</u> at the end of a word. You'll find this in words like:

autumn  column  condemn
damn   hymn   solemn

Note, however, that the <u>n</u> in these words is sounded when they become the base of another, longer word. It happens in *autum<u>n</u>al*, *dam<u>n</u>ation* and so on.

For more about silent letters, see **silent letters**.

### naive / naïve

These are equally good ways of writing this word.

It is a word we have borrowed from French. The two dots over the <u>i</u> are part of the original French spelling and show that the word is pronounced with two syllables (*nigh-eve*). See **dieresis** for more information about this accent.

Words like this gradually lose their accent as they become more settled into English. This word has been in our language for so long that it is much more common to see it spelled **naive**, without the accent.

Another spelling you might sometimes see in English is **naïf**, which is the French masculine form of **naïve**. See **gender**.

The noun from **naïve** also has several acceptable spellings in English, the most common one being **naivety**. The others, with varying degrees of remaining "Frenchness", are **naïvety**, **naïveté**, **naiveté**, and **naivete**.

### naivety / nativity

These words look similar but have different meanings.

We say that someone has an air of **naivety** if they are not sophisticated and have a childlike approach to life.

**Nativity** means "birth". The **Nativity** (always written with a capital <u>N</u>) is the birth of Christ.

## names

In your writing, you will often have to use names of people, places, institutions, and so on. It's important to get the spelling of names correct — there is very rarely any choice in how a name is spelled. If you are unsure, check in a reference book like an encyclopedia or atlas.

People's names generally have more than one part. In the UK, someone's last name is usually their *surname* or *family name*. So, in the names *Jane Roberts* and *David Lee*, the surnames are *Roberts* and *Lee*.

The family name or surname can appear first in some cultures, such as in China. For example, the surname of the famous Chinese leader, Mao Zedong (or Mao Tse-tung), was Mao. The other parts of someone's full name (such as *Jane* and *David* in the examples above) are their *given names*. These are sometimes called *Christian names*, but *given name* is a more accurate term, as many British people are not in fact Christians.

When you are writing people's names, you might have to use a title, like *Mrs*, *Dr*, *Lady*, or *Sir* before a name. For information about these words and abbreviations, and how to use them, see **forms of address**.

## narrative

A **narrative** is the story or account of something. It may be a true story, as when you describe what happened on your holiday, or relate the April Fools Day joke you heard. It can equally well be a tale about imaginary people and events — like a novel, a short story or a folktale.

When talking about a novel, people often distinguish the "narrative" from the dialogue in it. Used like this, the word **narrative** means whatever is narrated directly by the author, as opposed to the direct speech scripted here and there for the characters in the story.

For more about this, see **dialogue** and **direct speech**.

## narrator

Note the ending of this word. See **-ator**.

## nationalise / naturalise

These words sound similar but have different meanings.

To **nationalise** something, such as the health system or an airline, is to bring it under government ownership and control.

To **naturalise** someone is to make them a full citizen of a country.

## nativity

see **naivety/nativity**.

## naught

see **nought/naught**.

## naval / navel

These words sound the same but mean different things.

**Naval** means "of or belonging to a **navy**", as in *a naval battle* or *a naval officer*.

Your **navel** is the small hollow in the middle of your stomach.

## NB

This is an abbreviation for the Latin phrase *nota bene* which means "note well".

You use it when you want to draw your reader's attention to some particular point:
   *NB: There are several studies on this subject not yet published.*

As it is an abbreviation, you should avoid using it in your essays where it is best not to use shorthand expressions.

You might sometimes see this abbreviation written **n.b.** Because the letters are lower case here, full stops are needed. For more about this, see **abbreviations**.

## nebula

The plural of this word may be spelled **nebulas** or **nebulae**. For more about words like this, see **-a (as a singular ending)**.

## nectar

Note the ending of this word. See **-ar**.

## need / knead

These words sound the same but have different meanings.

To **knead** is to press and push something with your hands:
   *The pastry chef kneaded the dough.*

To **need** something is to want it urgently:
   *I need help. Quick!*

## negatives

There are several words in English which are used to make negative sentences. They include *no*, *not* and *never*.

You have to be careful not to use more negatives than you really need, since two negatives may be said to equal a positive:
   *I've never done nothing like that.*
This is not the same as:
   *I've never done anything like that.*
For more advice on this, see **double negatives**.

A common method of making words themselves negative is to use prefixes such as *in-*, *un-*, *dis-* and *non-*:

| | |
|---|---|
| likely | unlikely |
| decent | indecent |
| like | dislike |
| appearance | non-appearance |

For more about such words, see **dis-**, **in-/im-**, **in-/un-** and **non-**.

## negligible

Note the ending of this word. See **-able/-ible**.

## neither . . . nor

**Neither** is said to be a singular word, so in very formal writing
you say **neither** (of them) is, not **neither** (of them) are. However,
in speech and in informal styles of writing, **neither** is often
treated as if it were plural:

*Neither of the boys are getting paid.*

The same applies to **neither . . . nor**:

*Neither Tony nor Anna is going.*
*Neither Tony nor Anna are going.*

This is also the best solution when **neither . . . nor** is used with
two words which would take different verbs:

*Neither he nor I . . .*

We couldn't complete the sentence with *is going* or *am going.*
Neither of these sounds quite right. The usual way out is to
finish with

*. . . are going.*

## -ness

is an ending often used to make nouns out of adjectives. They
are usually abstract nouns. For example:

| calm | + | -ness | calmness |
| fresh | + | -ness | freshness |
| polite | + | -ness | politeness |
| wilful | + | -ness | wilfulness |

Other -ness words are formed with parts of verbs ending in -ing
or -ed:

tiredness    willingness

They may also be formed from compound adjectives:

kindheartedness    levelheadedness    shortsightedness
straightforwardness    waterproofness

When the compound adjective is a phrase, the hyphens in it are
kept in the abstract noun:

matter-of-factness    up-to-dateness

Note that adjectives that end in -y normally change it to i
before adding -ness, for example:

| ready | readi | + | -ness | readiness |
| weary | weari | + | -ness | weariness |

This is what has happened in our word *business*, which now
means "trade" or "affair", though it once meant "a state of being
busy". If you still need an abstract noun to express that idea of
being busy, you spell it *busyness*, without changing the -y.

## net / nett

These words sound the same but mean different things.

A **net** is a material made of fine threads knotted or woven
together with holes in between.

There is another word **net** which means "not counting packaging" or "after the expenses have been paid". It can also be spelled **nett**:

> *The net* (or *nett*) *weight of this coffee is 500 grams.*
> *The net* (or *nett*) *profit was £5000.*

### neuter gender

The pronouns *it* and *its* are said to be in the **neuter gender**. They usually refer to objects which are not living and cannot be said to be either masculine or feminine.

In some languages other than English, all nouns and pronouns are divided into groups labelled *masculine, feminine* and *neuter*. This is just a matter of grammar, and does not have anything to do with whether the objects are living or non-living, or whether they're male or female. In German, the word for girl (*Mädchen*) is neuter.

**Neuter gender** is different from **common gender**. *Common gender* is the label given to nouns when they refer to both genders, like *student*.

For more information, see **gender**.

### nevertheless

is always written as one word. The same applies to *nonetheless*.

### new / knew

These words sound the same but mean different things.

People or things are **new** if they have arrived recently or have just come into being. The word can also refer to something fresh or unused.

**Knew** is the past tense of the verb **know**, to feel certain that something is true, or to have learned and understood it:

> *I knew that carbon was an element.*

### news reporting

When news is reported by journalists for a newspaper, it is presented in a special way. The structure of news reports is explained in WRITING WORKSHOP pp 52–3.

### night / knight / nite

These words sound the same but have different meanings.

**Night** is the time between sunset and sunrise, when it is dark.

**Nite** is another spelling for **night** that is used in informal writing and advertising:

> *Buy Nite-Lites! Nite-Lites make night light!*

A **knight** in medieval times was an armed soldier on horseback. To be made a **knight** in the 20th century is an honour.

### nit

See **knit/nit**.

## no

When this word is a noun, its plural is usually spelled **noes,** though you may sometimes see **nos** and even **no's**.

Note that you shouldn't use **no** instead of *any*. It's wrong to say:
*I don't want no more pavlova.*
It should be:
*I don't want any more pavlova.*
For more information, see **double negatives**.

## no / know

These words sound the same but have different meanings.

**No** is the opposite of yes. We use it to deny, disagree with or refuse something.

To **know** something is to feel certain that it is correct or true. If you **know** someone, then you have met them before.

## nobody / no-one

These words are singular, and so should be followed by singular verbs such as *is* or *has*:
*Nobody has left yet.*
For advice on the best pronoun to use with **nobody** and **no-one** (should it be *his? her? their?*), see **somebody/someone**.

## nominative case

See **subjective case**.

## non-

This means "not", and it makes many words into their opposites:
non- conformist   nonconformist
non- existent     nonexistent
non- sense        nonsense
non- resident     nonresident
It was originally used in legal language, and *non-parole* (period) is one of the examples you're likely to know. But nowadays it is used everywhere. Words with non- are often created when people want words to stress their awareness of a problem and the fact that they have a solution. For example:
non-nuclear (without nuclear complications)
nonstop    (without unwanted interruptions)
non-toxic   (without harmful chemicals)
Advertisers use non- words to emphasise the virtues of a product:
nonskid (tyres)   nonslip (soles)

When they are new, words with non- are often written with hyphens. It helps to make clear whatever word is being negated. The hyphens gradually disappear when the new words become more familiar, as they have from most of those above.

For other negative prefixes, see **dis-, in-/im-** and **in-/un-**.

## none

**None** is a singular word and, according to most grammar books, should be followed by a singular verb such as *is* or *has*:

*None* of it *is* quite ready yet.
*None* of them *is* ready yet.

For most of us, though, the second example doesn't work as well as the first. Increasingly, we accept that **none** in such examples can be seen as meaning *not any*. It is commonly used as a plural in both formal and informal writing:

*None* of them *are* ready yet.

## nonetheless

is always written as one word. The same applies to *nevertheless*.

## nonfiction

Writing can be divided into two broad categories – **fiction** and **nonfiction**. Most nonfiction is factual and can be informative or present a point of view, while fiction is made up or invented to entertain the reader.

Nonfiction includes factual or argumentative essays, science reports, and summaries. See **essays**, **report writing** and **summary**.

Journalism is another form of nonfiction writing. See **journalism**.

Biography and autobiography are usually regarded as categories of nonfiction. See **biography**.

Note that nonfiction is usually written in prose. But occasionally it's written as a poem (for example, Pope's poem called *An Essay on Man*).

## non-sexist language

The aim of non-sexist language, or "inclusive language" as it is sometimes called, is to avoid unnecessary or irrelevant reference to a person's gender. The problem comes up in three ways:
1  words which describe a person's job, occupation or role
2  words or phrases which mention a person's gender when that information is unnecessary
3  pronouns like *his/her*

1  Many names of occupations have the suffix -man. (See **-man**.) Some people argue that this seems to mean that only men can hold these positions. So people have tried to avoid these words. One method is to replace -man with -person. (See **-person**.) So instead of *chairman* you could use *chairperson*. Another method is to find different words which are neutral as to gender.
*So for* businessman *we have* executive

| | |
|---|---|
| chairman | convener *or* moderator |
| policeman | police officer |

There are other sets of words where there used to be paired forms, masculine and feminine, with the feminine form indicated by a feminine word ending attached to the masculine form. For example, we had *poet* and *poetess, author* and *authoress, editor* and *editress.* In these pairs the masculine form is neutral. It is the feminine form which has the gender marker. So the easiest solution is to drop the feminine form and use the neutral form for both male and female. Thus a poet is a man or a woman.

**2** Even though you use words which are neutral with regard to gender, like poet or doctor or plumber, some people add words which indicate gender. Often this is not necessary. For example:
*We interviewed a lawyer, a journalist and a lady doctor.*
In this instance it is the professions of the people interviewed that is important, not their gender. If that had been important it would have been given for all of them, not just for the doctor.

In most cases sexist language is the unnecessary indication of female gender. But it is sometimes the reverse, as in *male nurse.*

**3** Sometimes you can get into trouble with words like *his* and *her* that refer to someone already mentioned in your writing. For example:
*A doctor keeps medicine in his/her bag.*
Using *his/her* avoids assuming one gender or the other, but it's a rather clumsy expression. One simple way to avoid such problems is to turn this sentence into the plural:
*Doctors keep medicine in their bags.*
Another way out of the "his or her" difficulty is to use the neutral *their* for the singular. For example:
*Every child keeps their books in their desk.*
There are still a number of people who disapprove of this solution on grammatical grounds, since *their* is normally a plural pronoun. Nevertheless it is widely accepted in spoken language. It provides a simple solution to a real problem. Other solutions are on the whole more complicated and cumbersome, or they require a major re-working of the sentence.

There are no hard-and-fast rules to follow to avoid sexist language. The hardest part is to become aware of it as a problem and to form the habit of removing it from your writing.

## nosy / nosey

These are equally good ways of spelling this word. **Nosy** is the more common of the two, and is in keeping with the usual English pattern. For more about words like this, see **-y/-ey**.

## not / knot

These words sound the same but mean different things.

We use **not** to express something negative, or to deny or refuse something:
*I am not a blond bombshell.*
*I'm not going to eat my spinach.*

You can tie a **knot** in a piece of thread or rope. If your hair is tangled it has **knots** in it. A **knot** is also a measure of speed for ships.

## notable / noticeable

These words look similar but have different meanings.

A **notable** achievement is important and worth taking **note** of.

Something is **noticeable** if it grabs your attention, as in *a very noticeable hat*. This word relates to the verb **notice**.

## nothing

**Nothing** is a word that is often singular and so is followed by a singular verb:

*Nothing is known about him.*

Even when some plural words separate **nothing** from its verb, strictly speaking the verb should be singular too:

*Nothing except a few isolated facts is known about him.*

Notice that this sentence is equivalent to:

*Nothing is known about him except a few isolated facts.*

But you will often find a plural verb used in sentences like this:

*Nothing except a few isolated facts are known.*

Few people would object to this nowadays.

## noticeable

See **notable/noticeable**.

## not only . . . but also

We use these words in a sentence to connect two related things:

*I not only saw your children but also heard them shouting.*

The sentence flows more easily when **not only** and **but also** both have the same kind of word after them. In the sentence above, each of them is followed by a <u>verb</u> (*saw* and *heard*).

*I not only saw your children playing but also you.*

The second sentence sounds awkward because **not only** is followed by a <u>verb</u> and **but also** is followed by a different kind of word, a <u>pronoun</u>.

## nought / naught

These words sound the same but we use them for different things.

**Naught** is an old-fashioned word for "nothing":

*It was naught but the wind.*

It can also mean "ruin", or "complete failure", as in *to bring to naught* or *come to naught*.

**Nought** is a sign in maths (0) which stands for zero.

## noun clauses

are clauses which act like nouns. See **clauses**.

## noun phrases

A **noun phrase** is a group of words which has a noun as its main word. Note how, in the following examples, the noun *man* can have various words placed before it to construct phrases, while remaining the key word of the phrase:

*a man*
*an old man*
*a tired old man*
*a very tired old man*

Sometimes, the key word will have its secondary words placed after it:

*a man of many parts*

For more information, see **nouns** and **phrases**.

## nouns

**Nouns** are words that are commonly said to name people, places or things. They often act as the subject or object in a sentence.

**Proper nouns** name individual people or places: *Tony, David Gower, River Thames, Ben Nevis, Loch Ness*. They start with capital letters.

**Common nouns** start with lower-case letters and refer to ideas and types of things, such as *butter, dog, beauty* and *flying*. Some common nouns are called **abstract nouns**, and refer to such things as ideas and feelings: *beauty, flying, rudeness*. Other common nouns are called **concrete nouns**, and refer to things your senses can directly experience: *butter, dog, skateboard, vice-captain*.

Most concrete nouns refer to things that you can count, and so are called **count nouns**. *Dog, skateboard* and *vice-captain* are all count nouns. *Butter*, on the other hand, is a **mass noun**, like *rice, mud* and *water*. You can talk about *two dogs*, but you can't talk about *two rices*.

For more detailed discussions, see **proper nouns, common nouns, abstract nouns, concrete nouns, count nouns** and **mass nouns**.

## novel / novella / novelette

These words are all related but mean slightly different things.

A **novel** is a work of fiction. It is a long piece of prose writing which usually tells a story. That is to say, it has a plot and characters which are developed in the unfolding of the story.

A **novelette** has all the elements of a novel but it is shorter. Novelettes are often of a rather trite and sentimental nature.

A **novella** is a serious piece of prose somewhere between a novel and a short story in length. It is usually more limited in its scope than a novel, in terms of the number of characters and the complexity of its plot.

## nucleus

The plural of this word may be spelled **nucleuses** or **nuclei**. For more about words like this, see **-us**.

## number

**Number** is a term in grammar which refers to the fact that verbs, nouns, and pronouns can be either *singular* or *plural*.

In English, the number of the verb has to match the number of the noun or pronoun that acts as its subject:
*He + walks*         singular pronoun + singular verb
*The dogs + walk*   plural noun + plural verb

This is known as agreement, and it's one of the things you have to be careful about in writing. For more information, see **agreement**.

For a full list of singular and plural pronouns, see **pronouns**. See also **singular** and **plural**.

## number prefixes

In English we build numbers into words through a set of prefixes borrowed from Greek and Latin. They include:

| uni- | (Latin) | "one" | *as in* | unicorn |
|------|---------|-------|---------|---------|
| mono- | (Greek) | "one" | | monologue |
| bi- | (L) | "two" | | bicycle |
| di- | (G) | "two" | | dipole |
| tri- | (L) | "three" | | triangle |
| quadr- | (L) | "four" | | quadrangle (See also **quadr-**.) |
| tetra- | (G) | "four" | | tetrahedron |
| quin- | (L) | "five" | | quintuplets |
| pent- | (G) | "five" | | pentathlon |
| hex- | (L) | "six" | | hexagon |
| sept- | (L) | "seven" | | septet |
| hept- | (G) | "seven" | | Heptateuch (the first seven books of the Bible) |
| oct- | (L) | "eight" | | octopus |
| non- | (L) | "nine" | | nonagon |
| deca- | (L/G) | "ten" | | decahedron |
| deka- | (G) | "ten" | | dekalitre |
| cent- | (L) | "hundred" | | century |
| kilo- | (G) | "thousand" | | kilogram |
| mega- | (G) | "million" | | megaton (See also **mega-**.) |
| deci- | (L) | "one tenth" | | decilitre |
| centi- | (L) | "one hundredth" | | centimetre |
| milli- | (L) | "one thousandth" | | millimetre |
| micro- | (L) | "one millionth" | | microsecond (See also **micro-**.) |

For a complete list of number prefixes used in the metric system, see APPENDIX C.

## numbers

1 **Numbers in figures.** When you are writing large numbers there are two different ways to break them up, so that they are easy to read. One is to use spaces, the other is to use commas.

To use the first method, separate the figures with a space into groups of three to the left or right of the decimal point:

70 000
700 000
7 000 000
0.000 07
0.000 007
0.000 000 7

If the number has only four figures or less on either side of the decimal point there is no space:

700.007
7000.0007
70 000.0007
70 000.000 07

If you use commas, there are two main differences from what happens when you use spaces. Firstly, commas are never used *after* the decimal point. Secondly, you *do* use a comma with four-figure numbers.

700
7,000
70,000
7,000,000
7,000.007
7,000.0007
70,000.00007

The use of a comma rather than a space has a number of disadvantages. As you can see from the examples, this style makes long numbers after the decimal point difficult to read. Another problem is that in some countries the comma is also used to indicate the decimal place.

The use of spaces is recommended. It follows widespread international practice, and it makes tables of figures much easier to read.

**Groups of numbers – pages.** To write a group of page numbers you can use as few figures as possible for the last page, so long as your meaning is clear:

pp 184–9    i.e. pages 184 to 189
pp 184–99   i.e. pages 184 to 199
pp 184–209  i.e. pages 184 to 209

Note however that it is not usual to shorten the numbers between 10 and 19 in each hundred:

pp 10–14, *not* 10–4
pp 217–19, *not* 217–9

**Groups of numbers – years.** Writing groups of years follows the same rules, except that it is not usual to shorten the final year to three figures:

1884–6    1884–96    1884–1906, *not* 1884–906

2 **Numbers in words.** Numbers are usually written out as words in writing that is descriptive, or where numbers are unusual – writing such as English essays, history essays or stories.

But writing in maths and science involves lots of numbers, and there it is simpler and easier for the reader if you write them as figures.

Even in descriptive writing there are some kinds of numbers that you don't write out. For example, years, and numbers used with abbreviations or symbols are usually written as figures:

*Captain Cook landed in Australia in 1770.*
*He landed at Botany Bay, 34°S, 151°E.*

It is also usual to write large numbers in figures rather than words. Different writers choose different cut-off points — some write out all numbers under 100, some all numbers under 20, some all under 10. Whichever you choose, make sure you use the same rule throughout your work.

For information on special uses of numbers, see also **fractions** and **dates**.

## numerator

Note the ending of this word. See **-ator**.

# Oo

**-o**

Words which end in -o are an odd lot. There is a handful of very short ordinary ones: *do, go, no, so* and *to*. The rest are all either abbreviations, or foreign borrowings.

**The foreign borrowings ending in -o** have come into English from many parts of the world. Many came through Spanish and Portuguese:

| | | | | | |
|---|---|---|---|---|---|
| armadillo | avocado | banjo | buffalo | burro | bronco |
| cargo | flamingo | merino | mosquito | negro | poncho |
| potato | silo | sombrero | tomato | tornado | |

The words refer to new plants and animals found overseas, and to aspects of colonial life.

Other words ending in -o are part of our cultural inheritance from Italian and Latin. For example:

*from Italian*

| | | | | | |
|---|---|---|---|---|---|
| cello | concerto | crescendo | fiasco | fresco | grotto |
| inferno | motto | piano | portico | proviso | solo |
| stiletto | studio | | | | |

*from Latin*

| | | | | |
|---|---|---|---|---|
| echo | embryo | halo | hero | ratio | torpedo |

**Abbreviations ending in -o** are sometimes the standard short form of a word, for example:

| | | |
|---|---|---|
| auto | *for* | automobile |
| pro | | professional |
| radio | | radiotelegraphy |

**Which ones should have -es and which -s for their plural?**

Overall, there's a shrinking number of words ending in -o which make their plurals by adding -es. The following are a few of those remaining:

echoes  heroes  potatoes  tomatoes  torpedoes  vetoes

But others which have had -es plurals are going back to -s:

| | | | | | |
|---|---|---|---|---|---|
| banjos | buffalos | flamingos | frescos | ghettos | grottos |
| hobos | mangos | mosquitos | mottos | volcanos | zeros |

This spelling with -s is simpler and easier. It brings them into line with most other plurals.

313

Many -o words have always had -s plurals anyway. For example:

armadillos    cellos    merinos    pianos
ponchos    silos    sombreros    stilettos

Those with another vowel before the final -o have also always had just -s:

arpeggios    bamboos    embryos    cameos    folios    ratios
rodeos    studios    tattoos

(An extra -e before the plural -s would have made strange reading: *cameoes*.)

So an -s plural will now do for almost all words ending in -o, apart from that handful of ordinary ones like *echo*.

Note that a few of the Italian borrowings with -o, especially those used in music and architecture, can also form their plurals in the Italian way, with -i. For example, *concerti*.

### oar / or / ore / awe

These words sound the same but mean different things.

You use an **oar** for rowing a boat.

You use **or** to connect alternative words, phrases or clauses:
*I don't know which colour to choose — red, yellow or green.*

**Ore** is a rock or mineral which is mined for the metal it contains.

**Awe** is a feeling of great respect mixed with fear:
*The men were in awe of her bad temper.*

### oasis

The plural of this word is spelled **oases,** with the last syllable pronounced like *seas*. For more about words like this, see **-is**.

### object

The object of a verb is the person or thing that is affected by the action of that verb.

There are two different types of object:

1 **direct object**  To find the direct object, we simply ask "who?" or "what?" after the verb:
   *She stroked the cat.*
She stroked "who?" or "what?" The answer is the cat. So the cat is the direct object of the verb stroked. It is what is acted on by the verb.

2 **indirect object**  Some sentences have another kind of object as well. It is the person or thing that receives something through the action of the verb:
   *They sent him a book.*
In this example, him is the indirect object (the person who gets the book). See **indirect object**.

Note that *book*, the thing being sent, is the **direct object**.

In English, pronouns have a special form when they act as objects in a sentence. This form is known as the objective case. See **objective case**.

## objective case

If a noun or pronoun is the <u>object</u> of a verb, or if it follows a preposition, it is said to be in the **objective case**. Pronouns in the objective case change their form, but nouns don't. For example, when the pronoun <u>he</u> is the object of a verb, or follows a preposition, it becomes <u>him</u>.

> *The company called <u>him</u>.*
> (<u>him</u> is the object of <u>called</u>)

In the same way, <u>we</u> becomes <u>us</u>:

> *The joke's on <u>us</u>.*
> (<u>us</u> follows the preposition <u>on</u>)

The objective case pronouns are:

| *Singular* | *Plural* |
|---|---|
| me | us |
| you | you |
| him | them |
| her | |
| it | |

It's important to remember that, even when the pronoun is separated from the verb or from the preposition, it still should be in the objective case:

> *They called Terry and <u>me</u> on the phone.*   RIGHT
> *They called Terry and <u>I</u> on the phone.*   WRONG
> *Besides him and <u>me</u> . . .*   RIGHT
> *Besides him and <u>I</u> . . .*   WRONG

To help you decide which is the right pronoun in cases like this, there are two methods you can use:

Firstly, try removing the first object from the sentence and see how it reads:

> *They called . . . <u>me</u> on the phone.*

Secondly, try repeating the verb:

> *They called Terry and they called <u>me</u> on the phone.*

The **objective case** is also known as the **accusative case**.

For more information, see **case**.

## objector

Note the ending of this word. See **-er/-or**.

## obligatory

Note the ending of this word. See **-ary/-ery/-ory**.

## observatory

Note the ending of this word. See **-ary/-ery/-ory**.

## octopus

The plural of this word is usually spelled **octopuses**. You may also see **octopodes** and **octopi**. But if you are writing it yourself it's best to use the normal English **octopuses**.

For more about words like this, see **-us**.

## odes

An **ode** is a lyric poem of praise, often addressed to a particular subject as in *Ode on Melancholy, Ode to a Nightingale,* and always on a lofty theme such as beauty or death. In Greek poetry it had a special verse form, but in English poetry it comes in a variety of forms.

## -oe-

The letters o͟e are unusual in English, except at the ends of words like *shoe* and *toe.* However, they do occur in some scientific words which have come down to us from Greek. For example:

amoeba    diarrhoea    homoeopath    oesophagus

The -o͟e- makes an awkward spelling in such words, because few of us know the Greek roots they relate to. More and more, the -o͟e- is being written as just -e͟- in such words. So they appear as:

ameba    diarrhea    homeopath    esophagus

These spellings aren't generally acceptable in the UK yet, but they have a lot going for them — they are simpler and follow normal English spelling patterns. In the USA they are already the standard ones.

There is a longer discussion of this type of spelling problem under **-ae-**.

## oesophagus

The usual spelling of this word is **oesophagus**, but it can be spelled **esophagus**. For more about words like this, see **-oe-**.

The plural is spelled **oesophaguses/esophaguses** or **oesophagi/esophagi**. For more about plurals like this, see **-us**.

## of / have

When you abbreviate **have** in contracted forms like *could have* (could've), *would have* (would've) and *should have* (should've), the 've͟ sounds like **of**. It is a fairly common mistake to write *could of, would of,* and *should of,* but this is not correct.

## of / off

These words look similar but have different meanings.

We use **of** after nouns indicating:

**1** distance or direction: *a few kilometres east of London*
**2** contents or material: *a packet of biscuits, cloth of gold*
**3** belonging or possession: *an uncle of mine*

For other uses look up your dictionary.

We usually use **off** to mean "away from" or "no longer in a particular place or position":

*The hat blew off her head.*
*The garden gnome's nose has broken off.*

## off / from

These words are both often used as prepositions in the following way:
> *I'll buy that book off you.*
> *I'll buy that book from you.*

Note that some people consider this use of **off** to be incorrect so it's better to avoid it in formal essays.

## offence / offense

These are equally good spellings for this word.

**Offence** is the usual spelling in the UK.

**Offense** is the usual spelling in the USA.

Even in the UK, this word is spelled with s̲ not c̲ when it is made into an adjective by adding -ive̲:
> *Their offensive remarks made me furious.*

For more about words like this, see **-ce/-se**.

## older

See **elder/eldest/older/oldest**.

## oldest

See **elder/eldest/older/oldest**.

## omelette / omelet

These are equally good ways of spelling this word. It comes from French and **omelette** is the original spelling in that language.

**Omelet**, on the other hand, is a simpler spelling, in keeping with English spelling patterns.

For more about the -ette̲ ending, see **-ette**.

## one

Some people like to avoid speaking too personally and directly, and instead of using *I* and *you*, they use **one**. You might say or write:
> *What can one possibly do about it?*

It could mean *you* and it could mean *I* (or both of us).

**One** is rather a detached form of address, with no fixed or regular place in our pronoun system. This is why it often causes problems when you try to continue the sentence with it. Which possessive pronoun should you use?

1 One can only do his̲ best.
2 One can only do her̲ best.
3 One can only do their̲ best.
4 One can only do one's̲ best.

The first two sentences draw attention to gender, which many people prefer to avoid. (See **non-sexist language**.) The third sentence is neutral in gender, but moves from singular to plural in a way that some people feel is ungrammatical. The fourth sentence has an unusual and rather self-conscious tone because of the pronoun **one's**. Whichever pronoun you choose, you will need to stay with it, to be consistent. So after *his*, you would have to use *himself*, after *one's* it would have to be *oneself*, and so on.

With all these complications, it is probably easier not to use **one** at all. For most British people, it has a slightly old-fashioned and pompous ring to it these days.

For other ways of achieving a more impersonal style, see WRITING WORKSHOP pp 26–31.

## only

We often use **only** to spotlight something in a sentence:
*John only got his work back today.*

In speech it doesn't matter too much where we put the **only**, because we can show by the rising pitch of the voice just which word it is meant to spotlight. In our example, the speaker's voice could rise all the way from *only* to *today*, to show that *today* was the point of surprise.

But in writing there is no voice to guide the reader to the word we mean to spotlight. Instead it must be shown through the careful placement of words. **Only** draws most attention to the word straight after it. So to emphasise *today* we would have to write:
*John got his work back only today.*
Note the difference of meaning if we write:
*John got only his work back today . . . (Something else was kept back)*
or
*Only John got his work back today . . . (Others didn't)*

Other words which help to spotlight those next to them are:
even     exactly     just     merely     nearly     simply
Like **only**, they must be carefully placed to create the meaning you intend.

## onomatopoeia

is the name we give to the way the sound of a word can echo its meaning or sense. For example, ducks quack, cows moo and cats miaow. *Quack, moo* and *miaow* are onomatopoeic words. They sound in our language something like the noise we think that these animals make.

But in other languages they are different words, possibly ones which bring out different qualities in the sound made. For example, in Japanese the ringing of a bell is not *ding-ding* but *chirin-chirin*, the noise a rooster makes is not *cock-a-doodle-doo* but *kokekokko*, the noise a dog makes is not *bow-wow* but *wa-wa*, and the noise a cat makes is not *miaow* but *nyao*.

Some poetry is made more effective by using onomatopoeic words. Indeed some poets set out to repeat a sound in a number of words to build up a special effect. For example in the phrase *the buzzing of busy bees*, the initial onomatopoeic word is *buzzing*, but that sound is repeated in *busy* and in *bees*. The total effect is that you can almost hear the bees.

Onomatopoeia is the English spelling of a Greek word, which is why it looks so strange. It breaks up into onomato-, from the Greek word for a name or word, and -poeia from the Greek word for "making", so it means literally "the making of words for things". In particular it is the making of words which imitate sound.

Note that onomatopoeia is never spelled with just an e instead of the oe (as in *f(o)etus*). The last part of the word breaks up into -po-ei-a, even though the pronunciation has slipped into two syllables *pee-a*.

### operator

Note the ending of this word. See **-ator**.

### opposites

For information about words with opposite meanings, see **antonyms**.

### or

See **oar/or/ore/awe**.

### -or / -our

These are two different ways of spelling the ending of words like *colo(u)r*, *favo(u)r*, *hono(u)r* and *labo(u)r*. The spellings are left over from the mix-up in England in the seventeenth century, when people tried to spell words according to their origins. The words which came from French were supposed, in this case, to be spelled with -our and those from Latin with -or. But there was much confusion about which came from where, and more and more people began to feel that it would be best to use -or for all of them. The trend ran its full course in the USA, and so Americans always use *color*, *labor* etc.

But the trend was halted in England by Dr Johnson's dictionary of 1755. Even he let some words of this kind go to -or anyway. Examples are *error*, *horror* and *terror*, which we would never think of spelling with -our. The rest were fixed -our, whether they deserved it or not. (Some, like *harbour* and *behaviour* certainly didn't, because they weren't either French or Latin, but old English words!)

In the UK we use the -our spellings, even though it is actually harder for you to be sure how to spell other words related to them. For example, if you spell *humour* with the u, you must remember to leave it out in *humorous*. It is the same with *labour* and *laborious*, *vigour* and *vigorous*. Even worse is *honour*, which would remain the same in *honourable* but change in *honorary* and *honorific*.

### oral

See **aural/oral**.

### orator

Note the ending of this word. See **-ator**.

### oratory

See **rhetoric**.

### orbit

Note that you don't add another t to this word when you add the endings -ed, -ing, -er, or -al to form **orbited, orbiting, orbiter** or **orbital**. See **doubling of last letter**.

### ordinal numbers

See **cardinal numbers/ordinal numbers**.

### ore

See **oar/or/ore/awe**.

### organically

Note the ending of this word. See **-ally**.

### orient / orientate

These verbs can both be used to mean either "to aim or direct" or "to adjust or adapt":

*The lesson was oriented* (or *orientated*) *towards the younger students.*

*The house was oriented* (or *orientated*) *towards the north to catch the sun.*

*They oriented* (or *orientated*) *themselves quickly to their new school.*

**Orientate** has been formed by chopping the -ion off the noun **orientation** and adding an -e. This process is called **backformation**. The -ate ending adds nothing to the meaning of **orient**, which is the simpler and older verb, and does the same job perfectly as well.

Both words originally came from the Latin word *oriens*, meaning "the east" or "sunrise", and one meaning of **orient** or **orientate** is "to place something so that it faces the east".

### originator

Note the ending of this word. See **-ator**.

### orthopedic / orthopaedic

These are equally good ways of spelling this word. For more about words like this, see **-ae-**.

## ought to

Both **ought to** and **should** mean that something has to be done:
*You ought to turn the light on.*
*You should turn the light on.*
So *ought to* and *should* both combine with other verbs to make statements expressing obligation. But when it comes to making questions or negative sentences, **ought to** seems awkward, and perhaps a little old-fashioned:
*Ought you to turn the light on?*
*You oughtn't to turn the light on.*
It's easier to say:
*Should you turn the light on?*
*You shouldn't turn the light on.*
For more about words like this, see **modal verbs**.

## our

See **we/us/our/ours/ourselves**.

## ours

See **we/us/our/ours/ourselves**.

## ourselves

See **we/us/our/ours/ourselves**.

## -ous

is the ending which means "full of" or "similar to". So

| | | |
|---|---|---|
| courageous | *is full of* | courage |
| dangerous | | danger |
| poisonous | | poison |
| riotous | *like a* | riot |

In words like these, -ous is added straight on to the noun to make the new adjective.

With *adventurous, famous, virtuous,* the final e of *adventure, fame* and *virtue* have been dropped before the -ous.

With *furious, glorious* and *industrious,* the final y of *fury, glory* and *industry* have changed to i before the -ous.

In some other -ous words, the ending replaces the last two letters (-on) of the noun:

| | |
|---|---|
| caution | cautious |
| contagion | contagious |
| flirtation | flirtatious |
| oblivion | oblivious |
| rebellion | rebellious |
| repetition | repetitious |

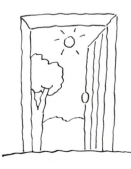

## outdoor / outdoors

These words both mean "outside (the house or building)" but **outdoor** is the adjective and **outdoors** is the adverb.

Here is a sentence showing **outdoor** the adjective:
*Playing soccer is an outdoor activity.*

Here is a sentence showing **outdoors** the adverb:
*We'll have breakfast outdoors today.*

## outfit

Add another t at the end of this word when you add the endings -ed, -ing or -er to form **outfitted**, **outfitting** or **outfitter**. See **doubling of last letter**.

## oversee

Note that the past tense of this verb is **oversaw**:
*She always oversaw the department fairly.*

The past participle is **overseen**:
*This project has been overseen by the same person for fifteen years.*

When you add -er to form a noun from this verb, you drop an e to form **overseer**. Otherwise there would be three e's in a row.

## ovum

The plural of this word from biology meaning "egg" is **ova**. It comes from Latin, and **ova** is its Latin plural. For more about words like this, see **-um**.

## ox

The plural of this word is spelled **oxen**.

There are only three words that have kept this old English plural ending. The others are *brethren* and *children*.

# Pp

## p as a silent letter

The letter p is written but not sounded in some English words.

It is silent before s and n at the beginning of a few words borrowed from ancient languages. For example, it is silent in *pneumatic, psychiatry, psychiatrist, psychology, psychologist, pseudonym* and other words with pseudo-, all of which are Greek. It is silent in both *psalm* and *psaltery* from Hebrew.

P is occasionally silent in the middle of a word, as in *receipt*. In this case the p was added by scholars in the sixteenth century, who thought its spelling ought to be more like other words from the same Latin root, such as *reception* and *receptacle*. The fact that the p was actually sounded in those other words didn't make them think twice about introducing it into *receipt*, where it had never been. *Receipt*, like *conceit* and *deceit*, was different because it came through French. But the pronunciation of *receipt* has never changed, in spite of its revised spelling.

At the end of the word *coup* (meaning "revolution") the letter p is also silent. This is because it has been borrowed from French, and has kept its French pronunciation.

## pail

See **pale/pail**.

## pain / pane

These words sound the same but mean different things.

**Pain** is the hurt or suffering you feel when you are injured, sick or unhappy.

A **pane** is a single plate or sheet of glass, usually in a window.

## pair / pear / pare

These words all sound the same but they mean different things.

Two things that go together, like shoes, are a **pair**.

A **pear** is a kind of fruit.

You **pare** an apple when you peel off the skin.

## palate / palette / pallet

These words all sound the same but their meanings are quite different.

Your **palate** is the roof of your mouth. It is also your sense of taste.

Painters mix their colours on a thin board called a **palette**.

A **pallet** is a wooden packing tray which can be moved from place to place in a factory.

## pale / pail

These words sound the same but they have different meanings.

Your face is **pale** if it looks rather white. A colour is **pale** if it isn't very bright or dark.

**Pail** is another word for "bucket".

## palette

See **palate/palette/pallet**.

## palindromes

A **palindrome** is a word or sentence which reads the same backwards or forwards. For example, the word *Madam* is a palindrome, as is the sentence *Madam I'm Adam*. Try reading these backwards.

## pallet

See **palate/palette/pallet**.

## palomino

The plural of this word is spelled **palominos**.

You may sometimes see **palomino** spelled **palamino**, but this is a rare spelling.

For more about the plurals of words like this, see **-o**.

## pane

See **pain/pane**.

## panel

For information about whether to double the l when you add endings like -ed, -ing, or -er, see **-l-/-ll-**.

## panic

Add a k to make the words **panicked**, **panicking**, and **panicky**. For more about words like this, see **-c/-ck-**.

## papaw

See **pawpaw/papaya/papaw**.

## papaya

See **pawpaw/papaya/papaw**.

## papier-mâché

The accents above the a and e in **mâché** show that the word comes from French. The accent above the a is a circumflex. The acute accent above the e shows that the e is pronounced to rhyme with *pay*.

While foreign accents sometimes give a useful hint about pronunciation, they tend to be used less often once a word becomes better known in English. So it may be that in the future you will see **papier-mâché** written without any accents.

For more about accents in English, see **accents**. See also **acute accents** and **circumflex**.

### papyrus

**Papyrus** usually stays singular even when you are writing about more than one plant, or when you are talking about lots of papyrus as a writing material:

*The papyrus was waving all along the banks of the Nile.*
*The papyrus was stacked neatly for the scribe.*

When it is used in this way, **papyrus** is a mass noun. For more information about this, see **mass nouns**.

**Papyrus** does sometimes need a plural, though. When you use this word to refer to documents written on papyrus, you will need the plural **papyruses**:

*There are five more papyruses in the British Museum.*

This plural can also be spelled **papyri**. For more about the plural of words like this, see **-us**.

### parables

A **parable** is a story which can be taken at face value as a simple story, or interpreted to explain some moral teaching or truth. When it is understood this way, each character can be seen to stand for something else and the events in it to symbolise some greater truth. See **allegory**.

A parable normally illustrates one issue and is intended to teach and persuade the listener. The parables of Jesus Christ are probably the best known part of his teaching.

### paragraphs

are the large building blocks of most kinds of writing in prose. They usually consist of a few sentences, which detail or develop one particular point.

In a narrative, the paragraphs help to build each stage of the story, as they do in the story entitled "The Mistake" in WRITING WORKSHOP pp 40–1.

In an essay, each paragraph holds a unit of information, or an argument, as shown in the two essays in WRITING WORKSHOP pp 48–9. The paragraphs of an essay usually begin with a topic sentence, which states what kind of information or argument is to come. See **topic sentences**.

Newspaper articles are unusual in that their paragraphs often only have one sentence in them. (Check the article in WRITING WORKSHOP p 53.) This is not good for essay (or story) writing, because if you have one short paragraph after another, it splinters things up too much for the reader. But of course you may want to use one on occasions, for special effect.

Note that while one-sentence paragraphs are too short, make sure you don't make your paragraphs too long either. If your paragraph lasts for a whole page, it usually means that its focus has shifted. There are probably two or more points in it, each of which needs its own paragraph.

See also **indent**.

### parakeet / parrakeet

These are equally good spellings for this word. **Parakeet** is the usual spelling in the UK. **Parrakeet** is the usual spelling in the USA. You may also find the word spelled **parroquet** and **parroket**, but these are rarer spellings.

### parallel

You have a choice whether or not to double the l when you add -ed or ing to this word. See **-l-/-ll-**.

Note that when you add -ist and ism, the l is never doubled: **parallelist, parallelism**.

### paralyse / paralyze

These are two possible spellings for this word. See **-yse/-yze**.

### paralysis

The plural of this word is spelled **paralyses**, with the last syllable pronounced to rhyme with *seas*. This is a Latin form of plural, and is used because **paralysis** came into English from Latin. For more about words like this, see **-is**.

### parameter / perimeter

These words look similar but mean different things.

The **parameters** of something are the limits that restrict it:
*I have to consider the parameters of your voice, like how high you can sing, before I write a song for you.*
In maths and science, a **parameter** is a variable factor.

A **perimeter** is the outside edge of a shape or an area, as in *the perimeter of a playing field.*

### paraphrasing

is finding other words or phrases to say the same thing. You do it to make a statement clearer, or to change its style of language. For example, the sentence:
*Children should be seen and not heard.*
could be paraphrased as:
*Kids shouldn't open their mouths when they're in the presence of adults.*
or as:
*The younger generation ought to impinge on us visually rather than aurally.*
As the examples show, you can paraphrase in different ways. You may want to make the language more informal, or more formal. See also **variety in writing**.

## parcel

For information about whether to double the <u>l</u> when you add endings like <u>-ed</u> or <u>-ing</u>, see **-l-/-ll-**.

## pardon

Don't double the <u>n</u> for any of the words that are made from **pardon: pardoned, pardoning, pardonable, pardonably, pardoner**. For more about words like this, see **doubling of last letter**.

## pare

See **pair/pear/pare**.

## parentheses

are a kind of bracket. For information about their use, see **brackets**.

## parody

When you imitate a serious piece of writing (or music) in a humorous way, you are using **parody**.

The most important thing to remember when writing **parody** is to <u>keep</u> the style of the original but to <u>change</u> it in a way that makes fun of it.

It is quite easy to **parody** poetry because you can keep the structure and rhythm of the original poem and substitute your own rhyming words. But to **parody** a piece of prose is more difficult because prose is usually longer and more complex.

The following example is a **parody** of a fairy story:

*Once upon a time there was a king and a queen and a beautiful princess. The princess was put under a spell by a wicked witch and carried off by a dragon. A handsome prince fought the dragon, and drove away the wicked witch. So they all lived happily ever after. Except for the dragon. The end.*

You will notice that the writer uses many of the familiar stock phrases common to all fairy tales but strings them all together in only five lines. Many of the stereotyped characters of fairy tales are introduced one after the other in rapid succession. Everything happens so quickly that it is obvious the writer is not taking this style of writing seriously. The example makes fun of that type of writing, which is what makes it a **parody**.

## parrakeet

See **parakeet/parrakeet**.

## participles

We say that verbs have two **participles**, the past and the present. The verb *to walk* for example, has:

1 the **present participle** *walking* (the action is going on)
2 the **past participle** *walked* (the action is in the past)

You can usually recognise them by their -ing and -ed endings. But the past participles of some verbs have unpredictable forms, such as -en and -n:

*Ride* becomes *ridden* in *I have ridden.*

*Tear* becomes *torn* in *I have torn.*

Some even keep their basic form (infinitive):

*Cut* remains as *cut* in *I have cut.*

For more information on this, see **-ed** and **-ed/-(e)n**.

Participles combine with the verbs *be* and *have* (auxiliaries) to make new verb forms that express a completed or incompleted action (aspect), or an action that may be in a past, present or future time (tense). Some examples of this are:

*was walking*
*have walked*
*has been walking*

and so on.

Many of the adjectives in our language have come from these two types of participles. For example, *interesting* in *an interesting book* and *exhausted* in *an exhausted student.*

## particular

Note the ending of this word. See **-ar**.

## parts of speech

The different classes or groups of words in a language are often called **parts of speech**. In English, we generally say that there are eight parts of speech:

| | | |
|---|---|---|
| nouns | *such as* | water, tree, wisdom |
| pronouns | | you, mine, them |
| adjectives | | yellow, wise, dog-eared |
| verbs | | walks, is, wondered |
| adverbs | | soon, never, quickly |
| prepositions | | in, through, under |
| conjunctions | | and, because, when |
| interjections | | hey! oh! |

Each of these is described in its alphabetical place in this book, and extra information about the various types is given there.

## passed / past

These related words sound the same but they are different parts of speech.

**Passed** is the past form of the verb **pass**:

*We passed the shop.*
*He passed me the ruler.*
*That time has passed.*

**Past** can be used as follows:

| | |
|---|---|
| as an adjective: | *the past fifteen years* |
| as a noun: | *in the past* |
| as an adverb: | *the soldiers marched past* |
| as a preposition: | *the house past the shop* |

## passive verbs

A **passive verb** is one whose subject is having an action done to it, rather than doing the action itself.

In the sentence
*The dog was hit by a car*
*the dog* is not doing the hitting. It is being hit by the car. Because the subject of the sentence (the dog) is not the "doer" of the action, we say that the verb is **passive**.

When the subject of a sentence carries out the action, we say that the verb is **active**. You can see an example of an active verb in the following sentence:
*A car hit the dog.*

When we change from passive to active or vice versa, the focus of our attention shifts. In the case of our two examples, it shifts from *the dog* (in the passive sentence) to *the car* (in the active sentence).

**Passive verbs** are said to be in the **passive voice**.

Note that using passive verbs is a way of making your writing more impersonal. For more information about this, see **impersonal writing**.

## passive voice

This is a grammatical term which describes how a subject is related to its verb. For examples see **passive verbs**.

## past

See **passed/past**.

## pastor

Note the ending of this word. It is -or, not -er, because it was borrowed straight from Latin. See **-er/-or**.

## past forms

The normal ending for the past tense and the present participle of verbs is -ed:
*I walked to town.*
*I have walked to town.*

There are some exceptions, however. Some verbs do not have an extra ending at all:
*I hit the ball and it smashed the window.*
*I have hit the ball.*
Some other verbs that act like this are *burst, cut* and *put*.

Other verbs (like *beat* and *show*) add -en or -n for the past participle:
*I have beaten him.*
*I have shown him.*

Still others (like *swim*) change the main part of the verb instead of adding an ending:
*I swam*          (past tense)
*I have swum*     (past participle)

For more information, see **past tense** and **irregular verbs**.

## past tense

We use the **past tense** of a verb for actions and events that have happened in the past.

We show this either by adding endings to the basic (infinitive) form of the verb (*walk* becomes *walked* and *finish* becomes *finished);* or by changing the spellings within the word itself (*fight* becomes *fought* and *run* becomes *ran.*

We can also show whether the events are completed or continuing by using the past tense in its *perfect* or *continuous* forms:

| | |
|---|---|
| *I walked* | (past – simple form) |
| *I was walking* | (past continuous) |
| *I had walked* | (past perfect) |
| *I had been walking* | (past perfect continuous) |

As you can see in the examples above, we use the verbs *be* and *have* to indicate the perfect and continuous aspects of the past tense. For more information about this, see **aspect**.

## pâté

The accents above the a and e in this word show that it comes from French. The accent above the a is a circumflex. The acute accent above the e shows that the e is pronounced to rhyme with *pay*.

While foreign accents sometimes give a useful hint about pronunciation, they tend to be used less often once a word becomes better known in English. So it may be that in the future you will see **pâté** written without any accents. (In this case, though, it will look identical to the word **pate**, meaning "the head", which is pronounced to rhyme with *gate*.)

For more about accents in English, see **accents**. See also **acute accents** and **circumflex**.

## pathetically

Note the ending of this word. See **-ally**.

## paw

See **pour/poor/paw/pore**.

## pawn / porn

These words sound the same but have different meanings.

A **pawn** is one of the pieces in chess. If you **pawn** your watch, you leave it with a **pawnbroker** when you borrow money, and collect it when you repay your debt.

**Porn** is art, photography or writing thought or designed to be obscene or indecent. It is short for **pornography**.

## pawpaw / papaya / papaw

These are equally good words for this fruit. **Pawpaw** and **papaw** are the usual spellings in the UK. **Papaya** is the spelling closest to the original Spanish word (of Caribbean origin).

### peace / piece

These words sound the same but have different meanings.

**Peace** is freedom from war, as in *a march for peace*. It can also be calm or quiet, as in *peace of mind*.

A **piece** of something is a bit or part of it, as in *a piece of cake*. It can also be a single or individual thing, as in *a piece of fruit*.

### peaceable

Note that you keep the final e̲ of **peace** when adding -able̲. For more about words like this, see **-able/-eable**.

### peaceable / peaceful

These words are both linked to **peace** but they have different meanings.

A **peaceable** person is someone who likes to keep the peace.

A **peaceful** scene is one in which everything is restful, tranquil and full of peace.

### peak / peek / pique

These words all sound the same but they have different meanings.

A **peak** is the top of a mountain.

To **peek** is to snatch a quick look, often when you are not supposed to.

**Pique** is a feeling of mild annoyance. To be miffed is to be **piqued**.

### peal / peel

These words sound the same but mean different things.

Bells **peal** when they ring out.

To **peel** an apple is to remove the skin from it.

### pear

See **pair/pear/pare**.

### pearl / purl

These words sound the same but they can mean different things.

A **pearl** is the precious bead that you find in an oyster.

**Purl** is a stitch in knitting. It can also be spelled **pearl**.

### pedal / peddle

These words sound the same but mean different things.

A **pedal** is something you push to make a wheel go round, as on a bike. To **pedal** a bike is to make it go by pushing the pedals.

For information about whether to double the l when you add -ed̲ or -ing̲ to **pedal**, see **-l-/-ll-**.

To **peddle** something is to sell it, usually in small quantities to individual buyers. The person who peddles is a **pedlar** or **peddler**. See **pedlar/peddler**.

## peddler

See **pedlar/peddler**.

## pedlar / peddler

These are equally good spellings for this word.

**Pedlar** is the usual spelling in the UK for someone who travels around selling goods. **Peddler** is the usual spelling in the USA for this sense of the word.

**Peddler** is the spelling for someone who sells illegal goods, such as drugs or stolen property. This spelling is usual in the UK and the USA.

For more about words like this, see **-ar** and **-er/-or**.

## peek

See **peak/peek/pique**.

## peel

See **peal/peel**.

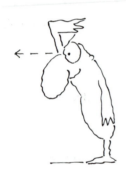

## peer / pier

These words sound the same but mean different things.

To **peer** at something is to look at it closely in an effort to see. Your **peers** are your equals, in age or rank. A **peer group** is a group of people of the same age or social position.

A **pier** is a jetty.

## pencil

For information about whether to double the l when you add endings like -ed, -ing, or -er, see **-l-/-ll-**.

## peninsula / peninsular

These two words sound the same and are closely related, but there is an important difference.

**Peninsula**, without the r, is a noun:
*The windsurfers sailed round the peninsula.*

**Peninsular**, with the r, is an adjective:
*The peninsular landscape is rugged and beautiful.*

## per cent / percent

These are equally good spellings for this term:
*A small per cent of tigers eat people.*
*A large percent of people are afraid of tigers.*

**Percentage** may also be used here instead of **per cent**:
*A small percentage of people eat tigers.*

Be careful about agreement:
*Five per cent of the population is bald.*
*One per cent of the apples are rotten.*

Note that in these sentences the verb agrees with the nouns rather than the per cent number. So it is *the population is*, not *five per cent . . . are*. And it is *the apples are*, not *one per cent . . . is*.

**Per cent** is often replaced by the symbol **%**. It is usually best to keep this symbol for writing in which you're quoting a lot of numbers.

## percentages

For information about writing percentages, see **fractions**.

## perceptible

Note the ending of this word. See **-able/-ible**.

## perfect aspect

We use the term **perfect** in grammar to mean "completed". We say that a verb like *have run* is perfect because it expresses a completed action. This differs from *was running* which is **continuous**. For more information about these two grammatical categories, see **aspect**.

You can express a completed action in the present or past tense:
*have run*    (present perfect)
*had run*     (past perfect)

See also **past tense**.

## perimeter

See **parameter/perimeter**.

## period

See **full stops**.

## periodically

Note the ending of this word. See **-ally**.

## permissible

Note the ending of this word. See **-able/-ible**.

## permissible / permissive

These words are both linked to **permit** but they mean different things.

Something is **permissible** if it is allowed or permitted.

Someone is **permissive** if they permit lots of things that others wouldn't:
*Permissive parents allow their children to do pretty well anything they like.*

## perpetrate / perpetuate

These words look similar but they mean different things.

To **perpetrate** a crime is to commit it:
*He perpetrated a fraud against his employer.*

To **perpetuate** something is to make it last or keep it happening:
*Our economic system perpetuates poverty in society.*

## perpetrator

Note the ending of this word. See **-ator**.

## perpetuate

See **perpetrate/perpetuate**.

## persecute / prosecute

These words look similar but they mean different things.

You **persecute** people if you treat them cruelly or unjustly, often because of their political or religious beliefs.

You **prosecute** someone if you take legal action against them.

## persecutor

Note the ending of this word. See **-er/-or**.

## person

**Person** is a term we use in grammar to distinguish three kinds of pronouns.

The **first person** is the person speaking (usually *I* or *we*). The **second person** is the person spoken to (*you*). The **third person** is the person or thing spoken about (*he, she, it, they*, or *him, her, it, them*):

> *I'll tell*     *you about*     *her.*
> (first person)    (second person)    (third person)

Some verbs also have a special ending for the third person. The third person singular of verbs in the present tense usually ends with -s or -es. For example:

> *I walk* but *she walks*
> *I finish* but *it finishes*

WRITING WORKSHOP pp 26 and 29 for more information on the use of **first person** in narrative.

## -person

This ending doesn't show the sex of whoever it refers to, so it can be useful as a way of avoiding sexist language. *Chairperson* can be used instead of *chairman* or *chairwoman*, either of which may draw attention to the sex of the person referred to. Other cases like this in which a word with -person may be used are *draftsperson, spokesperson* and *tradesperson*.

But as things are, -person words mostly get used when a woman is being mentioned (only rarely do they refer to a man). So the -person ending comes to mean "female" for many people, and doesn't really beat the sexist problem.

It is perhaps better to find some other kind of non-sexist word. Some alternatives are discussed at **-man** and **non-sexist language**.

## personal / personnel

These words look similar but they mean different things.

If something is **personal** then it is something that relates to you as a person and is usually private, such as *a personal diary*.

The **personnel** of a business or an institution are the people employed there.

## personal pronouns

Pronouns are words that can stand in place of nouns that have already been mentioned.

We use **personal pronouns** to substitute for any noun that refers to a person or thing already mentioned:
*Where's Helen? I need her.*
The personal pronoun *her* stands for *Helen* in the example above.

The full set of personal pronouns in English is displayed in the box alongside. The different forms are explained at **person**, **number**, **gender** and **case**.

| Personal pronouns |
|---|
| I me my mine |
| we us our ours |
| you your yours |
| he him his |
| she her hers |
| it its |
| they them their theirs |

## personal writing

is writing about things from your own experience and your own viewpoint. You may write this way to express your ideas and feelings, or as a stepping stone to other kinds of writing. For many writers it is the easiest way to begin writing.

Ways of turning personal and subjective writing into more objective forms of writing are discussed in WRITING WORKSHOP p 29.

## personification

is a device we use in writing for special effect. We **personify** objects when we treat them as if they were a person. For example, people often talk about boats and cars as if they were female. Instead of talking about your car as an "it", you might refer to it as a "she". This can indicate a special affection for the car. It is as if it had a personality of its own.

The thing to watch with personification is that once you have begun to write about an object in this way, you must make all references to it match up. If you have talked about your car as "she", then you must talk about her steering wheel, not its steering wheel. Once you have referred to the object as a person, you cannot suddenly go back to talking about it as if it were a thing.

## personnel

See **personal/personnel**.

### perspective / prospective

These words look similar but they mean different things.

A **perspective** is a particular view you have of something. This can be what you see with your eyes, or a way of thinking about something. To have things in the right perspective is to be looking at things the right way.

Something that is **prospective** is likely to happen. You can look towards it as a **prospect**:

> *Your prospective increase in income will mean that you can buy a car.*

A **prospective** student is someone who intends or looks forward to becoming a student.

### petrol / petrel

These words sound the same but mean different things.

**Petrol** is the fuel that a car runs on.

A **petrel** is a kind of seabird, like the **stormy petrel**.

My name's Phideaux, what's yours?

### ph / f

Which English words can be spelled with either <u>ph</u> or <u>f</u>? See **f/ph**.

### phantasy

See **fantasy**.

### pharynx

The plural of this word may be spelled **pharynxes** or **pharynges**.

**Pharynxes** follows the normal English pattern for making plurals – simply add <u>-es</u> (or <u>-s</u>).

**Pharynges** is the Latin plural. It is sometimes used because **pharynx** came into English from Latin. It's the spelling used in other words made from **pharynx: pharyngeal** ("connected with the pharynx"), **pharyngitis** (a disease of the pharynx), and so on.

For more about words like this, see **-x**.

### phase

See **faze/phase**.

### phenomenon

The plural of this word is **phenomena**.

Because **phenomena** is already a plural, it is a mistake to "pluralise" this plural with the spelling *phenomenas*, although this form is becoming more widespread.

**Phenomenon** needs a singular verb, and **phenomena** needs a plural:

> *This phenomenon <u>is</u> most unusual.*
> *The phenomena <u>are</u> many and varied.*

For more about words like this, see **-a (as a plural ending)**.

## phony / phoney

These are equally good spellings for this word.

If you use **phony**, the plural is spelled **phonies**. If you use **phoney**, the plural may be spelled **phonies** or **phoneys**. For more about words like this, see **-y/-ey**.

## phosphorus / phosphorous

These words sound the same but mean different things.

**Phosphorus** is the noun, and **phosphorous** is the adjective that comes from it:

*They found some phosphorus at the back of the cave.*
*The rock had a phosphorous glow.*

## phrases

A **phrase** is a group of words that act together as a unit within a sentence:

*standing on the corner*
*the old man*
*was singing*
*at the top of his voice*

are all phrases.

As you can see from the examples above, **phrases** can't stand on their own and make a sensible message, except in answer to a question:

*What are you doing? Standing on the corner!*

Note that **phrases** like those above are all different from **clauses** in that they don't have both a *subject* and a *predicate*. Thus the following words make a clause:

*He* (subject) *was standing on the corner* (predicate).

For more information, see **clauses**.

## phylum

The plural of this word is spelled **phyla**. **Phylum** came into English from Latin, which is why we use its Latin plural. For more about words like this, see **-um**.

## physically

Note the ending of this word. See **-ally**.

## physiologically

Note the ending of this word. See **-ally**.

## piano

The plural of this word is spelled **pianos**. For more about words like this, see **-o**.

## picket

Note that you don't add another t to make **picketing, picketed** and **picketer**. For more about words like this, see **doubling of last letter**.

## picnic

Note that you add a <u>k</u> to make the words **picnicking**, **picnicked** and **picnicker**. For more about words like this, see **-c/-ck-**.

## picture / pitcher

These words sound similar but have different meanings.

A **picture** can be a drawing, painting or photo.

A **pitcher** is a large jug. It can also be the baseball player who throws the ball to the batter.

## piece

See **peace/piece**.

## pier

See **peer/pier**.

## pigeon / pidgin

These words sound the same but have different meanings.

A **pigeon** is a common bird which is often a pest in cities.

**Pidgin** is a basic language made up of bits of other languages and used by people who have no regular language in common.

## pigmy / pygmy

These are equally good spellings. See **i/y**.

## pillar

Note the ending of this word. See **-ar**.

## pique

See **peak/peek/pique**.

## pistol / pistil

These words sound the same but have different meanings.

A **pistol** is a type of small gun that fits into a holster.

A **pistil** is a botanical word for the seed-bearing part of a flower.

## pitcher

See **picture/pitcher**.

## pixie / pixy

These are equally good spellings for this word. The plural, however, is always **pixies**. For more about words like this, see **-ie/-y**.

## placenta

The plural of this word may be spelled **placentas** or **placentae**. For more about words like this, see **-a (as a singular ending)**.

## plagiarism

is using the words of another writer as if they were your own. It is bad writing practice. How to avoid it is explained in WRITING WORKSHOP p 63.

### plain / plane

These words sound the same but have different meanings.

A **plain** is a large flat area of land. If something is **plain** then you see, hear or understand it clearly.

A **plane** is a tool for smoothing wood. It is also a shortened form of **aeroplane**.

Note that both these words are linked to the same Latin word *planus*. The spelling of **plain** changed because it came into English through French, whereas **plane** came directly from Latin.

### plaintiff / plaintive

These words sound similar but mean different things.

In law a **plaintiff** is a person who brings a court case against someone else.

A voice or cry is **plaintive** if it is sorrowful or complaining.

### plane

See **plain/plane**.

### plateau

The plural of this word may be spelled **plateaus** or **plateaux**. For more about words like this, see **-e(a)u**.

### plausible

Note the ending of this word. See **-able/-ible**.

### plectrum

The plural of this word may be spelled **plectrums** or **plectra**. For more about words like this, see **-um**.

### plot

The **plot** is the backbone of any story. There are features common to all plots — an opening in which the scene is set, a development in which complications occur, and a climax which is the high point in the story. Often there is a denouement where everything is explained or resolved. See **climax** and **denouement**.

### plough

This is the usual spelling of this word. You may sometimes see it spelled **plow**, which is the way it is spelled in the USA.

### plum / plumb

These words sound the same but mean different things.

A **plum** is a soft smooth-skinned fruit.

A **plumb** is a lead weight on a string, used to measure depth or to test if something is exactly upright. **Plumb** can also mean "exactly":
*The picture is plumb in the middle.*
The b is not pronounced but is in the spelling because the word comes from the Latin word for lead *plumbum*.

### plummet

Note that the t remains single in **plummeted** and **plummeting**. For more about words like this, see **doubling of last letter**.

### pluperfect

is another name for the **past perfect**. For more information on this, see **perfect aspect**.

### plural

When a noun, verb or pronoun refers to more than one person or thing, we say it is **plural** in number. We call it singular if it refers to just one.

For nouns in English, adding -s or -es is the most common way of forming the plural:

*one cat          five cats*
*one box          fifteen boxes*

Some nouns form their plurals in a different way:

*child   children        criterion   criteria*
*ox      oxen            thesis      theses*
*man     men             mouse       mice*

Some don't change at all:

*one sheep        two sheep*

All of these are known as *count nouns* because they refer to things you can count, and they usually have a distinct plural form. Other nouns (*mass nouns*) don't normally occur in the plural at all:

*butter   rice   mud*

Most pronouns have a special plural form. *I* is singular, for example, but *we* is plural.

Verbs have different singular and plural forms, at least in the present tense. In these cases it's important to make sure that you follow a plural noun or pronoun with a plural verb:

*She wants* . . . but *They want* . . .

For more information on difficult cases, see **agreement**.

### plus

We are familiar with **plus** used in at least three different ways:

1 *One plus one equals two.*
2 *My teacher is giving me ten piano lessons, plus an extra one he owes me from last term.*
3 *Surely the extra attention he's giving you is a plus, not a minus.*

In the first two sentences **plus** is being used as a preposition. In the third it is used as a noun.

Nowadays many people use **plus** in a different way – as a conjunction meaning "and in addition":

*All his family gave him presents, plus he got gifts from all his friends as well.*

This use of **plus** is so widespread that it is likely to continue and be completely accepted. Note that some people still frown on it.

### p.m.

This abbreviation can be used when writing the time, to show that it is between noon and midnight. For example, *6.30 p.m.* means that it is 6.30 <u>in the evening</u>.

The letters **p.m.** stand for the Latin words *post meridiem*, meaning "after noon". They are often written without full stops: *6.30 pm*.

For more information, see **abbreviations**.

### poems

A **poem** is a piece of writing in which all the words have been selected for their imagery and qualities of sound. They are arranged in a particular form, which usually has a rhythmic pattern. Sometimes the words at the end of the lines rhyme, but this isn't always the case. When you are writing poems you are making **poetry**. Compare poetry with **prose**.

### poet / poetess

The suffix -<u>ess</u> is a common feminine ending in English. So **poetess** is the feminine form of **poet**.

Nowadays it is desirable to avoid words that refer to gender unnecessarily, and there is no need to turn **poet** into **poetess**. **Poet** describes someone who writes poetry, either a man or a woman.

For more information, see **feminine word endings** and **non-sexist language**.

### poetic form

The most striking features of poetic form are rhyme and rhythm. For more about these, see **rhyme** and **rhythm**.

The basic structural unit of a poem is the stanza or verse. See **stanza**.

### poisonous / venomous

These words have meanings that are similar but not the same.

If food or drink is **poisonous,** it contains a substance which can kill you or make you very sick if you swallow it:
*Snow White didn't know that the apple was poisonous.*

We say that an animal is **venomous** if its fangs contain a dangerous venom:
*The adder is the UK's only venomous snake. If treated with caution, it need not prove dangerous however.*

### polar

Note the ending of this word. See **-ar**.

### pole / poll / Pole

These words sound the same but mean different things.

A **pole** is a long thin piece of wood.

A **Pole** is someone from Poland. This word has a capital letter because it's a name. The **Poles** mark the southernmost (South Pole) and northernmost (North Pole) points of the earth.

When someone takes a **poll** they count and record the number of people, votes or opinions in favour of or opposed to an important issue.

## politics

You may use either the singular or the plural form of a verb with **politics**, depending on the situation.

The verb is most often plural when **politics** means "political opinions" or "political actions":
*Her politics are totally different from mine.*
*The politics of that situation are a little difficult to follow.*

For other meanings the singular verb is normally used:
*Politics is a tough business to be in.*
*Politics is an easy subject for me to study.*

## poll

See **pole/poll/Pole**.

## poly-

is a Greek prefix meaning "many". You'll find it in words like:
polygon (many-sided figure)
polygamy (marriage with many wives)
polyphonic (having several musical parts)
polysyllabic (having several syllables — like this very word!)

It's also used in naming chemicals, some of which are household words:
polyester   polythene   polyunsaturated

Note that the islands of *Polynesia* have the same prefix built into their name. The second part of the name is just the Greek word for "islands".

## poor

See **pour/poor/paw/pore**.

## pore

See **pour/poor/paw/pore**.

## porn

See **pawn/porn**.

## portion / potion

These words look similar but have different meanings.

A **portion** is a part or share of something, as in *my portion of dessert*.

A **potion** is an old-fashioned word for something you drink, often something poisonous or magical.

## portmanteau

The plural of this word may be spelled **portmanteaus** or **portmanteaux**. For more about words like this, see **-e(a)u**.

## portmanteau words

are those in which the start of one word is blended in with the latter part of another. For example, *telecast*, which is a blend of "<u>tele</u>vision" and "broad<u>cast</u>".

Some other common examples are:

| | |
|---|---|
| bit (in computing) | binary + digit |
| breathalyser | breath + analyser |
| electrocute | electro- + execute |
| guesstimate | guess + estimate |
| heliport | helicopter + airport |
| motel | motor + hotel |
| newscast | news + broadcast |
| paratroops | parachute + troops |
| smog | smoke + fog |

## possessive adjectives

See **possessive case**.

## possessive case

We use the **possessive case** for nouns and pronouns when we want to show that they "own" something.

Singular nouns end in <u>-'s</u> when they're in the possessive case:
*John's book   the dog's tail*
With plural nouns the possessive is shown by <u>-s'</u>, as in *the students' exercises*. For more information, especially on how to treat plural nouns, see **apostrophes**.

Pronouns in the possessive case include *my, your, his, her, its, our* and *their*. These are also called **possessive adjectives**. For a full list of personal pronouns, see **personal pronouns**.

Note that the **possessive case** is also called the **genitive**.

## possessive pronouns

Some pronouns that indicate ownership (possession) can be used instead of a noun which has already been mentioned, and they take a special form. These pronouns are called **possessive pronouns**:

*That book is <u>mine</u>.*
*Is that one <u>yours</u>?*
*<u>Yours</u> is the red one.*

They contrast with **personal pronouns** in the possessive case which are sometimes called **possessive adjectives** . These always come with a noun:

*That's <u>my</u> book.*
*Is <u>your</u> umbrella the one with stripes?*

For more information on this, see **personal pronouns** and **possessive case**.

## possible

Note the ending of this word. See **-able/-ible**.

## possible / probable

These words have similar meanings.

Something is **possible** if it can exist, happen, be done or be used:
*This new drug is a possible cure for AIDS.*
*Is it possible to walk all that way in one day?*

Something is **probable** if it is likely or expected to happen or be true:
*It is probable that they will get there in one day.*

## posterity / prosperity

These words look similar but mean different things.

**Posterity** refers to all the people who will live in the future:
*I'm leaving my art collection to posterity.*

**Prosperity** is success or good fortune, often in relation to wealth:
*The farmers have enjoyed two years of prosperity after the drought.*

## potato

The plural of this word is spelled **potatoes**.

This is one of the few surviving English nouns ending in -o which does not form its plural by simply adding -s.

For more about words like this, see **-o**.

## potion

See **portion/potion**.

## pour / poor / paw / pore

These words sound the same but have different meanings.

You can **pour** a liquid from one container to another.

Someone is **poor** if they don't have much money or property.

A **paw** is the foot of an animal with nails or claws.

A **pore** is a small hole. Sweat comes out through the **pores** in your skin. To **pore** over something is to read or study it carefully:
*He watched the pirates pore over the secret treasure map.*

## practically

Note the ending of this word. See **-ally**.

## practise / practice

These words sound the same and are closely related, but there is an important difference.

**Practise** is always a verb:
*We need to practise this tune a lot more.*

**Practice** can be a noun or an adjective:
*You need some practice on the piano.* (noun)
*That was just a practice run.* (adjective)

You may sometimes also see **practice** used as a verb, since that is the verb spelling in the USA.

For more about words like this, see **-ce/-se**.

## pray / prey

These words sound the same but mean different things.

**Pray** means "to talk to God":
*The minister always prays for people who are sick.*

To **prey on** something is to hunt and eat it. It can also mean "to affect something harmfully":
*Cats prey on mice.*
*The cause of his death still preys on my mind.*

## pre-

This prefix means "before in time", as in *prehistoric*, *preschool* and *preselect*. It is used a lot in English, to make new verbs, adjectives and nouns:

| | | | |
|---|---|---|---|
| preadvertise | predate | predawn | predestined |
| preheat | prejudge | prenatal | prepaid |
| preshrunk | prestressed | preview | prewar |

In such words it is usually written without a hyphen. But when it combines with historical or geological names which have a capital letter, pre- is written with a hyphen. For example:
pre-Cambrian  pre-Christian  pre-Darwinian  pre-Raphaelite

Pre- is a Latin prefix, so it's also built into many words we've borrowed straight from Latin. For example:
predict    preliminary    prepare    prevent

Pre- overlaps with ante-, which means "before in time or space". In fact, pre- may be taking over from ante- in some words, because ante- is easily confused with anti- (meaning "against"). This is probably why we have both:

| | |
|---|---|
| antecede | *and* | precede |
| antedate | predate |
| antenatal | prenatal |

These pairs of words have similar meanings. In each case, the form with pre- is gaining ground at the expense of the other one.

## precede / proceed

These words sound similar but they have different meanings.

To **precede** someone is to go in front of them:
*The headmistress will precede the other teachers as they enter the hall.*

To **proceed** is to go on or forward:
*The winners will proceed to the victory stand.*

## precis

A **precis** is a summary version of a piece of writing. It expresses the main facts or points of the original, but uses different words to express them.

The word comes from French and is pronounced *pray-see*. In French it is written with an accent (*précis*) and the accent still appears on it sometimes in English.

It can be either a noun or a verb. As a noun, the spelling remains exactly the same whether it is singular or plural:

*I made a precis of the chapter on volcanos.*
*I actually made three precis from that book.*

Note that the plural, although spelled the same as the singular, is pronounced *pray-seez*.

As a verb it takes the normal past endings:

*I precised it.*    *I have precised it.*

Note that *precised* is pronounced *pray-seed*.

See **summary**.

## predatory

Note the ending of this word. See **-ary/-ery/-ory**.

## predecessor

Note the ending of this word. See **-er/-or**.

## predicate

We commonly divide sentences into two parts:

**1** What is being talked about (the **subject**)
**2** What is being said about it (the **predicate**)

*She* (subject) *laughs a lot* (predicate).
*Really ordinary people that you meet in the street* (subject) *are nice* (predicate).
*The snowy peaks* (subject) *were beginning to turn pink in the sunset* (predicate).

Usually the predicate is the latter part of the sentence (that is everything that follows the subject). But occasionally, especially in literary styles of writing, the predicate can come first:

*With great ceremony, and without a flicker of emotion, in walked* (predicate) *Eustace* (subject).

## preface

A **preface** is a statement made by the author or editor of a book, and printed at the front before the real content begins. It explains the book's aims or contents. You'll find one at the front of this book. See also **foreword/preface**.

## prefer

Remember to double the last r̲ to make **preferred, preferring** and **preferrer**.

All the other words that come from **prefer** have a single r̲. For example, **preference, preferable, preferential, preferment**.

For more about words like this, see **doubling of last letter**.

## prefixes

A **prefix** is a unit at the front of a word which changes the word's meaning in some way. For example:

| | |
|---|---|
| anti- | makes *anticlockwise* mean "the opposite of *clockwise*" |
| ex- | makes *ex-president* mean "the former *president*" |
| pre- | makes *preheat* mean "*heat* beforehand" |

For more information about prefixes and other affixes, see **affixes**.

### preliminary

Note the ending of this word. See **-ary/-ery/-ory**.

### premier / premiere

Both these words are linked to a Latin word meaning "first", but they mean different things.

To be **premier** is to be first in rank or the leader in the field.

A **premiere** is the first performance of a play or screening of a film. This word has come into English from French and used to be spelled **première** with an accent. However it has become such a familiar word that we have dropped the accent.

### premise

In the singular, **premise** means "a logical proposition which is the basis of an argument or case":

*The argument that your income should increase is based on the premise that the cost of living has gone up.*

The plural, **premises**, means "a building":

*The estate agent took me to view the premises.*

Note that **premise**, the logical proposition, can also be spelled **premiss**.

### preposition / proposition

These words look similar but have different meanings.

A **preposition** is a part of speech. See **prepositions**.

A **proposition** is a suggestion or proposal:

*Your proposition that we should have a picnic lunch is a good one.*

### prepositions

Words such as *through, under, in, on* are **prepositions** in English. They are placed before nouns or pronouns to show how they relate to other words in the sentence:

*the man in the moon*
*I walked through the mud.*

### prescribe / proscribe

These words look similar but have different meanings.

A doctor **prescribes** medicine to take when you are ill.

To **proscribe** something is to condemn it and forbid people to do it.

### present

This word has several meanings, with different pronunciations. It can be an adjective, a noun or a verb.

**Present**, pronounced with a stress on the <u>pres-</u>, means "happening or existing now":

*The present school captain is the worst we've had so far.* (adjective)
*There's no time like the present.* (noun)

It can also mean "something given":

*That brooch is a birthday present from my brother.* (noun)

---

**Common prepositions**

above   after
among   at  before
beside  between
by  for  from  in
near  of  off  on
over  through  to
under  up  upon

**Present**, pronounced with a stress on the -sent, is a verb meaning "to give something in a formal way":
*The mayor has been asked to present the prizes.*
It can also mean "to introduce one person to another":
*I'd like to present my wife Belinda.*

## presently

**Presently** means "soon":
*I'm reading the newspaper now so I'll tidy up presently.*
It also means "now" or "at the moment":
*I am presently staying in a big hotel.*

It used to mean "immediately or at once", but nowadays this use is pretty rare, particularly since it could be misunderstood. If you say *"I will do it presently"*, people are most likely to think that you will do it soon, but not immediately.

## present tense

You use the **present tense** of the verb to show or suggest that actions and events are happening at the very time you are writing. The following sentence is in the present tense:
*I look out on this wonderful park.*

The present tense suggests to the reader that things are going on at the very time they are reading. So you can use it to bring the past into the present. For example:
*He comes into the room and is blinded by the light. He puts on his dark glasses and sees . . .*
This is called the **narrative present**.

We can also distinguish whether the events are completed or are continuing by using the present tense in its *perfect* or *continuous* forms:
*I walk* (present – simple form)
*I am walking* (present continuous)
*I have walked* (present perfect)
*I have been walking* (present perfect continuous)

The perfect and the continuous forms of a verb are called *aspects* of tense, and they are indicated by the auxiliary verbs *be* and *have*. You can see them used with the verb *walk* in the examples above. For more information on this, see **aspect**.

## pretence / pretense

These are equally good ways of spelling this word. **Pretence** is the usual spelling in the UK. In the USA, this word is usually spelled **pretense**. For more about words like this, see **-ce/-se**.

## preventive / preventative

These words both mean "helping to prevent".

The word **preventive** is the earlier one in English. **Preventative** came later, adding two letters without adding anything to the meaning.

## prey

See **pray/prey**.

## priceless

This word does not mean "having no price or value" but rather "of such great value that no price can be put on it".

## primaeval / primeval

These are equally good spellings. See **-ae-**.

## primary

Note the ending of this word. See **-ary/-ery/-ory**.

## primeval / primaeval

These are equally good spellings. See **-ae-**.

## principal / principle

These words sound the same but mean different things.

To be **principal** is to be first or most important:
*The principal reason I came here was to talk to you.*
And so the most important person in a school is the **principal**.

A **principle** is a general truth or rule of conduct:
*Whatever the temptation, I will stick to my principles.*

## principal parts

The **principal parts** of a verb are the infinitive (or basic form), the past tense and the past participle. We usually add -ed to the basic form for both the past tense and the past participle. So for a verb like *walk*, the principal parts are:
*walk, walked* and (have) *walked.*

For more about the forms of verbs, see **regular verbs** and **irregular verbs**.

## principle

See **principal/principle**.

## prize / prise

These words sound the same but mean different things.

A **prize** is a reward for success.

To **prise** something open is to force it open, usually with a lever.

## pro-

is a prefix with several meanings:
**1** in favour of
**2** forward, in front of
**3** instead of

The first meaning, "in favour of", is the only one used to form new words in English. It appears in words such as *pro-American, pro-communist* and *pro-hanging,* to express a political attitude. In such words, it is written with a hyphen.

The second meaning, "before, forward", is built into many words borrowed from French and Latin, like:

*prologue*   (a speech which comes at the beginning)
*promote*   (move forward)
*propel*   (push forward)

In these the prefix has long ago merged into the whole word, and the hyphen is never used.

The third meaning, "instead of", is found in the word *pronoun*, which is a word that is used instead of a noun.

## probable

See **possible/probable**.

## problems of language and expression

Some aspects of language can cause particular difficulty for both writer and reader. Anything that is confusing, distracting or unnecessarily difficult will interfere with what you're trying to communicate.

For information on what makes language confusing or vague, see **ambiguity, clichés, double negatives, redundancy** and **tautology**.

For information on language that distracts the reader because of inbuilt racism or sexism, see **racist language** and **sexist language**.

For information on what can make language difficult for the reader, see **-ese, jargon** and **technical writing**.

## proceed

See **precede/proceed**.

## professor

Note the ending of this word. See **-er/-or**.

## profit

Note that the <u>t</u> remains single in **profited, profiting, profiteer, profitably**, and any of the words that come from **profit**.

## profit / prophet

These words sound the same but have different meanings.

A **profit** is the money you make from selling something at a higher price than you paid for it. It can also be an advantage or benefit:

*There is no profit in regretting the mistakes you made in your youth.*

A **prophet** in biblical times was someone who spoke on behalf of God. It can also mean "a great teacher or leader".

## prognosis

See **diagnosis/prognosis**.

## program / programme

These are equally good spellings for this word. The word was actually spelled **program** until the beginning of the nineteenth century, when it was respelled **programme** under French influence. But the spelling **program** follows the same pattern as other English words such as *diagram, telegram* and *anagram*.

Note that it should be spelled **program** whenever you're writing about computer programs.

## projector

Note the ending of this word. See **-er/-or**.

## prologue

The usual spelling of this word is **prologue**, though you may sometimes find it spelled **prolog**, a spelling sometimes used in the USA. For more about words like this, see **-gue/-g**.

## prone

See **likely/liable/apt/prone**.

## pronouns

**Pronouns** are words like *it, them* or *who*. They often stand in place of *nouns* we have mentioned before:

> The <u>surfers</u> finished waxing their <u>surfboards</u>. Then <u>they</u> ran into the water with <u>them</u>.

The pronouns *they* and *them* (in the second sentence) stand for *surfers* and *surfboards* (in the first sentence).

The six types of pronouns are:

| | |
|---|---|
| **personal pronouns** | *me, our, them* and so on |
| **possessive pronouns** | *mine, ours, theirs* and so on |
| **reflexive pronouns** | *myself, ourselves, themselves* and so on |
| **interrogative pronouns** | *who, which* and so on |
| **relative pronouns** | *who, that* and so on |
| **demonstrative pronouns** | *that, these* and so on |

Note that some words appear in more than one list. For more information on each type of pronoun, see under the separate headings.

## pronunciation

Of course this noun is related to the verb **pronounce**, but it is not in fact formed from it. Instead it's based on the Latin word *pronuntiatio*. This is why it does not have two o's like **pronounce**.

There is a similar pattern in a number of other English verbs and nouns. For example: *denounce/denunciation, renounce/renunciation*, and so on.

## pronunciations

How to pronounce a word can often be quite tricky to work out, because the way the word is written and the way it is pronounced don't necessarily match up. For example, look at *rough, bough* and *though* which have three different vowel sounds although they are all spelled with -**ough**. The same thing can happen at the beginning of words, as in *aid, air* and *aisle*.

When you know a word only by its pronunciation, it can be hard to find it in an alphabetical list. To help you with this problem, there's a list of alternative spellings for the same sound in APPENDIX A.

## proof

The plural of this word is spelled **proofs**. For more about words like this, see -**f/-v-**.

## proofreading

is the process of checking your writing before it is published. It means looking for all kinds of mistakes with words, spelling and grammar which you wouldn't want the reader to see. The verse below contains six mistakes which a proofreader ought to correct. (The words which need correcting are ringed.)

Their was a yung lady from Bright
Who moved with the spead of light
She set out one day
In a rellative way
And returned hom the preveous night.

A checklist for proofreading is given in WRITING WORKSHOP pp 14 and 16.

The word **proofreading** comes from the printing industry. A first *proof* is a sample page which the author gets to check before the book is printed. An editor then reads and checks each proof before it is mass-produced.

## propaganda

**Propaganda** is the spreading of information which is intended to affect people's thinking about something. But the writers of propaganda want people to accept their point of view without question. They may also stoop to unfair tactics like smearing the reputations of the people who oppose their point of view, leaving out facts that don't fit their point of view, and telling deliberate lies.

The word comes from the name of a kind of committee in the Roman Catholic Church, the *Congregatio de Propaganda* (the Board for Propagating the Faith). This 17th century committee comprised a group of Cardinals who published material aimed at spreading Catholicism. What they produced came to be called **propaganda**.

## propeller

Note that this word ends in -er, even though many words to do
with machinery end in -or. For more about words like this, see
**-er/-or**.

## proper names

are more often called **proper nouns**. See under that heading for
more information.

## proper nouns

**Proper nouns** name individual people or places: *Tony, David
Gower, Ben Nevis*. They start with capital letters. Occasionally
the definite article *the* (without a capital) is part of the name: *the
River Thames, the Black Mountains, the Tower of London*.

**Proper nouns** contrast with **common nouns**, which are the
general names of things rather than an individual one: *river,
house, policeman*.

## prophecy / prophesy

These words are closely related, but there is an important difference.

**Prophecy** is the noun, while **prophesy** is the verb:
  *She looked into the fire and made a prophecy.*
  *I prophesy the toast will burn.*

The -cy of **prophecy** sounds like *sea*, while the -sy of **prophesy**
sounds like *sigh*.

## prophet

See **profit/prophet**.

## proposition

See **preposition/proposition**.

## proscribe

See **prescribe/proscribe**.

## prose

is ordinary written language. It contrasts with poetry because it
has no regular rhyme or rhythm. It contrasts with dialogue,
because it doesn't have the exchange of words between two or
more people.

Yet **prose** can take many forms and styles, some of which are
talked about and illustrated in WRITING WORKSHOP, Part 3:
Forms of Writing.

## prosecute

See **persecute/prosecute**.

## prosecutor

Note the ending of this word. See **-er/-or**.

## prospective

See **perspective/prospective**.

## prosperity

See **posterity/prosperity**.

### protector

Note the ending of this word. See **-er/-or**.

### protégé

The acute accents above the e's in this word show that it came into English from French. Their main use is to show that the e is pronounced to rhyme with *day*, although in English this applies only to the second e. The first e is pronounced like the e in *open*.

As words borrowed from foreign languages become better known in English they tend to lose their special accents. So it may be that you will find **protégé** written with only the last accent, or with no accents at all.

For more about accents in English, see **accents**. See also **acute accents**.

### protein

Note that e comes before i in this word. See **i before e**.

### protester

This is the most common spelling for this word. You may sometimes see it spelled **protestor**, perhaps because it means the same as the word *demonstrator*, which does end in -or.

Nevertheless the -er spelling is the original one and the one most often used in dictionaries. The -er ending is the most common English ending for words of this type.

For more about words like this, see **-er/-or**.

### protractor

Note the ending of this word. See **-er/-or**.

### proved / proven

These are equally good spellings for the past participle of **prove**: I have **proved**, I have **proven**. For more about words like this, see **-ed/-(e)n**.

### proviso

The plural of this word may be spelled **provisos** or **provisoes**. For more about words like this, see **-o**.

### publicly

This is the only commonly used adverb in English where ic is not followed by -ally. For more about the -ally ending, see **-ally**.

### pulley

The plural of this word is spelled **pulleys**. For more about words like this, see **-ey**.

## pummel

For information about whether to double the l when you add
endings like -ed or -ing, see -l-/-ll-.

## punctuation

These are the punctuation marks used in writing:

### Punctuation for sentences

| brackets<br>  (parentheses) | ( ) | exclamation mark<br>full stop | ! <br>. |
| colon | : | question mark | ? |
| comma | , | quotation marks | " " |
| dash | — |   (inverted commas) | |
| ellipsis | . . . | semicolon | ; |

### Punctuation for words

accents:

| acute | ´ | grave | ` | apostrophe | ' |
| cedilla | ، | háček | ˇ | hyphen | - |
| circumflex | ^ | tilde | ~ | | |
| dieresis | ¨ | umlaut | ¨ | | |

## puns

A pun is a play on words, often for humorous effect. Puns are
often used in advertisements, like the one for a new kind of
pillow, which said: *"What we tell you about our pillow will send
you to sleep."* Puns like this one play on two different meanings
for the same word, in this case *sleep*. The sentence that carries
the pun has to be very carefully worded, to allow both meanings
to come out.

Some puns play on two different words with the same sound
*(homophones)*. This type of pun was used by the doctor who
joked to his wife: *"I've been losing patients all day."* Here of
course the play was on *patients/patience*. Puns like this one are
less effective when written down, because you have to choose
one word or the other through the spelling.

Many puns are uttered and forgotten, though some have an
extended life in literature. Shakespeare often used them in his
writing; and the author of the following epitaph made an
immortal pun about a dead dentist:
> *As we, his patients, pace this earth with gravity:*
> *Dentist Brown is filling his last cavity.*

## pupa

The plural of this word may be spelled **pupas** or **pupae**. For
more about words like this, see **-a (as a singular ending)**.

## purl

See **pearl/purl**.

## purposely / purposefully

These related adverbs are both linked to **purpose** but they have
different meanings.

If you do something **purposely**, you do it intentionally and not by chance:

*They purposely went early to avoid the crowds.*

If you do something **purposefully**, you do it with determination and resolution:

*She began walking towards him slowly but purposefully.*

## putrefy

This is one of the few English verbs left that ends in -efy rather than -ify.

Note that there is also an e in **putrefaction**, but an i in **putrid**.

For more about words like this, see **-ify/-efy**.

## pygmy

See **pigmy/pygmy**.

## pyjamas / pajamas

These are equally good ways of spelling this word.

**Pyjamas** is the usual spelling in the UK. In the USA, this word is usually spelled **pajamas**.

# Qq

## quadr-

is a prefix meaning "four", as in *quadrangle* (a shape with four angles) and *quadruped* (a four-footed animal).

The hardest thing with many quadr- words is knowing what vowel to write straight after the prefix. There are quadr- words with all five vowels of the alphabet. In some cases, you can tell which vowel it is by the way it is pronounced:

| | | |
|---|---|---|
| quadrangle | quadratic | quadrella |
| quadrennial | quadric | quadrille |
| quadrillion | quadruple | quadruplicate |

Some of the others can be linked up with these:

quadrant *is like* quadrangle

quadruped *and* quadruplex *are like* quadruple

The other ones from mathematics (*quadrilateral, quadrinomial, quadrivalent*) are all like quadrillion.

This leaves a handful of new ones whose spelling varies. The sound of the vowel in the all-important second syllable is unclear. (It is in fact a schwa. See **schwa**.)

Three may be spelled with a or i:

| | | |
|---|---|---|
| quadracycle | *or* | quadricycle |
| quadraplegic | | quadriplegic |
| quadrasonic | | quadrisonic |

Two others are written with a or o:

| | | |
|---|---|---|
| quadraphonic | *or* | quadrophonic |
| quadraphony | | quadrophony |

## qualifiers

are words which affect the force of others, like *very* and *rather*.

> He was *very* rich.

> She was *rather* annoyed.

Some of them (like *very*) intensify other words, or reinforce their meaning. (For more about them, see **intensifiers**.)

Other qualifiers, like *rather, quite* and *somewhat*, serve to soften the impact of the words they go with. For more about these words, see **hedge words** and **modifiers**.

## quarrel

You have a choice whether or not to double the l when you add -ed, -ing or -er to this word. See **-l-/-ll-**.

Note that when you add -some, the l is never doubled: **quarrelsome**.

## quartet

You may sometimes see this word spelled **quartette**. This is the spelling of the original French word, but it is the less common spelling in English.

## quarts / quartz

These words sound the same but mean different things.

**Quarts** is the plural of **quart**, a measure of liquid in the imperial system. One **quart** is equal to 1.136 litres.

**Quartz** is a common mineral found in rocks. A **quartz** crystal is used inside some watches.

## quatrain

A **quatrain** is four lines of verse that make a unit. It can be a complete poem or it can be part of a longer poem, like a stanza.

## quay

See **key/quay**.

## question marks ( ? )

A **question mark** can be used in a number of ways to indicate a question:
1 *How are you going?*
2 *Well? What?*
3 *That's all you've got to say?*
4 *I said, "How are you going?"*
5 *"Are you going to answer me?" I asked.*

Example 1 shows the most common use of the question mark, at the end of a sentence which is a question.

Example 2 shows that you can use a question mark for a question that isn't a complete sentence — it may only be one word.

Questions sometimes use the same word order as statements. But when they are spoken, you know they are questions by the special pitch of the voice of the speaker. When such questions are written, the only indication that they <u>are</u> questions is the question mark at the end, as in example 3.

Examples 4 and 5 show how to use question marks with quotation marks. The question mark comes just before the final quotation mark, and there is no need for a comma if the sentence continues after the quotation.

Note that there is no need for a question mark when you write an indirect question:
*I asked how she was going.*

Note also that it is not necessary to use a question mark when the sentence is a request:
*Would you pass the butter, please.*

## questions

A **question** is a request for information. Questions may differ from statements in several ways. Often, instead of the subject of the verb beginning the sentence, part of the verb itself is placed first:

*He is leaving home.* (statement)

becomes

*Is he leaving home?* (question)

Alternatively, a question word such as *who, what* or *where* may begin the sentence:

*Where is he going?*

Sometimes, a question tag such as *won't you* or *doesn't she* ends the sentence:

*He's leaving home, isn't he?*

Note that all these forms have one thing in common: they end with a question mark.

Sometimes in speech the only difference between a statement and a question is the pitch of your voice. And when you write them down, the only difference would be the punctuation you use:

*He's leaving now.*
*He's leaving now?*

For more information, see **indirect questions** and **question marks**.

## queue

Note that you drop the final <u>e</u> from **queue** when you add <u>-ed</u> and <u>-ing</u>: **queued, queuing**. For more about words like this, see **-e**.

## quick / quickly

**Quickly** is an adverb:

*Come here quickly.*

**Quick** is an adjective:

*I just have time for a quick drink before I leave.*

Note that **quick** can be an adverb:

*Come here quick.*

It is mostly used in this way in informal language.

## quiet / quite

These words sound similar but they have different meanings.

**Quiet** (with the <u>e</u> before the <u>t</u>) means "silent" or "peaceful".

**Quite** (with the <u>e</u> after the <u>t</u>) means "completely":

*I'm sure you are quite right.*

It can also mean "fairly or considerably":

*He's really quite handsome.*

See **quite**.

## quintet

You may sometimes see this word spelled **quintette**. This is the spelling of the original French word, but it is the less common spelling in English.

## quit

There are two ways of making the past forms of this word: **quit** and **quitted**.

| | |
|---|---|
| I quit | I quitted |
| I have quit | I have quitted |

Both ways are grammatically correct and quite common:
*He quit his job yesterday.*
*He quitted the field after being injured.*

For more about words like this, see **-ed/-t**.

## quite

This word can be used in the following two ways.

Firstly, as an <u>intensifier</u> meaning "completely or entirely":
*You're quite correct to think that.*
*"That's quite enough", she said sternly.*

Secondly, as a <u>hedge word</u> or <u>modifier</u> meaning "fairly or rather":
*She's really quite clever.*
*I chose his birthday present quite easily.*

For more about words like this, see **modifiers**, **intensifiers** and **hedge words**.

## quiz

The plural of **quiz** is **quizzes**. For more about words like this, see **doubling of last letter**.

## quorum

The plural of **quorum** is **quorums**.

Although it is a Latin word, **quorum** has only an English plural because it became a noun only in English. In Latin it was a pronoun.

Compare **-um**.

## quotation marks ( " " or ' ' )

These punctuation marks are also known as **quote marks**, **quotes** and **inverted commas**. Their main use is to show that you are quoting someone exactly, and especially to show that you are quoting someone's spoken words:
*George told them to "push off".*
This shows that "push" and "off" are exactly the words that George spoke. Compare:
*George told them to push off.*
Here George still tells the people to go away, but because there are no quotation marks it may be that he used some expression other than "push off".

Quotation marks can sometimes be used to indicate the titles of short pieces of writing — for example, essays, poems, or the chapters of a book. The names of planes, trains and other vehicles can similarly be written with quotation marks.

Another use for quotes is to highlight a word or to show that you've made it up:

*I think the word "yuppies" is a bit old-fashioned.*

*Why don't we call them "amans" for all money and no sense?*

When using quotation marks, there are two things to consider: (**1**) whether to use double quotes (" ") or single quotes (' '), and (**2**) how to punctuate with quotation marks.

**1  Double quotes or single quotes?** In your writing you must choose one or other as your basic system. There are good arguments in favor of each.

Double quotes are useful because you can tell them apart easily from apostrophes:

*'I've visited all my friends' houses,' Harry said.*

*"I've visited all my friends' houses," Harry said.*

The first sentence is slightly confusing to read because the apostrophes after *I* and *friends* look the same as the closing quotes. You are not sure till the very end just where the quotation stops. Double quotes, then, often make your writing easier to understand.

The main argument for single quotes is that they are less fussy, both to look at and to write.

Your choice, then, depends on which of these arguments you think is more important. (For this book we have chosen double quotes.)

Once you have chosen one style as your basic quotation marks, you should use it throughout your written work. The second style can then be used for quotations within quotations:

*She told me, "George saw them and said 'push off' to them."*

*She told me, 'George saw them and said "push off" to them.'*

**2  Punctuation with quotations.** When you are writing speech you often introduce a quotation with a phrase like *he said, she replied* and so on. There are three common ways to punctuate between the phrase and the quote. You can simply leave a space, add a comma, or add a colon:

*George said "Push off."*

*George said, "Push off."*

*George said: "Push off."*

All of these are correct. Your choice depends on whether you think a punctuation mark helps or hinders the meaning and flow of the sentence. The trend these days is to use as little punctuation as possible.

Once you are inside the quotation marks you should use exactly the same punctuation as you would in your normal writing. If the quotation is a sentence, it should start with a capital letter, and should usually end with a full stop:

*George said "You've all got to push off."*

If the sentence continues after the quotation is ended, the full stop changes to a comma:

*George said "You've all got to push off," and went to bed.*

It is important to remember that punctuation <u>inside</u> the quote marks relates to the quote, while punctuation <u>outside</u> the quote marks relates to the surrounding sentence. For example, compare the position of the exclamation mark in these two sentences:

*George said "push off!"*
*George said "push off"!*

The change of position completely changes the effect. In the first sentence the exclamation mark is part of George's speech, and shows that he is making a forceful command. The second exclamation mark is part of the sentence outside the quote, and shows that the writer is surprised at what George has said.

Since punctuation that does not relate to the quote should be outside the quote marks, you should be careful where you put your commas and full stops. Note that in the following sentences the full stop and comma come <u>after</u> the closing quote, because they really belong to the main sentence:

*George said "push off".*
*George said "push off", and went to bed.*

## quotations

A **quotation** is an exact repetition of the words said or written by someone else. The quotation can be as short as a word or phrase, or as long as one or more paragraphs. Whatever its length, you always put **quotation marks** (or inverted commas) at the beginning and end:

*Nelson said: "England expects every man to do his duty."*

When adding a quotation into a sentence, you should make sure that it fits in with the words around it. There must be no gaps in the grammar, and no surplus words either. How to blend your quotation smoothly into a sentence is explained in WRITING WORKSHOP p 63.

When you make a proper quotation in an essay, you're showing you know that the words belong to someone else. It's important to do this to avoid plagiarism. Check **plagiarism** if you're not sure what it is.

See **quotation marks**.

# Rr

## r as a silent letter

The letter r is written but not sounded in many English words, when it comes after a vowel. See for example:

car  card  cork  fear  fir  fur  fewer

You may not notice that the r is silent until you hear an American saying these words.

But when r comes between two vowel sounds, it is no longer silent. See for example:

arouse  derive  irate  moron  several  very

The only word in which it is silent between vowels is *iron*.

Note that these rules hold for English as it is spoken in southern Britain, and in the north-east and south of the USA. In the rest of Britain and the USA, as well as Canada and Ireland, r is <u>never</u> a silent letter.

For more about silent letters, see **silent letters**.

## racist language

There are words in English that express racial prejudice – just like those that express sexist prejudice. Some examples are:

coon  wog  (for a dark-skinned or olive-skinned immigrant)
nigger  (for a negro)
Itie  eyetie  (for an Italian)
frog  (for a French person)
pommy  (for an English person)
gook  slope  slap (head)  slit-eye  (for a person from Asia)
Yank  (for a person from the USA)

All such words have negative overtones for most people. They are derogatory and off-handed, and they put people of other races and nationalities at an immediate disadvantage. Whether you mean it or not, the words suggest a bias against those people – or at least a readiness to stereotype them.

The UK has provided a home for many immigrants from different countries for hundreds of years. The blend of their cultures with ours is a national strength. It is a pity to make life hard for others by careless use of racist words. You should avoid them whether you are writing or speaking.

## racket / racquet

These words sound the same but have different meanings.

A **racket** is a loud confused noise. It can also be an illegal way of making money.

A **racquet** is the bat you use for playing tennis and squash. You can also spell this **racket**.

## racy

Note that you drop the -e from the end of **race** when you add y. For more about words like this, see **-e**.

## radiator

Note the ending of this word. See **-ator**.

## radical / radicle

These words sound the same but mean different things.

You would call a political party **radical** if it was in favour of extreme social or political reforms. **Radical** can also mean "going to the bottom of things":

*The new government made radical changes to the health system.*

The **radicle** is the largest and most important root of a young plant.

## radio

The plural of this word is spelled **radios**. For more about words like this, see **-o**.

## radio-

This prefix has several meanings:

1 with a radio, as in *radiogram*

2 using radio waves, as in *radioastronomy, radiotelephony*

3 using X-rays, as in *radiography, radiology*

4 emitting radiation, as in *radioactive, radioisotopes*

Note that in some words, two of these meanings overlap. For example, in *radioastronomy* you use a radio (of a special kind) to pick up radio waves from outer space. And in *radiography* you sometimes use X-rays to trace the radioactive sources implanted in the body.

## radius

The plural of this word may be spelled **radiuses** or **radii**. For more about words like this, see **-us**.

## rain / reign / rein

These words all sound the same but they have different meanings.

**Rain** is water falling from the sky in drops.

The **reign** of a king or queen is the period during which they rule.

A rider uses a **rein** to guide a horse.

Note that in **reign** and **rein** the e comes before the i. See **i before e**.

## raise

See **rise/raise**.

## raise / raze

These words sound the same but have different meanings.

To **raise** something is to lift it up, or to increase it:
*Raise your hands above your head.*
*We will have to raise prices from next week.*

To **raze** something is to knock it down flat:
*The wreckers have been told to raze the damaged building.*

## -rance

When a verb ending in -er is turned into a noun with -ance, it loses a syllable. What happens is that the e before the final r drops out. So *enter* becomes entr- + -ance, that is *entrance*. Some other cases are:

hinder      hindr + -ance      hindrance
remember    remembr + -ance    remembrance

## rap / wrap

These words sound the same but mean different things.

To **rap** something is to strike it with a quick light blow:
*Rap on the window and I'll let you in.*
It also means "to talk about something" and "to compose verses off the top of your head".

To **wrap** something is to fold paper or material around it:
*I'll wrap the present for you.*

## rapped / rapt / wrapped

These words sound the same but have different meanings.

**Rapped** is the past form of the verb **rap**, to hit or knock sharply or lightly:
*She rapped my knuckles.*

**Wrapped** is the past form of the verb **wrap**, to fold material or paper around someone or something:
*I wrapped the blanket around him.*

When someone says that they're really **wrapped** in someone or something, it means that they're very enthusiastic about them. You can also spell this **rapt**.

Note that **wrapped** implies being wrapped up in someone and **rapt** describes being enraptured by someone. When used in this way, both these words are part of everyday language, and you should try to avoid them in your essay writing.

If you are **rapt** in your own thoughts, you are thinking so deeply that you're unaware of what is happening around you.

## rarefy

Note that this word ends in -efy, even though it sounds as if it could end in -ify. To spell it correctly, think of **rare**, not **rarity**. **Rarity** is formed on a regular pattern. See **-e**.

For more about words like this, see **-ify/-efy**.

## ravage

See **ravish/ravage**.

## ravel

For information about whether or not to double the l when you add -ed, -ing or -er, see **-l-/-ll-**.

## ravenous / ravishing

These words both begin with rav- but their meanings are very different.

If you are **ravenous**, you are very hungry.

We say someone is **ravishing** if they are enchanting or delightful.

## ravish / ravage

These words sound similar but have different meanings.

To **ravish** a woman is to rape her.

To **ravage** something is to damage it badly:
*The landscape had been ravaged by bushfire.*

## ravishing

See **ravenous/ravishing**.

## raw / roar

These words sound the same but mean different things.

Food is **raw** if it hasn't been cooked.

Lions **roar** when they make a loud deep sound.

## raze

See **raise/raze**.

## razor

Note the ending of this word. See **-er/-or**.

## re

is a word found mostly in business letters. It means "regarding", and points out the main subject of the letter. For instance:

Dear Sir,
Your letter re additional copies of *Education News* arrived after we had dispatched your regular order. We have therefore sent them separately and you should receive them in the next few days.
Yours faithfully


Terry Learner
Manager

## re-

is a prefix which usually means "again", as in *rebuild*, *re-enter*, *refill*, *reopen*, *reprint* and many others. In just a few words, like *recall*, *recover* and *replace*, it means "back".

In older verbs borrowed from French and Latin, re- has lost its sense of "again" and is just part of the total meaning of the word, as in *recount* and *reform*. We notice this when we compare:

   *recount* (tell a story)   with   *re-count* (count again)
and
   *reform* (change to a better state)   with   *re-form* (form again)

In the list below you'll find a number of other words where the hyphen makes quite a difference in meaning:

| | | | | |
|---|---|---|---|---|
| re-act | re-cede | re-collect | re-cover | re-create |
| re-lay | re-lease | re-mark | re-petition | re-present |
| re-press | re-serve | re-sort | re-sound | re-store |
| re-trace | re-view | | | |

Ask yourself what each one means when it's written without the hyphen.

## -re / -er

A number of words which we spell with -re are spelled with -er in North America. The best known cases are *centre/center* and *theatre/theater*. Other examples are:

| | | | |
|---|---|---|---|
| calibre | fibre | litre | louvre |
| lustre | meagre | metre | sabre |
| sepulchre | sombre | spectre | |

All these are spelled with -er by Americans.

If you use the conventional -re spelling for all of these words, there is clearly less to worry about. In addition, you do not have to change the core of the word when you build them into other words. For example, *centre* and *central* have the same core (centr-), as do *fibre* and *fibrous* (fibr-). If you work with *center* and *fiber* the words have to change rather more to become *central* and *fibrous*.

The -re spellings also look better than -er after the letters c or g. With -er spellings you get *acer* and *meager*, where you might expect the c to become an s sound and the g to become a j sound, following a common spelling rule. (See **-ce/-ge**.)

The -re spellings are the more useful ones overall.

Note that some words like this are spelled with -re everywhere in the world (even in North America):

| | | | |
|---|---|---|---|
| acre | cadre | lucre | macabre |
| massacre | mediocre | ogre | timbre (tone quality) |

## reactionary

Note the ending of this word. See **-ary/-ery/-ory**.

## reactor

Note the ending of this word. See **-er/-or**.

## read

See **red/read**.

### read / reed

These words sound the same but have different meanings.

Children learn to **read** books at school.

A **reed** is a tall kind of grass growing in marshes and swamps.

### real / really

These related words are different parts of speech.

**Real** is an adjective meaning "true, or genuine", as in *the real reason* and *a real moustache*.

**Really** is an adverb meaning "actually, or truly":
*It really is hot after all.*
*He's a really honest politician.*
**Really** can also mean "very or extremely":
*You are really pretty.*

Note that in casual talk **real** can also mean "very":
*That's a real good idea.*

### real / reel

These words sound the same but have different meanings.

Something is **real** if it is true, or genuine:
*Tell me a story from real life.*
*Is she wearing real diamonds?*

A **reel** is a cylinder onto which thread or something similar is wound. To **reel** is to sway or stagger, often from a blow. A **reel** can also be a lively Scottish dance.

### realism

is a style of writing in which the subject matter is taken from the real world. The characters are true to life and the events of the story are limited to what is possible in real life. The opposite is **fantasy**.

### realistically

Note the ending of this word. See **-ally**.

### reality / realty

These words look similar and are both related to **real** but they have different meanings.

**Reality** is the real world of things which exist.

**Realty** is property or real estate.
*My wealth is based on realty rather than shares.*

### really

See **real/really**.

### rebuff

See **reject/rebuff**.

### receipt

See **recipe/receipt**.

### receptor

Note the ending of this word. See **-er/-or**.

## recession

See **depression/recession**.

## recipe / receipt

These words look similar but have different meanings.

A **recipe** gives you a list of ingredients and the instructions for cooking something.

You get a **receipt** to prove that you have paid for goods in a shop.

## reconnoitre / reconnoiter

These are equally good ways of spelling this word. **Reconnoitre** is the usual way of spelling this word in the UK, whereas **reconnoiter** is more common in the USA. For more about words like this, see **-re/-er**.

## rector

Note the ending of this word. See **-er/-or**.

## rectum

The plural of this biological word may be spelled **rectums** or **recta**. For more about words like this, see **-um**.

## recur

Add another r at the end of this word when you add the endings -ed, -ing, -ence, and -ent to form **recurred, recurring, recurrence**, and **recurrent**.

For more about words like this, see **doubling of last letter**.

Note that there is no word spelled reoccurrence though **recurrence** is often misspelled this way.

## red / read

These words can sound the same but they have different meanings.

**Red** is the color of a tomato when it's ripe.

**Read** (rhymes with *bed*) is the past form of the verb **read** (rhymes with *feed*):
*I read her a fairy story last night.*

## redundancy

is using more words than you need to say something, as in:
*The two twins are playing great football today.*

In speech, redundant words may help to stress something. But in writing they are more likely to clutter the point you want to make.

Redundant words are one of the things to check for when you are revising and editing your work. See **tautology**.

## reduplication

In English, some compound words have been made by repeating the first part of the word in a slightly different form:
*harum-scarum, hocus-pocus.* This is known as **reduplication**.

## reed

See **read/reed**.

## reek / wreak

These words sound the same but mean different things.

To **reek** is to give off a terrible smell.

To **wreak your revenge** on someone is to carry out a vengeful act against them. To **wreak havoc** is to bring about ruinous damage. **Wreak** is an old-fashioned word so both phrases sound rather formal.

## reel

See **real/reel**.

## refer

Remember to add another ‑r at the end of this word to form **referred**, **referring**, **referral**, and **referrer**.

But note that **referable**, **referent** and **reference**, have only a single r because of the difference in stress.

For information about the way stress affects words like this, see **doubling of last letter**.

## referendum

The plural of this word may be spelled **referendums** or **referenda**. For more about words like this, see **-um**.

## reflection / reflexion

These are equally good spellings. See **-ction/-xion**.

## reflector

Note the ending of this word. See **-er/-or**.

## reflexion / reflection

These are equally good spellings. See **-ction/-xion**.

## reflexive pronouns

| Reflexive pronouns | |
|---|---|
| myself | ourselves |
| yourself | yourselves |
| himself | themselves |
| herself | |
| itself | |

**Reflexive pronouns** are those that end in -self or -selves. We use them to show that both the subject and the object of a verb refer to the same person or thing. That is, the reflexive pronoun refers back to the subject:

*She cut herself.*

In this sentence, she (personal pronoun) is the subject, while herself (reflexive pronoun) is the object, but they both refer to the same person.

*They surprised themselves.*

In this sentence, they (personal pronoun) and themselves (reflexive pronoun) both refer to the same people. Similarly, in the following sentence, George (noun) and himself (reflexive pronoun) refer to the same person:

*George shot himself.*

For more information, see **pronouns**.

### reflexive verbs

are ones which have the same person as subject and object. For example:

*He taught himself to play the guitar.*

In English we make reflexive verbs simply by adding a reflexive pronoun after the verb. In the example above, *himself* is a reflexive pronoun which refers back to *he*. For more about this, see **reflexive pronouns**.

In other languages, reflexive constructions are always used with some verbs. In both French and German, for example, the verb *remember* is always reflexive, though it never is in English.

### refrigerator

Note the ending of this word. See **-ator**.

### refuse

This word has two pronunciations and two meanings — one for the verb and one for the noun.

To **refuse** (with a stress on -*fuse*) is to say you will not accept, give or do something:

*Don't refuse my offer of help.*
*They refuse to go home.*

**Refuse** (with a stress on ref-) is rubbish:

*Refuse is clogging up all the gutters in town.*

### regret

Remember to add another -*t* to this word to form **regretted, regretting**, and **regrettable**.

But note that **regretful** has only a single t.

For more about words like this, see **doubling of last letter**.

### regretful / regrettable

These words are both linked to **regret** but they mean different things.

Someone is **regretful** if they are sad about something that has happened. They are full of **regret**.

Something is **regrettable** if it has happened but you wish it hadn't. It is to be **regretted**.

### regular verbs

In English, the tenses of most verbs are formed according to a set pattern. For instance, the verb *walk* forms its past tense by just adding -*ed*:

*I walked*

its past participle also by adding -*ed*:

*I have walked*

and its present participle by adding -*ing*:

*I am walking.*

Some verbs need a slight change to their spelling before these endings are added. *Hate*, for instance, drops its final -*e*, and *skim* doubles its final letter. Since these verbs are otherwise following the set pattern, they are generally regarded as behaving in the same way as *walk*.

Any verb which forms its past tense and past participle by adding -ed is known as a **regular verb**. Other verbs such as *swim* and *hit* are called **irregular verbs** because their past forms do not follow the set pattern:

> I <u>swam</u>   I have <u>swum</u>
> I <u>hit</u>    I have <u>hit</u>

Many languages have both irregular and regular verbs. The regular verbs are sometimes called *weak* verbs, and the irregular verbs are sometimes called *strong* verbs.

See **irregular verbs**.

## regulator

Note the ending of this word. See **-ator**.

## reign

See **rain/reign/rein**.

## rein

See **rain/reign/rein**.

## reindeer

**Reindeer** can refer to one or more than one animal, and although you may see the plural **reindeers**, it is more common to spell it **reindeer**.

When you are using this word as a plural, make sure the verb and pronoun you use with it are also in the plural:

> The reindeer <u>were</u> drinking at the waterhole when <u>they</u> were disturbed by the hunter.

For more about words like this, see **collective nouns**.

Note that <u>e</u> comes before <u>i</u> in **reindeer**. See **i before e**.

## reject / rebuff

These words have similar meanings.

To **reject** something is to refuse to accept or use it, as in *to reject an invitation* or *to reject someone's work*. A **reject** is someone or something that has been discarded or thrown away.

To **rebuff** someone is to snub them or refuse to accept any offers or suggestions they make:

> I felt hurt when he rebuffed my offer of help.

## relative pronouns

The relative pronouns are *who, whom, whose, which* and *that*. They begin adjectival clauses in the following examples:

> the lady <u>who/that</u> lost her umbrella
> the policeman <u>whose</u> foot you ran over
> the amplifier <u>which/that</u> overloaded
> the teacher <u>whom/that</u> you like the least

Note that in the last example you don't actually need a relative pronoun at all:

> the teacher you like the least

Except for the use of *whose* in the second example, you have a choice of relative pronouns. Some writers feel that you should choose *that* only when you are writing informally, but in fact your writing will be quite acceptable no matter which you use. **Relative pronouns** do the same job that all pronouns do — they stand in for nouns. In particular they stand in for the subject or object of adjectival clauses (as shown by the examples above). The clauses which they begin are often called <u>relative clauses</u>.

*Who, whom, which* and *whose* are not always relative pronouns. Sometimes their job is to begin questions. For more information on this, see **interrogative pronouns**.

Note that *that* can also be used as a demonstrative and is often used to introduce a noun clause. See **demonstratives** and **noun clauses**.

### remembrance

Note that **remember** loses its last <u>-e</u> before <u>-ance</u> is added. For more about words like this, see **-rance**.

### remodel

For information about whether to double the <u>l</u> when you add endings like <u>-ed</u> or <u>-ing</u>, see **-l-/-ll-**.

### rent / lease / let / hire

These words have similar meanings but there are some differences.

To **rent** or **lease** property is to have the use of it in return for payments made to the owner:
> *I am renting a flat in town from a millionaire.*
> *I am leasing a television rather than buying it.*

To **rent** or **lease** property is also to give temporary possession of it to someone else. Sometimes this is **rent out**:
> *I will rent (out) my flat in town to you.*

The verb **rent** has developed from the noun **rent**, the payment made to the owner. The document you sign when **renting** a property is a **lease**.

To **let** property is to put it up for rent:
> *I have made the decision to let my flat in town. If you want it*
> *I will rent it to you.*

Property which is available for rental in this way is said to be **to let**:
> *My flat in town is to let.*

To **hire** something is to have temporary use of it in return for payment:
> *We are hiring a hall for the wedding.*

To **hire** something is also to give others the temporary use of it in return for payment. Often this is **hire out**:
> *I will hire out this hall to you for the wedding.*

To **hire** someone is to employ them:
> *We are hiring a band for the occasion.*

## repel / repulse

These words have similar meanings.

To **repel** something is to drive it back, or keep it away:
*They managed to repel the enemy.*
*This spray is meant to repel mosquitoes.*
**Repel** can also mean "to disgust":
*Such cruelty repels us.*
*The smell of rotting food repelled them.*

To **repulse** something is to drive it back:
*They managed to repulse the attack.*
**Repulse** can also mean to reject or refuse something coldly:
*He repulsed all my efforts to befriend him.*

Didn't you find the insect repellent?

No, I found it fascinating!

## repellent / repellant

These are both possible spellings for this word though **repellent** is now more common, whether it is a noun or an adjective. For more about words like this, see **-ant/-ent**.

## repetition

When you repeat something, it may be by accident or design. Writers often repeat a word or phrase to emphasise a point. They may also want to make a link with something that was mentioned earlier, and this is most obvious if you provide an echo with the same word. Some ideas and concepts, especially in maths and the sciences, can only be expressed through one word, and so of course it has to be repeated.

But words also get repeated when writers are absent-minded or in a mental groove, not really thinking about their expression. Other things being equal, you need to think of different ways of expressing things, because it makes your writing more interesting to read. A thesaurus would help you to find other words.

For more about this, see **variety in writing**.

## replace / substitute

These words describe the same event from different angles.

You **replace** an <u>existing</u> person or thing <u>with</u> something else:
*We'll replace Jim with George as fullback.*

You **substitute** a <u>new</u> person or thing <u>for</u> something else:
*We'll substitute George for Jim as fullback.*

In these two sentences exactly the same thing is happening. Jim is going and George is coming. Note that the names appear in a different order.

## report writing

Reports may be either formal or informal. Formal reports are the type usually used to present scientific experiments, both at school and later. They have a standard format with five basic parts: Aim, Apparatus, Method, Results, Conclusion. A sample chemistry report is reproduced and discussed in WRITING WORKSHOP p 50.

Informal reports are used to present a set of observations (as on a field trip), or to describe a particular process (in technology, for example). They have no fixed format. See WRITING WORKSHOP pp 51–2.

### repulse

See **repel/repulse**.

### research

is the background work of reading which you do for an essay. You will need to gather facts and information for the contents of your essay, unless you are doing personal or imaginative writing (and even then you often need to do research of some kind). Your teachers or the librarian will suggest which books would be most useful for you to research.

### reserve

See **reverse/reserve**.

### resin / rosin

These words are linked in origin but they mean different things.

**Resin** is a substance, sometimes hard, sometimes sticky, which comes from some trees.

**Rosin** is the resin of the pine tree which has been treated so that impurities are removed.

### resistance

Note the ending of this word. See **-ance/-ence**.

### resistor

Note the ending of this word. See **-er/-or**.

### resolution

See **denouement**.

### respectable / respectful

These words are both linked to **respect** but they mean different things.

You are **respectable** if you are of such good character that you can be respected.

You are **respectful** if you are full of respect or admiration for someone else and behave in a way that shows this.

### respectfully / respectively

These words look similar but they mean different things.

**Respectfully** is the adverb from **respectful**, meaning "full of respect or admiration":
*She bowed her head respectfully.*

**Respectively** is the adverb from **respective**. It is used in situations where you have a number of things which have to be matched up with other things in corresponding order:
*Mice, horses, and rabbits eat cheese, hay, and carrots respectively.*

### respirator

Note the ending of this word. See **-ator**.

### responsible

Note the ending of this word. See **-able/-ible**.

### rest / wrest

These words sound the same but mean different things.

To **rest** is to relax and take life easy.

To **wrest** something is to remove it with difficulty, especially by giving it a violent twist or pull.

### resume / résumé

These related words look similar, but mean different things and are pronounced differently.

To **resume** something is to continue it.

A **résumé** is a summary. It is a French word, and the acute accent over the final e̠ indicates that the last syllable is pronounced *may*. You'll notice that there can also be an acute accent over the first e̠ but this no longer affects its pronunciation.

Words like **résumé** gradually lose their accents as they become more settled into English. But you can see that the accents are particularly useful in this case because without them **resumé** would look exactly the same as **resume**. For more about accents in English, see **accents**. See also **acute accents**.

### retch / wretch

These words sound the same but mean different things.

To **retch** is to try to vomit.

A **wretch** is a poor miserable person.

### retina

The plural of this biological word may be spelled **retinas** or **retinae**. For more about words like this, see **-a (as a singular ending)**.

### revenge / avenge

These words have the same basic meanings but are usually different parts of speech.

**Revenge** is most often used as a noun. It is the hurt or damage done to pay someone back for the bad things they have done to you. Another noun like this is **vengeance**. You can use **revenge** as a verb if you want to, although it isn't very common.

**Avenge** is always used as a verb. It means "to pay someone back for a wrong they have done":

*"I will avenge my father's murder!" cried the princess.*

### reverse / reserve

These words look similar but mean different things.

To **reverse** is to make something go backwards:
*You need to reverse the car up the drive.*

To **reserve** something is to keep it for a particular person or use:
*I'll reserve you a seat next to mine.*
*She wants to reserve this book for her project.*

### reversible

Note the ending of this word. See **-able/-ible**.

### revert

This word means "to go back to the way things were before". It comes from Latin and is made up of <u>re-</u> meaning "back" and <u>-vert</u> meaning "turn". You will often hear people use <u>back</u> after it:
*Don't <u>revert back</u> to your old style of writing.*

As **revert** already includes the idea of returning or going back in its meaning, you don't need to use "back".
*Don't revert to your old style of writing.*

For more information about this, see **tautology**.

### review / revue

These words sound the same but have different meanings.

A **review** is a newspaper or magazine article which describes a book or film and gives you the reviewer's opinion of it.

A **revue** is a musical show with songs, dances and skits making fun of recent events or popular fashions.

### reviews

A review is a piece of writing in which the writer assesses the value of a book or film, or how well a play or piece of music has been performed.

### revise

This is one of the few words ending in <u>-ise</u> that cannot also be spelled with an <u>-ize</u> ending. It is always spelled **rev<u>ise</u>**. For more about words like this, see **-ise/-ize**.

### revising

Writers always need to revise or fix up the mistakes in their drafts before showing them to a reader. This revision is part of editing your writing, to make sure it says exactly what you mean. For some tips on how to revise, see WRITING WORKSHOP pp 7, 12, 14 and 16.

### revue

See **review/revue**.

### rhetoric

**Rhetoric** is speech that is intended to persuade the listener. The word comes from the Greek *rhetor*, a person who stood in the assembly and argued a case. Another word for rhetoric is *oratory*.

Many of the things which are important in writing speeches are important in writing generally. You have to think up ideas and arguments, arrange them in the right order, and find the right words to express them.

Nowadays, the word **rhetoric** is usually applied to forms of expression which are artificial and striving for effect.

### rhetorical questions

Some questions are used just for the stylistic (or rhetorical) effect they will have on an audience. Such **rhetorical questions** do not expect an answer from the listeners.

> *"What do I see before me?"* thundered the Prime Minister. *"I see a dispirited Opposition."*

These questions draw attention to the answer, which is then assumed or supplied by the speaker.

### rhombus

The plural of this word from mathematics may be spelled **rhombuses** or **rhombi**. For more about words like this, see **-us**.

### rhyme / rhythm

These words look similar but have different meanings.

**Rhyme** is when sounds at the end of words are the same or alike, as in <u>rat</u> and <u>mat</u> or <u>galore</u> and <u>rapport</u>. **Rhyme** is often used at the ends of the lines in a poem.

**Rhythm** is the pattern of beats in music, speech or poetry.

### rhyme / rime

These words sound the same but mean different things.

**Rime** is an old-fashioned word meaning "frost".

Words **rhyme** when the sounds at the end of them are alike. For more information on the meaning, see the entry above this one.

It is interesting to note that **rhyme** used to be spelled **rime** until the 16th century when it was respelled to make it look similar to *rhythm*. You may still sometimes see it spelled **rime**, especially in older poetry.

### rhythm

See **rhyme/rhythm**.

### ricochet

This verb may be spelled with either a single <u>t</u> or a double <u>t</u> when you are writing its past form:

    ricocheting/ricochetting
    ricocheted/ricochetted

See **doubling of last letter**.

The spellings with the one <u>t</u> usually correspond with the pronunciations *rico-<u>shay</u>-ing* and *rico-<u>shay</u>-ed*.

The spellings with the double <u>t</u> usually correspond with the pronunciations *rico-<u>shet</u>-ing* and *rico-<u>shet</u>-ed*.

### rid

This word may be spelled in this way whether it is present tense or past tense:

*We always rid ourselves of our uniforms as soon as we get home.*
*Last week, he finally rid the house of cockroaches.*

You may also see the past tense spelled **ridded**:

*She has ridded herself of that job forever.*

### rigger / rigour

These words sound similar but have different meanings.

A **rigger** is someone who fits sails and rigging to the mast of a ship. It can also be a construction worker on a building site who works with cranes. Such a worker is also known as a **dogman**.

**Rigour** is strictness, or hardship:

*You'll have to train for the Olympics with the utmost rigour.*
*I hope he'll survive the rigours of prison life.*

### right / write / rite / wright

These words sound the same but have different meanings.

If you get an answer **right**, then it is correct. If an action is **right**, it is thought to be good or acceptable. Your **right** hand is the opposite of your left hand.

To **write** is to form letters or words with a pen or something similar. You **write** a poem when you create it using words.

A **rite** is a ceremony, often a religious one, as in *the holy rite of baptism*.

A **wright** is an old-fashioned word for a worker who constructs things. You will find it nowadays only as a suffix in words like *wheelwright* and *playwright*.

### rime

See **rhyme/rime**.

### ring / wring

These words sound the same but have different meanings.

You wear a **ring** on your finger. Bells **ring** when they give out a clear musical sound. When you **ring** someone, you telephone them.

To **wring** is to twist and squeeze something:

*I'll wring the water out of my wet socks.*
*I saw her wring her hands in grief.*

### rise / raise

These words look similar but have different meanings.

To **rise** is to get up, or go upwards:

*I rise at dawn each morning.*
*Their voices rise when they get angry.*

A **rise** is an upward movement, or an upward slope, as in *a price rise* or *a rise in the ground*.

To **raise** is to lift up, or bring up something:
*They tried to raise the bucket from the well.*
*I'm trying to raise this family by myself.*
A **raise** is an increase in wages, as in *a raise in salary*. For this meaning, you may also use the word **rise**.

### rite

See **right/write/rite/wright**.

### rival

You have a choice whether or not to double the l when you add -ed and -ing to this word. See **-l-/-ll-**.

Note that when you add -ry, the l is never doubled: **rivalry**.

### rivet

Note that you don't add another t when you add -ed or -ing to this word: **riveted, riveting**. For more about words like this, see **doubling of last letter**.

### road / rode / rowed

These words all sound the same but they have different meanings.

Cars, people and animals travel along a **road**.

**Rode** is the past tense of the verb **ride**, to sit on and control something:
*I fell off that horse the first time I rode it.*

**Rowed** is the past form of the verb **row**, to move using oars:
*I rowed the boat right around the island.*

### roar

See **raw/roar**.

### rocket

Note that you don't add another t when you add -ed or -ing to this word: **rocketed, rocketing**. For more about words like this, see **doubling of last letter**.

### rode

See **road/rode/rowed**.

### rodeo

The plural of this word is spelled **rodeos**. For more about words like this, see **-o**.

### roe

See **row/roe**.

### role / rôle

These are equally good ways of writing this word.

This is a word we have borrowed from French, and in the French spelling there is a circumflex over the o. This is to show that a long time ago there used to be another syllable in the middle of the word.

Words like this gradually lose their accent as they become more settled into English.

For more about accents in English, see **accents**. See also **circumflex**.

## roll / role

These words sound the same but mean different things.

When balls **roll** they move along, turning over and over many times. When trucks or cars **roll** along, they are carried along on wheels. Paper, material or food made into the shape of a cylinder is a **roll**, as in *a roll of carpet* or *a sponge roll*.

A **role** is the part or character that a person plays either in an organisation, or in a play or movie:
*Tell me about your role in the new movie.*

## romance

A **romance** is a novel which deals with romantic love. The basic notion is that true love wins in the end, although there are various obstacles that must be overcome along the way.

## Romania / Rumania

These are equally good spellings for this word. **Romania** is closer than **Rumania** to the original Latin word. You may also find this word spelled **Roumania**, but this is not a very common spelling.

## romantically

Note the ending of this word. See **-ally**.

## roof

The plural of this word is spelled **roofs**.
For more about words like this, see **-f/-v-**.

## root

The **root** of a word is its core, a string of letters which carry its basic meaning. The root of *spacious* is spac- because it carries the meaning "space". The rest of the word -ious is the suffix or ending which just shows that it is an adjective. Below are some more examples, with the root underlined in each case:

| | | |
|---|---|---|
| garden | gardener | gardening |
| differ | different | indifferent |
| reflect | reflector | unreflective |

In compounds there may be two (or more) roots, whether they are written as separate words or not. There are two roots in both *backyard* and *back garden*.

For more about this, see **stem**.

## root / route

These words can sound the same but they have different meanings.

A **root** is the part of a plant which grows downwards into the soil. A **root** in maths is a number which, when multiplied by itself a certain number of times, produces a given quantity:
*3 is the square root of 9 and the cube root of 27.*

A **route** is a way or road from one place to another:
*The bus takes the longest possible route to the station.*

Note that you usually pronounce this word like *root*, but it is sometimes pronounced to rhyme with *out*.

See also **rout/route**.

### rosin

See **resin/rosin**.

### rostrum

The plural of this word may be spelled **rostrums** or **rostra**. For more about words like this, see **-um**.

### rote / wrote

These words sound the same but have different meanings.

If you learn something **by rote**, you repeat it over and over again until you memorise it, but you don't try to understand what it means.

**Wrote** is the past tense of the verb **write**, to form words with a pen, or to compose something with words:
*She wrote a long letter to her friend in New Zealand.*

### rout / route

These words look similar but have different meanings.

If an army **routs** its enemies, it defeats them easily. We pronounce **rout** to rhyme with *out*.

A **route** is a way of going from one place to another:
*I'll show you the route I take from my place to school.*
We usually pronounce this to rhyme with *shoot*, but it can also be pronounced to rhyme with *out*.

See also **root/route**.

### route

Note that you drop the -e from the end of this word when you add -ed to form **routed**.

But when you add -ing you have a choice of keeping the -e, or dropping it. Both **routeing** and **routing** are equally good spellings, but the -eing spelling helps to show it is related to **route** and not *rout*.

For more about words like this, see **-e**. See also **rout/route**.

### row / roe

These words can sound the same but they mean different things.

**Roe** is the mass of eggs inside a female fish. This word rhymes with *slow*.

A **row** (also rhyming with *slow*) is a line of people or things, as in *a row of houses*. Also, you **row** a boat with oars.

When **row** means "a noisy quarrel or fight" we pronounce it to rhyme with *cow*.

### rowed

See **road/rode/rowed**.

## RSVP

stands for the French words *répondez s'il vous plaît* which means "respond if you please" or "please reply".

It is usually written on invitations in front of a date, and is asking for the invitation to be answered by that date.

Note that you do not need to use stops after the letters. See **abbreviations**.

## Rumania

See **Romania/Rumania**.

## rung / wrung

These words sound the same but have different meanings.

**Rung** is a past form of the verb **ring**, to make clear musical sounds. It is the past participle:
*They have rung the bell but no-one answers.*

**Wrung** is the past form of the verb **wring**, to twist and squeeze something:
*They wrung their hands in grief.*
*I have wrung the water out of the washer.*

## -ry

is the ending of a number of abstract nouns or nouns to do with an occupation, such as *artistry* or *carpentry*. It is really a shortening of the -ery ending the words once had. (*Carpentry* was *carpentery* a few hundred years ago.) For more about -ery words see **-ary/-ery/-ory**.

Other common examples of -ry words are:
(abstract nouns)

| ancestry | bigotry | citizenry |
| husbandry | peasantry | rivalry |

(nouns of occupation)

| chemistry | dentistry | heraldry |
| masonry | palmistry | |

(place of occupation)

| foundry | laundry | pantry |
| vestry | | |

Just one word may be spelled with either -ery or -ry:
jewellery *or* jewelry

For more about words ending in -y, see **-y**.

## rye / wry

These words sound the same but mean different things. **Rye** is a grain like wheat, that is ground into flour. You make a **wry** face to show displeasure or disgust.

# Ss

### s as a silent letter

The letter s̲ is written but not sounded at the end of a number of words we've borrowed from French. For example:

chassis    corps    debris    fracas    precis

It is also silent in *aisle, island, isle* and *islet*. In *isle* and *islet* the s̲ is part of the original word, and would have been pronounced many centuries ago. But in *aisle* and *island* the s̲ would never have been sounded because it's there by mistake. Scholars thought they were both related to *isle*, but in fact they aren't at all.

For more about silent letters, see **silent letters**.

### -s

This ending has two important roles, one with nouns, the other with verbs. It shows:

1 that a noun is a plural, as in *roles, nouns* and *verbs*, in the first sentence above.

You'll find the -s̲ plural more often than any other in English. It makes the plural for most ordinary English nouns, like *cats* and *dogs, sticks* and *stones, tables* and *chairs*. It becomes -es̲ when the word ends in s̲, ss̲, z̲, zz̲, ch̲ or tch̲, as in *buses, glasses, quizzes, riches* and *matches*.

It is also the plural for many words borrowed from French, such as *chateaus*; from Italian, such as *concertos*; from Latin, such as *formulas*, and other foreign languages too. Though borrowed words often bring their foreign plurals with them into English, for example, *chateaux, concerti, formulae*, sooner or later the English -s̲ plural comes to replace it.

For more about this, see **-um, -us** and **-a (as a plural ending)**.

The -s̲ ending also shows:

2 that a verb is singular (third person) in the present tense. It is the only verb form to have an -s̲, as the following example shows:

I drive    you drive   he/she drives
we drive  you drive  they drive

Note that when the verb ends in s̲, ss̲, z̲, zz̲, ch̲ or tch̲, this ending is -es̲, as in *passes, buzzes* and *catches*.

For more about this, see **present tense** and **plural**.

### 's

This is the "apostrophe s". Most often it shows that the word is possessive, as in:
> *the teacher's book*   (the teacher owns the book)

or that the word is specially associated with what follows:
> *the student's answer*   (the student gave the answer)

For more about this, see **apostrophes**.

But 's can also be a contraction of either *is* or *has*, as in:
> *that's* (that is)
> *he's got to* (he has got to)
> *Where's the cat?* (Where is the cat?)
> *Where's she put it?* (Where has she put it?)

Note that you often have to work out whether it is *is* or *has* from the rest of the sentence.

We use contractions like these all the time in speech. People also use them in their writing when they want it to be informal. See **contractions**.

### sabre / saber

These are equally good spellings for this word. **Sabre** is the usual spelling in the UK. **Saber** is the usual spelling in the USA. For more about words like this, see **-re/-er**.

### sac

See **sack/sac**.

### saccharine / saccharin

These are equally good spellings for this word. Either spelling may be used for both adjective and noun senses:
> *He put some saccharin(e) in his tea.*
> *It was a rather saccharin(e) movie.*

For more about words like this, see **-ine/-in**.

### sack / sac

These words both mean "a bag". They sound the same but they have developed differently.

A **sack** is a large strongly-made bag, as in *a sack of potatoes*. If your boss gives you **the sack**, you have lost your job.

A **sac** is a small bag-like part of an animal's body, usually containing liquid:
> *Bees have a honey sac for carrying nectar.*

### saga

A **saga** has come to mean a long and involved story:
> *Did I ever tell you the saga of my trek through the jungles of Borneo?*

Originally it was a story in medieval Icelandic or Norse literature which told the history of a person or a family:
> *I've just read a saga about Eric the Viking.*

## sail / sale

These words sound the same but mean different things.

A **sail** is the part of a boat which catches the wind and makes it move through the water.

A **sale** is when something is sold or offered for sale, usually by auction or at a reduced price.

## sailor

Note the ending of this word. See **-er/-or**.

## sale

See **sail/sale**.

## salesperson / salesman / saleswoman

The non-sexist word **salesperson** is often used to refer to a person who sells goods in a shop. The ending -person applies equally to both men and women. It is replacing the traditional names **salesman** and **saleswoman**. The endings -man and -woman are being avoided nowadays because they draw unnecessary attention to whether it's a man or woman.

Another option is to use a different expression altogether, such as *shop assistant*.

For more information, see **non-sexist language** and **-person**.

## salon / saloon

These words look similar but have different meanings.

A **salon** is a fashionable shop, such as *a beauty salon* or *a dress salon*. We pronounce this with a stress on the first syllable sal-.

A **saloon** is a well-furnished bar room in a hotel. This word rhymes with *balloon*.

## salvage / selvage

These words sound similar but mean different things.

To **salvage** something is to rescue it from fire, shipwreck or other damage.

**Selvage** is the edge of fabric or wallpaper sewn or finished to stop it from fraying. Another way of spelling this is **selvedge**.

## sarcasm

is a form of mockery or humour intended to belittle someone. In a sarcastic remark you often say the opposite of what you mean, in an ironical way. For example:
*Look at that mess! You have been clever!*

Often it is your tone of voice that makes it quite clear that you are not paying someone a compliment — quite the reverse. See **irony**.

## sarcastically

Note the ending of this word. See **-ally**.

### sardonically

Note the ending of this word. See **-ally**.

### satire

is a literary style which uses irony and sarcasm to ridicule vice, stupidity or foolish behaviour. It can be used in plays, poems, essays, television shows and so on. *Gulliver's Travels* is an example of a famous English satire.

### sauce / source

These words sound the same but mean different things.

**Sauce** is a thick cooked liquid used to flavour food, such as *tomato sauce*.

The **source** of something is the place, thing or person from which it comes:
> *He travelled up the River Thames towards its source.*
> *Which book was the source of your information?*
> *My mother is the source of that rumour.*

### sauté

Note that when you add -<u>ed</u> and -<u>ing</u> to this word the spelling is **sautéed** and **sautéing**.

**Sauté** originally came into English from French, which is why there is an acute accent above the <u>e</u>. The accent shows that the <u>e</u> is pronounced to rhyme with *day*.

As words like this become more widely used in English they tend to lose their foreign accents. So in the future you may find this word written without the acute: **saute**.

For more about accents in English, see **accents** and **acute accents**.

### savanna / savannah

These are equally good spellings for this word, though **savanna** is used more often and is closer to the original Spanish word.

### saw / sore / soar

These words sound the same but have different meanings.

A **saw** is a cutting tool with sharp teeth on a thin blade.
**Saw** is also the past tense of the verb **see**, to take things in with your eyes or your mind:
> *I saw your photo in the paper.*

If your leg is **sore**, it hurts or feels painful. If you feel **sore** about something, you are annoyed or offended.

To **soar** is to fly upwards, or to rise to a great height:
> *Jets soar into the air.*
> *House prices are about to soar.*

## scallop

Note that you don't add another <u>p</u> when you add the endings <u>-ed</u>, <u>-ing</u> or <u>-er</u> to this word: **scalloped, scalloping, scalloper.**

You may sometimes find this word spelled **scollop,** which is a spelling closer to the word's pronunciation. This is a much rarer spelling.

For more about words like this, see **doubling of last letter.**

## scapula

This is the technical name for the shoulder-blade. Its plural may be spelled **scapulas** or **scapulae.** For more about words like this, see **-a (as a singular ending).**

## scarcely

Like *hardly,* **scarcely** is an adverb that has negative meaning, so it should not be used after the word *without* (which already has a negative meaning).

For example:
> *We can fix it <u>with</u> <u>scarcely</u> any effort.*     RIGHT
> *We can fix it <u>without</u> <u>scarcely</u> any effort.*     WRONG

Note that *scarcely* is one of the few adverbs that require you to change around the word order when a verb follows it:
> *Scarcely <u>had I</u> gone when . . .*     RIGHT
> *Scarcely <u>I had</u> gone when . . .*     WRONG

For more information on this, see **word order.**

## scarf

The plural of this word may be spelled **scarfs** or **scarves.** For more about words like this, see **-f/-v-.**

## scene / seen

These words sound the same but have different meanings.

A **scene** is a place where something happens, as in *the scene of the crime.* In a stage play, a number of **scenes** make an act.

**Seen** is a past form of the verb **see,** to take things in with your eyes or mind. It is the past participle:
> *Have you seen the circus?*
> *He hasn't seen the joke yet.*

## scent

See **cent/sent/scent.**

## sceptic / skeptic

These are equally good spellings for this word. **Sceptic** is the usual spelling in the UK. It is closer to the Latin spelling. **Skeptic** is the usual spelling in the USA. It is closer to the earlier Greek word.

## sceptre / scepter

These are equally good spellings for this word. **Sceptre** is the usual spelling in the UK. **Scepter** is the usual spelling in the USA. For more about words like this, see **-re/-er.**

## schwa

is the sound you use more than any other in English. It's also the least well-known one, because it has no special letter of the alphabet to stand for it. Instead, it is spelled in quite a number of different ways. **Schwa** is the weak vowel which is the first sound in *abroad* and *amount*, and the last one in *sailor* and *water*. It is the vowel sound in the first and third syllables of *delicious*, and in the second and fourth syllables of *conversation*. In spite of their different spellings, all those vowel sounds are alike. They all sound rather unclear, and rather like a small grunt. In the phonetic alphabet this vowel has its own special symbol: **ə**.

**Schwa** is an unclear or indeterminate vowel because it has only weak stress on it. All the syllables in which it occurs are unstressed syllables. The **schwa** vowel often makes spelling harder, because you can't tell which vowel it is standing for.

See **pronunciation** and APPENDIX A.

## science fiction

A **science fiction** novel is one which is set in a world full of the imagined wonders of science and technology. It often assumes that we have developed the means of travelling to other worlds where there are different forms of life.

## scientific symbols

See APPENDIXES C and D.

## scissors

Although the word **scissors** refers to a single object, we treat the word as a plural in English:

*Are there any scissors in the house?*

Because *scissors* are really a single unit, we often refer to them as *a pair of scissors*. When we do, the verb we use with this phrase is singular:

*Is there a pair of scissors in the house?*

## scrotum

The plural of this word may be spelled **scrotums** or **scrota**. For more about words like this, see **-um**.

## scull

See **skull/scull**.

## sculpture / sculptor

These related words have different meanings.

**Sculpture** is the art of making figures or designs in marble, clay or bronze. A **sculpture** is an object you make this way.

A **sculptor** is a person who makes **sculptures**.

## sea

See **see/sea**.

## sealing

See **ceiling/sealing**.

### seam / seem

These words sound the same but mean different things.

A **seam** is the line where two pieces of material like fabric or metal have been joined together. It can also be a layer of rock or mineral in the ground, as in *a coal seam*.

To **seem** is to appear to be a certain way:
*They seem happy together.*

### seance / séance

These are equally good ways of writing this word.

**Seance** first came into English from French, where it is always written with the acute accent over the first e: **séance**. In French, as in English, this shows that the s̲é̲ is pronounced *say*.

This word has become so widely known in English that it is no longer necessary to use the foreign accent to show this special pronunciation. So it is quite common nowadays to see the word written **seance**.

For more about accents in English, see **accents**. See also **acute accents**.

### seas

See **sees/seize/seas**.

### second person

Pronouns such as *you*, *yourself* and *yourselves* are said to be in the **second person**, which is the person being spoken to. (**First person** is the one speaking; **third person** is the one spoken about.) For more information, see **person**.

### sector

Note the ending of this word. See **-er/-or**.

### sedimentary

Note the ending of this word. See **-ary/-ery/-ory**.

### see

The verb **to see** is an irregular verb in English. That is, it does not follow the normal and regular pattern of forming its past tense and past participle by simply adding -ed.

The past tense is *saw*: *I saw a star.*
The past participle is *seen*: *I have seen a star.*

Note that the use of *seen* as a past tense is not acceptable in writing:
*I seen him this morning.*        WRONG
*I have seen him this morning.*   RIGHT

### see / sea

These words sound the same but mean different things.

You **see** things with your eyes. **See** can also mean "to understand".

A **sea** is a large stretch of water.

### seem

See **seam/seem**.

### seen

See **scene/seen**. See also **see**.

### sees / seize / seas

These words sound the same but mean different things.

**Sees** is a part of the present tense of **see**:
*He sees the pen on the table.*

To **seize** something is to grab hold of it:
*He seized the pen and wouldn't let it go.*
Note that e comes before i in this word. See **i before e**.

**Seas** is the plural of **sea**:
*We went sailing on the high seas.*

### selector

Note the ending of this word. See **-er/-or**.

### self

The plural of this word is **selves**. For more about words like this, see **-f/-v-**.

### sell / cell

These words sound the same but mean different things.

To **sell** something is to hand it over to someone in exchange for money.

A **cell** is a small bare room, like a *prison cell*. A **cell** is also a small unit of living matter, as in a *plant cell*.

### seller

See **cellar/seller**.

### selvage

See **salvage/selvage**.

### semi-

is a prefix meaning "half" or "partly". You'll find it in *semicircle* and *semiconscious*.

In technical words, it usually means exactly "half". For example, in music, with *semibreve*, *semiquaver* and *semitone*; in architecture, with *semiarch* and *semidome*; and in mathematics, with *semicircumference* and *semicylinder*.

But in ordinary words, semi- generally means "partly", as in
semiautomatic      semidesert
semiskilled        semitrailer

In punctuation, a *semicolon* (;) is the top half of a colon (:) with a comma added in. But it is stronger than either colon or comma as a punctuation mark. See **semicolons**.

Nowadays words with semi- are usually written without a hyphen, except before a word beginning with i, for example, *semi-intoxicated*.

## semicolons ( ; )

You generally use a semicolon to divide parts of a sentence which could each stand on their own as separate sentences. The semicolon shows that the separate parts are related in some way:

*The telephone rang; his sister ran inside.*
*The telephone rang. His sister ran inside.*

The first example suggests much more strongly than the second that the two events are related (perhaps the sister ran inside <u>because</u> the telephone rang).

Note that it is quite acceptable to use connecting words like *and, but* and *however* after a semicolon:

*The telephone rang; and his sister ran inside.*

Semicolons can also be used to separate lists of different sets of things — that is, to form a large list made up of smaller lists:

*At the jumble sale there were books, magazines and newspapers; records, cassettes and CD's; and tables, chairs and sofas.*

The small lists in this sentence are the lists of printed works, musical recordings and furniture. The individual items in these small lists are separated by a comma. The small lists together make up the larger list of "kinds of things sold", and the three kinds of things are separated by a semicolon.

## sensible

Note the ending of this word. See **-able/-ible**.

## sensible / sensitive

These words look similar but mean different things.

If you are **sensible** then you show good sense or common sense.

If you are **sensitive** then your senses are keen and you respond quickly to outside events and influences. Sometimes it means that you are too easily affected by these things.

## sensor

Note the ending of this word. See **-er/-or**. See also **censor/sensor**.

## sent

See **cent/sent/scent**.

## sentence fragments

Groups of words which are punctuated as sentences but which are not fully formed are known as **sentence fragments** or **fragmentary sentences**. They usually occur as responses to questions, and leave out some parts of their structure as "understood" or assumed:

*Tomorrow night.*

This would be an acceptable answer to the question *"When are you coming back?"*

For more information, see **sentences**.

## sentences

In writing, sentences always begin with a capital letter and end with a full stop, a question mark or an exclamation mark.

What we call "fully formed" sentences are those which have a main clause (with a subject and a predicate).

There are three main types of sentences:

1 **Simple sentence** This consists of a single main clause (that is, a clause that can stand on its own):
   > *They       are going home now.*
   > subject    predicate

2 **Compound sentence** This consists of at least two main clauses, joined by a conjunction:
   > *They are going home now        and        I'm going with them.*
   > main clause 1                 conjunction    main clause 2

   The conjunction has to be what is called a coordinating conjunction — for more information, see **conjunctions**.

3 **Complex sentence** This consists of at least two clauses, one of which is a dependent clause (that is, a clause that can't stand on its own):
   > *They are going home now       because it's so late.*
   > main clause                   dependent clause

From time to time you may discover groups of words which are punctuated as if they were sentences but which do not have both subject and predicate and so do not fall into any of the three categories above. These pieces of sentences are often called **sentence fragments** or **fragmentary sentences**. They usually occur as answers to questions, and some parts of their structure are left out, so the readers have to complete the rest of the sentence for themselves.
   > *When are you getting home?* Question: <u>simple sentence</u>
   > *Sometime after nine.* Answer: <u>fragmentary sentence</u>

The fragmentary answer is really saying.
   > *I'm getting home sometime after nine.*

This is what actually happens in real conversation, so you'll find it particularly in written dialogue.

## sept-

is a Latin prefix meaning "seven", as in *septet* (a group of seven performers, or music written for them). It is also in *September*, which was the seventh month of the Roman year. (For us, of course, it is the ninth month.)

Note that the <u>sept-</u> prefix in *septic* and *septicemia* is a different one. In those words it is the Greek root meaning "putrid".

## septic / sceptic

These words look similar but have different meanings.

When something is **septic** it is infected with germs, as in *a septic wound*.

A **sceptic** is someone who doesn't believe things that most other people accept without question. For more about this word, see **sceptic/skeptic**.

## sequel

A **sequel** is a novel, play or film which is written to follow on from an existing work. It uses the same characters but tells a new story about them. So *The Empire Strikes Back* is a sequel to *Star Wars*.

## serf

The plural of this word is spelled **serfs**. For more about words like this, see **-f/-v-**.

## serge

See **surge/serge**.

## serial

See **cereal/serial**.

## serum

The plural of this word may be spelled **serums** or **sera**. For more about words like this, see **-um**.

## servant

Note the ending of this word. See **-ant/-ent**.

## serviceable

Note the ending of this word. See **-able/-eable**.

## serving / servicing

These words look similar but mean different things.

**Serving** is the present participle of **serve** meaning "to attend or wait on someone":
*The waiter is serving me now.*

**Servicing** is the present participle of **service** meaning "to repair":
*The garage is servicing my car.*

## sew

See **so/sew/sow**.

## sewage / sewerage

These words look similar because both are linked to **sewer**, but they mean different things.

**Sewage** is the stuff that goes down the sewer.

**Sewerage** is the process of removing waste material or sewage by means of sewers. It can also apply to the network of sewers which does this.

## sexist language

is language which presents a view of the world which either excludes or demeans one or other sex. Given our social history, it usually refers to language which presents a world dominated by men, in which men are the real people and women are shadowy figures in the background. For example, terms like *businessman* or *newsman* inevitably give the impression that only men can have jobs in business or can report the news. See **-man**.

The attitude of mind that is behind sexist language is revealed in other less obvious ways. Look at the following examples and note the underlying assumptions about men and women which they reveal:

1 *A boy and his sister were sitting in their father's fine watermelon patch. The gingerbread man ran past. "Stop!" commanded the boy. "Oh please stop!" pleaded the little girl.*

In this example the assumption is that boys command and that girls plead. That is, that men have the authority to give orders but women should just ask very nicely.

2 *The Abkhasian people of Soviet Georgia are famous for their longevity. Many of them live vigorous lives well past their hundredth birthday. Most have their own teeth, under flamboyant silver moustaches.*

In this example the writer has drifted from talking about people, which ought to mean men and women, to talking about men with their "flamboyant silver moustaches". This implies that the only people who count are the men.

For ways to avoid sexist language, see **non-sexist language**.

## shall / will

These words are both used to indicate the future, but they have different uses.

**Will** is used for most ordinary cases, where no special meaning or emphasis is needed:

*I will come tomorrow.*

You use **shall** rather than **will** when you want to make it clear that something is going to happen in the future because you want it to happen and because you are going to make sure that it does:

*You shall go to the party tomorrow.*

If you read this sentence aloud you will find that you have to emphasise the word **shall**.

Often you get the feeling that **shall** is needed if there is something or someone opposing what you want, as in:

*I shall go to the party tomorrow, even if it rains.*

It is also needed where some threat of force is implied, as in:

*The holder of this policy shall pay the company £200 a month.*

However, sometimes when you read **I shall**, it doesn't mean "I intend to". This is because people used to regard **shall** as the proper future form to use after I or we. But there is no reason these days for not saying **I will** or **we will** to indicate the future.

Note that the people who wrote **I shall** and **we shall** for the future tense would then have used **I will** and **we will** to show a clear intention to do something in the future. This is exactly the opposite of what happens nowadays.

### shallot / eschalot

These are two spellings for the same vegetable. **Eschalot** is closer to the original French word. **Shallot** is the spelling used more commonly in the UK.

### shammy

See **chamois/shammy**.

### shan't

This is a short form of **shall not**. See **contractions**.

### she / her / hers / herself

These personal pronouns are all third person, singular and feminine.

**She** is in the <u>subjective</u> case (it is the subject of a verb):
 *She rang me.*
See **subjective case**.

**Her** is in the <u>objective</u> case:
 *I talked to her.*
See **objective case**.

**Her** is also the personal pronoun in the <u>possessive</u> case. It is sometimes called a possessive adjective:
 *It was her umbrella.*

**Hers** is the possessive pronoun:
 *I didn't know it was hers.*

**Herself** is the reflexive pronoun:
 *She bought it herself.*

For more information, see **case, personal pronouns, possessive pronouns** and **reflexive pronouns**.

### sheaf

The plural of this word is spelled **sheaves**. For more about words like this, see **-f/-v-**.

### shear

The past tense of **shear** is **sheared**: *I sheared the sheep.*

The spelling **shore** for the past tense is now very rare.

For the past participle you can use either **sheared** or **shorn**: *I have sheared the sheep, I have shorn the sheep.*

### shear / sheer

These words sound the same but have different meanings.

To **shear** a sheep is to cut off its fleece.

Cloth is **sheer** if it is so thin that you can see through it.
A **sheer** cliff is very steep. To **sheer** away is to change course
suddenly.

## she'd

is a short form of **she had** or **she would**. See **contractions**.

## sheer

See **shear/sheer**.

## shelf

The plural of this word is spelled **shelves**. For more about
words like this, see **-f/-v-**.

## she'll

is a short form of **she will** or **she shall**. See **contractions**.

## she's

is a short form of **she is** or **she has**. See **contractions**.

## ship

See **boat/ship**.

## -ship

is a suffix which makes abstract nouns out of words that
describe a person's role. It turns *friend* into *friendship*, *leader* into
*leadership* and *scholar* into *scholarship*.

Some -ship words refer to a community, like *fellowship*, *kinship*,
*membership* and *township*.

Others refer to a particular status, such as *apprenticeship*,
*championship* and *lectureship*.

A few -ship words are used as terms of honour, as in *Your
Ladyship* or *Your Worship*.

Certain -ship words become a term of commendation for
particular skills, for example, *craftsmanship*, *horsemanship* and
*showmanship*. New ones are sometimes invented in the same
way: *brinksmanship*, *oneupmanship*.

## shoot / chute

These words sound the same but mean different things.

A **shoot** is a new part that grows from a plant. You **shoot** at
something when you fire a gun at it. Look up your dictionary
for other meanings.

A **chute** is a sloping channel for sending things like water,
grain, rubbish or coal to a lower level.

## shore / sure

These words sound the same but have different meanings.

The **shore** is the land along the edge of the sea or a lake.

If someone is **sure** of something, they are certain or confident of
it, as in *sure of success*.

## short story

A **short story** is a piece of prose fiction. As the name suggests, a short story is much shorter than a novel. It usually has a small number of characters and just one main theme or topic. Many British writers have written short stories – D. H. Lawrence is a famous example.

## should

is one of a set of words called *modal verbs*. It is the past tense form of *shall*. For more information, see **modal verbs**.

## shouldn't

This is a contraction of **should not**. See **contractions**.

## should've

When you say **should've** it may sound like the words "should of", but in fact it is short for "should have". While it is correct to use **should've**, it is wrong to use *should of* because *should* is never followed by *of*.

See **contractions**.

## shovel

You have a choice whether or not to double the l when you add -ed, -ing or -er to this word. See **-l-/-ll-**.

Note that when you add -ful, the l is never doubled: **shovelful**.

## shrivel

For information about whether to double the l when you add endings like -ed or -ing, see **-l-/-ll-**.

## sight / site / cite

These words sound the same but mean different things.

Your **sight** is your ability to see things. It can also be something worth seeing: *a great sight*.

A **site** is the land where something is built or will soon be built.

To **cite** something is to quote it as an authority, or to refer to it as an example.

## sign / sine

These words sound the same but have different meanings.

Anything that shows that something exists or is likely to happen is a **sign**:
*These black clouds are the sign of a thunderstorm.*
A **sign** can also be something such as a mark or symbol that stands for something else:
*Could you write a pound sign in front of the amount of money on this form.*
A notice giving information is a **sign**.

**Sine** is a mathematical term used in trigonometry. It is the ratio of the side opposite a given angle in a right-angled triangle to the hypotenuse.

## signal

You have a choice whether or not to double the l when you add -ed or -ing to this word. See **-l-/-ll-**.

Note that when you add -ise, the l is never doubled: **signalise**.

## silent letters

When a letter is written but not sounded in a word, we call it a **silent letter**. The same letter may be sounded in one word and silent in another. For example, the second b in *bomb* is silent, but in *bombardment* it is sounded. Many silent letters (though not all) were once sounded. Those at the beginning of words like *knee* and *knife*, *write* and *wrong* used to be pronounced in Old English.

Silent letters are often important in helping to identify words. The silent b in *jamb* (as in *doorjamb*) makes it look different from *jam*. The silent b in *comb* matters because it makes *combing* different from *coming*.

The following letters are all silent in some English words:
    b  e  g  gh  h  l  n  p  r  s  t  u  w
Check under each of those letters for details. The entries are **b as a silent letter**, **g as a silent letter**, and so on.

## silicon / silicone

These words look similar but have different meanings.

**Silicon** is a chemical element, as in the *silicon chips* used in computers.

**Silicone** is the name for any of a group of chemical compounds that include the element **silicon** as part of their structure. Some oils and synthetic rubbers are **silicones**.

## silo

The plural of this word is spelled **silos**. For more about words like this, see **-o**.

## similar

Note the ending of this word. See **-ar**.

## similes

A **simile** is a writing device in which something is likened to something else. It can be the whole thing or just one particular aspect of the thing that we observe to be similar to something else.

Similes usually start with the word *like* or *as*, as in the following examples:
    *The sun is like a golden orange in the sky.*
    *He wandered lonely as a cloud.*

Compare this with the metaphor:
    *The sun is a golden orange in the sky.*

The image presented as a simile is less vivid and direct than the metaphor. Similes do not make the same imaginative leaps as metaphors. See **metaphors**.

## simple / simplistic

These related words are used in different ways.

If we speak about a point of argument being **simple**, we mean it is not complicated and is easy to understand.

If we say something is **simplistic**, we mean that it has been made much simpler than it really is. So **simplistic** expresses disapproval for something not properly thought out or based on reality.

## simple sentences

A **simple sentence** is one that consists of just one main clause:
*They are going home now.*

It contrasts with **compound sentences** and **complex sentences**. For more information, see **sentences**.

## simplistic

See **simple/simplistic**.

## simulator

Note the ending of this word. See **-ator**.

## sine

See **sign/sine**.

## singular

If a noun, verb or pronoun refers to one single person or thing, we say it is **singular** in number. If it refers to more than one, we say it is *plural* in number. For information on how we show whether nouns, verbs or pronouns are singular or plural, see **plural**.

Note how we spell the ending of this word. See **-ar**.

## sink

You may use either **sank** or **sunk** as the past tense of **sink**, though **sank** is used more often:
*The torpedo sank the cruiser.*
*The torpedo sunk the cruiser.*

For the past participle you should use **sunk**:
*The torpedo has sunk the cruiser.*

**Sunken** is used as an adjective: *sunken treasure.*

## siphon / syphon

These are equally good spellings for this word, though **siphon** is closer to the original Latin word. For more about words like this, see **i/y**.

## sirup

See **syrup/sirup**.

### sister-in-law

The plural of this word is **sisters-in-law**. The possessive is **sister-in-law's**: *My sister-in-law's husband.*

### site

See **sight/site/cite**.

### sizable / sizeable

These are equally good spellings for this word. For more about words like this, see **-able/-eable**.

### skein

Note that e̲ comes before i̲ in this word. See **i before e**.

### skeptic

See **sceptic/skeptic**.

### skilful / skillful

These are equally good spellings for this word. **Skilful** is the usual spelling in the UK. **Skillful** is the usual spelling in the USA.

Note that there are three l̲'s in **skilfully**.

See **-l-/-ll-**.

### skull / scull

These words sound the same but have different meanings.

Your **skull** is the bony part of your head, which encloses your brain and supports your face.

A **scull** is a type of oar used for rowing a boat.

### slander

See **libel/slander**.

### slang

**Slang** is very informal language. For that reason, it is found more in speech than in writing.

When you comment on how good something is by saying it's *unreal*, you're using slang. *Ace* and *brill* are used to describe experiences that are exciting and rewarding, and *to snuff it* is slang for "to die".

The occasional use of slang in speech and informal writing can be effective because it can capture the flavour of everyday situations.

### slashes ( / )

The slash is a punctuation mark sometimes used to separate items that are equally good alternatives.

For example if you write *he/she/it comes*, this means that *he, she* and *it* are all possible as pronouns with the verb *comes*.

Slashes are a convenient way of conveying this information, though some writers prefer to avoid them if possible in formal essay writing.

Note that the technical name of the slash is the *solidus*.

## slay / sleigh

These words sound the same but have different meanings.

To **slay** something is to kill it:
*St George set off to slay the dragon.*

A **sleigh** is a sledge, usually one pulled by animals.
Note that e comes before i in this word. See **i before e.**

## slow / slowly

**Slowly** is an adverb:
*How slowly do you want me to play it?*

**Slow** is an adjective:
*It is a slow piece of music.*

Note that **slow** can be an adverb:
*How slow do you want me to play it?*
It is mostly used in this way in informal language.

## smelled / smelt

These are equally good spellings for the past forms of **smell**:
I smelled          I smelt
I have smelled   I have smelt
For more about words like this, see **-ed/-t.**

## snivel

For information about whether to double the l when you add
endings like -ed, -ing or -er, see **-l-/-ll-.**

## snorkel

For information about whether to double the l when you add
endings like -ed or -ing, see **-l-/-ll-.**

## so / sew / sow

These words sound the same but mean different things.

**So** means "therefore":
*He asked me and so I will go.*
For information about this use of **so**, see **link words** and
**conjunctions. So** has other meanings. Check your dictionary if
you are unsure.

To **sew** is to stitch something with a needle and thread.

To **sow**, rhyming with *go*, is to scatter seed on the ground.
But a **sow**, rhyming with *cow*, is a female pig.

## so / that

One common way of using **so** is as an intensifier meaning
"very":
*I'm so tired after all this walking.*

You will hear **that** used in the same way:
*I'm that tired after all this walking.*
Note that it is best not to use **that** as an intensifier in formal
writing. See **intensifiers.**

### soap operas

A **soap opera** is a radio or television play such as *Coronation Street* or *Neighbours*. It is presented as a serial in short regular programmes, and deals with domestic problems, usually in a highly emotional manner.

### soar

See **saw/sore/soar**.

### socks

You may sometimes see this word spelled **sox**, especially in advertising. **Sox** is also sometimes used for **socks** in the USA.

### soft sell

Advertisers may choose a **soft sell** or **hard sell** method when writing advertising copy. The soft sell is the one they adopt when they feel they can appeal to readers by indirect means – appealing to their values and hidden desires, rather than putting direct pressure on them to buy. The high-pressure method is the hard sell.

Both soft sell and hard sell advertisements are illustrated in WRITING WORKSHOP pp 54–5.

### solar

Note the ending of this word. See **-ar**.

### sole / soul

These words sound the same but mean different things.

Your **sole** is the underneath part of your foot.

Your **soul** is the spiritual part of you, contrasted with your body.

### solicitor

Note the ending of this word. See **-er/-or**.

### soliloquy

A soliloquy is a speech an actor makes in a play where he or she thinks out loud. Sometimes the actor pretends that there are other characters there and talks as if they had said something. But the essential thing about a soliloquy is that the actor is all alone. For an example you could look at Hamlet's famous soliloquy "To be or not to be" in which he broods over the possibility of killing himself.

### solo

The plural of this word may be spelled **solos** or **soli**. For more about words like this, see **-o**.

### soluble / solvable

These words look similar and are linked in origin but they are not exactly the same in meaning.

**Soluble** means "able to be dissolved", as a chemical, or "able to be solved", as a problem.

**Solvable** means "able to be solved", so only a problem is **solvable**. A chemical is not.

## -some

You'll find the ending -some in a few words referring to small groups of people: a *threesome*, a *foursome*. Here -some is the fossil of an old English word meaning "together".

There is a different -some in some adjectives like:
    fearsome     lonesome     tiresome     troublesome

In those, -some just makes an adjective out of some other word. *Handsome* ("good-looking") is another example. The first part of the word (hand) is a lost adjective which once meant "convenient", and then "pleasing".

## some / sum

These words sound the same but mean different things.

**Some** means "a few or a little":
    *I will have some jam on my bread.*

A **sum** is a calculation in arithmetic:
    *I am doing my sums now.*
It is also an amount of money:
    *That is a big sum to pay out.*

## somebody / someone

These words are singular and so should be followed by singular verbs such as *is* and *has*:
    *Somebody has left.*
The real problem arises when you have to choose the right pronoun to follow. You could write
    *Somebody has left his headlights on.*
which assumes the person is male, or
    *Somebody has left her headlights on.*
which assumes the person is female, or
    *Somebody has left his or her headlights on.*
which doesn't assume the gender of the person, but is awkward to write all the time.

One solution is to break the singular agreement and use the plural pronoun *their*:
    *Somebody has left their headlights on.*
This is the usual way of solving the problem in our speech, and is increasingly common even in formal writing. Some people, however, object to this and would prefer you to rewrite the sentence:
    *Somebody's headlights have been left on.*

For more information on this, see **agreement**, and compare **everyone/everybody/everything**.

## sometime / sometimes

These words are obviously linked but they have different meanings.

**Sometimes** means "on some occasions":
    *Sometimes I give myself a real treat.*

**Sometime** means "at some indefinite or unspecified point in time": *He will come sometime next week.*

Note that **sometime** is written as two separate words whenever it's part of a phrase: *at some time in the future, for some time to come.*

### son-in-law

The plural of this word is spelled **sons-in-law**. The possessive is **son-in-law's**: *my son-in-law's car.*

### sonnets

A **sonnet** is a special kind of poem which has fourteen lines. The way the rhymes are arranged within the lines can vary but the most usual pattern is shown in the following sonnet by William Shakespeare:

> Shall I compare thee to a summer's day?
> Thou art more lovely and more temperate:
> Rough winds do shake the darling buds of May,
> And summer's lease hath all too short a date:
>
> Sometime too hot the eye of heaven shines,
> And often is his gold complexion dimmed;
> And every fair from fair sometimes declines,
> By chance, or nature's changing course untrimmed;
>
> But thy eternal summer shall not fade,
> Nor lose possession of that fair thou ow'st;
> Nor shall death brag thou wander'st in his shade,
> When in eternal lines to time thou grow'st;
>
> So long as men can breathe, or eyes can see,
> So long lives this, and this gives life to thee.

Note that in the first four lines, the first line rhymes with the third line, and the second with the fourth. The next four lines follow the same pattern (but with different rhymes) as do the next four. Then there is a rhyming couplet (two lines) to finish off.

There is an Italian form of the sonnet which follows a different pattern. It has a major group of eight lines, followed by a minor group of six lines.

### soprano

The plural of this word may be spelled **sopranos** or **soprani**. For more about words like this, see **-o**.

### sore

See **saw/sore/soar**.

### sort / sought

These words sound the same but mean different things.

A **sort** is another word for "a kind or type". To **sort** something is to separate it into different classes or types.

**Sought** is the past form of **seek**, to look for:
> *I sought him here, I sought him there.*
> *I have sought an answer to this question for a long time.*

## soufflé

is a word which we have borrowed from French and which has not lost its French appearance in English.

It is written with an acute accent over the e to show that the last syllable is pronounced to rhyme with *lay*.

As words like this become more widely used in English they tend to lose their written accents. So in the future you may find this word written without the acute accent: **souffle**.

For more about accents in English, see **accents**. See also **acute accents**.

## sought

See **sort/sought**.

## soul

See **sole/soul**.

## source

See **sauce/source**.

## sovereign

Note that the e comes before the i in this word. See **i before e**.

## sow

See **so/sew/sow**.

## spaghetti

In English, **spaghetti** is normally a singular noun. It stays singular even when you are talking about lots of spaghetti:
*I can't hold this much spaghetti. It is sliding off my plate.*

This kind of noun is called a mass noun, since it refers to a group or mass of things. See **mass nouns**.

The plural (if you had to have one) is spelled **spaghettis**:
*All the different spaghettis were lined up for the spaghetti tasting contest.*

## specialty / speciality

Nowadays **speciality** seems to be taking over from **specialty**. They used to have separate roles.

A **specialty** used to refer to a special interest or study:
*His specialty was the history of clocks in medieval times.*

A **speciality** used to mean "something that you are especially good at doing":
*My speciality is pavlova so I'll make dessert.*

But this distinction seems to be disappearing, and you are likely to find **speciality** used with both these meanings.

## specks / specs

These words sound the same but have different meanings.

**Specks** are tiny marks or particles of something, as in *specks of dust*.

**Specs** is an informal word for spectacles or glasses.

### spectator

Note the ending of this word. See **-ator**.

### spectre / specter

These are equally good ways of spelling this word. **Spectre** is the usual spelling for this word in the UK, whereas **specter** is more common in the USA. For more about words like this, see **-re/-er**.

### spectrum

The plural of this word which is used in physics may be spelled **spectrums** or **spectra**. For more about words like this, see **-um**.

### spelled / spelt

These are equally good ways of spelling the past forms of the verb **spell**:

I spelled   I have spelled
I spelt     I have spelt

For more about words like this, see **-ed/-t**.

### spelling rules

Spelling rules are few and far between in English, and every "rule" has exceptions. This is partly because the English language has borrowed words from many different languages, and they have kept their foreign spellings.

It is also because the spelling of English words was very fluid up to about 1600, and the same word could be spelled and printed in several different ways. Then during the seventeenth and eighteenth centuries, people wanted to fix spellings once and for all, and their choices weren't always consistent. Pronunciation was still changing too, and so we get strange pairs like *great* and *treat*, *horse* and *worse*.

This book explains some of the more useful "rules". Perhaps we should call them **spelling points**, because there are always exceptions. Both the general pattern, and the exceptions to it, are found under the following headwords:

| -ae- | -c/-ck- | doubling of last letter | -e | -f/-v- |
| i → y | i before e | -ise/-ize | -l-/-ll- | -o | -oe- |
| -or/-our | y → i | | | |

### spelt

See **spelled/spelt**.

### spilled / spilt

These are equally good ways of spelling the past forms of the verb **spill**:

I spilled   I have spilled
I spilt     I have spilt

For more about words like this, see **-ed/-t**.

### spiral

For information about whether to double the l when you add endings like -ed or -ing, see **-l-/-ll-**.

## split infinitives

When a verb starts with the word *to*, it's called an **infinitive**: *to walk, to respond, to develop*. Yet the infinitive is also found without *to* beside it at all — whenever it is used with an auxiliary verb, as in: *can walk, do respond* or *will develop*. Those who think of the infinitive as *to walk* have been inclined to say that it is a single unit which should never be split up. So they object to **split infinitives**.

To split an infinitive is to insert a word between *to* and the verb, as in *to slowly walk, to quickly respond*. It happens quite often when we speak and often seems the most natural thing to write.

Your efforts not to split infinitives can sometimes alter the meaning of a sentence. Compare:
  *I like to really understand things.*
with
  *I like really to understand things.*
The second sentence keeps the infinitive unsplit, but does it mean quite the same as the first sentence?

Getting the meaning right is the most important thing, and you will find that splitting the infinitive is accepted without comment these days.

## spoiled / spoilt

These are equally good ways of spelling the past forms of the verb **spoil**:
  I spoiled   I have spoiled
  I spoilt    I have spoilt

For more about words like this, see **-ed/-t**.

## spokesperson

This word has been made up to avoid referring to the gender of the person speaking. After all, the important thing usually is that the person is speaking on behalf of others. It generally doesn't matter in the least whether they are a man or a woman.

Sometimes **spokesman** or **spokeswoman** is used when it is clear what gender the speaker is.

See **non-sexist language** and **-person**.

## spongy

Note that you drop the -e from the end of **sponge** when you add y. For more about words like this, see **-y**.

## sponsor

Note the ending of this word. See **-er/-or**.

## spoof

The plural of this word is spelled **spoofs**. For more about words like this, see **-f/-v-**.

## spoonerisms

A **spoonerism** happens when you say something and it doesn't come out quite right because the first letters of words have swapped places. For example, you might set out to say "the barking dog" and end up with "the darking bog". It quite often happens because you are tired. Spoonerisms were named after an English clergyman, William A. Spooner, 1844–1930, who was noted for making such slips. His original remark to his history students was "You have hissed my mystery lessons and tasted the whole worm".

## spy story

See **thriller**.

## stadium

The plural of this word may be spelled **stadiums** or **stadia**. For more about words like this, see **-um**.

## staff

This word can be used to refer to a group of people helping or working for the same leader or employer. In this case it is a **collective noun**.

It can be used with either a singular or plural verb:
*The staff were keen to finish the job.*
*The staff at our school is a most conscientious one.*

The plural of this kind of **staff** is spelled **staffs**:
*The staffs of the two schools held a joint end-of-term party.*

When **staff** refers to a stick or a rod, the plural is spelled **staves**.

In music, **stave** is an equally good spelling for **staff** when the word refers to the lines and spaces on which music is written. The plural of this kind of **staff** is also spelled **staves**.

## stair / stare

These words sound the same but have different meanings.

A **stair** is one of a series of steps.

To **stare** at someone is to look directly at them for a long time with your eyes wide open.

## stake

See **steak/stake**.

## stalactite / stalagmite

A **stalactite** is a deposit formed by dripping water, which hangs like an icicle from the <u>roof</u> of a limestone cave.

A **stalagmite** is a deposit formed by dripping water, which builds up on the <u>floor</u> of a limestone cave.

The first parts of these words make some difference to the meaning. <u>Stalact-</u> comes from a Greek word meaning "dripping". <u>Stalagm-</u> comes from a Greek word meaning "dropping". But the easiest way to remember which is which is to say <u>t</u> is <u>top</u> for **stalactite**, and <u>g</u> is <u>ground</u> for **stalagmite**.

### stalk / stork

These words sound the same but have different meanings.

A **stalk** is the stem of a plant. To **stalk** something is to follow it quietly and carefully:
*My cat likes to stalk mice.*

A **stork** is a large bird with long legs and a long beak.

### stamen

The plural of this botanical word may be spelled **stamens** or **stamina**.

**Stamens** follows the normal English pattern for making plurals — simply add -<u>s</u> (or -<u>es</u>).

**Stamina** is the Latin plural for this word. It is sometimes used because **stamen** was borrowed from Latin. Note that **stamina** has developed another meaning, that of endurance and strength. With this meaning it is always singular:
*Her stamina <u>is</u> amazing.*

### standard units

The **standard units** of measurement used in Europe are those of the metric system. For information on these units and their symbols, see APPENDIX C.

### stanza

A **stanza** is a section of a poem. It consists of two or more lines and often has a particular pattern of rhyme or rhythm which is then repeated in following stanzas. Another word for a stanza is a **verse**, although verse can also refer to the kind of metre a poem is in, as in *hexameter verse, pentameter verse.* See **verse**.

### stare

See **stair/stare**.

### statements

**Statements** are sentences in which you state or declare something:
*I'm going home.*
*It's getting pretty late.*
Statements contrast with *questions, commands* and *exclamations* as one of the four functions of sentences. A statement is perhaps the most basic type of sentence, and in writing usually begins with a capital letter and ends with a full stop.

### stationary / stationery

The <u>a</u> and the <u>e</u> in the ending of these words make all the difference to their meanings.

Something is **stationary** when it is not moving.

**Stationery** is writing paper and writing materials, such as pens and pencils.

You can remember the difference by saying that the <u>e</u> in **stationery** stands for *envelopes*.

For more about words like this, see **-ary/-ery/-ory**.

## statistics

There are several nouns ending in -ics that can take either a singular or a plural verb, and *statistics* is one of them.

When the word refers to a subject of study, it's treated as a singular:
> *Statistics is not my strong point.*

When it refers to a set of figures or results, then it becomes a plural:
> *This month's statistics are being released today.*

Other -ics words which show the same switching from singular to plural include *acoustics* and *politics*. For more information on this ending, see **-ic/-ics**. For advice on writing sets of figures, see **numbers**.

## stature / statue

These words look similar but have different meanings.

Someone's **stature** is their height.

A **statue** is an image of a person or animal, made out of stone, wood or bronze.

## steak / stake

These words sound the same but have different meanings.

**Steak** is a thick slice of meat or fish which is usually grilled or fried.

A **stake** is a stick with a pointed end. A **stake** can also be the amount bet in a race or game:
> *He knew the stakes were high as he began to deal the cards.*

## steal / steel

These words sound the same but have different meanings.

To **steal** is to take something that doesn't belong to you.

**Steel** is iron mixed with other metals and carbon to make it very hard and strong.

## stem

In English the **stem** of a word is the base part to which prefixes and suffixes are added. So educat- is the stem in all the following:
> educated education educator re-educating uneducated

As the examples show, the stem remains unchanged, whatever is added to it.

Note that in Latin you might distinguish the **stem** educat- from the **root** educ-. See **root**.

## stencil

For information about whether to double the l when you add endings like -ed or -ing, see **-l-/-ll-**.

### step / steppe

These words sound the same but mean different things.

You take one **step** after another when you walk. A **step** is one of a set of stairs.

A **steppe** is one of the large treeless plains found in south-eastern Europe and Asia.

### stigma

The plural of this word may be spelled **stigmas** or **stigmata**. For more about words like this, see **-a (as a singular ending)**.

### stile / style

These words sound the same but have different meanings.

A **stile** is a step or steps for climbing over a fence where there is no gate.

**Style** means "a kind of design" or "way of making something":
*The architecture of our new house is modern in style.*
A **style** can also be a way of doing something:
*I can't understand his style of writing.*

### stiletto

The plural of this word is spelled **stilettos**. For more about words like this, see **-o**.

### stimulus

The plural of this word may be spelled **stimuluses** or **stimuli**. For more about words like this, see **-us**.

### stop

See **full stops**.

### stork

See **stalk/stork**.

### story / storey

These words sound the same but have different meanings.

When someone tells a **story** they are telling of something that has happened, either made up, as in *a fairy story*, or in real life. The plural of this is **stories**.

A **storey** is one whole level or floor of a building. Note that in the USA **storey** is spelled **story**.

### straight / strait

These words sound the same but mean different things.

Something is **straight** if it is not bent or curved, as in *a straight road*. **Straight** can also mean "directly" or "immediately":
*I'll come straight home.*

A **strait** is a narrow channel connecting two large bodies of water, as in *Bass Strait*.

### straitjacket / straightjacket

These are equally good spellings for this word.

### stratum

The plural of this word may be spelled **stratums** or **strata**. For more about words like this, see **-um**.

### studio

The plural of this word is spelled **studios**. For more about words like this, see **-o**.

### stupefy

This word ends in -efy, even though it sounds as if it could end in -ify. Note that *stupid* and *stupidity* are spelled with an i. For more about words like this, see **-ify/-efy**.

### stupor

Note the ending of this word. See **-er/-or**.

### sty / stye

You can use both these spellings for a small, red and painful swelling on your eyelid:

*The doctor has given me some ointment to put on this sty* (or *stye*).

**Sty** is the only spelling for the name of the place where you keep pigs.

Note that the plural of both these spellings is **sties**.

### style

The language you write all adds up to a style. It may be formal or informal, bright or dull, clear or muddy, depending on how you choose your words and control your sentences.

How to manage and modify your style is explained in WRITING WORKSHOP pp 28–9.

### stylus

The plural of this word may be spelled **styluses** or **styli**. For more about words like this, see **-us**.

### sub-

is a prefix meaning "under", as in *submarine*, *subsoil* and *subway*.

It can also mean "under" in terms of organisation, as in:
subcommittee    subdivide    sublet    subsection

The prefix also appears in words which rank someone as being one level below a particular office. For example:
subdean    subeditor    sublieutenant

### subconscious

See **unconscious/subconscious**.

### subject

We commonly divide sentences into two parts: what is being talked about, and what is being said about it:

*She / laughs a lot.*
*The elephant in the corner that keeps waving its trunk / eats strawberries.*

The first part (what's being talked about) is called the **subject** of the sentence. The rest is called the **predicate**.

The easiest way to find the subject is to ask the question *who?* or *what?* before the main verb of the sentence (*laughs* and *eats* in the examples above).

**1** Who or what laughs?   *She . . .*
**2** Who or what eats?    *The elephant in the corner that keeps waving its trunk . . .*

## subjective case

If a pronoun is the subject of a verb it is said to be in the **subjective case:**

*We will be there soon.*
*You and I are going to be late.*

The subjective case pronouns are

| Singular | Plural |
|----------|--------|
| I | we |
| you | you |
| he she it | they |

The subjective case is also known as the **nominative case,** especially in the study of other languages. For more information, see **case.**

## subjunctive

A sentence which expresses something which is uncertain or possible may use a special **subjunctive** verb.

**Subjunctive** verbs are not very common in modern English. They most often appear in clauses beginning with *if* or *as if,* or in clauses after verbs like *wish:*

*I'd go if he were going.*   (instead of *was*)
*You may do that, if you be so inclined.*   (instead of *are*)
*I felt as if* (or, *as though*) *I were dead.*   (instead of *was*)
*I wish she were coming.*   (instead of *was*)

Some common expressions use the subjunctive, even though most people are probably not aware of it:

*God save the Queen.*   (means *May God save the Queen*)
*Come what may.*   (means *Whatever may come*)

Note that subjunctives are quite formal in English and much more common in writing than in speech. Some languages, however, make much more use of the subjunctive both in writing and in speech.

## subordinate clauses

**Subordinate clause** is another name for **dependent clause.** *Subordinate* means "lower" or "not as important". For more information, see **clauses.**

## subordinating conjunctions

See **conjunctions.**

## substitute

See **replace/substitute.**

## successor

Note the ending of this word. See **-er/-or.**

## suffixes

are the endings which tell you something about the grammar of English words. Some tell you what part of speech a word is:

<u>-ance</u> and <u>-tion</u> are noun endings, as in *assistance* and *situation*
<u>-ive</u> is usually an adjective ending, as in *festive*
<u>-ly</u> is usually an adverb ending, as in *brightly*
<u>-ate</u> is usually a verb ending, as in *pulsate*

Some suffixes also change the meaning of a word. For example:
<u>-ful</u> and <u>-less</u> in *hopeful* and *hopeless*.

English has a very large number of endings like these, what with some from Old English, as well as many from French and Latin. As all these examples show, the suffixes often help to create new words in English.

There are other suffixes which don't make new words, but show how words relate to each other in a sentence. For example:
<u>-'s</u> on a noun makes it possessive, as in:
*the neighbour's new garbage bin*
<u>-s</u> on a verb makes it singular, third person, present tense, as in:
*George plays saxophone, and I play the flute.*

These are inflectional suffixes. Given below is a complete set of them, for nouns, verbs and adjectives.

| | |
|---|---|
| noun inflections: | neighbour's (possessive) |
| | neighbours (plural) |
| | neighbours' (plural possessive) |
| verb inflections: | plays (singular, 3rd person, present) |
| | playing (continuous) |
| | played (past form) |
| adjective inflections: | brighter (comparative) |
| | brightest (superlative) |

English has many more suffixes than prefixes. For more about both, see **affixes**.

## sugar

Note the ending of this word. See **-ar**.

## suggestible

Note the ending of this word. See **-able/-ible**.

## suit / suite / sweet

These words are similar in spelling or sound, but they mean different things.

A **suit** is a set of clothes. It rhymes with *boot*.

A **suite** is a set of connecting rooms that make one living area. It is also a set of furniture, as in *a dining room suite*. In music it is a set of pieces written to go together. It rhymes with *beat*.

A **sweet** is a lolly or a dessert.

## sum

See **some/sum**.

## summary

A **summary** is a brief account of the points argued in a speech, or piece of writing. The following are often used as synonyms, though some writers keep their meanings distinct:

A *precis* is a restatement of the contents of a piece of writing in compact form.

An *abstract* is a very brief statement of the importance of a document, by its author. It shows the issues it tackled, and the results or conclusions drawn.

An *abridgement* gives you the text of a book in a shortened form, with the less important parts cut out, and the main ones left in the author's own words.

See also **synopsis**.

## summary / summery

These words sound the same but mean different things.

A **summary** is a brief account or summing up. See **summary**. **Summary** justice is justice delivered swiftly and without ceremony.

**Summery** means "suitable for summer" or "suggesting summer": *She wore such a light and summery dress.*

## summons

is a singular noun:
*The summons was handed to him. It was a couple of pages long.*

The plural is spelled **summonses**.

## super-

is a Latin prefix meaning "above". You'll find it in words like *superhuman* and *superstructure*.

In some words it means "beyond the range of", as in *supernatural* and *supersonic*.

It appears in a few scientific words meaning "above the normal level". This is its meaning in *superconductor* and *superheat*.

In advertising and promotion, super- is used to mean "bigger or better than anything of its kind", as in *supermarket, superproduct* and *superwoman.*

Compare **hyper-**.

## superior

Note the ending of this word. See **-er/-or**.

## superlatives

For information on these, see **degrees of comparison**.

## superstitious

See **suspicious/superstitious**.

### sur-

is a French prefix meaning "above". You'll find it in a few English words such as:

surcharge (an extra cost)          surface (the upper face)
surmount (get on top of)           surpass (be ahead of)
surplus (an extra amount)          surrealism (beyond what is real)

Note that sur- is also in *surprise*. It originally meant "to overtake or catch someone from above". Make sure you put an r in the first syllable, even though you don't hear it pronounced. See **r as a silent letter**.

### sure

See **shore/sure**.

### surely / surly

These words look similar but they don't sound the same and they mean different things. The e makes all the difference.

**Surely** means "certainly" or "of course". It sounds like *shore-ly*:
*Surely he will remember to bring the lunch.*

**Surly,** rhyming with *curly,* means "gruff and bad-tempered".

### surf / serf

These words sound the same but mean different things.

The **surf** is the waves breaking on the beach.

A **serf** was a peasant in medieval times.

### surge / serge

These words sound the same but have different meanings.

A **surge** is a sudden rush or upward sweep, as of water.

**Serge** is a kind of rough material.

### surly

See **surely/surly**.

### surplus / surplice

These words sound the same but mean different things.

A **surplus** is an excess amount:
*After we had distributed everyone's share we still had a surplus.*

A **surplice** is a garment worn by a member of the clergy.

### susceptible

Note the ending of this word. See **-able/-ible**.

### suspense / suspension

These words are both linked to **suspend** but they mean different things.

**Suspense** is the feeling of tension or anxiety that you feel when things are left hanging or unresolved:
*Don't tell me how the thriller ends — I like to be kept in suspense.*

**Suspension** is the state of being suspended or hung. A **suspension bridge** is a bridge which is hung from a cable above, rather than being supported by pillars beneath, like the Golden Gate Bridge. A **suspension** in chemistry is a liquid with tiny solid particles mixed through it. The particles are left hanging in the liquid. Chalk particles form a **suspension** in water. A **suspension** is also a punishment, for example, in sport, where the person who has broken the rules is excluded from the game for a period of time:

*The footballer was given a suspension of four weeks for striking an opponent.*

### suspicious / superstitious

These words look similar but they have different meanings.

When a person is **suspicious** of someone or something, they feel wary and distrustful of them:

*"I'm suspicious of these newfangled ideas," grumbled my grandfather.*

People who are **superstitious** believe that certain things or events bring them good or bad luck:

*He's so superstitious that he won't walk under a ladder in case something disastrous happens.*

### sustain / sustenance

The noun **sustenance** is related to the verb **sustain** in spite of the different spelling. For more about words like this, see **-aim/-ain**.

### swap / swop

These are equally good ways of spelling this word. **Swap** is the more usual spelling in the UK even though **swop** is the spelling closer to its pronunciation.

### swat / swot

These are equally good ways of spelling this word. **Swat** is the spelling used most commonly to refer to striking a sharp blow: *to swat a fly.*

**Swot** is the spelling used most commonly to refer to studying hard: *to swot for exams.*

### swear words

A **swear word** is an offensive word used in swearing or as an expression of anger or excitement. Swear words were originally words to do with God or religion — their shock value lay in their blasphemous use. But now the term covers all kinds of other words which offend people. For more about this, see **taboo words**.

### sweet

See **suit/suite/sweet**.

## swivel

For information about whether to double the l when you add endings like -ed or -ing, see **-l-/-ll-**.

## swop

See **swap/swop**.

## swot

See **swat/swot**.

## syllables

A **syllable** is a unit or section of pronunciation which may be part of a word, or may be the whole word. It usually contains a vowel, and often some consonants before and/or after it.

The word *cat* is made up of just one syllable, with the vowel a in the middle, and the consonants c and t on either side. Some other one-syllable words are:

stop
tie
through
my (here the y stands for a vowel sound)

Note that the words don't have to be short to be only one syllable: for example *through*.

Note also that you don't have to have a consonant on both sides of the vowel. For example, *tie* and *my* have only one consonant.

A word can be made up of several syllables.

Some two-syllable words:

has ty       pos ter       sci ence (note that the final e is not pronounced)

Some three-syllable words:

el e phant       por cu pine

Some four-syllable words:

el e va tion       tra di tion al

## syllabus

The plural of this word may be spelled **syllabuses** or **syllabi**. For more about words like this, see **-us**.

## symbolism

In writing, people or things may stand for something other than themselves. That is to say, as well as being themselves, they are symbols of some bigger idea or general truth.

Symbols are especially important in poetry. A poem uses symbolism to lift it from the literal level to a higher or broader level of meaning. For example, the following poem by William Blake can be read as a simple poem about a rose which has a worm in it, or the rose can be seen as a symbol of innocence and beauty corrupted by evil.

**The Sick Rose**
O Rose, thou art sick!
The invisible worm
That flies in the night,
In the howling storm,

Has found out thy bed
Of crimson joy,
And his dark secret love
Does thy life destroy.

Symbolism also has an important role to play in allegories. An allegory is a kind of story that is based on a set of symbols, so that as well as working as a simple story, it tells you something about life in general. See **allegory**.

## symbols

Many words used in scientific writing have shortened forms called symbols. Chemical elements and formulas have symbols, for example *C* for *carbon* and *CO$_2$* for *carbon dioxide*. Units of measurement also have symbols, for example *m* for *metre* and *kg* for *kilogram*.

Unlike some abbreviations, symbols are <u>never</u> written with full stops.

For information on chemical elements and their symbols, see the periodic table at APPENDIX D. For more on the symbols of units of measurement, see APPENDIX C.

## sympathetically

Note the ending of this word. See **-ally**.

## sympathy for / sympathy with

When **sympathy** is followed by **for** it means something quite different from **sympathy** followed by **with**.

To have **sympathy for** someone is to have concern for them, to feel sorry for them.

To have **sympathy with** a point of view or attitude is to have the same point of view or attitude, to feel the same way about something.

## synonyms

are words with the same meaning, such as *start* and *begin*. You could say either:
*I'll start reading today.*
or
*I'll begin reading today.*
It would mean exactly the same thing. So *start* and *begin* are synonyms in that context.

Yet it's hard to find words which are synonyms in every context. Often they belong to a slightly different style of language. For example, the word *commence* means the same as *start* and *begin*, yet it has a more formal feeling about it. You would be unlikely to say:
*The dog commenced chasing the cat.*

Synonyms have to be chosen for the particular context. A thesaurus will help you to find synonyms, but you should always check whether they suit the context. For more about using synonyms to vary your style, see WRITING WORKSHOP p 28.

**Synonyms** contrast with **antonyms**.

## synopsis

A **synopsis** is an overview of a piece of writing. It means "taking it all in together in a glance". The plural of synopsis is **synopses**, pronounced to rhyme with *seas*.

A synopsis summarises the contents of the writing, giving an outline of the plot, if it is fiction, or of the topics covered, if it is nonfiction.

Compare **summary**.

## syntax

**Syntax** is a technical word used by linguists to mean "the way words are placed together to form sentences". (We sometimes use the word *grammar* for this meaning.) But **syntax** refers particularly to the *order* of words in sentences. For example, to say *I will tomorrow go* is peculiar syntax. *I will go tomorrow* would be the normal word order.

## synthesis

The plural of this word is spelled **syntheses** with the last syllable sounding like *seas*. For more about words like this, see **-is**.

## syphon

See **siphon/syphon**.

## syrup / sirup

These are equally good ways of spelling this word. **Syrup** is more common than **sirup**, although **sirup** may be found occasionally in the USA. For more about words like this, see **i/y**.

## systematically

Note the ending of this word. See **-ally**.

# t as a silent letter

The letter t is written but not sounded in a number of words we've borrowed from the French. For example:

> *ballet*   *beret*   *bouquet*   *cabaret*   *chalet*   *crochet*
> *depot*   *debut*   *haricot*   *parquet*   *sachet*   *valet*

The t is still usually silent when you add inflections like -ed and -ing to these words:

> crocheted   *is pronounced*   *crow-shayed*
> debuting                      *day-boo-ing*

For more about silent letters, see **silent letters**.

# tableau

The plural of this word may be spelled **tableaus** or **tableaux**. For more about words like this, see **-e(a)u**.

# taboo / tabu

These are equally good spellings for this word.

**Taboo** is the more common spelling, and the more natural spelling in English. Its plural is spelled **taboos**. When you add -ed and -ing the spellings are **tabooed** and **tabooing**.

**Tabu** is the Tongan spelling for this word. It was from the Tongan language that the word came into English.

For more about words like this, see **-o**.

# taboo words

A **taboo word** is one which people avoid using because it will give offence. Swear words are the most common example of taboo words, usually because they confront people with some aspect of life which they consider distasteful or unpleasant, such as excrement. A number of four-letter words are in this field. But after all we do have to talk about unpleasant things from time to time so we do need acceptable words for them. To avoid giving offence we may use very formal words (like *excrement*).

Taboo words change from one society to another and from one generation to another. For example, there are a whole set of swear words that are based on the notion that it is forbidden to talk about sex. Books were banned and people put in jail because they dared to use these words. Now society has changed and such words are not as widely condemned as they used to be.

Society is not uniform in its attitude to taboo words. Expressions which one person uses as part of general, if colloquial, language can be regarded as "improper" by another. A speaker may use taboo words with the deliberate intention of shocking the listener, but the listener's reaction cannot be assumed, since "tabooedness" is relative. It may be quite offensive to say you are "pissed off" to one person, and yet perfectly natural to say it to someone else. You should be careful to get the effect you intend.

The point about taboo words is that they can provoke powerful and irrational reactions. Mere words should not have this power over us.

See also **swear words** and **four-letter words**.

### tabu
See **taboo/tabu**.

### tail / tale
These words sound the same but mean different things.

Some animals have **tails**.

A **tale** is a story, as in *a fairy tale*.

### tailor
Note the ending of this word. See **-er/-or**.

### tale
See **tail/tale**.

### talk / torque
These words sound the same but mean different things.

To **talk** to someone is to speak to them.

**Torque** is a special term in physics and motoring. It is a measurement of force in engines that relates to rotating power, and so to the power of the motor vehicle.

### tangible
Note the ending of this word. See **-able/-ible**.

### target
Note that you don't add another t when you add the endings -ed and -ing to this verb as in **targeted, targeting**:
*They targeted the bank for their robbery.*

For more about words like this, see **doubling of last letter**.

### tassel
For information about whether to double the l when you add endings like -ed or -ing, see **-l-/-ll-**.

## tattoo

The plural of this word is spelled **tattoos**.

When you add **-ed**, **-ing** and **-ist** the spellings are **tattooed**, **tattooing** and **tattooist**.

For more about words like this, see **-o**.

## tautology

is saying the same thing over again in another way. It adds nothing to the message, and is unnecessary:

*The two twins have returned back to the team . . .*

Here the sports commentator is uttering more than one tautology. Twins by definition come in "twos", and if you return, you "come back". The sentence doubles up on both points.

You'll hear tautologies on the lips of many people who have to give on-the-spot interviews. It's the way they manage to keep talking when they really have nothing more to say.

See also **redundancy**.

## taw

See **tore/taw/tor**.

## taxi

The plural of this word is spelled **taxis**. When you add **-ed** the spelling is **taxied**. When you add **-ing** the spelling may be either **taxiing** or, less commonly, **taxying**.

## tea / tee

These words sound the same but mean different things.

**Tea** is a kind of hot drink, made by soaking part of a plant, usually the leaves, in boiling water.

A **tee** is a small support for the ball that you use in golf.

## teach

See **learn/teach**.

## team / teem

These words sound the same but their meanings are different.

A **team** is a group of people who work together, particularly in sport. You can also have a team of animals, like *a bullock team*.

To **teem** is to rain very hard. It can also mean "to swarm with small animals":

*This river teems with fish.*

## tear / tier

These words can sound the same but mean different things.

A **tier** is one level in a series of levels:

*The wedding cake had three tiers in it.*

A **tear** rolls out of your eye when you feel sad. Note that this **tear** rhymes with *dear*. When it rhymes with *pair*, **tear** means "to rip or pull apart".

## teaspoonful

The plural of this word is **teaspoonfuls**, though you may sometimes find the plural **teaspoonsful**. For more about words like this, see **-ful**.

## technical writing

is writing which is meant for the specialists in a particular subject, such as science, engineering, economics and linguistics. You'll know it by the technical words and phrases it uses, which may not make sense to you. It is not necessarily that the writer is being deliberately difficult. Rather the writer assumes you have the specialised knowledge that goes with the technical words.

For example, a scientist might write:
*There was excess sodium chloride in its nutrients . . .*
This assumes that you know some basic chemistry and biology. The sentence only says that there was too much salt in the food. If the writer had put it in nontechnical language like that, you would assume it was meant for the general reader. For the scientist there are many kinds of salt, so it is important in scientific writing to specify whether you mean sodium chloride or not.

Writers need to be able to adjust the technicality of their language for their audience. For more about this, see WRITING WORKSHOP pp 31–2.

## technologically

Note the ending of this word. See **-ally**.

## tee

See **tea/tee**.

## teem

See **team/teem**.

## teeth / teethe

These words are related but mean different things.

**Teeth** is the plural of **tooth**. It is pronounced to rhyme with *beneath*.

To **teethe**, rhyming with *breathe*, is to grow teeth.

## tele-

is a Greek prefix meaning "far, over a distance". You'll find it in words such as:

telegram    (message sent from a distance)
telephone   (instrument for transmitting sound over a distance)
telephoto   (lens for taking photographs at long distance)
telescope   (instrument which gives you a long distance view)
television  (device for receiving visual material transmitted over a distance)

Some tele- words are blended words, for example:
telecast    (television + broadcast)
teledex     (telephone + index)
For more about this, see **portmanteau words**.

## tempo

The plural of this word may be spelled **tempos** or **tempi**. For more about words like this, see **-o**.

## temporary

Note the ending of this word. See **-ary/-ery/-ory**.

## tenor

Note the ending of this word. See **-er/-or**.

## tense

We are able to show in English whether events have happened (past time), are happening (present time), or will happen (future time). We do this in one of two ways:

1 by changing the verb a little: *sing, sang, sung;* or adding an ending to it: *walk, walks, walked.*
2 by bringing in an auxiliary (or helping) verb: *I will sing.*

The examples above are the simple tenses — present, past and future. There are other more complicated forms of each which we call compound tenses:

| | | |
|---|---|---|
| *I am walking* | *I have walked* | *I have been walking* |
| *I was walking* | *I had walked* | *I had been walking* |
| *I will be walking* | *I will have walked* | *I will have been walking* |

Compound tenses use the auxiliaries *have* and *be,* and the present or past participles. See **participles**.

These tenses express different ways of looking at the action of the verb. We call this "aspect". See **aspect**.

In other languages such as French and Italian, some of the compound tenses are made without auxiliaries, just by adding extra endings to the verb.

## terminus

The plural of this word may be spelled **terminuses** or **termini**. For more about words like this, see **-us**.

## terrible

Note the ending of this word. See **-able/-ible**.

## -th

This is an old English suffix which we still have in words such as:

| | | | | | |
|---|---|---|---|---|---|
| breadth | death | depth | faith | filth | growth |
| health | length | strength | truth | wealth | width |

It was used to turn verbs into nouns (*grow* into *growth*), and adjectives into nouns (*warm* into *warmth*). But the adjective we know has often changed a bit, for example:

| | | |
|---|---|---|
| breadth | *is related to* | broad |
| depth | | deep |
| length | | long |
| width | | wide |

Note that *height* (related to *high*) does not end in -th, though you might expect it to. In fact it did many centuries ago. But *height, weight* and *drought* have all lost the -h from the -th they once had.

## than

Sometimes people use *than what* when a simple **than** is all that's needed:

*They always stay longer than what I do.*

The sentence above is not acceptable usage. Write instead:

*They always stay longer than I do.*

For more information, see **different to/from/than**.

## that

See **so/that**, **this/that/these/those** and **which/that**.

## that / which / who / whom / whose

These words are all *relative pronouns*. That is, they are the words which begin adjectival clauses, and they may be either the subject or the object of that clause:

*I danced with a man who danced with a girl who danced with the Prince of Wales.*

*Where's the chocolate that you bought this morning?*

For more information on these, and advice on which one to use, see **relative pronouns**.

Note that these words are not always used as relative pronouns. **Which, who, whom** and **whose** can be used to introduce questions. See **interrogative pronouns**.

The word **that** is also used as a *demonstrative*:

*that centipede*

*that is the one*

See **demonstratives**.

Sometimes it is a *conjunction* introducing noun clauses:

*I know that you're coming.*

See **conjunctions**.

## the

**The** is the definite article in English. It contrasts with the indefinite articles such as *a* and *an*. For more information, see **definite articles**.

## theatre / theater

These are equally good spellings for this word. **Theatre** is the usual spelling in the UK. **Theater** is the usual spelling in the USA. For more about words like this, see **-re/-er**.

## thee

See **thou/thee/thy/thine**.

## their

See **they/them/their/theirs/themselves**.

## theirs

See **they/them/their/theirs/themselves**.

## them

See **they/them/their/theirs/themselves**.

## themselves

See **they/them/their/theirs/themselves**.

### there / their / they're

These words sound the same but mean different things.

**Their** is the possessive form of the pronoun **they**:
*They have their belongings.*
Note that e comes before i in this word. See **i before e**.

**There** means "in that place":
*I found my keys there.*

**They're** is a form of *they are*:
*They're going to visit us today.*
See **contractions**.

### therefore

is a connecting word meaning "as a result or consequently". You use it to show that one statement is a consequence of another. For example:
*My grandfather is rather hard of hearing. You must therefore talk a bit louder than usual when you meet him.*

**Therefore** makes a strong connection from one step to the next in an argument. You use it to stress that the conclusion you're drawing arises logically out of whatever you have just said. Make sure you don't use **therefore** too often, out of sheer habit, or it will lose this force in your writing.

For more about connecting words in argument, see **link words** and **conjunctions**.

### these

See **this/that/these/those**.

### thesis

The plural of this word is spelled **theses**, with the **-ses** pronounced like *seas*. We use this unusual spelling because **thesis** came into English from Greek, and **theses** is its Greek plural. For more about words like this, see **-is**.

### they / them / their / theirs / themselves

These personal pronouns are all third person and plural.

**They** is in the subjective case (it is the subject of a verb):
*They rang me.*
See **subjective case**.

**Them** is in the objective case:
*I talked to them.*
See **objective case**.

**Their** is the personal pronoun in the possessive case. It is sometimes called a possessive adjective:
*This is their country.*

**Theirs** is the possessive pronoun:
*This country is theirs.*

**Themselves** is the reflexive pronoun:
*Cats are always washing themselves.*

For more information, see **case, personal pronouns, possessive pronouns** and **reflexive pronouns**.

Note that these pronouns are sometimes used when you want to avoid using a pronoun that indicates the sex of the person you're referring to. For more information about this, see **non-sexist language**.

### they'd

is a short form of **they had** or **they would**. See **contractions**.

### they'll

is a short form of **they shall** or **they will**. See **contractions**.

### they're

is a short form of **they are**. See **contractions**. See also **there/their/they're**.

### they've

is a short form of **they have**. See **contractions**.

### thief

The plural of this word is spelled **thieves**. For more about words like this, see **-f/-v-**.

### thine

See **thou/thee/thy/thine**.

### third person

Pronouns such as *she, him* and *themselves* are said to be in the *third person*, which is the person being spoken about. (**First person** is the one speaking, **second person** is the one spoken to.) For more information, see **person**.

### this / that / these / those

These words are *demonstratives*, or words that point something out. **This** and **these** point to things that are close, **that** and **those** to things more distant:

*This book here, not that one over there.*

Sometimes the demonstratives act as adjectives, with nouns following them:

*this book/those people*

On other occasions, they act as pronouns, standing in place of nouns:

*I like this, so you can have that.*

For more information, see **demonstratives**.

### this kind

**Kind** is a singular collective noun, so it takes singular agreement. *This kind of apple* is an acceptable use; *these kind of apple* is not.

On the other hand, the whole phrase may be used in the plural:

*These kinds of apples.*

For more information, see **agreement** and **collective nouns**.

### thorax

The plural of this word may be spelled **thoraxes** or **thoraces**.

**Thoraxes** follows the normal English pattern for making plurals – simply add -es (or -s).

**Thoraces** is the Latin plural for this word. It is sometimes used because **thorax** came into English from Latin.

Note that the adjective from thorax is always spelled **thoracic**, meaning "relating to the thorax".

For more about words like this, see **-x**.

### those

See **this/that/these/those**.

### thou / thee / thy / thine

These pronouns are old-fashioned forms of *you* used in the singular.
thou = you (as the subject): *Thou art (= are) an ass, sir!*
thee = you (as the object): *I will follow thee.*
thy = your (personal pronoun): *Give me thy hand.*
thine = yours (possessive pronoun): *My heart is thine.*

These pronouns lasted in poetic writing long after they were replaced by *you* in ordinary speech and prose; and even today, they are still heard in some churches being used to address God:
*Hallowed be Thy name.*

### thrash / thresh

These words look similar but they mean different things.

To **thrash** someone is to beat them soundly as a punishment. It also means "to defeat someone easily":
*I know that you'll thrash me at tennis.*

To **thresh** is to separate grain or seeds from cereal plants, by beating or with a machine.

### threw / through

These words sound the same but mean different things.

**Threw** is the past tense of the verb **throw**, to fling or send something through the air:
*He threw the ball over the fence.*

The most common meaning of the preposition **through** is "in at one place and out at the other":
*The train went through the tunnel.*

### thriller

A **thriller** is a novel or a film which deals with crime or mysterious events, usually in an exciting and sensational way. The plot is important in a thriller because it relies on suspense and surprise. We never know what is going to happen next, or why.

Closely related to the thriller are the detective story and the spy story. In these the plot is often complicated with numerous sub-plots, usually intended to distract the reader and create suspense. This leads up to the resolution where all is explained.

### throne / thrown

These words sound the same but have different meanings.

A **throne** is the special chair used by a king, queen or bishop on important occasions.

**Thrown** is a past form of the verb **throw**. It is the past participle: *My ball was thrown over the fence by my brother.*

### through

See **threw/through**.

### thus

is a connecting word with two meanings:
1 "in this way":
*You use the equipment thus: first blow into the bag . . .*
2 "as a result of this":
*His head was aching and thus he couldn't take part in the discussion.*

Make sure you don't overuse **thus** in your writing, or it will lose its meaning for the reader.

See **link words** and **conjunctions** for more words of this kind.

### thy

See **thou/thee/thy/thine**.

### thyme

See **time/thyme**.

### tick / tic

These words sound the same but have different meanings.

A **tick** is a small mark (✓) used to show that something has been done correctly. To **tick** is to make the clicking sounds of a clock. A **tick** is also a tiny blood-sucking creature whose poison can paralyse animals.

**Tic** is the medical word for a sudden twitching in the muscles of your body, in particular your face.

### tie

Note that when you add -ing to this word, it is usual to drop the e and change the i to y: **tying**. You may sometimes see the spelling **tieing**, usually when this means "having the same score".

For more about words like this, see **i→y**.

### tier

See **tear/tier**.

### tight / tightly

**Tightly** is an adverb:
*Screw the lid on tightly.*

**Tight** is an adjective:
*What a tight jacket he's wearing!*

Note that **tight** can also be an adverb:
*Screw the lid on tight.*
It is mostly used in this way in informal language.

## tilde (~)

The **tilde** is an accent used in writing languages such as Spanish and Portuguese. It shows that certain letters have a special sound.

In Spanish the tilde is used with n̲, as in the word *señor*. It indicates that the n̲ should be pronounced as if it were followed by a y̲. Without the tilde the n̲ would sound like the n̲ in *tenor*.

In Portuguese the tilde is used with a̲ (and occasionally o̲) to show that the vowel has a nasal sound.

For more about accents in English, see **accents**.

## till / until

These words are both correct.

In more formal writing you usually use **until**:
*India was under British control until the Government announced in 1947 its intention to withdraw from the scene and leave India to settle its problems by itself.*

If you were to use **till** in this sentence, it would sound more informal.

Note that **till** shouldn't be written 'til or 'till because it is not an abbreviation of **until** but is a word in its own right.

## timber / timbre

These words look similar but have different meanings.

**Timber** is wood that has been sawn ready for building.

**Timbre** is the particular sound that an instrument or voice makes:
*The violin has a different timbre from the double bass.*
This word can sound the same as **timber** or you can pronounce the first syllable to rhyme with *jam*. On rare occasions you may find this spelled **tambre**.

## time / thyme

These words sound the same but mean different things.

**Time** is the passing of hours, days, weeks, months and years.

**Thyme** is a common garden herb.

## -tion

This is the ending of many abstract nouns in English. See **-ation** and **-ion**.

## tire / tyre

These words sound the same but have different meanings.

To **tire** is to become or make someone sleepy or weak:
*I tire easily since my illness.*
*All this strenuous exercise should tire the children.*

A **tyre** is the rubber or metal band fitted round the rim of a wheel. Note that in the USA **tyre** is usually spelled **tire**.

## titles

The way **book titles** are written is explained in WRITING WORKSHOP p 64.

To show the titles of full-length films and plays you can use underlining. The names of poems and songs are usually put in quotation marks. See **quotation marks**.

For the **titles** that go with people's names, see **forms of address**.

## titre / titer

These are equally good spellings for this word, a technical term in science. **Titre** is the usual spelling in the UK. **Titer** is the usual spelling in the USA. For more about words like this, see **-re/-er**.

## to / too / two

These words sound the same but they mean different things.

The preposition **to** expresses many things. The most common way it is used is to indicate movement in the direction of a place or person:

*Tomorrow I'm flying from London to Paris.*
*Can you walk over here to me?*

The most common meanings of the adverb **too** are "also or in addition" and "more than is required":

*I want to come too.*
*Your voice is too soft to hear.*

**Two** is a number and is a noun or an adjective.

## to be

For information on this verb, see **be**.

## toe / tow

These words sound the same but have different meanings.

People have **toes** at the end of their feet.

To **tow** a vehicle is to drag or pull it along using a rope or chain.

## tolerance

Note the ending of this word. See **-ance/-ence**.

## tomato

This is one of the few surviving English nouns ending in -o which does not form its plural by simply adding -s. The plural of this word is spelled **tomatoes**. For more about words like this, see **-o**.

## too

See **to/too/two**.

## topic sentences

are the sentences at the start of a paragraph that tell you what it's about. They are often general statements which lead on to some particular examples, or other relevant detail. The following paragraph shows you how the **topic sentence** works:

> *Whatever most people believe, Manchester does not have worse weather than London. The average rainfall in both cities is about the same. Manchester is subject to less fog . . .*

The main point of the topic sentence (underlined) is the false reputation of Manchester for bad weather. The paragraph goes on with sentences which support the topic sentence and help to detail it.

Topic sentences help the reader to understand the structure of your essay, stage by stage. They also help to remind you as a writer what your point is in each paragraph, so that you don't ramble away from it.

For examples of topic sentences in action, see WRITING WORKSHOP pp 12–13 and 48. See also **paragraphs**.

## tore / taw / tor

These words sound the same but mean different things.

**Tore** is a past form of **tear**, to pull apart or into pieces:
> *I tore my shirt on a nail.*

A **taw** is a kind of marble, or a token used in games like hopscotch.

A **tor** is a rocky outcrop or hill.

## tormenter / tormentor

These are equally good spellings for this word. For more about words like this, see **-er/-or**.

## tornado

The plural of this word may be spelled **tornados** or **tornadoes**. For more about words like this, see **-o**.

## torpedo

This is one of the few surviving English nouns ending in -o which does not form its plural by simply adding -s. The plural of this word is spelled **torpedoes**. For more about words like this, see **-o**.

## torque

See **talk/torque**.

## total

You have a choice whether or not to double the l when you add -ed and -ing to this word. See **-l-/-ll-**.

Note that when you add -ise, the -l is never doubled: **totalise**.

## tow

See **toe/tow**.

## toward / towards

These words are both correct:
*The duck came waddling toward me.*
*The duck came waddling towards me.*

You will find **towards** used more often in the UK and **toward** in the USA. For more information, see **-ward/-wards**.

## towel

For information about whether to double the l when you add endings like -ed or -ing, see **-l-/-ll-**.

## tractor

Note the ending of this word. See **-er/-or**.

## traffic

Note that you add a k to make the words **trafficking, trafficked** and **trafficker**. For more about words like this, see **-c/-ck-**.

## tragedy

A **tragedy** is a kind of play which has a serious theme. It usually has a very sad ending, and the mood of the whole work is bleak and unhappy. Some of Shakespeare's greatest tragedies are *Macbeth, Hamlet,* and *King Lear.*

## tragically

Note the ending of this word. See **-ally**.

## trail / trial

These words look similar but the order of the a and i makes all the difference to the meaning.

A **trail** is a path or a track made across rough country.

A **trial** is the testing of something, especially a case to test a person's guilt or innocence in a law court.

For information about whether to double the l when you add endings like -ed or -ing to **trial**, see **-l-/-ll-**.

## trait

See **tray/trait**.

## traitor

Note the ending of this word. See **-er/-or**.

## tranquility

See **tranquillity/tranquility**.

## tranquillise / tranquillize

These are equally good spellings for this word. Note that the usual US spelling for this word is **tranquilize**. For more about words like this, see **-ise/-ize** and **-l-/-ll-**.

## tranquillity / tranquility

These are equally good spellings for this word. **Tranquillity** is the usual spelling in the UK. **Tranquility** is the usual spelling in the USA. For more about words like this, see **-l-/-ll-**.

## trans-

is a Latin prefix meaning "across or through". It helps to make new geographical adjectives, such as *trans-European*, *transcontinental* and *transpolar*. Notice that it only takes a hyphen when the second part of the word begins with a capital.

Trans- is also an element in a large set of words we have borrowed from Latin, though we aren't always aware of it as a separate prefix. For example:

| | |
|---|---|
| transfer | (move across) |
| transform | (change from one state through to another) |
| transmit | (send across distance) |
| transparent | (allowing light through) |
| transplant | (relocate from one place across to another) |

## transfer of classes

This is when you use a word as if it belonged to a different grammatical class from its usual one. You make it change its part of speech:

*James is monstering his brother again.*

Here *monster* has become a verb, though it's normally a noun. *Monster* has temporarily transferred from one grammatical class to another.

It's quite easy to transfer words from one class to another, and it has been happening all through the history of English. Shakespeare was a master at it, with examples such as:

*He dukes it well.* (The noun *duke* used as a verb.)

This means he acts like a duke. Many of Shakespeare's examples are so familiar to us that we don't think of them as transfers any more. But when a word is newly transferred from one class to another, people sometimes disapprove. Recent examples are *impact* and *interface*, nouns which are being used more and more as verbs. The process is happening all the time.

The most obvious cases of transfer are those where nouns become verbs, as in our examples above. But it also happens when adjectives become verbs, as with *to brown the meat*, or when verbs become nouns, as in *a reject* or *a transfer*. Verb participles ending in -ing, or -ed or -(e)n often become adjectives. For example, the participle from *he was fighting* becomes an adjective in *a fighting chance*. It is the same when the participle from *they had loved* moves into the phrase *a loved friend*, or when the one in *we had spoken* moves into *the spoken word*.

For more about these, see **participles**, **-ed** and **-ing**.

## transformer

Note the ending of this word. See **-er/-or**.

## transistor

Note the ending of this word. See **-er/-or**.

## transitive verbs

A **transitive verb** is one that has a direct object. You can tell a verb is transitive if you can answer the question "who?" or "what?" after it. The verbs underlined in the following sentences are all transitive:

*I closed the door.* ("door" is the object – it answers the question "You closed what?")
*It surprised everybody.*
*They dropped their books.*

**Transitive verbs** contrast with **intransitive verbs,** such as *rang* in:
*The phone rang.*

Some verbs can be used transitively or intransitively:
*He was flying a kite.* (transitive)
*The plane was flying at a low altitude.* (intransitive)

For more information, see **object**.

## transitory

Note the ending of this word. See **-ary/-ery/-ory**.

## translation

When you make a **translation** you change the words of one language into another.

A literal translation is one in which you translate a text one word at a time. This approach does not take into account the natural way things are expressed in the original language or the language into which the translation is being made. See **idioms**.

The following example of a translation from French shows you the difference between the literal English translation and a more natural (or idiomatic) version:

*Bien entendu, je le sais.* (French)
*Well understood, I it know.* (literal translation)
*Of course, I know.* (idiomatic translation)

## translator

Note the ending of this word. See **-ator**.

## transparent / translucent

These words both begin with trans- but they have different meanings.

A **transparent** substance allows light to completely pass through, so that you can see through it.

A **translucent** substance allows some light to come through but not enough to see clearly.

Compare these with an *opaque* substance which doesn't allow any light to pass through, so that you can't see through it.

## trapezium

The plural of this term from geometry may be spelled **trapeziums** or **trapezia**. For more about words like this, see **-um**.

### trauma

The plural of this word may be spelled **traumas** or **traumata**. For more about words like this, see **-a (as a singular ending)**.

### travel

For information about whether to double the l when you add endings like -ed, -ing or -er, see **-l-/-ll-**.

### tray / trait

These words can sound the same but mean different things.

A **tray** is a flat piece of wood, plastic or metal used for holding or carrying things.

A **trait** is a particular quality or characteristic that someone has:
*Being boastful is one of the bad traits of his personality.*
Note that you will sometimes hear **trait** pronounced to rhyme with *plate*.

### tread

The past forms of this verb are **trod** and **trodden**: *I trod, I have trodden.*

**Trod** is sometimes used instead of **trodden**, though this is not a common practice:
*I have trodden on your foot.*
*I have trod on your foot.*

### tri-

is a Latin prefix meaning "three". You'll find it in ordinary words like *triangle*, *tricycle* and *tripod*. And you may come across it in more technical words such as *trinomial* (in mathematics), *trichloride* (in chemistry) and *trivalve* (in biology).

Tri- is also used in words which refer to time periods, such as:
trimonthly   (appearing every three months)
triweekly    (appearing every three weeks)
triennial    (appearing every three years)
But note that something which celebrates three centuries is a *tercentenary*.

Note also that tri- is pronounced with a shorter vowel in:
trilogy     (a creative work in three parts)
Trinity     (three persons of the Christian God)
trivial     (from *trivium*, the basic three-part curriculum of medieval schools)
It is still the same prefix, though we're not so aware of it.

### trivia

This noun can be either singular or plural:
*Such trivia is of interest to me.*
*These trivia are not worth collecting.*

There is no plural *trivias*.

### trolley

The plural of this word is spelled **trolleys**. For more about words like this, see **-ey**.

### troop / troupe

These words sound the same but have different meanings.

A **troop** is an organised group of people or a gathering of animals, as in *a troop of scouts* or *a troop of monkeys*. **Troops** are a large number of soldiers.

A **troupe** is a group of entertainers, as in *a troupe of actors*.

### trousseau

The plural of this word may be spelled **trousseaus** or **trousseaux**. For more about words like this, see **-e(a)u**.

### try to / try and

There is some argument about whether you should use *and* or *to* after **try**. Some people don't like **try and** because, they argue, *try* in this situation is followed by a verb in its infinitive form which should be indicated by *to*. For example, *try and climb the mountain* should be *try to climb the mountain*. But there is no doubt that **try and** is a common expression, and widely accepted and understood.

### tsar / czar

These are equally good ways of spelling this word.

**Tsar** is the spelling closest to the Russian form of the word. You may also find the similar spelling **tzar**, though this is less common.

**Czar** is a spelling which reflects the ultimate origin of the Russian word itself: the Latin *Caesar*.

The commonly used feminine form may equally be spelled **tsarina** or **czarina**. Note, however, that strictly speaking the English spelling of the regular Russian feminine form is **tsaritsa**, which may also be spelled **czaritsa**.

### tuba / tuber

These words sound the same but have different meanings.

A **tuba** is a very low-pitched brass wind instrument.

A **tuber** is the underground stem of a plant, thickened or rounded like a potato.

### tubular

Note the ending of this word. See **-ar**.

### tunnel

For information about whether to double the l when you add endings like -ed, -ing or -er, see **-l-/-ll-**.

### turf

The plural of this word is spelled **turfs**. For more about words like this, see **-f/-v-**.

### turkey

The plural of this word is spelled **turkeys**. For more about words like this, see **-ey**.

**tutor**

Note the ending of this word. See **-er/-or**.

**two**

See **to/too/two**.

**-ty**

This is a suffix found in abstract nouns formed from adjectives, such as *cruelty* from *cruel*, *certainty* from *certain*, *loyalty* from *loyal*, and *safety* from *safe*.

Some of the nouns formed in this way come to have more concrete meanings. See for example:

casualty (a victim of accident or war)
realty  (real estate, property)
royalty (members of the royal family)
surety  (a pledge of money)

**tyre**

See **tire/tyre**.

# Uu

## u as a silent letter

The letter u is often written but not sounded when it is paired with either g or q.

It has no sound in:

  guarantee  guard  guerilla  guest  guide
  guilt      guise  guitar    guy
or in:
  catalogue  dialogue  epilogue  fatigue  fugue  intrigue
  morgue     plague    tongue    vague    vogue
In most such words, the u helps to separate the g from an e or i, and ensures that it is sounded as g (not j).

The u is also silent in:

  antique  cheque     conqueror    grotesque  mosquito  opaque
  plaque   physique   picturesque  queue      technique  unique

But in other words, the u sounds as w after g or q, as in:

  anguish   distinguish   language   linguist   penguin
and:
| adequate | aquarium | banquet | conquest | delinquent |
| equal | equator | equip | frequent | liquid |
| quality | quantity | quaver | queen | question |
| quick | quite | quote | sequel | square |
| squeeze | squirrel | | | |

For more about silent letters, see **silent letters**.


## ukulele

This is the usual spelling for this word and is the spelling of the original Hawaiian word. (In Hawaiian, it means "flea".) You may sometimes see it spelled **ukelele**.


## ulna

The plural of this word (the name for a bone in the forearm) may be spelled **ulnas** or **ulnae**. For more about words like this, see **-a (as a singular ending)**.

## ultimatum

The plural of this word may be spelled **ultimatums** or **ultimata**. For more about words like this, see **-um**.

## -um

Most words that end in -um have been borrowed from Latin. For example:

| | | | |
|---|---|---|---|
| aquarium | curriculum | gymnasium | podium |
| referendum | stadium | stratum | ultimatum |

Their plurals in Latin were made by removing the -um and replacing it with -a.

So the plural of *aquarium* was *aquaria*, of *referendum* was *referenda*, and so on.

But many of these words now make their plurals in the English way, by just adding -s to the end. For example:

aquariums    referendums    ultimatums

With a few of these words, the English plural means something different from the Latin one, when both are still used:

mediums   (the means or material for doing something, including people who claim to communicate with spirits)

media     (channels of mass communication, or artistic expression)

stadiums  (sports grounds)

stadia    (ancient units of measurement; the stages of a disease)

stratums  (levels in society)

strata    (layers of rock, or biological tissue, or the atmosphere)

The English plurals are generally for things closer to everyday life, while the Latin ones are linked with specialised fields of study.

See also **-a (as a plural ending)**.

## umlaut (¨)

This is an accent sometimes placed above the vowels a, o or u in German and some languages related to German. It shows that the vowel should be pronounced differently from the unaccented vowel. The German word *Mann* rhymes with *sun*, while *Männer* is pronounced *menner*.

This accent is only rarely used in English, mainly when a proper noun from German is written. An example is the word **Führer**, meaning "a leader" or referring particularly to Adolf Hitler.

Sometimes an extra e is added in English instead of using the umlaut. For example, the Swiss German word *müsli* has become *muesli*.

Note that while the umlaut looks the same as the dieresis, they work in different ways. See **dieresis**.

For more about accents in English, see **accents**.

## un-

is a prefix with two similar meanings.

The first meaning is simply "not", and it is the one in many words like those in the following list:

| | | | |
|---|---|---|---|
| unable | unaware | uncertain | uncomfortable |
| uncommon | unconscious | unemployed | unfit |
| unhappy | unjust | unlike | unlimited |
| untidy | unusual | unwell | unwise |

With the second meaning, un- turns a word into its opposite. You'll find it in words like:

uncover    undo    unfasten    unlock    untie    unwind

This prefix is one of the few that can pair up with other prefixes at the front of a word. You see this in cases like:

unbeknown       (un + be + known)
unforeseen      (un + fore + seen)
unpremeditated  (un + pre + meditated)

Note that un- seems to be replacing in- in words such as:

unadvisable     (inadvisable)
uncontrollable  (incontrollable)
unescapable     (inescapable)

For more about this, see **in-/un-**. See also **dis-**.

## unbent

This is the usual spelling for the past forms of **unbend**: *he unbent, he has unbent.*

You may sometimes find the spelling **unbended**, but this is less common.

For more about words like this, see **-ed/-t**.

## unconscious / subconscious

The prefixes un- and sub- can make all the difference to the meaning of these two words.

Someone who is **unconscious** has fainted or lost consciousness:
*He lay unconscious beside the wrecked car.*
**Unconscious** can also mean "not at the level of awareness":
*We often cannot remember all the information held in our unconscious mind.*
In both cases un- means "not".

Your **subconscious** is the part of your mind below consciousness or awareness:
*Your dreams reflect the state of your subconscious.*
Sub- means "under" or "beneath".

## under-

is an English prefix with three meanings:

**1** below or underneath

**2** less than normal

**3** lower in rank

The first meaning, "below or underneath" is found in many words, such as:

| underclothes | underground | undergrowth | undermine |
| underpants | underpass | underwater | |

The second meaning, "less than normal", is in words like:

| undercooked | underdone | underestimate | underfed |
| undersell | undersized | understatement | |

The third meaning, "lower in rank" is found in only a few words, such as:

| undergraduate | underofficer | undersecretary | understudy |

See also **sub-**.

## understatement

Sometimes we can achieve a particular dramatic effect by understating things rather than exaggerating. For example:

*My head ached, my heart pounded. I had stabbing pains in my side. You could say that I was a trifle unwell.*

The effect is often humorous and is popular in colloquial language.

## under way / underway

These are two ways of writing this expression. It is most common to see it written as two words in the UK, but there is no difference in meaning if you write it as one word.

## uni-

is a Latin prefix meaning "one". You'll find it in words like:

| unicorn | (mythical animal with one horn) |
| unicycle | (cycle with only one wheel, ridden by circus performers) |
| uniform | (one style of clothes worn by all members of a group) |
| unilateral | (on one side only) |

Note that in *unanimous* (of one mind or in complete agreement) this prefix is just un-.

Compare this prefix with **mono-**.

## unintelligible

Note the ending of this word. See **-able/-ible**.

## unique

Something is **unique** if it is the only one of its kind, as in *a unique ring*. You cannot say more unique or most unique when the word has this meaning, because it doesn't make sense.

These days **unique** has extended its meaning to refer to something "very, very special", as in *a unique occasion*. When the word has this meaning you can use rather, most or more with it.

Note that you should decide which meaning you want before you use this word.

## units of measurement

When writing abbreviations for units of measurement, do not use a full stop:

kilometre   km
litre          l

For more about particular measurements, see APPENDIX C. For more about writing abbreviations, see **abbreviations**.

## unless / without

**Unless** is a conjunction and **without** is a preposition. They work in different ways in a sentence although the end result, the meaning, can be the same. **Unless** must be followed by a verb, and **without** must be followed by a noun. For example, compare the following sentences:

*I won't go unless you say I can.*
*I won't go without your approval.*

It would be quite wrong to say:

*I won't go without you say I can.*

## unmistakable / unmistakeable

These are equally good spellings. See **-able/-eable**.

## unshakable / unshakeable

These are equally good spellings. See **-able/-eable**.

## until

See **till/until**.

## upper case letters

are capital letters. See **capital letters**. Compare with **lower case letters**.

## urn

See **earn/urn**.

## us

See **we/us/our/ours/ourselves**.

## -us

is the ending on a number of words borrowed from Latin. In Latin most of them made their plurals by removing the -us and replacing it with -i.

So the plural of focus      *was*   foci
                 octopus            octopi
                 stimulus           stimuli

But most words like these make their plurals in the English way now. The -es is just added on:

focuses    octopuses    platypuses    syllabuses

Note that in mathematics, the Latin plurals are still used as much as the English ones. So *radii* is as common as *radiuses*, and so on.

## usable / useable

These are equally good spellings. See **-able/-eable**.

## use

See **ewes/use/youse**. See also **utilise/use**.

## usher / usherette

The feminine ending -ette makes all the difference to the meanings of these words.

An **usher** is a person who takes people to their seats in a church or theatre.

An **usherette** is a female attendant, especially one who shows people to their seats in a theatre or cinema.

Nowadays, although it is the job that people consider most important and not the sex of the person who does it, **usherette** is still widely used. It does not seem to be losing favor.

For more about this, see **feminine word endings** and **non-sexist language**.

## uterus

The plural of this word may be spelled **uteruses** or **uteri**. For more about words like this, see **-us**.

## utilise / use

The original distinction between these words is disappearing.

Strictly speaking to **utilise** something is a formal way of saying to use it in a practical or effective way:
*We can utilise solar power to make electricity.*

Nowadays many people choose **utilise** in a context where **use** would be clearer. This has the effect of making what they say sound pretentious — why use a long word when a short word is better? It would be better to say:
*If you use your brain, you'll find the answer to the riddle.*
rather than:
*If you utilise your brain, you'll find the answer to the riddle.*

## utterance

Note the ending of this word. See **-ance/-ence**.

# Vv

### vacuum

The plural of this word may be spelled **vacuums** or **vacua**. For more about words like this, see **-um**.

### vagina

The plural of this word may be spelled **vaginas** or **vaginae**. For more about words like this, see **-a (as a singular ending)**.

### vain / vein / vane

These words sound the same but mean different things.

To be **vain** is to be conceited.

A **vein** is a blood vessel taking the blood back to the heart. Note that in **vein**, the e comes before the i. See **i before e**.

A **vane** is a flat piece of metal, or something similar, designed to move with the wind. A **weather vane** shows the direction the wind is blowing.

### vale

See **veil/vale**.

### valency / valence

These are equally good spellings for this word. **Valency** is the usual spelling in the UK. **Valence** is the usual spelling in the USA, although it is sometimes used here in compound words, such as **valence electrons**.

### valley

The plural of this word is spelled **valleys**. For more about words like this, see **-ey**.

### valuable / invaluable / valueless

These words are all linked to **value** but mean different things. They form a scale of worth.

Something **invaluable** is so precious that no value or price can be attached to it. It is not, as you might think, the opposite of **valuable**.

Something **valuable** is of great worth or value.

Something **valueless** is worthless and has no value at all. Compare **priceless**.

## vane

See **vain/vein/vane**.

## variety in writing

Writing which repeats the same words over and over again quickly becomes boring and dull. To make sure your style of writing is interesting, you should think of different ways of saying things. You can do this in several ways:

**1** Look for synonyms. There may be different words which mean pretty much the same thing. Check a thesaurus to find them, and then a dictionary, to make sure that they're the right kind of word for the particular spot.

**2** Turn the sentence around. Try making your verb a noun for a change, and rephrasing the sentence around it. Or make a noun into the verb. Either way you'll get some variety in expression. See also **-ate**, **-ion** and **-ive**.

**3** Pretend you're writing for a different reader. It might suggest different words for something which would help to vary the style. See WRITING WORKSHOP p 28.

Note that whenever you are ready to replace a word or expression with some other one, you must check:
  – that the new word blends in with others in the same sentence
and
  – that the new word still keeps up the line of argument or discussion in the sentences before and after.

Special note: There is no need to vary technical terms in your writing in science, economics, geography and so on. Technical words have to be repeated, because no other word will do. No other word means exactly the same. You can't call *sodium bisulphate*, *duodenum*, *inflation* or *catabatic winds* anything else without confusing the reader.

## vector

Note the ending of this word. It is -<u>or</u>, not -<u>er</u>, because it was borrowed straight from Latin. See **-er/-or**.

## veil / vale

These words sound the same but mean different things.

A **veil** is a piece of light transparent fabric such as one which screens a woman's face. Note that the <u>e</u> comes before the <u>i</u> in **veil**. See **i before e**.

**Vale** is an old-fashioned word for "valley".

## vein

Note that <u>e</u> comes before <u>i</u> in this word. See **i before e**. See also **vain/vein/vane**.

## vendor / vender

These are equally good spellings for this word, though **vendor** is the one used more often. For more about words like this, see **-er/-or**.

## venomous

See **poisonous/venomous**.

## ventilator

Note the ending of this word. See **-ator**.

## veranda / verandah

These are equally good spellings for this word. Choose whichever spelling you like, but make sure you use the same one throughout your work.

## verbal

For information about whether to double the l when you add endings like -ed or -ing, see **-l-/-ll-**.

## verbal nouns

See **gerunds**.

## verb phrases

**Verb phrases** are groups of words which contain a main verb as the most important word:
> *The cat must have left.*

In the sentence above *must have left* is a **verb phrase**. *Left* is the main verb while *must* and *have* are auxiliary verbs.

**Verb phrases** are also called **compound verbs**. For more information, see **verbs**.

## verbs

A **verb** is a word that tells you what someone or something is, does or feels. It is often said that a **verb** is the most important word in a sentence. Some sentences (those that express commands) may consist of verbs alone:
> *Go!*
> *Shoot!*

Verbs usually come after the subject of a sentence. Many sentences are made up of just the subject and a verb:
> *She arrived.*
> *The cat left.*

Some verbs are made up of more than one word (and are referred to as compound verbs or verb phrases):
> *She has arrived.*
> *The cat must have left.*

The last word in each case (*arrived* and *left*) is the **main verb**. The other words that help make up the full verb (*has*, *must* and *have*) are called **auxiliaries**. For more information on these, see **main verbs** and **auxiliary verbs**.

There are a number of other things to say about the way verbs are used in sentences:

For the way verbs are connected with the subject of the sentence, see **active verbs** and **passive verbs**.

For information on how verbs relate to their objects, see **intransitive verbs** and **transitive verbs**.

For information on how verbs help show the time of an action, see **tense**.

For information on how verbs are used in making statements, asking questions, giving orders and so on, see **mood**.

For some general comments on how verbs use different endings for different purposes, see **regular verbs**, **irregular verbs** and **principal parts**.

## vermin

This is a plural noun, and there is no singular form:
*Vermin have invaded the flats.*

For more about words like this, see **collective nouns**.

## verse

is another word for poetry, but it has come to mean poetry with a rather simple rhythm.

The word **verse** can also refer to a group of lines in a poem which have a particular rhyme and rhythm. The pattern in one verse is then repeated in the other verses of the poem. Another word for this meaning of verse is **stanza**.

## vertebrae

This is a plural noun:
*Five of his vertebrae were broken.*

If you want to write about only one, you use the word **vertebra**.

**Vertebra** came into English from Latin, and **vertebrae** is the Latin plural. However, the plural may also be spelled **vertebras**. See **-a (as a singular ending)**.

## vertex

The plural of this word, meaning "apex or top", may be spelled **vertexes** or **vertices**. For more about words like this, see **-x**.

## veto

The plural of this word is spelled **vetoes**. This is one of the few surviving English nouns ending in -o which do not form their plurals by simply adding -s.

When you add -ed and -ing the spellings are **vetoed** and **vetoing**.

For more about words like this, see **-o**.

## vibrator

Note the ending of this word. See **-ator**.

## vice-

is a Latin prefix meaning "in place of" or "next in rank to". You'll find it in the names of ranks and offices, including:

vice-admiral     vice-chairman     vice-marshal
vice-president     vice-principal     vice-roy

Note that this prefix has nothing to do with the ordinary word *vice*, meaning "a bad practice or habit".

### victor

Note the ending of this word. It is -or not -er, because it was borrowed straight from Latin. See **-er/-or**.

### vie

Note that you drop the e and change the i to y when you add -ing: **vying**. When you add -ed the spelling is **vied**. For more about words like this, see **i → y**.

### villain / villein

These words look similar but mean different things.

A **villain** is a wicked person. This is a rather old-fashioned word these days, unless you are talking about the **villain** in a story.

A **villein** was a member of the peasant class in the feudal system of the Middle Ages. Note that e comes before i in this word. See **i before e**.

### virtuoso

The plural of this word may be spelled **virtuosos** or **virtuosi**. For more about words like this, see **-o**.

### virus

See **germ/bacterium/virus**.

### visible

Note the ending of this word. See **-able/-ible**.

### visor / vizor

These are equally good spellings, though **visor** is more common than **vizor**. Note the ending. It is -or not -er, because it was borrowed straight from French. See **-er/-or**.

### vocabulary

is a collective word for words. In writing you need a much wider vocabulary than you use in talking. This is because writing has to be more specific than speech normally is, and because you need to vary your expression.

For ideas on how to vary your expression, see **variety in writing**. For more about the different kinds of words and how they are built, see **words, complex words, compound words, affixes** and **parts of speech**.

### vocative case

The **vocative case** is used to show that you are addressing someone. English does not have a vocative case, but in some languages (such as Latin) the vocative case is shown by special endings on nouns and pronouns.

If you were translating:
   *O Julius, I salute you!*
into Latin, *Julius* would be in the vocative case. It would need the vocative ending.

For general information about case, see **case**.

### volcano

The plural of this word may be spelled **volcanos** or **volcanoes**. For more about words like this, see **-o**.

### volley

The plural of this word is spelled **volleys**. For more about words like this, see **-ey**.

### vowels

There are only five **vowel** letters in the English alphabet: a̱, e̱, i̱, o̱, u̱. All the others are called **consonants**.

Sometimes y̱ can be used as a **vowel** instead of a consonant as, for example, in *rhythm*.

### vulgar

Note the ending of this word. See **-ar**.

### vulva

The plural of this word may be spelled **vulvas** or **vulvae**. For more about words like this, see **-a (as a singular ending)**.

## w as a silent letter

The letter <u>w</u> is written but not sounded at the beginning of words like:

wreck    wring    wrist    write    wrong

Note also that it is always silent in *sword* (though not in any other words where it is paired with <u>s</u>, such as *swallow, swell, switch, swoop* and *swollen*).

For more about silent letters, see **silent letters**.

## wagon / waggon

These are equally good spellings for this word, though **wagon** is closer to the original Dutch word.

## wail / whale

These words sound the same but have different meanings.

To **wail** is to give a long sad cry or to cry continuously.

A **whale** is a very large mammal that lives in the sea.

## waist / waste

These words sound the same but they mean different things.

Your **waist** is the part of your body between your ribs and hips.

To **waste** something is to use it up or spend it without much result:

*Try not to waste too much money on cheap gimmicks.*

## wait / weight

These words sound the same but they have different meanings.

To **wait** is to stay or rest until something happens:
*Please wait until the doctor is ready to see you.*

**Weight** is how heavy something is. Your **weight** is how heavy you are.

### wait on / wait for

There is a difference in meaning between **wait on** and **wait for**. The preposition which follows **wait** makes all the difference.

To **wait on** someone is to act as a servant to them, particularly by serving meals to them.

To **wait for** someone is to stop so that someone else can catch up.

People sometimes use **wait on** to mean **wait for**. For example:
*We are waiting on Frank. He's always late.*
But this has a colloquial or informal flavor.

### waste

See **waist/waste**.

### watt

See **what/watt**.

### wander / wonder

These words look similar but have different meanings.

To **wander** (rhymes with *yonder*) is to go about with no definite aim or fixed course:
*I watched him wander about the garden, pulling out an odd weed here and there.*

To **wonder** (rhymes with *under*) is to think about something with curiosity or surprise:
*I wonder why she decided to change schools.*

### war / wore

These words sound the same but have different meanings.

**War** is any fighting or conflict between countries.

**Wore** is the past tense of the verb **wear**, to carry or have on your body:
*I wore a red dress to the disco.*

### -ward / -wards

Both these endings help to show the direction in which something is going, for example:

| | |
|---|---|
| backward(s) | going back |
| homeward(s) | going home |
| westward(s) | going west |

The trend in the UK is to use -ward when the word is an adjective, and -wards when it is an adverb. For example:
*a backward step* (adjective)
*We stepped backwards.* (adverb)
This difference holds for all the words in the following list:

| | | | |
|---|---|---|---|
| backward(s) | downward(s) | eastward(s) | homeward(s) |
| inward(s) | northward(s) | outward(s) | southward(s) |
| upward(s) | westward(s) | | |

Note however that *forward* is much more common than *forwards*, for both adverb and adjective. So you'd write:
> *a forward step* (adjective)

and
> *We stepped forward.* (adverb)

Note also that *towards* is much more common than *toward* in the UK. It is actually a preposition (neither adverb nor adjective):
> *We stepped towards the river.*

## ware

See **wear/where/ware**.

## warn / worn

These words sound the same but mean different things.

To **warn** is to tell someone of possible danger:
> *They warned us that the road was flooded.*
> *Flashing lights warn of roadworks ahead.*

Something is **worn** if it is shabby or damaged from frequent use, as in *a worn bedspread*. **Worn** is also a past form of the verb **wear**:
> *I have worn the same coat for four winters.*

## was / were

are forms of the verb *to be* in the past tense. For more information, see the entry at **be**.

## wasn't

is a short form of **was not**. See **contractions**.

## wave / waive

These words sound the same but mean different things.

To **wave** is to move up and down or from side to side, as in *to wave a flag* or *to wave your hand*.

To **waive** is to decide not to insist on something that is your right:
> *He waived his claim to be the next king.*

## way / weigh / whey

These words sound the same but have different meanings.

A **way** of doing something is the manner or fashion in which you do it:
> *Are you sure that's the right way to ride a skateboard?*

**Way** can also mean "direction":
> *You should go that way.*

To **weigh** something is to measure how heavy it is:
> *The greengrocer weighed the apples on the scales.*

Note that e comes before i in **weigh**. See **i before e**.

**Whey** is the watery part of milk separated from the curd, formed in cheese-making.

## we / us / our / ours / ourselves

These personal pronouns are all first person and plural.

**We** is in the <u>subjective</u> case (it is the subject of a verb):
*We heard Tony.*
See **subjective case**.

**Us** is in the <u>objective</u> case:
*Tony heard us.*
See **objective case**.

**Our** is the personal pronoun in the <u>possessive</u> case. It is sometimes called a possessive adjective:
*Tony heard our car.*

**Ours** is the possessive pronoun:
*The car is ours.*

**Ourselves** is the reflexive pronoun:
*We heard ourselves.*

For more information, see **case, personal pronouns, possessive pronouns** and **reflexive pronouns**.

## weak / week

These words sound the same but have different meanings.

To be **weak** is to be feeble or frail.

A **week** is seven days.

## wear / where / ware

These words sound the same but they have different meanings.

To **wear** is to carry or have something on your body, as in *to wear a hat.*

**Where** asks the question "at what place?":
*Where has my gnome gone to?*

We usually use **ware** as part of a combination word. It is a particular kind of manufactured article that you can buy, such as *silverware, tinware* or *software*. The word **wares** means "things for sale".

## weather / whether / wether

These words sound the same but have different meanings.

The **weather** is sunshine or rain.

**Whether** is a word which introduces the first of two alternatives. For example:
*I do not know whether to come or to go.*

A **wether** is a sheep. In particular it is a ram castrated when young.

## weave

When you use this verb in writing about textiles, the past forms are **wove** and **woven**:
*They wove a delicate pattern into the tapestry.*
*The shirt was woven of pure silk.*

When you use **weave** to mean "to follow a winding path", you could also use **wove**, but the past form is more commonly **weaved**:

*She weaved a path through the crowd at the fete.*

## we'd

**We'd** is a short form of **we had**:
*We'd better do this immediately.*
**We'd** is also a short form of **we would**:
*We'd go if it was fine.*
See **contractions**.

## week

See **weak/week**.

## weigh

See **way/weigh/whey**.

## weight

See **wait/weight**.

## weights

For information about weights and their abbreviations, see APPENDIX C.

## weird

Note that e̱ comes before i̱ in this word. See **i before e**.

## we'll

is a short form of **we shall** or **we will**. See **contractions**.

## went

**Went** is the past tense of the verb *to go*. See **go**.

## we're

is a short form of **we are**. See **contractions**.
*We're ready now.*

## were

See **was/were**.

## were / whirr

These words sound the same but have different meanings.

**Were** is a past tense of the verb *to be*:
*We were all different then.*

Something **whirrs** if it moves so fast that it makes a low humming sound:
*The insects whirred as they beat their wings.*

Note that this word can also be spelled **whir**.

## weren't

is a short form of **were not**. See **contractions**.

## werewolf

The plural of this word is spelled **werewolves**. For more about this plural spelling, see **-f/-v-**.

The word **werewolf** comes from Old English, where *wer* means "man". You may also sometimes find the word spelled **werwolf**, without the second e̲. This was a medieval spelling.

## western

A **western** is a novel or a film which is based on the "cowboys and Indians" stories of the American Wild West. In this setting you will often find the pioneer town (representing civilisation) opposed to the Indians and Nature (presented as hostile elements). In this kind of story there are usually goodies and baddies, and the goodies finally win.

## wet / whet

These words sound the same but have different meanings.

Water is **wet**.

To **whet** a knife is to sharpen it. If something **whets** your appetite then it sharpens your hunger.

## wether

See **weather/whether/wether**.

## we've

is a short form of **we have**. See **contractions**.

## whale

See **wail/whale**.

## wharf

The plural of this word may be spelled **wharfs** or **wharves**. For more about words like this, see **-f/-v-**.

## what / watt

These words sound the same but have different meanings.

**What** is a word that introduces a question:
  *What bird is that?*
For more information, see **interrogative pronouns**.

A **watt** is a unit of power in the SI system. (See APPENDIX C.) The watt was named after James Watt, the man who invented the steam engine.

## where

See **wear/where/ware**.

## whereabouts

As a noun, **whereabouts** is always plural and so takes a plural form of the verb:
*His whereabouts are unknown.*
**Whereabouts** can also be used as a conjunction:
*I don't know whereabouts in the world we are.*
And it can be used as an adverb that introduces questions:
*Whereabouts did you last see your pen?*

## whether

See **weather/whether/wether**.

## whey

See **way/weigh/whey**.

## which

See **that/which/who/whom/whose**.

## which / that

These are equally good alternatives in sentences such as:
*The bus which goes to the station.*
*The bus that goes to the station.*

For further information on their use, see **relative pronouns**.

## which / witch

These words sound the same but have different meanings.

A **witch** is the female equivalent of a wizard.

**Which** is a pronoun that introduces a question:
*Which witch did you like best?*

For more information, see **interrogative pronouns**.

## while / wile

These words sound the same but have different meanings.

A **wile** is a cunning trick. It is a rather old-fashioned word, although the adjective from it, **wily**, is still well-known.

**While** is a conjunction meaning "during the time that":
*While I cook dinner you can tell me the news.*
**While** is also a noun meaning "a space of time":
*He was here for a long while.*

## whine / wine

These words sound the same but have different meanings.

When animals like dogs **whine**, they make a noise that means they are unhappy.

**Wine** is an alcoholic drink that is made from grapes.

## whinge

When you add **-ed** or **-ing** the spellings are **whinged, whingeing**.
For more about words like this, see **-e**.

## whirr

See **were/whirr**.

## whisky / whiskey

These are equally good spellings for this word.

**Whisky** is the standard spelling for the drink made in Scotland and England. Its plural is **whiskies**.

**Whiskey** is the standard spelling for the drink made in Ireland and the USA. Its plural is **whiskeys**.

## whiz / whizz

These are equally good spellings for this word. Choose whichever you like, but make sure you use the same spelling throughout your work.

## who

See **that/which/who/whom/whose**.

## who / whom / whose

These words are all **relative pronouns**.

**Who** is in the <u>subjective</u> case:
*The teacher who saw me*

**Whom** is in the <u>objective</u> case:
*The teacher whom I saw*

**Whose** is in the <u>possessive</u> case:
*The teacher whose car I saw*

For more information, see **relative pronouns** and **case**.

## whoever / whomever

These words are relative pronouns and differ only in their case. **Whoever** is in the <u>subjective</u> case and stands for the subject of the verb:
*Whoever turns up should get a prize.*

**Whomever** is in the <u>objective</u> case:
*I'll give one to whomever turns up.*
Note that **whomever** is not very common these days. It's generally acceptable to use **whoever** in all cases.

For more information, see **case** and **relative pronouns**.

## whole

See **hole/whole**.

## who'll

is a short form of **who will** or **who shall**. See **contractions**.

## wholly

See **holy/wholly/holey**.

## whom

See **that/which/who/whom/whose**. See also **who/whom/whose**.

### who's / whose

These words sound the same but mean different things.

**Who's** is a short form of **who is** or **who has**:
*Who's ready for sweets?*
For more information, see **contractions**.

**Whose** is a word which introduces a question:
*Whose car is that?*

For more information, see **interrogative pronouns**.

### whose

See **that/which/who/whom/whose**. See also **who/whom/whose**.

### who've

is a short form of **who have**. See **contractions**.

### widow / widower

A **widow** is a woman whose husband has died, and a **widower** is
a man whose wife has died. In Old English there were two
words, *widowa* for a man whose wife had died, and *widewe* for a
woman whose husband had died. These both became **widow**.
But in Middle English an -er ending was added to **widow** for
the man whose wife had died. So there are now two words,
**widow** (female) and **widower** (male).

### wife

The plural of this word is spelled **wives**. For more about words
like this, see **-f/-v-**.

### wile

See **while/wile**.

### wilful / willful

These are equally good spellings for this word. **Wilful** is the
usual spelling in the UK. **Willful** is the usual spelling in the
USA.

### will

See **shall/will**.

### will've

is a short form of **will have**. See **contractions**.

### wily

See **while/wile**.

### wind

This word has two different meanings and two different
pronunciations to match them.

To **wind** is to change direction many times or to turn or twist
around. **Wind** in this sense rhymes with *kind*:
*This road winds a lot.*

When **wind** refers to moving air, it rhymes with *tinned*.

## wine

See **whine/wine**.

## wiry / wirey

These are equally good spellings. See **-y/-ey**.

## -wise

is an English suffix meaning "in the manner or way of". You'll find it in words like:

clockwise    (moving in a circle like the hands of a clock)
lengthwise   (going by length)

People also use -wise in a slightly different way to create new words on the spur of the moment. For example:

*Timewise he's hopeless; fashionwise he knows his business.*

Here the words with -wise help to state a topic quickly. Though it's done quite often in speaking, it's felt to be informal, so it would be best to avoid it in your essay writing.

## witch

See **which/witch**.

## woeful

You may sometimes find this word spelled **woful**, though **woeful** is used more often. For more about words like this, see **-e**.

## wolf

The plural of this word is spelled **wolves**. For more about words like this, see **-f/-v-**.

## woman

See **lady/woman**.

## wonder

See **wander/wonder**.

## won't

is a short form of **will not**. See **contractions**.

## wood / would

These words sound the same but have different meanings.

**Wood** is the hard substance that the trunk and branches of a tree are made of.

**Would** is an auxiliary verb, so you will always find it used with another verb:

*I would like to help you.*
*I would have helped you if you'd asked me.*

## woollen / woolen

These are equally good spellings for this word. **Woollen** is the usual spelling in the UK. **Woolen** is the usual spelling in the USA.

## wordbreaks

When the word you want to write is too long for the rest of the line, you can often divide it into two, and put the second part on the next line. You simply put a hyphen after the first part to show that there's more to come on the next line.

### Where to break words

It's important to divide words without misleading your reader. Don't for example divide *mother* into *moth-er*! Some of the guiding rules are:

1 Don't divide words of less than six letters.
2 Don't divide words of one syllable.
3 Try to have at least three letters of the word on each line.
4 Don't separate vowels which are part of the same syllable. For example, *crea-ture* is fine, but *cre-ature* is not.
5 Try to have a consonant at the beginning of the second part — except when it's misleading, as with a word like *dra-wing*.

## word order

In English, getting the words of a sentence in the right order is important. For example, the normal position for the subject of a sentence is before the verb:

subject    verb
*You       will go*

Changing the order of the words turns the statement into a question:

*Will       you go?*

There are some adverbs too, like *hardly* and *scarcely*, that change the usual order of words in a sentence:

*Scarcely had you gone when . . .*

And words like *only*, which are used to emphasise other words in a sentence, must be carefully placed or they will have the wrong effect. For more information, see **hardly**, **scarcely** and **only**.

## words

It is very difficult to define what a **word** is.

We could say that a word is a string of letters that always has spaces before and after it in a sentence: *cat, claustrophobia, up-to-date*. This definition would also include items like *NUT, a.m., NATO*. Many people would object that these are not words but abbreviations. And is *National Union of Teachers* really four words? Or is it just one? And what about *trade union* — is it two words or one?

People also disagree over whether *I'm* is one word or two. Our "simple" definition would force us to say that it's only one word. We would have to say, too, that *up-to-date* was one word with hyphens but three words if someone wrote it without the hyphens.

Even if everyone agreed on what a word looked like in a sentence, the meaning of *word* would still cause problems. Sometimes, for instance, we talk about the two words *child* and *children*; on other occasions we say that *child* and *children* are two forms (singular and plural) of the same word. Similarly, we'd probably agree that *gipsy* and *gypsy* are two spellings of the "same word"; but what would we say about *preventive* and *preventative*? Are they two spellings of the same word, or two different words?

The sensible approach probably is not to attempt a firm and accurate definition that will cover all cases, but to recognise that our writing system creates borderline cases, and that we also mean different things at different times when we talk about "words".

## wore

See **war/wore**.

## worn

See **warn/worn**.

## worship

When you add -ed or -ing to this word, the p is usually doubled: **worshipped, worshipping**.

In the USA, however, the p remains single: **worshiped, worshiping**.

For more about words like this, see **doubling of last letter**.

## would

is one of a set of words called *modal verbs*. It is the past tense form of *will*. For more information, see **modal verbs**. See also **wood/would**.

## wouldn't

is a short form of **would not**. See **contractions**.

## would've

When you say **would've** it may sound like the words "would of", but in fact it is short for "would have". While it is correct to use **would've**, it is wrong to use **would of** because **would** is never followed by **of**.

See **contractions**.

## wound

This word has two different meanings and two different pronunciations to match them.

A **wound** (rhymes with *crooned*) is an injury such as a cut, burn or bruise.

**Wound** (rhymes with *sound*) is the past form of the verb **wind** (rhymes with *find*):

The path wound up the mountain.
She has wound the wool into a ball.

### wrap

See **rap/wrap**.

### wrapped

See **rapped/rapt/wrapped**.

### wrapped / wrapt

These are equally good ways of spelling the past forms of **wrap**:

I wrapped     I wrapt
I have wrapped   I have wrapt

For more about words like this, see **-ed/-t**.

### wrath / wroth

These words look similar and both have to do with anger, but there is a difference.

**Wrath** is a noun, and means "anger":
*Beware the wrath of the gods.*

**Wroth** is a much rarer word. It is an adjective, meaning "angry":
*He was wroth with you.*

### wreak

See **reek/wreak**.

### wreath / wreathe

These words look similar but have different meanings.

A **wreath** (rhymes with *teeth*) is a ring of flowers and leaves tied together.

To **wreathe** (rhymes with *seethe*) is to surround or cover something:
*Mist wreathed the valley.*
*Smiles wreathed their faces.*

### wrest

See **rest/wrest**.

### wretch

See **retch/wretch**.

### wright

See **right/write/rite/wright**.

### wring

See **ring/wring**.

## write

The past forms of this verb are **wrote** and **written**:
*I wrote, I have written.*

In earlier centuries the spelling **writ** was also used for both these senses:
*He writ her a letter.*
*A reply was writ.*

Nowadays **writ** is not used as a verb, except in the phrase **writ large**. It <u>is</u> used, however, in law as a noun, the name for a special type of order.

See also **right/write/rite/wright**.

## wrote

See **rote/wrote**.

## wroth

See **wrath/wroth**.

## wrung

See **rung/wrung**.

## wry

See **rye/wry**.

## -x

Nouns that end in <u>-ax</u>, <u>-ex</u>, <u>-ix</u>, <u>-ox</u>, <u>-ux</u> and <u>-nx</u> form their plurals in the normal English way, by adding <u>-es</u>. For example:

| | |
|---|---|
| climax | climax<u>es</u> |
| complex | complex<u>es</u> |
| prefix | prefix<u>es</u> |
| equinox | equinox<u>es</u> |
| influx | influx<u>es</u> |
| larynx | larynx<u>es</u> |

Many words with these <u>-x</u> endings come from Latin or Greek, where their plurals were formed in a different way. A few of these plurals can still be found in English, as alternative plurals to the usual <u>-es</u> ending. For example:

| | |
|---|---|
| appendix | appendix<u>es</u> *or* append<u>ices</u> |
| apex | apex<u>es</u> *or* ap<u>ices</u> |
| index | index<u>es</u> *or* ind<u>ices</u> |
| matrix | matrix<u>es</u> *or* matr<u>ices</u> |
| pharynx | pharynx<u>es</u> *or* phary<u>nges</u> |

The words which can have plurals like these are generally longer than one syllable. For example, the plural of *box* can only be *boxes*, the plural of *hex* is always *hexes* and the plural of *jinx* is *jinxes*.

## -xion

is the ending of a few English words. For more about them, see **-ction/-xion**.

## Xmas

This word is an abbreviation for **Christmas**.

Like most abbreviations, you should generally try to avoid it in formal essay writing.

The X is used in **Xmas** because it is the closest letter in our alphabet to the Greek letter which begins the Ancient Greek spelling of Christ's name.

# Yy

**y**

See **i/y**.

**-y**

is a very common English ending for both adjectives and nouns.

The <u>adjectives</u> ending in -y are very many. The following list has just a few of them:

| | | | | | |
|---|---|---|---|---|---|
| cloudy | crazy | creamy | dirty | dusty | feathery |
| healthy | hilly | icy | misty | risky | roomy |
| shady | stony | stormy | thorny | velvety | watery |
| wealthy | windy | woody | | | |

In most of these words, the adjective has been made simply by adding -y to a noun. In just a few cases (such as *crazy, icy* and *stony*), the noun (*craze, ice* and *stone*) loses its <u>e</u> before the -y is added. (For more about words ending in -e, see **-e**.) Note that when the adjective is made from a noun ending in <u>y</u> (such as *clay*), the ending to be added is actually -ey (as in *clayey*).

Many of the <u>nouns</u> ending in -y are abstract nouns, like:

| | | | | | |
|---|---|---|---|---|---|
| beauty | envy | fury | glory | plenty | victory |

They have usually come ready-made from French or Latin. See also **-ity**, **-ry** and **-ty**.

A small group of nouns ending in -y are words with an informal character. Some are made specially for talking with small children, for example:

doggy   nanny   piggy

Others, like *brolly, footy, hippy* and *telly*, may be used with anyone. Note that many of these are spelled with -ie rather than -y at the end. For more about this, see **-ie/-y**.

Note also that -y becomes -i before other endings are added.
So cloudy *becomes* cloudier cloudiest
fury furious
hippy hippies

For more about this, see **y→i**.

## -y / -ey

Words like *chanc(e)y, fog(e)y, mous(e)y, phon(e)y* and *wir(e)y* are quite new in English – and their spelling hasn't settled down. So for the moment you can write them with -ey or just -y at the end.

Some people would say that they're easier to recognise with -ey. (*Mousey* shows you the link with *mouse* better than the spelling *mousy*.) But in the long run, *mousy* is likely to win. It's in keeping with the general rule that words ending in -e lose the e when -y is added on. This is what has happened with *crazy, greasy, spicy, shady, stony* and many more. For more about this, see **-e**.

## y→i

When y is at the end of a word, it sometimes changes to i before you add certain inflections.

Verbs ending in -y change it to -i before -ed, as in:

| | | | |
|---|---|---|---|
| fry | fried | apply | applied |
| try | tried | copy | copied |

Adjectives ending in -y change it to -i before -er and -est, as in:

| | | |
|---|---|---|
| gloomy | gloomier | gloomiest |
| merry | merrier | merriest |

Nouns ending in -y change it to -i before adding -es, as in:

| | | | |
|---|---|---|---|
| fly | flies | city | cities |
| spy | spies | estuary | estuaries |

Note that when you make a plural with a proper name ending in -y, it stays as y:

*the two Germanys*
*the three Kathys in my class*

When you add a suffix beginning with a consonant to a word ending in -y, the y changes to an i:

| | | |
|---|---|---|
| glory + -fy | → | glorify |
| beauty + -ful | → | beautiful |
| merry + -ment | → | merriment |

Note that one-syllable words ending in -y nowadays often keep it before -er, -est and -ly:

| | | |
|---|---|---|
| drier | driest | drily |
| dryer | dryest | dryly |

*Drier* and *dryer* are alternatives for both the comparative form of the adjective and the noun, which refers to a machine for drying, such as a *hair drier/dryer*.

When -y is paired with a vowel (for instance -ay, -ey, -oy or y), it usually stays as y, whatever endings are added. For example:

| | | | | |
|---|---|---|---|---|
| delay | → | delayed | alloy → | alloys |
| employ | | employed | day | days |
| survey | | surveyed | guy | guys |

| | | |
|---|---|---|
| coy | → | coyer, coyest |
| grey | | greyer, greyest |

The only exceptions to this rule are:

| | | |
|---|---|---|
| lay | → | laid |
| pay | | paid |
| say | | said |

## ye / you

**Ye** is an old-fashioned plural form of the pronoun **you**. In earlier times, when Shakespeare was writing his plays and the Bible was first being translated into English, **ye** was used for the subjective case and **you** for the objective case:

*Ye are my friends.* (subjective)
*I know you.* (objective)

For more information, see **personal pronouns** and **case**.

## yen

When you are writing about this Japanese money unit, the plural is simply **yen**:

*This book cost me 50 yen.*

**Yen** is also used as an informal word to mean "desire":

*Sarah has a yen to go on a walking holiday in Tibet.*

## yes

This word is only rarely used as a noun, but when it is, the plural is spelled **yeses**:

*There were many yeses when the offer was made.*

## yew

See **ewe/you/yew**.

## yodel

You may sometimes find this word spelled **yodle**, though **yodel** is the more common spelling. For more information about whether to double the l when you add -ed, -ing or -er, see **-l-/-ll-**.

## yoghurt / yogurt

These are equally good spellings for this word, though **yoghurt** is the one most commonly used. You may also find the spelling **yoghourt**, but this is a rare spelling.

**Yoghurt** comes from a Turkish word. Turkish is not written with the alphabet we use in English, and there are several ways of spelling Turkish words in our alphabet. This is why the three different spellings remain in use in English.

## yogi

The plural of this word is spelled **yogis**. **Yogi** comes from an Indian language and is the name for someone who has mastered **yoga**.

## yogurt

See **yoghurt/yogurt**.

## yolk / yoke

These words sound the same but have different meanings.

The **yolk** is the yellow part of an egg.

A **yoke** is a wooden cross-piece with curved ends, used for pulling or carrying loads.

## you

See **ewe/you/yew**. See also **ye/you**.

## you / your / yours / yourself / yourselves

These personal pronouns are all second person.

**You** can be in the <u>subjective</u> and the <u>objective</u> case:
*You love yellow.* (subjective)
*Yellow suits you.* (objective)

**Your** is the personal pronoun in the <u>possessive</u> case. It is sometimes called a possessive adjective:
*Are these your yellow sneakers?*

**Yours** is the possessive pronoun:
*The yellow sneakers are yours.*

**Yourself** and **yourselves** are the reflexive pronouns:
*Don't cut yourself.* (singular)
*Behave yourselves.* (plural)

For more information, see **case, personal pronouns, possessive pronouns,** and **reflexive pronouns.**

## you'd

is a short form of **you had** or **you would.** See **contractions.**

## you'll

is a short form of **you will** or **you shall.** See **contractions.**

## your

See **you/your/yours/yourself/yourselves.**

## your / you're

These words sound the same but mean different things.

**Your** is a pronoun used before a noun to describe something belonging to or done by you:
*Your good work has pleased your mother.*

**You're** is short for **you are.** See **contractions.**

## yours

See **you/your/yours/yourself/yourselves.**

## yourself

See **you/your/yours/yourself/yourselves.**

## yourselves

See **you/your/yours/yourself/yourselves.**

## you've

is a short form of **you have.** See **contractions.**

## -yse / -yze

These are alternative spellings for the ending of a number of words borrowed from Greek. For example:

| | | | |
|---|---|---|---|
| analyse | catalyse | electrolyse | paralyse |
| analyze | catalyze | electrolyze | paralyze |

The spelling -yse is the usual one in the UK. In the USA, -yze is often used, probably because Americans also prefer -ize in words like *organize*. For more about this, see **-ise/-ize**.

## yuppie / yuppy

These are equally good ways of spelling this word.

This is quite a new word that was invented to give a name to a group of people that have suddenly sprung up in our society: wealthy young people who work in the city.

It was created by using the first letters of a phrase that describes someone from this group: *young urban professional*. This is an *acronym* and gives you the first part of the word, **yup**.

Then the -ie (or -y) ending was added. This ending is often used to make nouns out of adjectives, as in *goodie*, *baddie* and *hippie*. It also adds an informal and slightly humorous feeling to the word.

When the acronym and the ending are put together you get **yuppie**, a new word to describe something new in our society.

A similar word, **yumpie**, is an acronym of *young upwardly-mobile professional*. For some reason this word failed to gain popularity, and is now only rarely seen.

For more about the ending, see **-ie/-y**. See also **acronyms**.

# Zz

### zero

The plural of this word may be spelled **zeros** or **zeroes**.

When you add -ed and -ing the spellings are **zeroed** and **zeroing**.

For more about words like this, see **-o**.

### zigzag

When you add -ed and -ing to this word, the spelling is **zigzagged** and **zigzagging**. For more about words like this, see **doubling of last letter**.

### zinc

When you add -ed and -ing to this word you usually add a k: **zincked**, **zincking**.

However it is possible to leave the c as it is: **zinced**, **zincing**. There is never a k in **zincify**, **zinciferous** or **zincite**.

For more about words like this, see **-c/-ck-**.

### zombie / zombi

These are equally good spellings for this word. It comes from an African name for a good-luck charm: *zumbi*.

# Appendices

# Appendix A
## SPELLING GUIDE

### The different ways sounds are spelled at the beginning of words

If you're having difficulty finding a word in a dictionary, it may be that the sound at the beginning of the word is spelled in an unusual way. For example, the word we pronounce *foe-toe* is actually spelled with *ph* at the start: *photo*. The word you are looking for might even start with a silent letter — *write* sounds as though it should start with the letter *r*, not *w*.

The following table lists the different spellings a sound can have at the beginning of a word. So it should help you track down some of these difficult words.

The table is arranged in groups, with each group devoted to one sound and its different spellings.

The sounds are in roughly alphabetical order to make it easy to find the one you're looking for.

The last sound in the table is the vowel we call "schwa". It's the neutral, "swallowed" vowel that we use a lot in English. For more about it, see **schwa** in the "A to Z Guide to Writing and Language".

| | | |
|---|---|---|
| The sound **ar** | *in* | art |
| is also spelled **a** | *as in* | after |
| **al** | | almond |
| **au** | | aunt |
| | | |
| The sound **ai** | *in* | aid |
| is also spelled **eigh** | *as in* | eight |
| **a** | | ate |
| | | |
| The sound **c** | *in* | cat |
| is also spelled **k** | *as in* | koala |
| **kh** | | khaki |
| **ch** | | chemistry |
| **qu** | | quiche |
| | | |
| The sound **ch** | *in* | chin |
| is also spelled **c** | *as in* | cello |
| | | |
| The sound **er** | *in* | ermine |
| is also spelled **ear** | *as in* | early |
| **ur** | | urban |
| **ir** | | irk |

| | | |
|---|---|---|
| The sound **ee** | *in* | eel |
| is also spelled **e** | *as in* | ego |
| **ea** | | each |
| **ei** | | either* |
| **ae** | | aeon |
| | | |
| The sound **air** | *in* | air |
| is also spelled **aer** | *as in* | aerial |
| | | |
| The sound **f** | *in* | fog |
| is also spelled **ph** | *as in* | photo |
| | | |
| The sound **g** | *in* | gap |
| is also spelled **gh** | *as in* | ghost |
| **gu** | | guide |
| | | |
| The sound **h** | *in* | hat |
| is also spelled **wh** | *as in* | who |
| | | |
| The sound **i** | *in* | ivy |
| is also spelled **ai** | *as in* | aisle |
| **ei** | | eiderdown |
| **eye** | | eye |
| | | |
| The sound **ear** | *in* | ear |
| is also spelled **er** | *as in* | era |
| **eer** | | eerie |
| | | |
| The sound **j** | *in* | jam |
| is also spelled **g** | *as in* | germ |
| | | |
| The sound **n** | *in* | net |
| is also spelled **gn** | *as in* | gnome |
| **pn** | | pneumonia |
| **kn** | | knee |
| **mn** | | mnemonic |
| | | |
| The sound **o** | *in* | otter |
| is also spelled **au** | *as in* | auction** |
| | | |
| The sound **o** | *in* | over |
| is also spelled **oa** | *as in* | oak |
| **ow** | | own |
| | | |
| The sound **or** | *in* | orbit |
| is also spelled **aw** | *as in* | awful |
| **a** | | all |
| **au** | | author |
| **oar** | | oar |
| **ough** | | ought |

\* Note that *either* is also pronounced *eye-ther*.
\*\* Note that *auction* is also pronounced *ork-shen*.

| | | |
|---|---|---|
| The sound **ow** | *in* | <u>ow</u>l |
| is also spelled **ou** | *as in* | <u>ou</u>t |
| | | |
| The sound **oi** | *in* | <u>oi</u>l |
| is also spelled **oy** | *as in* | <u>oy</u>ster |
| | | |
| The sound **r** | *in* | <u>r</u>at |
| is also spelled **rh** | *as in* | <u>rh</u>yme |
| **wr** | | <u>wr</u>ite |
| | | |
| The sound **s** | *in* | <u>s</u>at |
| is also spelled **c** | *as in* | <u>c</u>ell |
| **sc** | | <u>sc</u>ene |
| **ps** | | <u>ps</u>ychology |
| **sw** | | <u>sw</u>ord |
| | | |
| The sound **sh** | *in* | <u>sh</u>oe |
| is also spelled **ch** | *as in* | <u>ch</u>ampagne |
| **s** | | <u>s</u>ugar |
| **sch** | | <u>sch</u>edule★ |
| | | |
| The sound **sk** | *in* | <u>sk</u>in |
| is also spelled **sc** | *as in* | <u>sc</u>ar |
| **sch** | | <u>sch</u>ool |
| | | |
| The sound **t** | *in* | <u>t</u>op |
| is also spelled **th** | *as in* | <u>th</u>yme |
| **pt** | | <u>pt</u>erodactyl |
| **tw** | | <u>tw</u>o |
| | | |
| The sound **u** | *in* | <u>u</u>p |
| is also spelled **o** | *as in* | <u>o</u>ther |
| | | |
| The sound **w** | *in* | <u>w</u>ild |
| is also spelled **wh** | *as in* | <u>wh</u>ite |
| | | |
| The sound **u** | *in* | <u>u</u>nit |
| is also spelled **you** | *as in* | <u>you</u> |
| **ewe** | | <u>ewe</u> |
| **eu** | | <u>eu</u>calyptus |
| | | |
| The sound **z** | *in* | <u>z</u>ebra |
| is also spelled **x** | *as in* | <u>x</u>ylophone |
| | | |
| The "schwa" sound spelled **a** | *in* | <u>a</u>part |
| is also spelled **e** | *as in* | <u>e</u>lectric |
| **i** | | <u>i</u>mmediate |
| **o** | | <u>o</u>blige |
| **u** | | <u>u</u>pon |

★ Note that *schedule* is also pronounced <u>*sked-jool*</u>.

# Appendix B
## ABBREVIATIONS

Note that this list of abbreviations does not include the symbols for metric and imperial units (in Appendix C) or those for chemical elements (in Appendix D).

**A**  ampere
**AC** *or* **a.c.**  alternating current
**A/C** *or* **acc.** *or* **Acc**  account
**ACAS**  Advisory Conciliation and Arbitration Service
**AD**  in the year of our Lord (Latin: *anno domini*)
**adj.**  adjective
**adv.** *or* **advb**  adverb
**advert.** *or* **advt**  advertisement
**AGM**  Annual General Meeting
**AI**  artificial intelligence; artificial insemination
**AIDS**  acquired immune deficiency syndrome
**alt.**  alternative; altitude
**a.m.** *or* **am**  before noon (Latin: *ante meridiem*)
**amt**  amount
**ann.**  annual
**anniv.**  anniversary
**anon.**  anonymous
**Apr**  April
**approx.**  approximate(ly)
**ASAP** *or* **a.s.a.p.**  as soon as possible
**Assn**  Association
**Assoc**  Associate; Association
**asst**  assistant
**Aug**  August
**Av** *or* **Ave**  Avenue
**av.** *or* **avge**  average

**b.**  born; bowled; breadth
**BA**  Bachelor of Arts
**bal.**  balance
**b. & b.**  bed and breakfast
**BBC**  British Broadcasting Corporation
**BC**  before Christ
**bk**  bank; book
**BL**  Bachelor of Law
**BLitt**  Bachelor of Letters
**Blvd** *or* **Boul**  Boulevard
**BM**  Bachelor of Medicine
**BMX**  Bicycle Motorcross
**BO**  body odour
**Bros**  Brothers
**BSc**  Bachelor of Science
**B/W**  black and white

**C**  Cape; Celsius; Centigrade; century;
**c.**  cent; century; about (Latin: *circa*)

**CAB**  Citizens Advice Bureau
**cal**  calorie
**Cap** *or* **Capt**  Captain
**CB**  Citizens band
**cc**  carbon copy
**CD**  compact disc, civil defence
**Cdr**  Commander
**cent.**  Centigrade; central; century
**cert.**  certain; certificate; certified
**cf.**  compare (Latin: *confer*)
**c/f**  carried forward
**c.g.s.**  centimetre-gram-second (system)
**ch.** *or* **chap.**  chapter
**chq.**  cheque
**Co.**  Company
**c/o**  care of
**COD**  cash on delivery
**co-ed**  co-educational
**C of E**  Church of England
**Col**  Colonel
**conj.**  conjunction
**cont.** *or* **contd**  continued
**Cpl**  Corporal
**c.p.s.**  cycles per second
**Cres**  Crescent
**cu.**  cubic
**cwt**  hundredweight

**d.**  daughter; density; diameter
**dB**  decibel
**DC** *or* **d.c.**  direct current
**Dec**  December
**deg.**  degree
**dept** *or* **dpt**  department
**dip.**  diploma
**DNA**  deoxyribonucleic acid
**DOB**  date of birth
**doz.**  dozen
**Dr**  Doctor; Drive
**dup.**  duplicate

**E** *or* **e**  east; eastern
**ed.** *or* **edit.**  edited; edition; editor
**EDP**  electronic data processing
**e.g.**  for example (Latin: *exempli gratia*)
**enc.** *or* **encl.**  enclosed

**ENT**  ear, nose and throat
**env.**  envelope
**equiv.**  equivalent
**esp.**  especially
**ESP**  extrasensory perception
**Esq**  Esquire
**est.** *or* **estab.**  established
**ETA**  estimated time of arrival
**ETD**  estimated time of departure
**et al.**  and others (Latin: *et alii*)
**etc.**  and so on (Latin: *et cetera*)
**exc.**  except
**excl**  excluding; exclusive
**exp.**  experienced; export

**f**  (*music*) loudly (Italian: *forte*)
**F**  Fahrenheit
**Feb**  February
**fem.**  female; feminine
**ff.**  following
**fig.**  figure
**figs**  figures
**fol.**  following
**Fn**  footnote
**Fr**  Father
**Fri**  Friday
**Ft**  feet
**fwd**  forward

**G**  the constant of gravitation
**GDP**  Gross Domestic Product
**Gen**  General
**GM**  General Manager
**GMT**  Greenwich Mean Time
**GNP**  Gross National Product
**govt**  government

**h.**  height; hour
**h.c.f.**  highest common factor
**hcp**  handicap
**HM**  Her (His) Majesty
**Hon**  honorary; honorable
**HP**  hire purchase
**HQ**  headquarters
**hr**  hour
**Hts**  Heights

**i/c**  in charge; in command
**ID**  identification
**i.e.**  that is (Latin: *id est*)
**inc.** *or* **incorp.**  incorporated
**incl.**  including; inclusive
**ind.**  independent
**Insp**  Inspector

**inst.**  of the present month (short for *instant*)
**I/O**  input/output
**IOU**  I owe you
**Is**  Island
**ISBN**  International Standard Book Number

**Jan**  January
**jnr** *or* **jr**  junior
**JP**  Justice of the Peace
**Jul**  July
**Jun**  June

**K**  (*computers*) $2^{10}$ (1024); (*physics*) kelvin

**L**  learner (driver)
**l.**  left; length
**lat.**  latitude
**l.b.w.**  leg before wicket
**l.c.m.**  lowest common multiple
**l.h.s.**  left-hand side
**lic'd**  licensed
**log.**  logarithm
**long.**  longitude
**LPG**  liquefied petroleum gas
**l.s.d.**  pounds, shillings and pence (Latin: *librae,
    solidi, denarii*)
**Lt**  Lieutenant
**Ltd**  Limited

**m.**  male; married; mass; million; minute; month
**Maj**  Major
**Mar**  March
**masc.**  masculine
**matric.**  matriculation
**max.**  maximum
**med.**  medical; medicine; medium
**Messrs**  plural of *Mr* (French: *Messieurs*)
**mfd**  manufactured
**mfg**  manufacturing
**mfr**  manufacture; manufacturer
**Mgr** *or* **mgr**  manager
**m.g.s.**  metre-gram-second (system)
**min.**  minimum
**min**  minute(s)
**misc.**  miscellaneous
**m.k.s.**  metre-kilogram-second (system)
**Mon**  Monday
**MP**  Member of Parliament; Military Police
**m.p.g.**  miles per gallon
**Mr**  Mister
**Mrs**  Mistress (Missus)
**MS** *or* **ms.**  manuscript
**Mt**  Mount; Mountain

**N** *or* **n**   north; northern; name
**n/a** *or* **n.a.**   not applicable; not available
**NB**   note well (Latin: *nota bene*)
**nd**   no date
**NE** *or* **ne**   north-east
**No.** *or* **no.**   number (Italian: *numero*)
**Nos** *or* **nos**   numbers
**Nov**   November
**nr**   near
**NW** *or* **nw**   north-west

**Oct**   October
**OHMS**   On Her (His) Majesty's Service
**o.n.o.**   or nearest offer
**op.**   works (Latin: *opera*); work (Latin: *opus*)
**op.cit.**   in the work cited

**P**   provisional (driver's licence)
**p**   (*music*) softly (Italian: *piano*)
**p.**   page
**p.a.**   yearly (Latin: *per annum*)
**para.**   paragraph
**Parl** *or* **Parlt**   Parliament
**PAYE**   pay as you earn
**p.c.**   per cent
**pd**   paid
**Pen**   Peninsula
**perm.**   permanent
**pg.**   page
**Pk**   Park
**pkt**   packet
**Pl**   Place
**pl.** *or* **plur.**   plural
**p.m.** *or* **pm**   afternoon (Latin: *post meridiem*)
**PO**   post office; postal order
**pop.**   population
**POW**   prisoner of war
**pp**   pages
**pr**   pair
**PR**   public relations
**prelim.**   preliminary
**Prof**   Professor
**pro tem.**   for the time being (Latin: *pro tempore*)
**prox.**   in or of the next or coming month (Latin: *proximo*)
**PS**   postscript (Latin: *post scriptum*)
**pt**   point; pint
**p.t.**   part-time
**p.t.o.**   please turn over
**Pty**   Proprietary
**p.w.**   per week

**QC**   Queen's Counsel
**QED**   which was to be proved (Latin: *quod erat demonstrandum*)

**qt**   quart
**qtr**   quarter; quarterly
**qual.**   qualified; quality
**q.v.**   which see (Latin: *quod vide*)

**R**   River
**r.**   radius; right; (*cricket*) runs
**RC**   Roman Catholic
**Rd**   Road
**recd**   received
**ref.**   reference
**reg.**   registered; regulation
**rep.**   representative
**Rev.**   Reverend
**r.h.s.**   right-hand side
**RNA**   ribonucleic acid
**r.p.s.**   revolutions per second
**RSVP**   please reply (French: *Répondez s'il vous plaît*)
**Rt Hon**   Right Honorable

**S** *or* **s**   south; southern
**s.**   singular
**s.a.e.**   stamped addressed envelope
**Sat**   Saturday
**SE** *or* **se**   south-east
**sec.**   second(ary); secretary
**sect.**   section
**sen.**   senior
**Sep** *or* **Sept**   September
**sep.** *or* **separ.**   separate
**Sergt** *or* **Sgt**   Sergeant
**s.g.**   specific gravity
**SI**   International System of Units (French: *Système Internationale d'Unités*)
**sing.**   singular
**snr**   senior
**Soc**   Society
**Sq.**   Square
**Sr**   Senior; Sister
**St**   Saint; Strait; Street
**STD**   Subscriber Trunk Dialling
**Sth(n)**   south(ern)
**sub.** *or* **subj.**   subject
**Sun**   Sunday
**SW** *or* **sw**   south-west

**tech.**   technical; technology
**temp.**   temperature; temporary
**Thu** *or* **Thurs**   Thursday
**trad.**   traditional
**trans.**   translated; translation; translator
**Tu** *or* **Tue** *or* **Tues**   Tuesday
**TV**   television

**UFO**  unidentified flying object
**u.h.f.** *or* **UHF**  ultra high frequency
**ult.**  in or of the preceding month (Latin: *ultimo*)
**uni.**  university
**UV**  ultraviolet

**v.**  velocity; verb; versus; volume
**vac.**  vacancy; vacant; vacation
**VAT**  Value Added Tax
**vb**  verb
**VDT**  visual display terminal
**VDU**  visual display unit
**vel.**  velocity
**v.h.f.** *or* **VHF**  very high frequency
**viz.**  namely (Latin: *videlicet*)

**vol.**  volume
**vs.**  versus; verse
**v.v.**  vice versa

**W** *or* **w**  west; western
**w.**  week; weight; wide; width; with
**Wed**  Wednesday
**wk**  week; work
**wkly**  weekly
**WST**  Western Standard Time
**wt**  weight

**Xmas**  Christmas

**y.** *or* **yr**  year
**yr(s)**  your(s)

# Appendix C
## METRIC UNITS AND SYMBOLS

### The International System of Units (SI) and their symbols

#### 1. Base SI units

| Basic physical quantity | SI unit | Symbol |
|---|---|---|
| length | metre | m |
| mass | kilogram | kg |
| time | second | s |
| electric current | ampere | A |
| thermodynamic temperature | kelvin | K |
| amount of substance | mole | mol |
| luminous intensity | candela | cd |

#### 2. Supplementary units

| | | |
|---|---|---|
| plane angle | radian | rad |
| solid angle | steradian | sr |

#### 3. Some derived SI units with special names

| Physical quantity | SI unit | Symbol |
|---|---|---|
| frequency | hertz | Hz |
| energy | joule | J |
| force | newton | N |
| pressure | pascal | Pa |
| power | watt | W |
| electric charge | coulomb | C |
| potential difference | volt | V |
| resistance | ohm | Ω |
| capacitance | farad | F |
| conductance | siemens | S |
| magnetic flux | weber | Wb |
| inductance | henry | H |
| magnetic flux density | tesla | T |
| luminous flux | lumen | lm |
| illumination | lux | lx |

## 4. Prefixes for SI units

| Factor by which the unit is multiplied | | Prefix | Symbol | An example and its symbol | |
|---|---|---|---|---|---|
| $10^{18}$ | | exa- | E | exahertz | EHz |
| $10^{15}$ | | peta- | P | petahertz | PHz |
| $10^{12}$ | | tera- | T | terahertz | THz |
| $10^{9}$ | | giga- | G | gigametre | Gm |
| $10^{6}$ | $(=1\ 000\ 000)$ | mega- | M | megawatt | MW |
| $10^{3}$ | $(=1\ 000)$ | kilo- | k | kilogram | kg |
| $10^{2}$ | $(=100)$ | hecto- | h | hectogram | hg |
| $10$ | $(=10)$ | deka- | da | dekametre | dam |
| $10^{-1}$ | $(=0.1)$ | deci- | d | decigram | dg |
| $10^{-2}$ | $(=0.01)$ | centi- | c | centigram | cg |
| $10^{-3}$ | $(=0.001)$ | milli- | m | milligram | mg |
| $10^{-6}$ | $(=0.0000001)$ | micro- | $\mu$ | microvolt | $\mu$V |
| $10^{-9}$ | | nano- | n | nanometre | nm |
| $10^{-12}$ | | pico- | p | picofarad | pF |
| $10^{-15}$ | | femto- | f | femtogram | fg |
| $10^{-18}$ | | atto- | a | attogram | ag |

Note how capital letters and lower-case ones can be quite different symbols; for example *P* is *peta-* while *p* is *pico-*, and *H* is *henry* while *h* is *hecto-*.

## Metric measures, their symbols, and how to convert them to imperial measures

| Quantity | Metric unit | Symbol | Approximate conversion factor to imperial unit |
|---|---|---|---|
| length | centimetre | cm | 1 cm = 0.394 inches |
| | metre | m | 1 m = 3.28 feet |
| | | | 1 m = 1.09 yards |
| | kilometre | km | 1 km = 0.621 mile |
| mass | gram | g | 1 g = 0.0353 ounces |
| | kilogram | kg | 1 kg = 2.20 pounds |
| | tonne | t | 1 tonne = 0.984 ton |
| area | square centimetre | $cm^2$ | 1 $cm^2$ = 0.155 sq. inches |
| | square metre | $m^2$ | 1 $m^2$ = 10.8 sq. feet |
| | | | 1 $m^2$ = 1.20 sq. yards |
| | hectare | ha | 1 ha = 2.47 acres |
| | square kilometres | $km^2$ | 1 $km^2$ = 0.386 sq. mile |
| volume | cubic centimetre | $cm^3$ | 1 $cm^3$ = 0.0610 cubic inches |
| | cubic metre | $m^3$ | 1 $m^3$ = 35.3 cubic feet |
| | | | 1 $m^3$ = 1.31 cubic yards |
| | | | 1 $m^3$ = 27.5 bushels |
| volume (fluid) | millilitre | ml | 1 ml = 0.0352 fluid ounces |
| | litre | l | 1 l = 1.76 pints |
| | cubic metre | $m^3$ | 1 $m^3$ = 220 gallons |
| velocity | kilometre per hour | km/h | 1 km/h = 0.621 miles per hour |
| angular velocity | radians per second | rad/s | 1 rad/s = 9.55 revolutions per minute |
| energy | kilojoule | kJ | 1 kJ = 0.948 British thermal units |
| | megajoule | MJ | 1 MJ = $9.48 \times 10^{-3}$ therms |
| force | newton | N | 1 N = 0.225 pound-force |
| pressure (meteorology) | kilopascal | kPa | 1 kPa = 0.145 pounds per square inch |
| | millibar | mb | 1 mb = 0.0295 inch of mercury |
| power | kilowatt | kW | 1 kW = 1.34 horsepower |
| temperature | Celsius temp | °C | $(°C \times \frac{9}{5}) + 32 = °F$ |

## Imperial measures, their symbols, and how to convert them to metric measures

| Quantity | Imperial unit | Symbol | Approximate conversion factor to metric unit |
|---|---|---|---|
| length | inch | in | 1 in = 25.4 millimetres |
| | foot | ft | 1 ft = 30.5 centimetres |
| | yard | yd | 1 yd = 0.914 metres |
| | mile | | 1 mile = 1.61 kilometres |
| mass | ounce | oz | 1 oz = 28.3 grams |
| | pound | lb | 1 lb = 454 grams |
| | ton | | 1 ton = 1.02 tonnes |
| area | square inch | $in^2$ | 1 $in^2$ = 6.45 sq. centimetres |
| | square foot | $ft^2$ | 1 $ft^2$ = 929 sq. centimetres |
| | square yard | $yd^2$ | 1 $yd^2$ = 0.836 sq. metre |
| | acre | | 1 acre = 0.405 hectares |
| | square mile | sq. mile | 1 sq. mile = 2.59 sq. kilometres |
| volume | cubic inch | $in^3$ | 1 $in^3$ = 16.4 cubic centimetres |
| | cubic foot | $ft^3$ | 1 $ft^3$ = 28.3 cubic decimetres |
| | cubic yard | $yd^3$ | 1 $yd^3$ = 0.765 cubic metres |
| | bushel | bus | 1 bus = 0.0364 cubic metres |
| volume (fluid) | fluid ounce | fl oz | 1 fl oz = 28.4 millilitres |
| | pint | pt | 1 pt = 568 millilitres |
| | gallon | gal | 1 gal = 4.55 litres |
| velocity | mile per hour | mph | 1 mph = 1.61 kilometres per hour |
| angular velocity | revolution per minute | r/min; rpm | 1r/min = 0.105 radians per second |
| energy | British thermal unit | Btu | 1 Btu = 1.06 kilojoules |
| | therm | | 1 therm = 106 megajoules |
| force | pound-force | lbf | 1 lbf = 4.45 newtons |
| pressure (meteorology) | pound per square inch | psi | 1 psi = 6.89 kilopascals |
| | inch of mercury | inHg | 1 inHg = 33.9 millibars |
| power | horsepower | hp | 1 hp = 0.746 kilowatts |
| temperature | Fahrenheit temp | °F | $(°F - 32) \times \frac{5}{9} = °C$ |

# Appendix D
## CHEMICAL SYMBOLS

## Periodic table

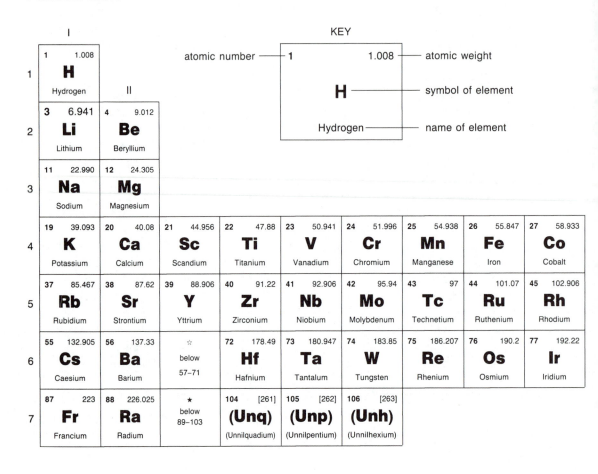

|   | I | | II | | | | | | | | |
|---|---|---|---|---|---|---|---|---|---|---|---|
| **KEY** |
| atomic number ——— 1 | | | | | 1.008 ——— atomic weight |
| | | | | | **H** ——— symbol of element |
| | | | | | Hydrogen ——— name of element |

**Periodic table**

| Period | Group I | Group II | | | | | | | |
|---|---|---|---|---|---|---|---|---|---|
| 1 | 1 1.008 **H** Hydrogen | | | | | | | | |
| 2 | 3 6.941 **Li** Lithium | 4 9.012 **Be** Beryllium | | | | | | | |
| 3 | 11 22.990 **Na** Sodium | 12 24.305 **Mg** Magnesium | | | | | | | |
| 4 | 19 39.093 **K** Potassium | 20 40.08 **Ca** Calcium | 21 44.956 **Sc** Scandium | 22 47.88 **Ti** Titanium | 23 50.941 **V** Vanadium | 24 51.996 **Cr** Chromium | 25 54.938 **Mn** Manganese | 26 55.847 **Fe** Iron | 27 58.933 **Co** Cobalt |
| 5 | 37 85.467 **Rb** Rubidium | 38 87.62 **Sr** Strontium | 39 88.906 **Y** Yttrium | 40 91.22 **Zr** Zirconium | 41 92.906 **Nb** Niobium | 42 95.94 **Mo** Molybdenum | 43 97 **Tc** Technetium | 44 101.07 **Ru** Ruthenium | 45 102.906 **Rh** Rhodium |
| 6 | 55 132.905 **Cs** Caesium | 56 137.33 **Ba** Barium | ☆ below 57–71 | 72 178.49 **Hf** Hafnium | 73 180.947 **Ta** Tantalum | 74 183.85 **W** Tungsten | 75 186.207 **Re** Rhenium | 76 190.2 **Os** Osmium | 77 192.22 **Ir** Iridium |
| 7 | 87 223 **Fr** Francium | 88 226.025 **Ra** Radium | ★ below 89–103 | 104 [261] **(Unq)** (Unnilquadium) | 105 [262] **(Unp)** (Unnilpentium) | 106 [263] **(Unh)** (Unnilhexium) | | | |

| ☆ LANTHANIDE SERIES | 57 138.905 **La** Lanthanum | 58 140.12 **Ce** Cerium | 59 140.908 **Pr** Praseodymium | 60 144.24 **Nd** Neodymium | 61 145 **Pm** Promethium | 62 150.36 **Sm** Samarium | 63 151.96 **Eu** Europium |
|---|---|---|---|---|---|---|---|

| ★ ACTINIDE SERIES | 89 227.027 **Ac** Actinium | 90 232.038 **Th** Thorium | 91 231.036 **Pa** Protactinium | 92 238.029 **U** Uranium | 93 237.048 **Np** Neptunium | 94 [244] **Pu** Plutonium | 95 [243] **Am** Americium |
|---|---|---|---|---|---|---|---|

VIII

| | | | | |
|---|---|---|---|---|
| 2 4.003 **He** Helium | | | | |

| III | IV | V | VI | VII |
|---|---|---|---|---|
| 5 10.81 **B** Boron | 6 12.011 **C** Carbon | 7 14.007 **N** Nitrogen | 8 15.999 **O** Oxygen | 9 18.998 **F** Fluorine |

| 10 20.179 **Ne** Neon |
|---|

| 13 26.982 **Al** Aluminium | 14 28.085 **Si** Silicon | 15 30.974 **P** Phosphorus | 16 32.06 **S** Sulphur | 17 35.453 **Cl** Chlorine | 18 39.948 **Ar** Argon |
|---|---|---|---|---|---|
| 28 58.69 **Ni** Nickel | 29 63.546 **Cu** Copper | 30 65.38 **Zn** Zinc | 31 69.72 **Ga** Gallium | 32 72.59 **Ge** Germanium | 33 74.922 **As** Arsenic | 34 78.96 **Se** Selenium | 35 79.904 **Br** Bromine | 36 83.80 **Kr** Krypton |
| 46 106.42 **Pd** Palladium | 47 107.868 **Ag** Silver | 48 112.41 **Cd** Cadmium | 49 114.82 **In** Indium | 50 118.69 **Sn** Tin | 51 121.75 **Sb** Antimony | 52 127.60 **Te** Tellurium | 53 126.905 **I** Iodine | 54 131.29 **Xe** Xenon |
| 78 195.08 **Pt** Platinum | 79 196.967 **Au** Gold | 80 200.59 **Hg** Mercury | 81 204.383 **Tl** Thallium | 82 207.2 **Pb** Lead | 83 208.980 **Bi** Bismuth | 84 209 **Po** Polonium | 85 210 **At** Astatine | 86 222 **Rn** Radon |

| 64 157.25 **Gd** Gadolinium | 65 158.925 **Tb** Terbium | 66 162.5 **Dy** Dysprosium | 67 164.930 **Ho** Holmium | 68 167.26 **Er** Erbium | 69 168.934 **Tm** Thulium | 70 173.04 **Yb** Ytterbium | 71 174.967 **Lu** Lutetium |
|---|---|---|---|---|---|---|---|
| 96 [247] **Cm** Curium | 97 [247] **Bk** Berkelium | 98 [251] **Cf** Californium | 99 [252] **Es** Einsteinium | 100 [257] **Fm** Fermium | 101 [258] **Md** Mendelevium | 102 [259] **No** Nobelium | 103 [260] **Lr** Lawrencium |

[ ] Values given in square brackets are the atomic mass number of the isotope of the element with the longest half-life.

( ) Names and symbols in parentheses are those recommended by the International Union of Pure and Applied Chemists (IUPAC).

# Appendix E
## LETTER FORMATS

### A format for personal letters

St Anne's Hotel,
Flapthorne,
Evesbury,
Worcs.
20th July 1989

Dear Julie,

Here we are in gorgeous Evesbury! Actually we're just outside it in what is jokingly called a village. It seems to consist of the hotel we're stopping in, a gypsy caravan parked in a lay-by down the road, a broken down old cottage and a telephone box. In fact, Evesbury's not much better. Have you ever been there? If you haven't you'd never believe such a place existed! I reckon life stopped in Evesbury in the fifties. I saw a gang of boys about our age walking down the High Street in Evesbury dressed in Teddy Boy gear! Yes, Teddy Boy gear – velvet collared jackets, brothel creepers, drainpipe trousers – the lot! I would have killed myself laughing if I hadn't been so depressed with the thought of having to spend another twelve days here.

I can't understand my mum and dad. They've been looking forward to this holiday for months. It's the highlight of their year. They seem to enjoy doing nothing all day. They don't think about what I'd like to do. I have to fit in with them. Take yesterday for instance, we got up at about eight, had breakfast, went for a drive, stopped at a local pub at about twelve, went for another drive, stopped at a tea shop at four for a cream tea, got back to the hotel at six, had dinner at 7.30, talked to the other guests in the hotel – two old-age pensioners – and went to bed at nine. Sounds fun, doesn't it? I told my dad that he ought to slow down or he'd give himself a heart attack. Too much excitement could be dangerous. He wasn't amused and gave me a lecture about "being grateful" and about all the other kids of my age who aren't lucky enough to have a holiday. Lucky? I'd change places with them any day. Why can't we go to Torremolinos or Corfu – somewhere exciting where there's a bit of night-life? Perhaps not. He really would have a heart attack if we went somewhere like that!

I'll have to go now. I need to save my strength for tomorrow. See you when I get back. I'll spend all of five minutes describing the exciting things that have happened to me on holiday. Hope you're having a better time at home.

Love,
Beth

*Sender's address* starts about middle of page.

*Date* is at right-hand side.

*Salutation* is at left-hand side. It is friendly and informal.

*Body of letter.* The start of each paragraph is indented. A line space is left after the salutation and before the complimentary close.

*Complimentary close* is about middle of page. It's friendly and affectionate because this is a personal letter.

This letter format is **semi-blocked** (not everything begins at the left-hand margin), and has **closed** (full) punctuation. (It uses punctuation marks all through the letter, not just in the body.)

# A format for business letters

---

*Sender's address* is in letterhead.

*Date of letter* is at left-hand side. No punctuation.

*Name and address of person being written to* is at left-hand side. If it is a company address, their position in the company is given.

*Salutation* is at left-hand side. It uses a formal title, but no initials or punctuation.

*Subject line* highlights the letter's business, in block capitals or underlined, at left-hand side.

*Body of letter*. Each paragraph starts at left-hand side (no indent). Leave a line before and after each paragraph, if needed.

*Complimentary close* is at left-hand side. Leave space for signature, but type name and position of sender after it, on separate lines.

---

*Surety Insurance Company*

Registered address:
19 Farrier Street, Bristol BS7 OTR


29 April 1989


Mr S Keating
29 Church Street
Hillfield
Cheltenham
GL54 2FG


Dear Mr Keating

Re: Insurance theft of boy's bicycle

In answer to your letter of 25 April, the company regrets to
inform you that your present insurance policy does not cover
the theft of your son's bicycle. Unfortunately your policy only
safeguards personal property of this nature when it is at home.
To provide insurance cover for personal property which is removed
from home, as was the case at the time of the theft of your son's
bicycle, you will need an additional policy made out against loss
and/or theft. It would nominate each item for which such cover
is required and declare the circumstances under which each may
come to be removed. Details are available on request.

Yours sincerely

*B. Reece*

B Reece
Manager

---

This letter format is **fully blocked** (every typed line begins at the left hand margin), and has **open** punctuation. (There's no punctuation except in the body of the letter.)

# Notes